The First American
Political Conventions

The First American Political Conventions

Transforming Presidential Nominations, 1832–1872

STAN M. HAYNES

To Boog,

As an American history professor,
Bob thought you would enjoy
this book.

Stan Wagner

McFarland & Company, Inc., Publishers
Jefferson, North Carolina, and London

LIBRARY OF CONGRESS CATALOGUING-IN-PUBLICATION DATA

Haynes, Stan M., 1957–
The first American political conventions : transforming
presidential nominations, 1832–1872 / Stan M. Haynes.
p.   cm.
Includes bibliographical references and index.

ISBN 978-0-7864-6892-8
softcover : acid free paper ∞

1. Political conventions — United States — History — 19th century.
2. Presidents — United States — Election — History — 19th century.
3. Nominations for office — United States — History — 19th century.
I. Title.
JK2255.H39 2012   324.273'15609034 — dc23   2012014895

BRITISH LIBRARY CATALOGUING DATA ARE AVAILABLE

Front cover images © 2012 Shutterstock

Manufactured in the United States of America

*McFarland & Company, Inc., Publishers
Box 611, Jefferson, North Carolina 28640
www.mcfarlandpub.com*

To my wife, Beth, and my son, Nate,
who over the years have accompanied me on tours of
what we refer to as "DPHs" (dead presidents' houses)
and who have patiently explored with me
many other lesser known and almost forgotten places
where someone once did something of note.

Table of Contents

Acknowledgments

No one writes a book alone. I want to thank my wife, Beth, for not only her moral support, but also in her professional capacity with the Howard County Library System for tracking down and obtaining copies of virtually any book I requested. The staff of the H. Furlong Baldwin Library at the Maryland Historical Society was very helpful during my many research visits. I am grateful to Jeff Korman, the manager of the Maryland Department at the Central Library of the Enoch Pratt Free Library in Baltimore for allowing me access to the thousands of photographs and illustrations of Baltimore history in the library's collection to find those suitable for inclusion in this work. The staff of the Library of Congress was also helpful with information concerning that library's vast collection of photographs and illustrations. My gratitude also goes out to the inventors of the internet, whoever they may have been. The amount of historical information available by computer at the click of a mouse is truly amazing. From Google Books and other websites of books concerning American politics from the nineteenth-century to those recently published, to the archives of major newspapers from the nineteenth-century, to the transcripts of many of the conventions discussed in this book, the internet made this project much more efficient and pleasant to complete than it would have been only a few short years ago. I also appreciate and thank the Honorable James F. Schneider and P. Matthew Darby for reading drafts of the book, and for their encouragement.

Stan M. Haynes • Ellicott City, Maryland

Preface

I consider the true policy of the friends of republican principles to send delegates, fresh from the people, to a general convention, for the purpose of selecting candidates for the presidency and vice-presidency.... — President Andrew Jackson, March 17, 1835

They are, in many ways, still the focal point of the modern American presidential campaign. Candidates work for months and years, for one purpose — to win delegates pledged to support them at their party's presidential nominating convention. They raise millions of dollars, flood the airwaves with campaign commercials, and travel incessantly from state to state to campaign in primaries and caucuses, all leading up to their party's midsummer moment in the spotlight. Party officials, officeholders, delegates, the media, and onlookers flood into the convention city. The modern convention is a four-day, carefully choreographed prime time television event designed to portray the party and its candidate for the presidency in the most favorable light. A dramatic roll call of the states seals the nomination, and the pinnacle of excitement is reached on the convention's last night with, hopefully, a spellbinding acceptance speech by the party's new standard-bearer. Balloons and confetti drop from the rafters of enormous convention arenas, falling on a sea of silly hats being worn by otherwise respectable-looking people. While a successful convention does not guarantee victory in the November general election, an unsuccessful one almost always guarantees a loss.

The orderly transfer of political power is necessary for the lasting existence of a democracy. For almost two centuries, in good times and in bad, Americans have relied upon political conventions to provide the nation with choices for new leadership. These gatherings, throughout their history, have exhibited both frivolity and weightiness. Delegates who dance in conga lines while blowing kazoos decide whose finger could launch nuclear weapons. As one commentator has noted, "It is hard not to wonder whether the American presidential nominating convention, by its very informality, by its confident and impromptu assumption of such awesome power, may not symbolize some larger and more ephemeral quality of the American experience than is contained within the diameter of simple politics."[1] Emotions at conventions run the gamut from boredom to excitement, from the routine to the unexpected. H. L. Mencken, a journalist and a critical observer of politics and life during the first half of the twentieth century, after sitting through many a convention, commented, that "There is something about a national convention that makes it as fascinating as a revival or a hanging....

1

One sits through long sessions wishing heartily that all the delegates and alternates were dead and in hell — and then suddenly there comes a show so gaudy and hilarious, so melodramatic and obscene, so unimaginable, exhilarating and preposterous that one lives a glorious year in an hour."[2]

Where did these creatures, these conventions, come from? Who conceived them, where were they born, and how have they developed over time? This book will attempt to answer these questions. The short answer is that political conventions were created during the second generation of the young United States as a more democratic way of selecting nominees for the presidency. Surprisingly, it was not the major political parties of the era but an obscure and now largely forgotten third-party movement that held the first presidential nominating convention during the campaign of 1832. Since then, conventions have been a fixture of the American political process. Baltimore, Maryland, hosted the first conventions and had a virtual monopoly on these quadrennial gatherings for a generation. In the presidential elections held between 1832 and 1864, a dozen major party conventions were held in Baltimore, compared to only two each in Chicago and Philadelphia, and one each in Harrisburg, Cincinnati, and Charleston.

The story of the origin and development of America's political conventions is also the story of the generation that spanned the middle third of the nineteenth century. Andrew Jackson and Abraham Lincoln stand as two pillars at its beginning and near its end. Both were strong presidents, some would say too strong, and both were reelected to second terms. In between them, eight men sat in the presidential chair, each serving only partial or single terms. Two, William Henry Harrison and Zachary Taylor, died in office and their terms were completed by their respective vice presidents, John Tyler and Millard Fillmore, who were not elected in their own right. The four others — Martin Van Buren, James K. Polk, Franklin Pierce, and James Buchanan — served their four-year terms and were out of office, with only Van Buren winning his party's nomination to seek a second term. There is not a candidate for Mount Rushmore among them. Likewise, the two presidents immediately following the Civil War, Andrew Johnson and Ulysses S. Grant, did not fare much better. Of these ten, arguably only Polk had a successful presidency, but his was one which many believe created more problems than it solved.

These were the first men who took office as the products of the new system for selecting presidential candidates that began in the 1830s, the presidential nominating convention. By this time, the first American party system, the Federalists and the Anti-Federalists, had dissolved. The second party system can properly be termed the Jacksonians versus the Anti-Jacksonians, as Andrew Jackson's Democratic Party became the dominant political force of the era, opposed first by the National Republicans, then by the Whigs and, finally, by the Republican Party. Analysis of the political conventions of this generation reveals, not only the origin and development of the process by which America has, for nearly two hundred years, picked the men who would be president, but also sheds light on the political issues that dominated one of the least studied eras of American history.

At the beginning of this era, presidential elections were fought mainly over economic issues and the scope of power of the federal government. The National Republicans and, later, the Whigs, favored federal expenditures for internal improvements, such as roads and canals, and a national bank to foster economic development. The Democrats opposed both internal improvements and a national bank as being unconstitutional. Slavery was always an area of disagreement between North and South, but both major parties had cross-sectional appeal and neither was interested in changing the status quo of slavery in the existing states. After the massive additional territory that the United States gained in the 1840s as a result of the annexation of Texas and the Mexican War, however, the issue of whether or not to expand slavery into the new territories came to dominate political debate and presidential campaigns. The nominating conventions of both political parties came to focus on slavery-related issues — support for or opposition to Texas annexation, the Wilmot Proviso, the Compromise of 1850, the Kansas-Nebraska Act, and popular sovereignty. So long as the nation's major political parties drew their support from both the North and South, the nation survived. When the bonds between the Northern and Southern wings of the major parties dissolved, so did the nation.

As with the making of laws and sausages, the process of making a president is often not pretty. As the procedures of the presidential nominating conventions were created and became standardized over a generation, these gatherings of the nation's political activists showed the best and worst of men. There was great oratory and not-so-great oratory. Unwise rules were adopted, which later came to be honored as precedent. The conventions at times demonstrated compromise for the sake of country and party, but also had their share of political dirty tricks and double-crossing. There were grand processions through the streets of the convention cities, and there was tragedy on the same streets. Delegates from different sections of the country sometimes came to work together as brothers; sometimes they physically assaulted one another. Crowds gathered; pickpockets thrived. There were outdoor evening rallies held on elaborate stages drenched in gaslight, with speeches being drowned out by supporters of rival candidates. There was action, drama, and conflict. For anyone who loves history, or who loves politics, the story of the nation's first generation of political conventions is a fascinating one.

CHAPTER 1

From Caucuses to Conventions

I would rather learn that the halls of congress were converted into common brothels, than that caucuses of the description stated should be held in them. — Hezekiah Niles, 1822

Since the Bush-Gore election of 2000, most Americans know that the president of the United States is not elected by the popular vote of the people but, rather, is elected by a majority vote of the Electoral College. Today, all the electoral votes of a state are cast for the candidate who wins the majority of the popular vote in that state.[1] What is less known is that the tying of a state's Electoral College votes to the popular vote of the people in that state, as well as the majority-takes-all rule, is nowhere contained in the Constitution of the United States. The states, using the discretion given to them under the Constitution, have chosen to use the popular vote as the method of selecting electors to the Electoral College and have adopted the majority-takes-all rule as a way to increase their power by casting their electoral votes as a block.[2] The system that we operate under today for electing the president is far different from the one envisioned by the founding fathers. Under the Constitution, a presidential election, as we know it, is not required, or necessary, and was likely never anticipated by the founding fathers.

The Constitution provides that "each State shall appoint, in such Manner as the Legislature there of may direct, a Number of Electors" equal to that state's total number of members in the House of Representatives and in the Senate. The electors are to meet in their respective states, and are given two votes each, of which "one at least shall not be an Inhabitant of the same State with themselves."[3] The person receiving the votes of the majority of the electors becomes the president. The only other requirement under the Constitution is that Congress can determine the time frame for the states to choose their electors, but the day on which their votes are counted shall be the same throughout the country.[4] Despite well-deserved reverence for the Constitution, its provisions for the election of the president have not escaped criticism. It has been said that "no other part of the great charter of the country has failed so completely to fulfill the intention of the fathers; has by its ambiguity of language, given rise to more, or more perplexing disputes; or been the occasion of more numerous and varied attempts at amendment."[5]

The choice of George Washington as the first president of the United States was easy. The man who was "first in war, first in peace, and first in the hearts of his countrymen"[6] was the unanimous choice of the Electoral College for president in 1789 and again in 1792. When Washington decided to voluntarily relinquish power after two four-year terms (one of his greatest legacies), there was no formal process to choose candidates as his successor. The Constitution prescribed only the last stage of this process, the election of the president by the casting of votes in the Electoral College. The process of nominating candidates whose names would be before the Electoral College was not specified and was open to interpretation.

The system likely envisioned by the founding fathers was that the two processes — nominating and electing — would be merged and that both would be performed by the Electoral College. Although the Constitution gave each elector two votes, one of their votes had to be for someone from a different state than the elector. Anticipating that many electors would cast one of their votes for a "favorite son" candidate from their own state, the founding fathers likely intended this process to result in the person receiving the most "second choice" votes becoming the president. The idea of the framers of the Constitution was that each state would select its "most capable individuals" as electors, who would meet and choose "the wisest and most virtuous member of the natural aristocracy ... who should serve as president." The runner-up in this talent search for wisdom and virtuosity would become the vice president.[7] But the founding fathers did not foresee the rise of political parties. With the development of political parties, a systematic method of nomination of a single candidate by the party was needed. Otherwise, votes in the Electoral College would be scattered among several candidates and it would be unlikely that one could attain the majority vote of electors required to win the presidency.

Into this void jumped members of Congress, and the congressional caucus system for nominating presidential candidates was created. The caucus consisted of each party's elected members of Congress in the House of Representatives and in the Senate gathered together for a single meeting held at the end of the congressional session in the spring of the presidential election year. A vote was taken and the winner became the party's presidential candidate. It was a simple and easy way to pick a nominee, but gave the people no voice in the selection of presidential candidates. This system lasted for a generation after George Washington left the presidency.

The first congressional nominating caucus was held in 1796 by the Anti-Federalists, or Republicans, and they nominated Thomas Jefferson and Aaron Burr as their two candidates for the Electoral College. The Federalists did not hold a formal caucus that year but, through various meetings, it was decided that their candidates would be John Adams and Thomas Pinckney. Of the sixteen states in the Union in 1796, half gave the people no direct vote in choosing electors. In those states, the electors were chosen by the state legislatures. This number varied with each election but, for the first generation of American presidential elections, a substantial number of states, sometimes a majority, had their presidential electors chosen by their state legislatures, rather than by a majority vote of the people.[8] In 1796, Adams won in the Electoral College with 71 electoral votes, to 68 for Jefferson, 59 for Pinckney, 30 for Burr, and various scattered votes.[9] Under the Constitution, Adams became the president and the second-place finisher, Jefferson, became the vice president.

The next election in 1800 showed the fundamental flaws of the Electoral College system as established by the founding fathers when operating in the context of political parties. In that year, the Republicans, through their party's congressional caucus, again nominated Jefferson and Burr as their candidates. A similar caucus of the Federalist members of Congress nominated the incumbent president, John Adams, and Charles Pinckney of South Carolina. While it was clear to all that Adams and Jefferson were the candidates for the presidency, and that Burr and Pinckney were the candidates for the vice presidency, there was nothing in the Constitution allowing electors to cast their two votes for specific offices.[10] Of the sixteen states in the Union in 1800, only five (Rhode Island, Maryland, Virginia, North Carolina, and Kentucky) held popular elections to choose electors; electors were chosen by the state legislatures in the remaining eleven states. The result was an electoral fiasco. The two Republican candidates, Jefferson and Burr, tied for the lead with 73 electoral votes each. The Federalists apparently foresaw the likelihood of a tie if all of their electors voted for their two caucus-nominated candidates and had one of their electors cast a vote for John Jay of New York, which gave Adams, with 65 electoral votes, one more than his would-be vice president, Pinckney.[11] The tied election was then moved, under the Constitution, to the House of Representatives where, after thirty-six ballots, Jefferson finally prevailed over the scheming Burr and only after Jefferson's political archenemy, Alexander Hamilton, an ardent Federalist, let it be known that he favored the Virginian over the character-challenged New Yorker. Burr did not forget this intervention by Hamilton. Within four years, he would kill Hamilton in a duel.

After the election of 1800, both the Electoral College system and the congressional caucus system came under attack. With respect to the Electoral College, Congress passed, and the states ratified, the Twelfth Amendment to the Constitution. It was enacted in June 1804, in time for the next election. This amendment fixed the electoral tie problem among candidates of the same party that occurred with Jefferson and Burr. Henceforth, each elector was required to designate which of his two votes was for president and which was for vice president.[12] The problems with the caucus system were not so readily changed, although calls for reform began to be heard. Who gave a party's members of Congress the right to select its nominees for the presidency? There was no constitutional basis for the system. It was, in a word, un-American. The caucus system gave the people no direct role in choosing candidates for the presidency and created presidents who, once in office, were totally beholden to their party's members of Congress for their nomination and election.[13] Citizens who lived in congressional districts with a congressman from the political party opposing their own had no representation in the process. Why should members of the national legislature be permitted to choose nominees for the national executive? Was not the Constitution intended to establish a system of checks and balances, and of separation of powers? Moreover, attendance at caucuses by members of Congress was never overwhelming, with an average turnout of less than seventy-five percent. Frequently, a caucus was called by, and run by, the friends and colleagues of the perceived front-runner for the nomination, and supporters of the other candidates would simply boycott the caucus to show their displeasure.[14] As one critic of the caucus system queried:

> Under what authority did these men pretend to dictate their nominations? ... Did they receive six dollars per day [the daily rate of pay for members of Congress] for the double purpose of caucusing and legislating? Do we send members of Congress to cabal once every four years for president? Or are we arrived at such a pitch of Congressional influence that what they decide is binding in the United States? Is there any paragraph in the Constitution which gives them such an authority, or even countenances such a proceeding? After Congress have accomplished their legislative business, have they a right to dictate the choice of an executive?[15]

Throughout the country, the caucus system came to be viewed as Washington insiders picking the president with no regard for the views of the people. Hezekiah Niles of the *Niles Weekly Register*, a weekly newspaper published in Baltimore that was a compendium of the nation's news, editorialized that it would be preferable to have the halls of Congress "converted into common brothels" than for them to be used for the tainted caucuses.[16]

Despite criticism, the caucus system continued over the next several elections. In 1816, calls for reform increased after an extremely close vote in the Republican caucus. James Monroe of Virginia received sixty-five votes, while William Crawford of Georgia received fifty-four. Monroe, the sitting secretary of state, was far more popular and well known nationally, and many believed that the supporters of Crawford in Congress had manipulated the calling and timing of the caucus in a nearly successful attempt to steal the nomination.[17] Monroe won the election and proved to be such a popular president that, in 1820, he had competition neither inside nor outside of his party and he ran unopposed for reelection. No formal caucus was held, nor needed, that year. Monroe became, and still is, the only president other than Washington to run unopposed for reelection.

In 1824, Crawford finally won the nomination of the Republican caucus for president but by then the process was so discredited that it was a pyrrhic victory. Supporters of rival candidates John Quincy Adams and Henry Clay boycotted the caucus and, of the approximately 260 Republican members of Congress, only about twenty-five percent attended the caucus meeting, where Crawford won sixty of the sixty-eight votes cast. In the week following the caucus, a Baltimore newspaper expressed its disdain:

> The poor little political bird of ominous note and plumage, denominated a CAUCUS, was hatched at Washington on Saturday last.... It is now running around like a pullet, in a forlorn and sickly state. Reader, have you ever seen a chicken directly after it was hatched, creeping about with a bit of egg shell sticking to its back? This is a just representation of this poor forlorn Congressional caucus. The sickly thing is to be fed, cherished, pampered for a week, when it is fondly hoped that it will be enabled to cry the name of Crawford, Crawford, Crawford.[18]

As a result, what was then referred to as the Democratic-Republican Party fielded three candidates in the election of 1824 — Crawford, Adams and Clay — who competed against Andrew Jackson, the candidate of the emerging Democratic Party. The trio split their party's votes. Jackson won a plurality of the popular votes, but did not gain a majority in the Electoral College. As in the election of 1800, under the Constitution, the election went to the House of Representatives, where each state was given one vote.[19] There, Adams prevailed, over outraged cries by Jackson and his supporters that a "corrupt bargain" had been struck between Adams and Clay — an endorsement in exchange for an alleged promise of the top cabinet post. Clay had thrown his support to Adams and, within weeks, was named the latter's secretary of state, the office which was then perceived as the stepping-stone to the presidency.

After the fiasco of 1824, the caucus system was dead. But what to replace it with? There began to be calls for national conventions to nominate candidates for the presidency. In 1822, a leading newspaper promoted a new system whereby the people would:

> [C]hoose delegates in all the States, to meet at some central place ... to select and recommend some suitable person for the Presidency.
> The delegates so chosen, must be specifically instructed by their respective States, whom to support; and the delegates so chosen must, in no case, be incumbents (or expectants) of office.
> That the result of the meeting of delegates be published for the consideration of the American people.
> That, notwithstanding any selection or recommendation by a convention of delegates, the electors when chosen, must vote independently of any previous recommendation or selection.
> That, from this combined expression of the public sentiment, first by delegates chosen to select and recommend, and, second by electors chosen to elect, no doubt the best and most honest selection and election would result.[20]

After a brief experiment with nominations of presidential candidates being made by various state legislatures, which Andrew Jackson used to his advantage in 1828, the era of national conventions for the nomination of candidates for the presidency began in the election cycle of 1832 and has continued ever since. This new process, unlike the congressional caucuses, would not be played out in Washington, the seat of the federal government. Interestingly, in what has now been almost two centuries of American presidential nominating conventions, no major political party has ever held its convention in Washington. The concept of "running against Washington" and playing to the country's anti-"inside the Beltway" mentality existed long before there was a paved Capital Beltway ringing the Federal City. Still, Washington politicians of the 1830s were not about to totally relinquish their control over president-making. They were, "like their species in all times, quick to detect the trend of popular sentiment and to get in step with it. While professedly yielding to the people's desires, they were already planning to get control of the new system for their own purposes."[21] If not in Washington, where would these conventions be held?

The first political conventions would not be held in New York City, the nation's most populous city and its financial center, nor would they be held in Philadelphia, the birthplace of the nation and of the Constitution. They would not be held in Boston, which had been the political powder keg of the country and where the first shots of the American Revolution had been fired. They would not rotate from city to city. Instead, with very few exceptions, the new process for selecting the president of the United States would be developed and played out in the meeting halls, hotels, taverns, and streets of Baltimore, a city that, theretofore, had been a mere onlooker to the national political scene. Beginning with the 1832 election and continuing for the next generation, every four years the nation's attention focused on Maryland, "the Old Line State," and the road to the White House passed through Baltimore.

CHAPTER 2

The Monumental City

To Baltimore — the Monumental City — may the days of her safety be as prosperous
and happy as the days of her danger have been trying and triumphant!
—President John Quincy Adams, 1827

As the 1830s dawned, Baltimore, with a population of approximately 80,000, was the third largest city in the still young United States, ranking behind New York and Philadelphia and just ahead of Boston. New York was more than twice as large as Baltimore, with just over 200,000 people. To a large extent, the city's economy at the time was based on the processing of grain into flour and in exporting flour by sea to the rest of the country and to Europe.[1] It has been said that Baltimore "was built by flour and war."[2] Baltimore was well known and respected throughout the country for successfully repelling the British army during the War of 1812. Still, it is surprising that Baltimore in the early 1830s was about to become the political center of the nation in selecting its president. Baltimore and, for that matter, the state of Maryland, had not been at the forefront of political discussion and debate in the first generation of the new republic. No national political leaders had emerged from Maryland and the state was not closely identified with a particular political party.

What Baltimore lacked in not being at the center of political activity it made up for by being at the geographic center of the country and by its proximity to Washington, D.C., located only forty miles to its south. It also had ease of transportation, both by land and by sea. As a large city, Baltimore had the hotels and meeting halls necessary to support a political convention. Despite this, the choice of Baltimore for political conventions was not a foregone conclusion. Philadelphia was also centrally located and had many of the same advantages as Baltimore. If proximity to Washington was the main criterion for the location of presidential nominating conventions, other cities, such as Wilmington, Richmond, and Harrisburg, all qualified. Each of these cities lacked, however, the combination of location, transportation, and facilities that made Baltimore America's first city of choice for conventions.

Known then and now as the "Monumental City," Baltimore acquired its famous nickname during a visit by the sixth president of the United States, John Quincy Adams. The year 1827 had not been a good one for the dour and disciplined New Englander, neither professionally nor personally. His proposals for federally financed internal improvements and other policy initiatives were blocked in Congress by the increasingly powerful and vocal supporters of

Andrew Jackson. He was still mourning the loss in 1826 of his beloved father, John Adams, and he was dealing with a wayward son, George Adams, who had significant alcohol and gambling problems. As was the custom with most government officials at the time, Adams had vacated Washington during the summer of 1827 and had spent most of August and September at his family home in Quincy, near Boston.[3] As he was preparing to depart Massachusetts, six prominent citizens of Baltimore sent the president a written invitation, dated October 6, 1827, asking him to make a stopover in Baltimore on his return trip to Washington "to enable us to pay to the chief magistrate of the nation, those marks of respect which are so justly due to one whose life has been dedicated to the service of his country."[4] Adams was already en route to Washington when he received the invitation, and he notified the Baltimoreans, in a note written from Philadelphia on October 13, of his acceptance of their invitation and advising that he would be in Baltimore the next day. His upcoming campaign for reelection in 1828 was obviously a consideration in the affirmative response. Why not do a little campaigning while on the way back to Washington?

One day's notice was not much time to prepare for a presidential visit. Adams arrived in Baltimore by steamship from Philadelphia on the afternoon of October 14, checked into Baltimore's finest hotel, Barnum's City Hotel, and promptly took a long nap. That evening, Adams received news that Maryland's foremost military hero from the American Revolution, John Eager Howard, had died on October 12 at his Baltimore home. Adams was asked, and agreed, to extend his stay in the city for an extra day to attend the funeral, which took place on October 15, and which delayed by one day the activities planned by the committee that had invited him to Baltimore. During his visit, the president could readily see the recently finished Battle Monument, located just outside his hotel, and the Washington Monument, located a few blocks to the northwest, nearing completion, but still without the statue of the first president adorning its top. On the morning of October 16, the committee that had invited the president took him to the North Point battlefield, located about nine miles from the city, where the Maryland militia had beaten back the British army during its attempted invasion of Baltimore in the War of 1812. Adams noted in his diary that, at the battlefield, he viewed a "small monument," about four feet high and dedicated to the memory of Aquila Randall, a twenty-four-year-old private in the Maryland militia, who was killed in the battle. Erected in 1817, the monument still stands and is located on Old North Point Road in Dundalk, Maryland.[5]

In the early afternoon, the president received and greeted an estimated 2,000 citizens of Baltimore, including a group of about one hundred students and faculty from the city's St. Mary's College. Noting that the students had studied the heroes of ancient Greece and Rome, Adams urged them to draw inspiration from the monuments that he had seen that very day in Baltimore: "Young gentlemen ... before we part let me remind you ... that you have in this city and its immediate vicinity, the monuments of the same exalted spirits exhibited in the defence of our own country ... and I hope that they will influence your future lives as deeply as the most exalted proofs of public spirit which you will find in the course of your studies."[6] Later in the day, following a dinner with the inviting committee, which also included several veterans of the Revolutionary War and of the War of 1812, Adams thanked the citizens of Baltimore "for the kindness of the reception they have given me." The commander-in-chief offered the event's final toast to "Baltimore — the Monumental City — may the days of her safety be as prosperous and happy as the days of her danger have been trying and triumphant!"[7] The nickname stuck. Adams had bestowed on Baltimore an identity that would last for generations.

Only a few years after President Adams' visit, delegates and others attending political conventions in Baltimore would not only see the monuments that inspired him, but would, like Adams, also stay in some of the country's finest hotels, arrive in the city by transportation systems unequalled in the era, and would be greeted by local citizens known for their hospitality.

Baltimore's Washington Monument had originally been proposed for "The Square" at Calvert and Fayette Streets, the site of many fashionable residences at the time. Those living in the area feared that the proposed 175-foot column would attract lightning or even topple onto their homes during a storm. The objections of the residents were accepted, and John Eager Howard, a Baltimore resident and one of Maryland's heroes from the Revolutionary War, offered an alternative site for the monument on land he owned called Howard Park, which was at that time "safely detached from the City." The cornerstone of the Washington Monument was laid on July 4, 1815, and construction continued for almost fifteen years. The massive statue of the nation's first president was hoisted to the top of the white marble column on November 28, 1829.[8] When built, the Washington Monument was several blocks north of what was then considered the center of Baltimore. Appropriately, the neighborhood came to be known as Mount Vernon. Engravings, prints, and, later, photographs of Baltimore show the Washington Monument dominating the city's skyline until the early twentieth century. Its larger namesake in Washington, D.C., would not be started until 1848 and was not completed until 1884. Travelers to Baltimore invariably commented on the beauty, gracefulness, and grandeur of the Washington Monument. Provided with lanterns, visitors ascended the dark winding staircase and, once atop the structure, saw the sixteen-foot statue of the great man up close and had an unobstructed view for miles in all directions.

The square originally proposed for the Washington Monument became the site of the city's other major monument, the Battle Monument, which is much smaller and less impressive to the eye. Built between 1815 and 1825, it honors Marylanders who were killed in the successful repulsion of the British attack on Baltimore during the War of 1812. The monument sits in the middle of Calvert Street, between Fayette and Lexington Streets. Its image has been the official symbol of the City of Baltimore since 1827. Approximately forty-three feet tall, the shaft of the Battle Monument rests on a base resembling an Egyptian tomb, with its eighteen layers representing the number of states at the time of the war. Arising from the base is a round column, circled with bands inscribed with the names of the soldiers who fell in the battle. A statue at the top, approximately ten feet tall, represents the City of Baltimore, her face looking eastward toward the scene of the battle. She holds aloft a laurel wreath in her right hand (representing the glory won in the battle), a ship's helm in her left hand (representing Baltimore's seaport), with an eagle (representing the United States) and a bombshell (representing the bombardment of Fort McHenry) at her side.[9] Four griffins guard the statue at the corners of the monument's base. The architecture was praised by a nineteenth-century American, who observed: "A single glance at this monument, strikes the beholder with admiration, and suffices to convince him, that its various parts have been designed and combined by the effort of talent and genius of the first order.... This elegant structure presents a glorious testimony of the patriotism, devotion, and gratitude of the citizens of Baltimore, and a no less gratifying evidence of the rapid advancement of arts in this country."[10]

Soon after the construction of the Battle Monument, the area surrounding it, known as Monument Square, became the heart and soul of Baltimore, much as Times Square is to modern New York and Trafalgar Square is to London. The square became the center of evening activity during Baltimore's political conventions. Thousands of people, multiple brass bands

Completed in 1829, Baltimore's Washington Monument was the nation's first monument honoring George Washington. It was visited by, and inspired, many of the delegates attending conventions in Baltimore *(Enoch Pratt Free Library)*.

BALTIMORE MD.

BATTLE MONUMENT-MONUMENT SQUARE.

Baltimore's Battle Monument and its surrounding square were the scene of many evening rallies during conventions held in the city *(Enoch Pratt Free Library)*.

playing on balconies overlooking the square, political speeches, and competing rallies for the various candidates filled the square during the conventions. The meeting halls of Baltimore's political conventions, and the lodging of most of the delegates, were all contained within a one-half mile radius of the Battle Monument.

Immediately southwest of the Battle Monument, at the southwest corner of Calvert and Fayette Streets, stood Barnum's City Hotel, the largest and grandest of all Baltimore hotels in the nineteenth century. Opened in September 1826, Barnum's was the most comfortable and prestigious address for any traveler to Baltimore. Some called it the best hotel in the country. A young Philadelphia lawyer staying at the hotel shortly after it opened wrote to his father that the "house of Barnum is the most splendid hotel I have ever seen."[11] When the president of the United States came to Baltimore, he stayed at Barnum's. John Quincy Adams, Martin Van Buren, Zachary Taylor, and James Buchanan, among other presidents, stayed there.[12] The English novelist Charles Dickens, who toured the United States in 1842, had criticisms of America and Americans, but he was full of praise for his luxurious accommodations in Baltimore. Dickens wrote in his journal of Baltimore and Barnum's: "The most comfortable of all the hotels of which I had any experience in the United States, and they were not few, is Barnum's in that city; where the English traveller will find curtains for his bed, for the first and probably the last time in America ... and where he will likely have enough water for washing himself, which is not at all a common case."[13] Six stories tall, the hotel occupied 120

As the convention era began in the 1830s, Barnum's City Hotel was the most luxurious hotel in Baltimore. Barnum's was the leading hotel for the lodging of delegates, as well as for deal making *(Enoch Pratt Free Library)*.

feet along Calvert Street and originally ran 213 feet along Fayette Street. In 1848, the hotel was enlarged and another 135 feet was added to its back, resulting in the hotel occupying virtually the entire city block.[14] Everything about Barnum's was first class: "No expense has been spared either for the materials used, or for the quality of the furniture."[15] One writer noted that the hotel's "food deserves a separate chapter," with its guests feasting on Maryland specialties of "terrapin and wine, the oysters and old ham, canvas backs and devilled crabs."[16]

After Barnum's, there was one close rival in Baltimore, and then many followers. A decade after the opening of Barnum's, a second grand hotel opened several blocks to the west. Located at the northwest corner of Baltimore and Eutaw Streets, the Eutaw House was a worthy competitor of Barnum's. The massive all-brick structure opened in 1835, its construction having taken three years. Fronting on 125 feet along Eutaw Street and 110 feet along Baltimore Street, the Eutaw House was an "elegant hostelry" of the first order[17] and was "celebrated as one of the best hotels in the country."[18] One foreign guest in about 1840 praised the Eutaw House as "equal to any in the Union," and said it "combines more of cleanliness, comfort, and adequate attendance, than any hotel we had yet visited in the country."[19]

Beyond these two large and elite hotels, there were several other smaller hotels that were all well known to visitors to Baltimore in the mid–nineteenth century and which also served as the temporary homes of delegates, reporters, and other visitors to Baltimore during the city's political conventions. The Old Fountain Inn stood at the northeast corner of Light Street and German (now Redwood) Street and dated from the American Revolution. George Washington had lodged there. A separate ballroom on the grounds was the scene of many of Baltimore's grand social events. The Indian Queen Hotel, at the southwest corner of Hanover and Baltimore Streets, also dated from the revolutionary era. The General Wayne Inn (corner of Baltimore and Howard Streets), the Exchange Hotel (Second Street near Gay Street), the Gilmor House (west side of Monument Square), Guy's Hotel (originally on the northeast

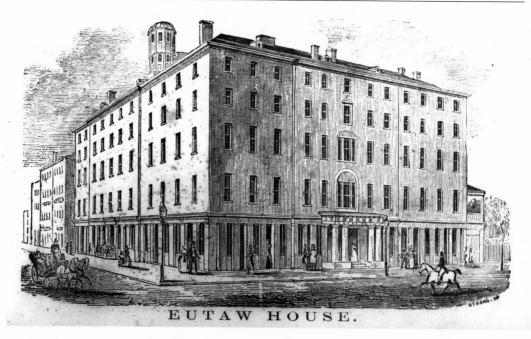

EUTAW HOUSE.

The Eutaw House was Baltimore's other luxury hotel during the city's convention era. Located several blocks west of Barnum's, it was a favorite of the large New York delegations (*Enoch Pratt Free Library*).

corner of Fayette Street and Monument Square), and the Maltby House (East Pratt Street near Light Street), were all part of the abundant lodging accommodations that attracted political conventions to the Monumental City.[20]

Convention cities, then and now, need not only hotels but adequate transportation to reach them. July 4, 1828, was a day that changed Baltimore's history. With the opening of the Erie Canal in 1825, New York City had a virtual East Coast monopoly on commerce with the rapidly westward-expanding United States and its territories. Baltimore, ideally situated at the midpoint of the original thirteen states of the eastern seaboard, desperately looked for a way to compete. On the fifty-second anniversary of the signing of the Declaration of Independence, Baltimore began its journey on the road to capturing its share of commerce with the West. In a grand ceremony held near Mount Clare Mansion in Baltimore, with Maryland's own Charles Carroll of Carrollton, the last surviving signer of the Declaration of Independence, turning over the first shovel, the cornerstone of the Baltimore and Ohio (the "B & O") Railroad was laid.[21] Two dozen leading citizens had successfully lobbied the Maryland legislature to incorporate the railroad, and the City of Baltimore invested a half million dollars in the corporation's stock. It was an ambitious plan — to build a railway 250 miles westward to the Ohio River. Baltimore had a geographic advantage, being located two hundred miles closer to the Ohio River than New York, and one hundred miles closer than Philadelphia. The enterprise was risky, as there were no real functioning railroads in America at the time. Only two short lines existed, one in Pennsylvania and one in Massachusetts, each only a couple of miles in length and which were used to haul raw materials from mines.[22] A reliable steam locomotive had not yet been built and, in the B & O's initial years, horses were used to pull the cars along the rails.

Remarkably, the venture worked and it prospered. The B & O placed Baltimore in the forefront of the railroad transportation revolution. By May 1830, one could travel thirteen miles from Baltimore to Ellicott's Mills (now Ellicott City) while sitting in a primitive horse-drawn railway car. The one-way travel time was two hours.[23] While westward construction continued, the owners of the B & O secured a second charter from the Maryland legislature in March 1833 that would closely link Baltimore with the nation's capital. Tapping into the existing rail line to Ellicott's Mills at Relay (located eight miles from Baltimore), the Washington branch line of the B & O Railroad was begun in October 1833. By the time that the B & O tracks to Washington opened in August 1835, horses had been replaced with four brand new steam locomotives, appropriately named the Thomas Jefferson, the James Madison, the James Monroe, and the John Quincy Adams. Passengers paid two and one-half dollars for a one-way fare between the Federal City and Baltimore. The state of Maryland had invested a half-million dollars in the project, with the condition that it receive twenty percent of the passenger revenues, plus stock dividends.[24] Travel time by locomotive between the two cities was approximately two hours. In reaching to the west with the B & O Railroad, Baltimore, through the secondary line to Washington, had, as the convention era began, unintentionally secured its future as the primary location for presidential nominating conventions. The political elite of both parties in Washington might be willing to share power in selecting presidents with their party's convention delegates, but they also had a vested interest in keeping the nominating conventions close by and as much under their watchful eyes and control as possible.

Within a decade of the opening of the B & O, two other major railroads laid tracks to Baltimore, connecting the city with the North. The Northern Central Railroad ran to Harrisburg, Pennsylvania, and its terminus in the city was at Calvert Station. This station was on the east side of Calvert Street near Franklin Street, where the main office of the *Baltimore Sun* is currently located. The Philadelphia, Wilmington, & Baltimore Railroad came from Philadelphia and its passengers arrived and departed from President Street Station, located on the east side of Baltimore's Inner Harbor. These three railroads made Baltimore a railroad hub, with trains from the north, the south, and the west funneling through the city.[25] The use of locomotives through the city was prohibited at the time and horse-drawn railcars shuttled passengers and cargo between the three stations on rail tracks along Pratt Street and Calvert Street.[26]

Railroads provided only one facet of Baltimore's transportation advantages as a host city for political conventions. As early as 1813, Baltimore, as a seaport, had steamboats linking it to other port cities on the East Coast.[27] In 1832, a steamboat trip to Philadelphia cost four dollars, and involved a partial overland route by stagecoach (and later by railroad) between Frenchtown, Maryland, and New Castle, Delaware, for total travel time of nine hours. A steamship to Norfolk cost seven dollars and took eighteen hours. Longer trips from Baltimore to further destinations could be specially booked, with travel to Savannah costing twenty dollars and to New Orleans fifty dollars. For those interested in more traditional modes of transportation, stagecoaches were available to Washington for three dollars, for four and one-half dollars to Harrisburg, and for fourteen dollars to Pittsburgh.[28] The stagecoaches traveled along turnpikes that connected Baltimore with other cities. The most famous of these was the National Road, begun in 1811, which consisted of a central carriageway of stone and gravel. It was financed by the federal government, and by 1818 the National Road extended to Wheeling, Virginia (now West Virginia), and by 1833 to Columbus, Ohio. It was the "longest, best known, and most extensive turnpike in the United States," and was a favorite route for western congressmen of the era to travel back and forth from their districts to Baltimore and then on to Washington.[29]

In addition to its location and transportation facilities, Baltimore also had intangibles that attracted political conventions to the city. Baltimore was viewed as a pleasant place to visit. As one writer noted of the city in the first half of the nineteenth century, "The first views of the skyline of domes, spires, and columns seldom failed to impress a traveler, and although here and there a sidewalk might be blocked by a pig searching for garbage, even the critics who were prepared to find fault were disarmed by Baltimore hospitality. No American city was reputed to be so gay and warmhearted; none was graced by so many beautiful women."[30] The friendly nature of Baltimoreans was often commented on by visitors to the city. One noted that "the trade of Baltimore is very considerable, yet there is less appearance of bustle and business than either in New York or Boston."[31] Compared to other large American cities, one observer wrote, Baltimore's "tone of conversation is lighter and more agreeable ... there is not much pretension of any sort."[32] Then, as now, Baltimore had a reputation as being less cosmopolitan than its northern counterparts: "Baltimore lagged far behind New York, Philadelphia, and Boston in the arts, music, and library facilities, and was generally not the regional cultural center its northern sister cities were."[33] Some thought that Baltimore had the best of both sections on the country: "Baltimore in the 1840s was the most northern of southern cities, or to put it another way, the Queen of the Patapsco was culturally southern and economically northern."[34]

There was one aspect of Baltimore's economy in the mid–nineteenth century that was that was distinctively southern. Maryland was a slave state and slavery existed in the city of Baltimore. Many of the staff of Baltimore's hotels were slaves hired out by their masters to the hotels to work as housekeepers, porters, and waiters. While there were slaves in Baltimore, the city was also a haven for free blacks, and the city's free black population in the middle third of the nineteenth century greatly outnumbered its slave population.[35] The extent to which some southern delegates brought slaves to Baltimore with them while attending conventions is unknown but, presumably, this occurred and there was less risk of a slave fleeing than if the convention had been held in a northern free state. As to slavery and delegates attending conventions in the city, Baltimore was unlikely to offend visitors from the North or the South. Northerners would not be exposed to the harshest features of slavery, and southerners would not encounter local abolitionists while visiting the city.[36]

By the early 1830s, with its monuments, hotels, meeting halls, railroads, steamships, and turnpikes all in place, Baltimore was ready for its role as convention city and to host visitors from throughout the nation.

CHAPTER 3

1832: Please Join Us, Mr. Carroll

Oh! Harry Clay's a lawyer, a fellow wise and rare;
He's going to try another heat, to reach the people's chair.

In Thirty-two you tried it, to beat old Hickory back;
But your horse was easy distanced, and flung you on the track.

Oh! No you don't, old Harry; the President's chair,
It is too far to suit your legs — you never will get there.[1]

Campaign song, 1844

The American presidential nominating convention was born in the campaign of 1832. With the old congressional caucus system fully discredited, this new system of choosing a party's candidates for president and vice president began. Between September 1831 and May 1832, three political parties would hold conventions and all three would choose Baltimore as the site of their meetings. The political activists and officeholders of each of the parties trekked to Baltimore from across the country for the first of these quadrennial gatherings, which quickly became the standard method for selecting a presidential candidate. The methodology lasted longer than two of the three parties, for the national conventions held the 1832 election cycle would be not only their first but also their last. The procedures used by the three conventions were similar in many ways, but different in others. There was one common theme for each of the conventions — an invitation to Maryland's most distinguished citizen to join their proceedings.

Anti-Mason Convention

The supposed murder of one man precipitated a third-party political movement that led to the first nominating convention for the presidency. William Morgan was a New Yorker and a disaffected member of the Masons. In 1826, shortly after he threatened to publish an exposé revealing the secrets of the Masonic Order, he disappeared and was rumored to have been kidnapped and murdered at the direction of Masons from lodges in upstate New York. Many elected officials in New York and throughout the country were Masons (George Washington had been a Mason) and the death of Morgan lit a spark that ignited a political firestorm. The

Anti-Mason movement began in New York in 1826 and quickly spread to neighboring states. Its goal was singular and simple — the removal of Masons from public office. Among the leaders of the Anti-Masons were young men such as William Seward and Millard Fillmore of New York, and Thaddeus Stevens of Pennsylvania, who would become leaders of the Whig and Republican parties later in their careers. Representatives of the movement met in Philadelphia in September 1830 for an initial national gathering and resolved to meet again in Baltimore in September 1831 for the purpose of nominating candidates for president and vice president of the United States. They needed their own candidate, since the incumbent president, Andrew Jackson, was a Mason, as was his expected opponent, Henry Clay.[2]

Whether Morgan was actually murdered has never been proven. According to New York editor Thurlow Weed, a leader of the Anti-Mason movement, something resembling a human body was produced, said to be the remains of the disgruntled former Mason, and the supposed body was a "good enough Morgan until after the election."[3] Morgan definitively was kidnapped and taken around a large part of upstate New York. One rumor favored by the Masons was that he was taken in a rowboat across the Niagara River to Canada and given five hundred dollars and a horse, and voluntarily agreed never to return to the United States.[4]

It was the intent and expectation of the party's leaders to nominate Justice John McLean of the United States Supreme Court as their candidate for the presidency. McLean, from Ohio, was a political chameleon whose party allegiance changed with the prevailing winds. He had served in the cabinet as postmaster general under the National Republican administrations of Presidents James Monroe and John Quincy Adams. He then became a supporter of Andrew Jackson, a Democrat, and secured an appointment, in 1829, from Jackson to the Supreme Court. He then became disenchanted with Jackson, flirted with the Anti-Mason Party, and would later move to the Whigs, the Free-Soilers, and eventually, to the Republicans. Known as "the politician on the Supreme Court," McLean surfaced as a would-be presidential candidate in several mid–nineteenth-century campaigns.[5] Former president John Quincy Adams wrote in his diary in 1833 that Justice McLean "thinks of nothing but the Presidency by day and dreams of nothing else by night."[6]

In response to inquiries from leaders of the Anti-Mason Party, McLean had initially advised that he was in agreement with their cause and would, if nominated, gladly be their candidate. Just prior to assembling in Baltimore for their convention, however, the leaders of the party were surprised to learn that they had been jilted by their prospective nominee. As Weed later recounted in his autobiography, the party leaders were "much embarrassed" by receipt of a letter from Justice McLean declining their nomination, if it was offered at the convention, which was totally contrary to his earlier indications. In the letter, written from Nashville on September 7, 1831, McLean stated that there were already three candidates for the presidency, Jackson, Clay, and Calhoun, and that adding a fourth name, "especially one so humble as mine ... would only distract the public mind." Therefore, he concluded, "I must respectfully decline the honor of being presented to that respectable body [the convention] for nomination to the presidency."[7] Stunned party leaders, with the convention scheduled to begin in only a few days, hastily began to look for an alternative candidate. McLean, who clearly wanted to be president, likely decided, after Henry Clay got into the race, that the anti–Jackson vote would be too fragmented and that he could never get to the White House as the candidate of an obscure third party.

The first presidential nominating convention in American history was held at the Athenaeum in Baltimore, located at the southwest corner of St. Paul and Lexington Streets. The building is often referred to as the "First Athenaeum," since a second building with the same name was built in Baltimore two decades later, in 1846, and was located a few blocks away.[8] In 1823, a group of prominent Baltimoreans had formed an association named "The Baltimore Athenaeum," which was incorporated by the Maryland legislature in 1824 and whose purpose was "the promotion of literature, and the encouragement of the arts and sciences by providing a library, reading rooms, and otherwise."[9] A building was then designed to fulfill the organization's needs. The cornerstone of the four-story structure was laid on August 10, 1824, and the project was completed on October 4, 1825. A visitor to Baltimore in the early 1830s described it as "a superb edifice built a few years ago, on a modern and beautiful design.... Lectures of various subjects are delivered in its spacious halls, and concerts and other public meetings held in its splendid saloon."[10] The Athenaeum's large meeting room, called the "grand saloon," was on the first floor and was the primary meeting place for large civic gatherings in the city. It was in this room that the Anti-Masons held their convention. The basement and second story of the building housed offices for local attorneys, the third floor was the home of the Maryland Institute, and the fourth floor housed the Maryland Academy of Arts and Sciences.[11]

The Anti-Mason Party's presidential nominating convention assembled in the Athenaeum on September 26, 1831. On the opening day, ninety-nine delegates were present from twelve states, which increased to one hundred and twelve delegates from thirteen states by the close of the proceedings.[12] More than half the delegates were from New York and Pennsylvania, where sentiments against the Masons were strongest, compared to only one delegate each from New Hampshire, Maryland, and Delaware. John C. Spencer of New York was named the president of the gathering. Each state was given the number of votes equal to its number of votes in the Electoral College (the number of seats held by each state in the House of Representatives, plus two more for the Senate).[13] The convention opened with a report of the corresponding committee that had been established at the Philadelphia meeting the previous year, which noted that a number of Anti-Mason newspapers had been established in several states and were, through the free press, exposing the evils of Masonry to the American public.[14]

The convention, in an attempt to give more credence to its deliberations, invited three distinguished Americans to attend. Chief Justice John Marshall was in Baltimore on other business and, "having been unexpectedly prevented from leaving the city," was extended an invitation, which he accepted.[15] The head of the federal judiciary attending a political convention was apparently not, at the time, considered injudicious. The Anti-Masons also invited William Wirt to attend their proceedings. Wirt, born and raised in Maryland, was a lawyer who had spent most of his adult life in Virginia. An ally of Thomas Jefferson, Wirt had been one of the prosecutors of former vice president Aaron Burr at his treason trial, held in Richmond in 1806. Wirt's skill as an attorney led President Monroe to name him attorney general of the United States, a post he held for twelve years, eight under Monroe and four under the second President Adams.[16] Upon his retirement as the country's top law enforcement officer in 1829, Wirt returned to Maryland and established a legal practice in Baltimore.[17] He represented the Cherokee Indians before the Supreme Court in their attempt to oppose Andrew Jackson's forced removal of the tribe to new land west of the Mississippi. By 1831, Wirt was firmly in the anti–Jackson camp.[18] Along with Marshall, Wirt, who lived and worked in Baltimore at the time, accepted the invitation of the Anti-Masons to attend their convention.

Attempting to derive the most benefit from and exposure for their Baltimore convention, the Anti-Masons also invited a third guest, Maryland's most famous citizen, to their gathering. A committee was appointed to go to the home of Charles Carroll of Carrollton and to extend

The Athenaeum in Baltimore was the site of the first three presidential nominating conventions in American history. During the 1832 election cycle, the Anti-Masons, the National Republicans, and the Democrats all gathered here *(Enoch Pratt Free Library).*

to him an invitation to attend. Carroll was the best known and most distinguished member of the Carroll family of Maryland. Modern residents of central Maryland can hardly travel more than a few miles without coming across a home that once belonged to some member of the family. The Maryland lineage of Carrolls began with Charles Carroll the Settler (1661–1720). He was a Catholic lawyer who was born in Ireland and who secured a commission from his friend and fellow Catholic, Charles Calvert, to be the attorney general of the Maryland Colony. The Settler arrived in Maryland in 1688 to assume his duties but, a year later, after the Glorious Revolution in England (in which King James II, a Catholic, was deposed and replaced with King William of Orange and Queen Mary, who were Protestants), Maryland's colonial government was controlled by Protestants, and Catholics were excluded from holding public office. Carroll then turned his talents to business, married well, and built a small fortune.

The Settler's son, known as Charles Carroll of Annapolis (1702–1782), maintained and increased the family's fortune. Also restricted by anti–Catholic laws from holding public office, and even from voting, he became involved in other matters and was a noted horse breeder and racer. In the 1720s he built a home next door to his father's home in Annapolis. The two houses, joined by a passageway, are still standing. They are now known as the Charles Carroll House of Annapolis, and are open to the public.[19]

It was the grandson of the Settler, Charles Carroll of Carrollton, who was by far the most famous member of the family. To distinguish himself from his father, Charles Carroll of Annapolis, he took his name from Carrollton Manor, a 17,000-acre family estate in Frederick County, Maryland, located near what is now Buckeystown. Carroll was born in 1737 in Annapolis, was educated in both England and France, and studied classics and the law. Like his grandfather and father, as a Catholic, he was prohibited from practicing law, and from

Charles Carroll of Carrollton, a Marylander, the last surviving signer of the Declaration of Independence, was invited to attend all three conventions held in Baltimore during the 1832 election cycle *(Enoch Pratt Free Library)*.

voting, in colonial America. He wrote anonymous pro-independence letters in newspapers and became a Maryland leader in the revolutionary movement. Elected to the Continental Congress as a representative from Maryland in early July 1776, he actually arrived in Philadelphia too late to vote for the Declaration of Independence, although he did get there in time to sign the document. After the American Revolution, he represented Maryland in the United States Senate, and served in the Maryland Senate.[20] When Thomas Jefferson and John Adams both died on July 4, 1826, the fiftieth anniversary of the signing of the Declaration of Independence, Charles Carroll of Carrollton became the sole surviving signer of that document and the last living link to the convention that had created the republic. It is not surprising that members of the nation's first presidential nominating convention, which was being held in Baltimore, would seek to have this venerated founding father and local citizen attend their proceedings.

Carroll was ninety-four years old in 1831. Rumored to be the richest man in America, he maintained a home in Baltimore located on the northeast corner of Lombard and Front Streets. This federal style brick home was built in 1811 and still stands. Now known as the Carroll Mansion and owned by the City of Baltimore, it has been used over the years as a home, a school, and as a museum. Carroll split his time between his city home and his much larger family estate known as Doughoregan Manor in Howard County, Maryland, located twenty miles from Baltimore. The aged patriot, upon receiving the invitation from the Anti-Masons to attend their convention, politely declined. The committee sent to invite him reported back to the convention that Mr. Carroll's secretary had told them that Mr. Carroll spent the summer at his Howard County estate, and although in good health, he was "desirous to avoid the fatigue of journeys to and from the city."[21]

Although Carroll was absent, the convention's other two distinguished guests, Marshall and Wirt, were given honored seats on the podium as the proceedings began.[22] At its opening session, the convention heard an extended report from one of its committees, the Committee on Masonic Penalties, which had been appointed at the Philadelphia gathering the prior year, and which outlined the levels of penalties established by Masonic orders for the disclosure of Masonic secrets.[23] The higher one rose in the order, the more grotesque the method by which one would pledge to meet his maker for disclosure of lodge secrets. A mere apprentice had only to agree "to have my throat cut across, my tongue torn out by the roots, and my body buried in the rough sands of the seas." That was minor compared to the Fellow Craft's oath, which compelled him, if secrets were revealed, "to have my left breast torn open, and my heart and vitals taken from thence, and given as a prey to the fowls of the air, and the wild beasts of the field." The level of pain and torture pledged by one who rose to the high level of Master Mason and who betrayed the order was even more intense: "to have my body severed in two in the waist, my bowels burnt to ashes and the ashes scattered to the four winds of heaven, that there might not the least track or trace of remembrance remain, among men or masons, of so vile and perjured a wretch as I."[24]

The convention then received a committee report retelling the saga of William Morgan, who, after disclosing Masonic secrets and apparently unwilling to agree to dismemberment, "was kidnapped and murdered by masons, and that at least five hundred of the fraternity must have been knowing to, and directly or indirectly implicated in." Further, the committee reported, it is "already too well known" that poor Morgan was forcibly carried a distance of more than one hundred and twenty miles to Niagara Fort, New York, and "was confined to that fort and finally murdered."[25]

The evils of Masonry having been detailed and exposed, the convention proceeded, for the first time in American history, to its main purpose — the nomination of a candidate for president of the United States by a group of citizens gathered together from throughout the country. With Justice McLean no longer a potential nominee, the attention of party leaders focused on their distinguished guests at the convention. McLean's boss on the Supreme Court, Chief Justice Marshall, was purportedly approached about his availability as a candidate, but he declined. According to Thurlow Weed, he and three other party leaders then met with the convention's other honored guest, William Wirt, who advised that he was "in cordial sympathy to our principles" and "finally consented to the use of his name" as a candidate.[26] With a prospective nominee finally lined up, the convention then moved to the establishment of its rules. The convention adopted a rule requiring a three-quarters vote of the delegates for nomination. Tellers were appointed to sit at a table in the center of the hall. Each delegate rose as his name was called, walked to the table, and deposited his ballot in an open box. When the tally took place, Wirt received 108 of the 111 votes cast, thereby winning the nomination on the first ballot. Anticipating his nomination and apparently feeling it would be unseemly to witness it in person, Wirt had stayed away from the proceedings on the day of the voting. The Anti-Mason convention then initiated a notification procedure that would be followed by virtually all political conventions over the next century — until the time when politicians would campaign openly for the presidency and attend conventions in person. A formal notification committee of three delegates was appointed to visit Wirt, to advise him of his nomination, and to obtain his reply.[27]

The convention then moved to the business of nominating a candidate for vice president. Only one name was placed in nomination, Amos Ellmaker of Pennsylvania, a lawyer who had served as attorney general of the Keystone State. A leader of the Anti-Mason movement in Pennsylvania, Ellmaker had been a delegate to the party's Philadelphia meeting in 1830 and had chaired the committee there that had recommended that the Baltimore convention be held the following year to nominate a candidate for the presidency.[28] To have any chance in the election, the Anti-Masons had to carry Pennsylvania, and the nomination of Ellmaker, a committed leader of the movement (unlike Wirt), was intended to fire up the party's base and to help in carrying a state with a large number of electoral votes. On the first ballot, the unopposed Ellmaker won the nomination for the second spot on the ticket, also getting 108 votes.[29]

By the time balloting concluded for vice president, the chairman of the notification committee Mr. Wirt reported that his committee had "performed that duty" and that a written response was promised from the nominee by 5:00 P.M. The convention then passed a resolution thanking the "City of Baltimore at whose expense this Convention has been accommodated with the use of the splendid hall of the Athenaeum; and that this Convention have felt peculiar pleasure in receiving such a proof of hospitality from the inhabitants of this elegant and polished city."[30]

The convention then proceeded to adopt the first political party platform in American history, which proclaimed that "the existence of secret and affiliated societies is hostile to ... free discussion ... and can subserve no purpose of utility in a free government."[31] As a single-issue political movement, the Anti-Mason platform would more properly have been called a plank. No resolutions were passed, nor even discussed, at the convention concerning the economic issues of the day, or on other pressing concerns of domestic or foreign policy. Revenge for the supposed murder of poor William Morgan, by the removal of Masons from public office at all levels, was the end-all and be-all of the movement.

Imagine the jaw-dropping reaction of the delegates when the written response of their nominee, William Wirt, was received later that evening. The nominee of the Anti-Mason

Party for president of the United States revealed to the convention that he had previously been, and might still be, a member of the secret society to which their venom was directed. Wirt was a Mason! In a candid letter, he advised the delegates that "very early in life, I was myself invited in the mysteries of free masonry," although he "never took the masters degree." Noting that George Washington had been a Mason and that he had viewed the organization as more of a social entity, Wirt stated that he had not been active in the Masons for thirty years. He politely offered the convention a way out of a potentially awkward situation, "so that you may be able to disembarrass yourself at once, by changing your nomination, if you find that you have acted under mistake."[32] After summarizing the charges against Masonic lodges over the Morgan kidnapping and alleged murder, Wirt renounced the organization and declared that "if this be masonry ... I have no hesitation in saying, that I consider it at war with the fundamental principles of the social compact, as treason against society, and a wicked conspiracy against the laws of God and man, which should be put down."[33] After hearing Wirt's letter, the delegates reaffirmed their nomination of him.[34] In reality, at this stage, any change would have been too embarrassing to the party and likely fatal to the movement.

Almost as soon as Wirt agreed to accept the nomination, he began to have regrets and looked for a way out. He had some explaining to do to his friends and colleagues, since he had previously agreed to attend the upcoming convention of the National Republican Party, to be held in Baltimore in December 1831, and to be a delegate there supporting the nomination of Henry Clay. He had written to his close friend Judge Dabney Carr of the Virginia Court of Appeals, in May 1831, concerning the National Republican Party convention, "If the people wish me to go to the Convention in December, I will go."[35] In another letter to Judge Carr only a few days after the Anti-Mason convention, Wirt pleaded that he was aware "an evening or two before, that such a thing was in agitation, and might possibly take place," but that he did not receive formal notice of his nomination until 1:00 P.M. on the day of the vote and a response was requested by the late afternoon. Pleading that the pressure of time left him without the opportunity to consult with "even a friend in this city," and being told by Anti-Mason Party leaders that Henry Clay could not possibly defeat Jackson, he had decided to accept the nomination.[36] The new and reluctant candidate explained to his friend Carr that he had been "drawn into a political scrape, which has taken me as much by surprise as if a thunderbolt had dropped at my feet on a clear day." He told Carr, "I am afraid you may think I have acted imprudently," and he feared that he would be "laughed at, abused and slandered." Yet, based on his newfound belief that Clay could not defeat Jackson, he reasoned: "I am still friendly with Mr. Clay, but I think I have done what is right."[37]

By January 1832, after Clay's nomination by the National Republicans in December, Wirt wanted out. He pleaded that he was no politician: "I have none of the captivating arts and manners of professional seekers of popularity. I do not desire them."[38] He wrote to leaders of the Anti-Mason Party and asked that his nomination be withdrawn, suggesting that Jackson was unbeatable and that the party should focus its energy on winning races below the presidential level. He wrote to Judge Carr, "I fear the Anti-Masons will not let me off."[39] In this, he was correct. He did not campaign, even in the limited campaigning that was done in that era by candidates for the presidency. He later wrote "In the canvass, I took no part; not even by writing private letters."[40] And so the American presidential nominating convention was born with a fringe party being jilted by its favored candidate, turning at the last minute in desperation to a reluctant nominee, who, after accepting, regretted his decision, tried to have his name withdrawn, and did nothing to campaign for the office. Maybe this wasn't going to be such a good way to pick a president after all.

The Anti-Masons were the first of many third-party movements in American history. Such movements have been likened to wildfires on the prairie—they have intense heat for a short period of time and then burn out quickly.[41] So it was with the Anti-Masons. Single-issue politics is not a basis upon which to build a national political party. As Wirt's biographer, John Pendleton Kennedy, wrote in 1849, during the peak of the Anti-Masonry movement in the late 1820s and early 1830s, "the zeal to destroy Masonry rose above all other subjects of public concern.... The most intractable of all men are those whose minds are engrossed with one idea.... We may now wonder, after this lapse of time, that intelligent and acute men could ever have persuaded themselves that it had a base broad enough upon which to build a party."[42]

The Wirt/Ellmaker ticket received only eight percent of the popular vote, just over 100,000 out of 1,200,000 cast, and won only one state, Vermont.[43] By the time of the next presidential election in 1836, the Anti-Masons would be organized only in a couple of states and, as a national political force, the movement, like poor William Morgan, would be missing and presumed dead. While the Anti-Mason Party did not last, its procedural innovation, the national nominating convention for the presidency, did, and ever since then, has been a fixture in the American election process.

National Republican Convention

Less than three months after the Anti-Mason convention vacated the Athenaeum in Baltimore, the National Republican Party met in the same building to hold its first presidential nominating convention. In the prior election of 1828, the party and its then incumbent president, John Quincy Adams, had been trounced by Andrew Jackson and the Democrats. Jackson had made the 1828 election a referendum on the 1824 contest, where he won the popular vote but failed to obtain a majority of the Electoral College votes needed for election.[44] As noted earlier, under the Constitution, the election went to House of Representatives, with the three top electoral vote finishers being the candidates. The fourth-place finisher, Henry Clay, was excluded from the contest, but threw his support to John Quincy Adams, who prevailed in the House over Andrew Jackson to become the nation's sixth president. When Adams then named Clay as his secretary of state, Andrew Jackson and the Democrats charged that a "corrupt bargain" between the two had robbed him of the presidency. The office of the secretary of state was viewed as a stepping-stone to the presidency, as Jefferson, Madison, Monroe, and John Quincy Adams himself, had each served as the nation's top diplomat before becoming chief executive.

In February 1831, six months after the Anti-Mason Party announced its intention to hold a presidential nominating convention in Baltimore, the *National Intelligencer*, the Washington newspaper of the National Republican Party, also called for a nominating convention, and suggested that it be held in Baltimore in December 1831. The call picked up support nationwide. In Maryland, a caucus of members of the legislature opposed to the Jackson administration met in Annapolis on February 17, 1831, and passed the following resolutions:

> Resolved, that it is the duty of all who love their country, to unite in strong endeavor, at the next presidential election, to deliver it from the hands of men who have threatened, assailed, and greatly endangered all that is valuable and venerable in our institutions.

> Resolved, That it is expedient that a national convention be held, to which the people of all states should be invited to send delegates, in which their will can be authentically ascertained, and that concert of action produced, which is essential to our cause.

Resolved, That it be, and it is hereby recommended to all persons of this state, opposed to the re-election of Andrew Jackson, to elect in such manner and in such time as they may deem convenient, one delegate from each congressional district, to meet in general convention in the city of Baltimore, on the second Monday of December next — and that this meeting will appoint two delegates — one from the eastern and one from the western shore, to attend the said convention.

Resolved, That our brethren of other states, who with us depreciate the re-election of Andrew Jackson, be, and they are hereby invited to meet in general convention, in Baltimore, on the second Monday of December next, by delegates equal in number to the electors for president to which their states are respectively entitled, in order that after full consultation, the convention may present as candidates for the presidency and vice-presidency, statesmen the best established in public confidence, and calculated to promote our common object, the safety and welfare of the country.[45]

Similar calls for a convention came from other states. Leading anti–Jackson politicians, most notably Henry Clay, also supported the call for a national nominating convention. Clay, as early as 1830, wrote in letters to friends and supporters that presidential nominations by state legislatures were not proper, since the legislators were not elected for that purpose. A nominating convention, however, would be "essentially a proceeding of the people," at which delegates from throughout the country would "form acquaintances, exchange opinions and sentiments, catch and infuse animation and enthusiasm, and return with a spirit of union and concert."[46] Thus, with widespread support, the convention became a reality.

There was no doubt as to the nominee going into the National Republican Party's first presidential nominating convention. Henry Clay had returned to Congress in 1831, this time to the Senate, and quickly became the primary opposition leader to Jackson and the Democrats. Although he carried the taint of the alleged "corrupt bargain" from the 1824 election, he was the consensus choice as the party's standard-bearer in 1832. The convention opened at the Athenaeum on December 12, 1831, almost eleven months before the election of 1832. A total of 156 delegates were certified, representing seventeen states and the District of Columbia.[47] James Barbour of Virginia was appointed president of the convention. At its outset, the convention resolved to send a committee to Charles Carroll of Carrollton inviting him to attend the proceedings as a guest.[48] The ninety-four-year-old Carroll resided in the winter months in his home in Baltimore, which was located several blocks from the Athenaeum. As with the Anti-Masons, it is not surprising that the National Republicans would want to have in their midst the sole surviving signer of the Declaration of Independence and the last living link to the 1776 Philadelphia convention that created the republic.

The convention then proceeded to the business of nominating a candidate for the presidency. The rules that were adopted gave each delegate a full vote, unlike the Anti-Masons, who had limited the number of votes from each state to that state's votes in the Electoral College. Also, a simple majority vote rule was adopted, again differing from the three-quarters rule set by Anti-Masons. Unlike modern conventions, which have an alphabetical roll call of the states, this convention designated that the states would be called "in their geographic order."[49] Maine, in the northeast corner of the country, was called first, with the roll call then moving south to the mid–Atlantic, to the southern states, and then westward. The rules dictated that when each state was called, each delegate "shall rise in his place as called and declare the name of the person for which he gives his vote."[50]

The rules thus established, the name of only one man was placed in nomination for the presidency — Henry Clay of Kentucky. At the time of the National Republican convention in 1831, Clay had been a national political figure for two decades. Born and raised near Richmond, Virginia, Clay had become a lawyer and, in the late 1790s, moved to Lexington, Kentucky, to begin his legal career. By 1811, while still a young man of thirty-four years of age, he was elected speaker of the United States House of Representatives. He served as one of President Madison's commissioners in Europe in 1814 to negotiate the Treaty of Ghent, which ended the War of 1812. After the war, he returned to the House and again won the job of speaker, greatly expanding the power and influence of that office. He served in Congress until he ran for and was defeated for the presidency for the first time in 1824. He then became the secretary of state under the second President Adams, serving from 1825 to 1829, and was then selected by the Kentucky legislature in 1831 to hold one of that state's seats in the United States Senate. He achieved his greatest successes in that body and was named by a panel of distinguished historians in the late twentieth century as the most effective senator in the history of the United States.[51] Henry Clay was a great orator and charmer, and he dominated any room he entered. He was also prone to vices, with rumors of gambling, drinking, and womanizing following him throughout his career.[52]

Convention president Barbour read to the delegates a letter that Clay had written to him from Washington on December 10, 1831, in which Clay congratulated Barbour on accepting his appointment to the upcoming convention in Baltimore the following week and noting that "notwithstanding the extraordinary inclement of the weather, you had proceeded to the city." Following the custom of the era, when it was taboo for any politician to openly declare that he wanted to be president of the United States, Clay nonchalantly mentioned that he heard his name might come up at the convention. "I must have been entirely regardless of passing events, if I had not observed that my name has been repeatedly mentioned as being likely to be brought before the Convention."[53] Clay's letter then launched into an attack on the policies of President Jackson and the Democrats and the need for change in Washington. The Kentuckian then began the tradition of the presumed presidential nominee not attending his party's nominating convention by making a request of convention president Barbour: "I have been very desirous to lay these sentiments before the Convention, but it has appeared to me that I could not formally do it, without incurring the imputation of presumptuousness or indelicacy. Will you then, my dear sir ... consent to be the organ of making them known, if necessary, to the Convention?"[54]

The reading of Henry Clay's letter completed, and with no other nominations having been made, the voting began. The roll call of the states commenced and each delegate, as his name was called, "rose in his place, and declared his vote." Clay received all of the 155 votes that were cast. One delegate from New York, for unknown reasons, was not present at the time of the voting.[55] Interestingly, the five delegates from Washington, D.C., were given equal votes with the other delegates, although at the time, as residents of the District of Columbia, they could not cast votes in the election for president, as the District of Columbia then had no electoral votes. Before adjourning for the day, the convention appointed two committees, one composed of one delegate from each state, to go to Washington to advise Mr. Clay of his nomination and to request his acceptance, while the other committee, of seven members, was assigned the task of preparing an address from the convention to the people of the United States.[56]

When the convention reconvened on December 14, it learned that its anticipated guest, Charles Carroll of Carrollton, who had initially accepted the invitation delivered to him the previous day, would be unable to attend. A letter was read from the old patriot stating that, due to the "severity of the weather and the apprehensions of my family on that account ... I must, therefore, claim the privilege of my advanced age, and apologize" for not attending as promised. The party leaders were not about to let a blessing from the venerated Carroll slip by, and appointed a committee to visit his nearby home to inquire, somewhat presumptuously, if he could not come to the convention, then could the convention come to him?[57]

The convention then proceeded with its remaining business. By then, the committee sent to Washington the previous day had returned from the Federal City with Clay's response. Again, in keeping with the fiction of the era that no politician would ever publicly state that he was qualified for the presidency or that he desired the job, the Kentuckian replied, "I should have been glad if the Convention had designated some citizen of the United States, more competent than myself ... [yet] I do not feel at liberty to decline their nomination."[58] Ten additional delegates to the convention arrived in Baltimore on December 14 and were permitted, although they had missed the roll call the previous day, to rise individually and openly state their support for the nominee.[59] Lateness was understandable. Although Baltimore was centrally located for easterners, getting to the city in the early 1830s from distant western locations was no easy task. It took one Ohio delegate two full weeks of travel, by horse, canal boat, steamboat, and stagecoach, to get to Baltimore for the convention.[60] Fortunately, the traveling delegates did not have to pay for the costs of the convention. In response to a question from a delegate as to how the costs of the convention were going to be paid, a delegate from Baltimore cheerfully advised his colleagues that "the expenses of the sitting were already provided for," presumably by the City of Baltimore, which was met with thanks from his fellow delegates.[61]

The matter of the vice presidential nomination was completed quickly and without controversy. Only one name, John Sergeant of Pennsylvania, a delegate to the convention, was placed in nomination and the vote in his favor was unanimous. Although a delegate, he left the hall at the time of his nomination and was not present at the time of the voting. A committee of five was named to report the nomination to him.[62] The fifty-two-year-old Sergeant was a prominent Philadelphia attorney with close ties to the Second Bank of the United States. By 1832, he had served a decade in the House of Representatives and was a strong proponent of federal support for internal improvements. He was anti-slavery and, as a congressman, had voted against the Missouri Compromise in 1820, taking the position that slavery should be prohibited in all of the nation's territories. As an easterner from a large state, Sergeant was a good balance to a ticket headed by the Kentuckian Henry Clay.[63]

On December 15, 1831, with most of the business of the convention completed, a resolution was passed thanking the citizens of Baltimore for their hospitality. The acceptance letter of vice presidential nominee John Sergeant was read to the convention. Perhaps more important, Charles Carroll of Carrollton sent a reply to the convention's latest invitation advising that yes, indeed, he would be willing to receive its members in his home and suggesting the time of four o'clock that afternoon.[64] Imagine the scene. In the late afternoon of an early winter day, more than one hundred and fifty well-dressed men walked a few blocks through the streets of Baltimore and "proceeded in a body to the residence of the venerable Charles Carroll ... where an interesting interview took place between the delegates and that venerable patriot, who received them with great hospitality and apparent gratification at this proof of their respect."[65] The National Republicans had touched the hand of the nation's last founding father, hoping that the connection between he and them would be of benefit in the coming election.

The convention assembled for its final session on December 16. No platform was adopted. Instead, the delegates of each state were instructed to prepare a written address to their constituents outlining the reasons for supporting the nominees of the convention. It then ordered that 10,000 copies of its proceedings be printed and distributed throughout the country. Finally, the convention received the report from its committee to prepare an address to the

Still standing, the Carroll Mansion in Baltimore was the home of Charles Carroll of Carrollton and is where the ninety-four-year-old patriot received delegates from two of the conventions held in the city during the 1832 election *(Enoch Pratt Free Library)*.

people of the United States, which outlined the party's view of the transgressions of President Jackson and his administration and urged support of the Clay/Sergeant ticket.[66]

The first presidential nominating convention of the National Republican Party was a united and successful gathering, but there were clouds on the horizon. The opposition to Jackson and the Democrats was split between the Anti-Masons and the National Republicans. Against a popular incumbent president, the prospects of victory were slim. Little did anyone know at the time that the first national convention of the National Republican Party would also be its last. By the next presidential election cycle in 1836, the party would be splintered and have no official nominee. By 1840 it would cease to exist and the Whig Party would emerge to take its place as the chief opposition party to the Democrats.

Democratic Convention

Five months after the National Republicans departed Baltimore, the Democratic Party came to the Monumental City for its own inaugural presidential nominating convention. More accurately, it was a vice presidential nominating convention. With Andrew Jackson occupying the White House, the Democrats had a popular incumbent holding the top office in the land and it was not felt that a formal nomination process for president was needed. Known as Old Hickory (a nickname first given to him by the soldiers that he commanded in the Tennessee militia because he was considered as tough as hickory, a particularly strong hardwood), Jackson had already been nominated by various state legislatures for reelection and the convention's delegates simply passed a resolution stating that they "repose the highest confidence in the purity, patriotism and talents of Andrew Jackson, and that we most cordially concur in the repeated nominations which he has received in various parts of the Union, as a candidate for reelection to the office which he now fills with so much honor to himself and usefulness to his country."[67] It was clear to all that the incumbent vice president, John C. Calhoun of South Carolina, would not be renominated at the convention. It was also clear that Martin Van Buren, a veteran New York political operative, had been successful during Jackson's first term in plotting to block others as potential successors to Calhoun and would be named to the second spot on the Democratic ticket in 1832.

How things got to this point requires a review of some of the intrigue during Jackson's first term. Van Buren, the son of a New York tavern owner, was a lawyer who had risen through the ranks of New York party politics. He became the head of the Albany Regency faction of what would become New York's Democratic Party, which he aligned with Jackson. He served in various offices, including in the New York Senate, as attorney general of New York, and in the United States Senate, earning in all a reputation as a cunning politician.[68] His shrewdness earned him the nickname "the Little Magician," a reference to his short stature and his ability to make seemingly impossible things happen in the political world. Calhoun, a South Carolinian and a Yale graduate, was a lawyer who began his political career in Washington in 1811 as a congressman and as a strong nationalist and a supporter of the War of 1812. He served with distinction as secretary of war during President Monroe's two terms and was elected vice president of the United States in 1824, the election in which John Quincy Adams was chosen president by the House of Representatives. He had an icy relationship with Adams and was reelected as vice president in 1828 on a ticket with Andrew Jackson. Calhoun is the only vice president to have served under two different presidents. A gifted thinker and orator, Calhoun became more oriented toward his home region as his career progressed and would become one of the nation's most vocal proponents of slavery and other southern interests.[69]

The relationship between Jackson and Calhoun soured shortly after the beginning of the Jackson administration in March 1829. The causes of the rift were both personal and professional. It was Washington's first major sex scandal that put Calhoun at odds with Jackson on a personal basis. Margaret O'Neale Timberlake, known as Peggy, was the daughter of a District of Columbia innkeeper and had a reputation for bestowing her favors on many men in the Federal City. She had been married to a sailor, John Timberlake, who had committed suicide in April 1828 while away at sea. It is unknown whether his wife's infidelities were a reason for his suicide. John Henry Eaton, a close friend of Jackson from Tennessee, was named by the president as secretary of war. Both Jackson and Eaton were widowers. Jackson's wife, Rachel, had died of a heart attack in December 1828, shortly after her husband was elected to the presidency. Young Peggy won the middle-aged Eaton's heart and they were married on New Year's Day in 1829, two months before the start of the Jackson administration. One Washington insider commented that "Eaton has just married his mistress, and the mistress of eleven doz. others."[70]

When the Jackson administration began in March 1829, Peggy Eaton was treated as a social outcast by Calhoun's wife, Floride, and by the wives of most of Jackson's cabinet members. Floride Calhoun refused to return a social call from young Peggy. Martin Van Buren, the secretary of state and a widower himself, did not have a wife to be offended by Peggy Eaton's morals, or lack thereof. Van Buren befriended her, many believe as a way to curry favor with the president. After months of this shunning and gossip, an enraged Jackson came to the defense of the Eatons, summoned his cabinet (except Eaton) and advisers to a meeting in September 1829, where he proclaimed of Peggy that "she is as chaste as a virgin!" and demanded that her mistreatment end. It did not. For one of the few times during his tenure in Washington, Andy Jackson did not get his way. The Eaton affair, most of which had been unknown to the public, burst forth in the headlines on April 20, 1831, when it was announced that the entire Jackson cabinet would be resigning. A deal had been struck, purportedly negotiated by Van Buren. The Eatons would be out of power, but so would their detractors. Jackson could not make his vice president resign, but he did not forget. He complained that Calhoun had conspired with the cabinet members "to put Major Eaton out of the Cabinet, & disgrace me, and weaken my administration."[71] Although Van Buren was one of the cabinet members who resigned, he was the big winner in the Eaton matter. His treatment of the Eatons brought him closer to Jackson, while Calhoun's alienated him from the president. They did not call Van Buren the Little Magician for nothing. One Washington observer, Amos Kendall, commented on how the New Yorker worked his magic: "Van Buren glides along as smoothly as oil and as silently as a cat. If he is managing at all, it is so adroitly that nobody perceives it. He is evidently gaining from the indiscretions of Calhoun's friends. He has the entire confidence of the president and all his personal friends, while Calhoun is fast losing it."[72] A generation later, a Jackson biographer would write of Van Buren's visiting Peggy Eaton and knocking on her door, with some truth and with some exaggeration, that "the political history of the United States, for the last thirty years, dates from the moment when the soft hand of Mr. Van Buren touched Mrs. Eaton's knocker."[73]

There was more personal animosity between the president and vice president when Jackson learned that Calhoun had taken a leading role in an old controversy that still had Jackson fuming. As a general in 1818, Jackson had been criticized by the cabinet of President James Monroe for exceeding his orders and invading Spanish Florida during the Seminole War. Calhoun had been secretary of war under Monroe, and only after Jackson was in the White House did he learn that it was his own vice president who had advocated his censure by the Monroe cabinet. More than a decade after they were written, old letters surfaced implicating Calhoun as the ringleader against Jackson. As with the Eaton matter, some saw the silent hand of Van Buren in bringing these letters to Jackson's attention years later. Jackson, known for his temper, was irate. He wrote, "I have this moment" seen evidence which "proves Calhoun a villain."[74] Jackson wrote to Calhoun with the evidence and demanded an explanation. Calhoun did not deny the charges, and responded that the real issue was that there was afoot against him a political conspiracy and that Jackson was naïve not to comprehend why all this was coming to light at that time. Needless to say, this did not go over well with Old Hickory, who fumed even more and vowed to destroy Calhoun.[75]

The final blow to whatever remained of any amicable or working relationship between Jackson and Calhoun came over the nullification crisis. Calhoun became a leading supporter of nullification, that is, the doctrine that a state could repudiate, or nullify, an act of Congress if it disagreed with it. South Carolina, Calhoun's home state, had repudiated increased tariffs passed by Congress and signed into law by the president. To Jackson, any recognition of a state's right to nullify federal laws would destroy the Union. On April 13, 1830, a public banquet in Washington honoring Thomas Jefferson's birthday was the scene of verbal jabs between the president and vice president. The banquet was being chaired by Senator Robert Y. Hayne of South Carolina (who had recently squared off with Massachusetts senator Daniel Webster in the Senate over nullification in the famous Hayne-Webster debates), and Jackson felt, correctly, that the event would be a pro-nullification celebration. After an evening of speeches extolling the virtues of state's rights, all eyes turned to the president of the United States who, by tradition, offered a toast. Jackson rose and proclaimed to the crowd: "Our Union. It must be preserved." The defiant Vice President Calhoun immediately responded with his own toast: "The Union. Next to our liberty, the most dear."[76] The breach was there for all to see—the president and vice president of the United States taunting each other with toasts at a public dinner.

Like Jackson, Calhoun was a man who was not above revenge. With some justification, he blamed the sly Van Buren for his troubles. Having resigned as secretary of state over the Eaton matter, Van Buren needed a job and was nominated by Jackson to be the minister of the United States to Great Britain, a post that required confirmation by the Senate. When his nomination came up for a vote on January 1832, Calhoun's Democratic friends in the Senate conspired with the National Republicans to arrange a tie vote, with twenty-three senators for and twenty-three against. The man presiding over the Senate, Vice President Calhoun, would break the tie and have the opportunity to extract his pound of flesh from his nemesis. As soon as the tie vote was announced, without hesitation, Calhoun voted no and the Van Buren nomination was defeated. He crowed to friends shortly after the vote that he had put the final nail in Van Buren's political coffin: "It will kill him, sir, kill him dead. He will never kick sir, never kick."[77] Calhoun could not have been more wrong. Jackson now knew for certain whom he wanted a heartbeat away from the presidency in his second term. He wrote to Van Buren shortly after the Senate vote: "The people will properly resent the insult offered to the Executive, and the injury intended to our foreign relations, in your rejection, by placing you in the chair of the very man whose casting vote rejected you."[78] The letter came as music to Van Buren's ears. He would, if elected vice president, be the heir apparent to the presidency once Jackson left office.

Jackson regularly met with a group of informal advisors, referred to as his "kitchen cabinet," where political and policy issues were discussed. The group consisted of four or five close friends of the president, two of whom were William R. Lewis and Amos Kendall.[79] This group decided that the best way to dump Calhoun as vice president would be to call for a national convention to nominate candidates for 1832. Calhoun had a majority support from the Democratic members of several of the state legislatures. Jackson's advisors feared that, if the decentralized nomination process by state legislatures that was used in 1828 was repeated in 1832, then Jackson "would be saddled with Calhoun for four more years."[80] To get rid of Calhoun, the method of nominating candidates needed to be changed. Lewis wrote to Kendall, who was in New Hampshire in the spring of 1831, and suggested that Kendall arrange to have the New Hampshire legislature issue a call for a convention. The legislature of the Granite State complied. The Democratic Party's Washington newspaper *The Globe* then promoted the call for a convention to its readers. The idea picked up steam and the convention became a reality. Thus, while being trumpeted to the public as a more democratic method of selecting candidates for the highest offices in the land, the 1832 Democratic convention, in reality, was conceived of and orchestrated by Jackson's closest advisors as a way of getting rid of Calhoun as vice president and naming Van Buren as Jackson's running mate.[81]

It was with this background that the first presidential nominating convention of the Democratic Party of the United States assembled in Baltimore on May 21, 1832. For the third time in the span of a few months, the Athenaeum played host to a political convention, at least initially. When 334 delegates from twenty-two states (all except Missouri) showed up in Baltimore, however, it became obvious that the Athenaeum was too small to host the large crowd and, on its second day, the convention reconvened a few blocks away to the more spacious accommodations in a nearly church building. Referred to as Warfield's Church (for the name of its owner), this structure was located on St. Paul Street near Saratoga Street and was being leased at the time by a congregation of Universalists.[82] Another structure built by the Universalists on Calvert Street a few years later would be the site of subsequent Baltimore conventions.

Since the public call for the convention initially came from a proclamation issued by the New Hampshire legislature, as the convention opened for its first morning session on May 21, a delegate from the Granite State explained the reasoning:

> The object of the representatives of the people of New Hampshire who called this convention was, not to impose on the people, as candidates for either of the two first offices in this government, any local favorite; but to concentrate the opinions of all the states. They believed that the great body of the people, having but one common interest, can and will unite.... They believed that the coming together of representatives of the people from the extremity of the union, would have a tendency to soothe, if not to unite, the jarring interests, which sometimes come in conflict, from the different sections of the country....
>
> They believed that the example of this convention would operate favorably in future elections; that the people would be disposed, after seeing the good effects of this convention in conciliating, the different and distant sections of the country, to continue this mode of nomination.[83]

He did not add that the idea of the convention had been conceived by Jackson and his advisors as a way to get rid of Calhoun as vice president.

The convention got off to a somewhat embarrassing start when the delegate initially nominated to be the temporary president of the gathering, Judge Overton of Tennessee, although in Baltimore, was not present in the hall and was discovered to be "confined to his room by indisposition."[84] An Ohio delegate, General Robert Lucas, was quickly named and approved as the substitute. The convention then set up a Committee on Credentials, with one member from each state, and adjourned for lunch.[85] When it resumed for its afternoon session, little was accomplished, perhaps because the search was on for a larger room in which to hold the convention. The Committee on Credentials reported that it was having difficulty deciding whether to seat delegates from the District of Columbia, and noted some inconsistencies in the lists of delegates from several of the states. Another committee, a Committee on Rules, was appointed, again with one member from each state, to decide not only the rules but also the permanent officers. Additionally, a resolution was passed "that the venerable Charles Carroll of Carrollton, the only survivor of that devoted band of patriots, who made and signed the Declaration of Independence, be invited to take a seat in this convention, during its deliberations, and that a committee of three members be appointed to present this invitation."[86] Like the Anti-Masons and the National Republicans before them, the Democrats wanted political mileage from an association of the aged Carroll with their proceedings. With that, they adjourned for the day.

The next day, Tuesday, May, 22, 1832, the convention reconvened in the morning at its new location, the Warfield's Church building. The Committee on Rules reported its recommendation that the temporary president, General Lucas of Ohio, be made the permanent president of the convention, and four vice presidents and three secretaries were also named, all of whom were approved by the delegates. Regarding the rules, the committee recommended, and the delegates approved, that each state be given votes equaling its total number of votes in the Electoral College, that "two-thirds of the whole number of the votes the convention shall be necessary" for nomination, and that "in taking the vote, the majority of the delegates from each state designate the person by whom the votes for that state shall be given."[87] This was the birth of the "two-thirds rule" and the "unit rule" that would be used, with much controversy, at Democratic conventions for much of the next century. The two-thirds rule was urged on the convention by Jackson as a way to make the nomination of Van Buren for vice president appear more impressive. In so doing, it has been argued, "He placed a shackle about the neck of his party"[88] that took a century to remove. Under the unit rule, a state's entire votes would be cast for the candidate with the majority of the delegate votes in that state, unless the majority agreed otherwise (which they rarely did). Both rules showed that the political leaders of the Democratic Party were not willing to totally relinquish control of matters to delegates in this new-fangled convention process. More than a simple majority of delegates would be required to nominate a candidate, and party bosses who controlled a majority of their state's delegates could silence the votes of the minority in their delegations. The committee also recommended that the sessions of the convention be opened with a prayer, which was approved, and then the gathering broke for lunch.[89]

In the afternoon session, a prayer now being officially sanctioned, one was given by a Baltimore clergyman. Then, the three delegates sent to Charles Carroll of Carrollton's nearby Baltimore home reported, with regret, that the ninety-four-year-old Marylander responded that he appreciated the invitation but that "owing to the state of his health, he would be unable to attend." The Committee on Credentials recommended denying delegate seats to the representatives from the District of Columbia, since the rules gave votes based on the Electoral College and, under the Constitution at that time, the nation's capital city had no such votes. This exclusion was affirmed by a vote of 153 to 126.[90]

Although it was known that President Jackson strongly favored Martin Van Buren as his running mate, many in the South were leery of the New Yorker, and suspected him of being a closet abolitionist. Other than Van Buren, the two other leading contenders for the vice presidential nomination were Phillip P. Barbour of Virginia and Richard M. Johnson of Kentucky. Johnson was viewed as a possible compromise candidate if Van Buren faltered. Van Buren's supporters, confident of victory, had supported the two-thirds rule for nomination proposed by the Committee on Rules, thinking that a super-majority vote for their man would be seen by the country "as a demonstration of party solidarity behind the candidate."[91] As will be seen later, it was a decision that would cost Van Buren dearly at a future convention. Only 283 of the 334 registered delegates voted, the non-voting delegates likely registering a silent protest against Van Buren. On the first ballot, Van Buren won the nomination with 208 votes, compared to only 49 for Barbour and 26 for Johnson, well over the two-thirds required.[92] Interestingly, John H. Eaton, whose marriage to the promiscuous Peggy Timberlake had helped to start the decline of Vice President Calhoun and the rise of Van Buren, was a Tennessee delegate to the convention and did not intend to vote for Van Buren. While the New Yorker had befriended Eaton's wife, "he had not won Eaton's affection." Eaton was sternly advised by a member of Jackson's kitchen cabinet that he must vote for Van Buren "unless he was prepared to quarrel with the General."[93] Eaton complied. This is but one example of the arm-twisting done by the Jackson men to accomplish their goal. As one writer has noted, "The 'spontaneous unanimity' of this convention was produced by the will of Andrew Jackson and the energetic discipline of the kitchen cabinet."[94] Calhoun was officially out and Van Buren was in. The president and vice presidents of the convention were named as a committee to notify Van Buren of his nomination. He was still out of the country, not having yet returned to the United States from his aborted stint as minister to Great Britain. No platform was adopted by the convention, although it did form another committee to draft an address from the convention to the people of the United States.[95] The gathering then adjourned for the day.

When the convention met for its third and final day on Wednesday, May 23, there was little official business to transact. Interestingly, the committee appointed the previous day to prepare and address the American people reported that it had met already and the members decided that they would rather not undertake the task. Instead, they suggested "in place of a general address from this body" that each state delegation "make such explanations by address, report, or otherwise, to their respective constituents of the objects, proceedings and result of the meeting as they may deem expedient." The delegates let the committee off the hook and approved this proposal. A resolution of thanks was passed "to the Baltimore committee of arrangement, for their hospitable and liberal exertions for the accommodations of this body, in a manner worthy of the patriotism and republican spirit, for which the citizens of Baltimore have been so long eminently distinguished."[96] One Pennsylvania delegate was so pleased with Baltimore as a convention city that he proposed that the Democrats agree to meet on the third Monday in May every presidential election year in the Monumental City for a presidential nominating convention.[97] His resolution did not pass, but, as will be seen, the Democratic Party would frequently return to Baltimore for its conventions.

There remained the matter of good old Mr. Carroll. Like the National Republicans before them, the Democrats did not take no for an answer, and they sent their committee back to Carroll's home to see if he would be willing to receive members of the convention there. Once again, as with the National Republicans, Carroll agreed and, after adjournment, the more than 300 delegates walked several blocks to the Carroll home at Lombard and Front Streets and were received by him.[98] Just a couple of weeks earlier, Carroll had also been besieged by a request from a Democratic Party convention of young men, some 300 of whom had met in Washington on May 10, 1832. After visiting George Washington's tomb at Mount Vernon, this group had also sent a request to Baltimore to have a committee from their gathering meet with the last living signer of the Declaration of Independence. The aged patriot had been gracious and had received the group of young men in his home on May 14. As reported at the time, "The scene presented by the young men gathering around this venerable patriarch, and catching the spirit of our constitution and of freedom from his lips, was truly solemn and impressive; and we have reason to believe, that no one who witnessed it, departed without entertaining the idea that this tribute was prompted by gratitude alone, that it was a deep earnest of love and country, and of affection for the memory of those who had called it into existence."[99] Perhaps fortunately for Charles Carroll of Carrollton, he would be deceased by the time the next round of presidential nominating conventions assembled in Baltimore, and he would not have to deal with politicians seeking to bask in his reflected glory.

The Campaign and Election

Campaigns and elections in the mid–nineteenth century had some similarities, but also significant differences, with the system we know today. The most obvious difference is that the electorate comprised only white males. Colonial and early American requirements that property be owned as a prerequisite to the right to cast a ballot were gradually abolished in the original states after 1815, and no new states admitted after that year required property ownership for voting. Still, Virginia kept this limitation on voting until 1850 and South Carolina kept it until the Civil War. Some states also limited voting to those who had paid taxes, but these requirements were also gradually eliminated.[100]

From a twenty-first-century perspective, it is easy to sneer at this limitation on the franchise. The proper comparison, however, is not with our own time, but with the rest of the world in the nineteenth century. The almost universal white male suffrage that existed in the United States in the early nineteenth century was revolutionary in a world where most people still lived under the rule of monarchs and, in those few places where voting was permitted, the franchise was far more restricted than it was in the United States, and voters did not elect the leaders of the nation. America was truly an experiment in democracy.

At the presidential level, campaigning by the candidates was virtually nonexistent. It was said that the office of the presidency sought the man, not the other way around. One stood for election; one did not run. Presidential candidates did not attend campaign rallies, and did not even attend their nominating conventions. The candidates made no speeches. Presidents were not orators. Perhaps the greatest speaker of the era, Henry Clay, silenced his lips on the occasions when he became his party's nominee. The presidential candidate generally stayed at home, or if he was the incumbent president or a sitting member of Congress, stayed in Washington. With few exceptions, the extent of campaigning done by candidates for president, both in seeking their party's nomination and after obtaining it, was in writing letters to supporters in response to specific inquiries on issues of the day, some of which, by intent, ended up being published in newspapers. On occasion, they wrote a newspaper editor directly and that letter would end up in print. Doing anything more, at least in public, was viewed as being unseemly.

Below the level of the presidential candidates, however, plenty of campaigning occurred. There was no pretense of nonpartisanship by newspapers, which were the primary source of campaign information to the public. The political parties had official or unofficial newspapers in most major cities, which blatantly trumpeted their own candidates and mercilessly criticized the opposition. Official documents from the parties' conventions, such as the platform adopted and an address to the people, were widely published. Campaign literature, both for and against candidates, was distributed in abundance and political rallies, picnics, and parades were commonplace.[101]

Once the campaigning was over, voting was a long and drawn-out process. Until 1848, there was no single presidential election day. State and local elections were generally held in September and October and their results usually provided a barometer as to the outcome of the separate federal elections for the Congress and the president, which were usually held in November. Voting in a state generally took place over two or three days, to allow those who lived long distances from the polling place time to travel. Each state set its own dates for its elections, even for federal offices. One state could set its presidential election for early November, while another could set its for late in the month. As a result, especially in close elections, the final results were often not known until December.

It was in this context that the campaign of 1832 was played out, with the candidates — Jackson for the Democrats, Clay for the National Republicans, and Wirt for the Anti-Masons — all, for the first time in American history, having been selected by party nominating conventions. Ironically, it was the National Republicans who gave the Democrats the issue that would be used to beat them. Clay and his supporters pushed through the Congress in the early summer of 1832 a bill rechartering the Second Bank of the United States, even though the bank's original charter did not expire until 1836. The National Republicans hoped to use the bill, and its expected veto by Jackson, as a campaign issue showing that they favored economic growth and were looking to the future. As expected, Jackson vetoed the bill and his veto was not overridden by Congress. Instead of the veto helping the National Republicans, however, Jackson turned the bank issue into one of rich and powerful bankers versus the common man and won the election in a landslide. Of the 1,217,691 votes cast, Jackson won 687,502, over 250,000 more than Clay's 530,189. The Anti-Mason Party was not a significant factor in the election, with Wirt getting only about 100,000 votes. The Electoral College count was even more lopsided for the Democrats, with Jackson winning sixteen states and 219 electoral votes, compared to only 49 for Clay (who won only his home state of Kentucky, Massachusetts, Connecticut, Rhode Island, Delaware, and a portion of Maryland's electors), 7 for Wirt (from Vermont), and South Carolina's 11 votes (with the electors chosen by the South Carolina legislature) going to a southern state's rights candidate, John Floyd.[102] Old Hickory had resoundingly won a second term, and now Martin Van Buren was at his side as vice president and heir apparent.

CHAPTER 4

1836: Hey Buddy, Wanna Be a Delegate?

Martin Van Buren — He's O.K.! — Democratic campaign slogan

As the election of 1836 approached, it was Andrew Jackson himself who issued a call for the Democratic Party to hold a nominating convention to name his successor. Jackson wrote a letter, published in the *Nashville Republican* newspaper on March 17, 1835, that would solidify conventions as a fixture in the American political process:

> I consider the true policy of the friends of republican principles to send delegates, fresh from the people, to a general convention, for the purpose of selecting candidates for the presidency and vice-presidency; and, that to impeach that selection before it is made, or to resist it when it is fairly made, as an emanation of executive power, is to assail the virtue of the people, and, in effect, to oppose their right to govern.[1]

As the opposition party would learn the hard way in 1836, without a convention, it would be impossible to solidify support behind a single candidate. Absent a convention, a party would, at best, hope that having multiple candidates in the race would keep any single candidate from gaining a majority in the Electoral College, and thereby force the election to be decided under the Constitution, as it was in 1824, by the House of Representatives.

Democratic Convention

Democrats rarely did anything to displease Andrew Jackson. He wanted a convention to name his party's next presidential nominee and he got one. Despite his professed non-interference with the process, there was no doubt that Jackson wanted to see his vice president, Martin Van Buren, as his successor in the White House. Van Buren had cunningly positioned himself as the heir apparent and, with Jackson's support, there was little that could be done to stop him from being the nominee of the Democratic Party for the presidency in 1836.

The timing of the second presidential nominating convention of the Democratic Party was unique in American political history. In an abundance of caution, and hoping to put the seal on the Little Magician's nomination before any effective opposition could develop, party leaders scheduled the convention for May 1835, only two months after Jackson's call for delegates "fresh from the people" to meet in a convention, and a full year and a half before the presidential election in November 1836. No other presidential nominating convention in American history has ever been held so far in advance of an election. Once again, the Democrats chose Baltimore as the location for their gathering. When more than 600 delegates showed up for the convention (almost twice the number of Democratic delegates in 1832), Baltimore, "which was abundantly supplied with hotels, taverns, and boarding houses, was hard pressed to provide accommodations."[2] An editor of a Democratic newspaper wrote to Jackson upon arriving in the city that "every tavern is full already and the delegates are hunting private houses to put up at."[3] It was more of a mass meeting than an organized convention. Maryland, which was also holding its state Democratic convention during that week, had 171 delegates in attendance, almost one-quarter of the overall delegates.[4] A formal process for the selection of delegates by state congressional district conventions, or by state conventions, would not be standardized until later conventions. There was also a large contingent from the Keystone State, as Pennsylvania had sent two competing delegations, which would be one of the major areas of controversy at the convention. There was a disproportionally large number of delegates from other nearby states, with another one-quarter of the overall delegates from Virginia and New Jersey. In contrast, only two delegates each were present from the states of Mississippi and Louisiana, and only one or two each from the territories of Missouri, Michigan, and Arkansas. Four states — Tennessee, South Carolina, Alabama, and Illinois — sent no delegates at all.[5]

The convention opened in Baltimore's Fourth Presbyterian Church on May 20, 1835. This church, located on Baltimore Street between Freemont and Poppleton Streets, began as a Sunday school of the First Presbyterian Church of Baltimore and then became its own separate congregation. The building was later purchased by Baltimore inventor and businessman Thomas Winans, who had a large home nearby, and became known as Winans' Chapel, or Winans' Soup Kitchen, and was then used for primarily for philanthropic purposes. The congregation of the Fourth Presbyterian Church later moved and became the Franklin Square Presbyterian Church.[6] At the opening session on Wednesday, May 20, 1835, it became apparent that the small church building was insufficient to handle the crowd. While the convention proceeded with its business, a search began for a new location, just as had happened with the first Democratic convention in 1832. The convention unanimously selected Andrew Stevenson of Virginia, a former Speaker of the House of Representatives, as president of the proceedings. At later conventions, a parliamentary procedure of initially naming a temporary president and then forming a committee to select a permanent president and officers would be used. Six vice presidents and four secretaries were named. At the outset, two committees, consisting of one delegate from each state, were appointed, one to establish the rules of the convention and one to examine the credentials of the delegates. Convention president Stevenson then gave his opening address, paying homage to the retiring incumbent Democratic president, Andrew Jackson: "Our venerable chief magistrate, following the example of illustrious predecessors, and with a patriotism worthy of himself, has already made known his determination, at the end of his present term, to retire to the shade of private life, and a successor is to be appointed!" Stevenson, echoing Jackson's call for a Democratic Party convention to pick a successor, stated that the people "look to a national convention, as the best means of concentrating the popular will, and giving it effect in the approaching election." Perhaps anticipating that all would not go well at the convention, he warned that "to secure the triumph of our principles, we must avoid everything like sectional feelings and jealousies and be willing to sacrifice all personal predilections and preferences."[7] At the conclusion of his opening address, around 10:30 A.M., Stevenson announced that "a more commodious room" had been located for the proceedings and that the convention would be moving to the larger First Presbyterian Church, which was located several blocks to the east in Baltimore.[8]

An hour and a half later, at noon, the more than 600 delegates reassembled at the First Presbyterian Church. Situated on the northwest corner of Fayette Street and North Street (now known as Guilford Avenue), the church building was the second one built by the congregation on the site, the first one having been on the property from 1766 to 1790. This second church, known as the Two Steeple Church, was completed in 1791. The current building on the site is Courthouse East of the Circuit Court for Baltimore City, a building which was originally built as the United States District Court for Baltimore and United States Post Office. The church was two stories tall, with galleries located ten feet above the main floor. Architecturally, it was "remarkable for its two steeples, and by its considerable spreading porticos in front, supported by four large lofty pillars."[9]

The use of the First Presbyterian Church for a political event, which was arranged on very short notice due to the lack of space at the Fourth Presbyterian Church, was not without later controversy and condemnation. The church's records indicate that one member of the congregation, James McCulloh, had asked a committee governing the church for permission to use the building for the convention, apparently on the opening morning of the convention, which was granted. This occurred while the pastor, Dr. William Nevins, was on a leave of absence in the West Indies due to health reasons.[10] The church's full congregation was not consulted. Shortly after the convention, a meeting of the congregation was held which "passed a resolution disapproving the use of the church building for other than religious purposes and proposing to the committee that neither body should in the future authorize the use of the church building or lecture room for any secular purpose without the concurrence of the other."[11] As will be discussed in a later chapter, this church building was again used as the site of a political convention in 1860, but only after the congregation had sold the building and land to the United States government and moved to a new church building located at Madison Street and Park Avenue in Baltimore, which still stands and is the home of the First Presbyterian Church of Baltimore today.[12]

After settling into its new home, the convention then heard the report of its Committee of Rules and Regulations, which recommended that each state receive the number of votes on any roll call equal to its number of votes in the Electoral College. This was consistent with the voting rule adopted at the prior convention in 1832. Thus, states which had large delegations at the convention received no voting advantage from their large numbers. The vote of the delegates from such states was watered down, as each could cast only a fractional vote. For example, while Maryland had 171 delegates present, they could cast only Maryland's total number of Electoral College votes, which was ten. In contrast, this rule enhanced the influence of delegates from states which sent only a few delegates to the convention, since those delegates could cast their state's entire number of electoral votes. The committee also recommended, as was done at the party's convention in 1832, that a two-thirds vote be required for nomination as president or vice president. The wisdom of the two-thirds rule was debated, with proponents arguing that "it would have a more imposing effect," and opponents arguing that it was undemocratic. The report of the committee was amended to require only a majority vote and the amended report was approved with 271 yeas and 210 nays.[13] Thus, under this amendment, only a majority vote would be necessary for nomination. The Committee of Rules and Regulations also recommended that five delegates be named to a separate committee to draft an address from the convention to the American people.[14] The convention then heard the report of the Committee on Credentials. The chairman advised that the committee was unable to

Baltimore's First Presbyterian Church was the controversial site of the 1835 Democratic convention, leading its members to ban future secular gatherings in the building without their permission *(Enoch Pratt Free Library)*.

"act definitely" as to which of the two Pennsylvania delegations was the valid delegation from the Keystone State, so it recommended seating both of them.[15] Of course, this pleased neither of them and they spent much of the convention sniping at one another. One newspaper referred to it as the battle of "brotherly hatred" between the competing Wolf and Muhlenberg factions in the Pennsylvania Democratic Party.[16] The committee also recommended that the delegates from the territories of Michigan and Arkansas be admitted "with the same power as delegates from those territories in Congress."[17] In other words, the committee's position was that delegates from the territories were welcome to stay, observe, and participate, but their votes would not be counted. The report of the Committee on Credentials was adopted by the convention and, with that, the meeting adjourned for the second day.

On the third day, Friday, May 22, the convention reassembled in the morning. No sooner had the opening gavel fallen, however, when the Virginia delegates asked for a recess until the afternoon because they "had under consideration important matters not yet concluded" concerning the nominations to be made. New York's Silas Wright, one of Van Buren's closest advisors and a floor leader for his candidate, also requested a recess because New York was likewise not ready to proceed.[18] Behind the scenes and off the floor, a major battle was being fought between Virginia and New York over the vice presidential nomination. Prior to the convention, the Virginians had promoted their own William C. Rives, a former ambassador to France in Jackson's first term, and a former United States senator, for the second spot on the ticket, to counter-balance the New Yorker, Van Buren. The Virginia delegation had received pre-convention assurances that Van Buren personally supported Rives and that he would also be supported by the New York delegation.[19] Combined with support for Rives from other southern states, his nomination was thought to be certain. Unfortunately for the Virginians, the man in the White House thought otherwise. President Jackson was concerned about the popularity of his in-state rival, Hugh Lawton White, a Democrat turned Whig, in Tennessee and in other western states. Jackson thought that a westerner, rather than a southerner, would bring more strength to the ticket, and his candidate was Richard M. Johnson.[20]

Richard Mentor Johnson was one of the more interesting figures in American politics during the first half of the nineteenth century. A native Kentuckian, Johnson was elected to Congress in 1807 as a supporter of President Thomas Jefferson and the Democratic-Republican Party. While in Congress, he was a strong advocate of the War of 1812, raised a regiment in Kentucky, and fought in the war. In October 1813, the United States Army, with General William Henry Harrison in command, and with Johnson serving as one of his top officers, defeated the British and their Indian allies at the Battle of the Thames. During this battle, Tecumseh, the chief of the Shawnee tribe, was killed and Johnson was given credit for his death, although historical proof that Johnson was the actual killer of the Indian hero is lacking.[21] Following the war, he continued in Congress, serving in both the House and the Senate for the next quarter-century, and became a friend and ally of Andrew Jackson. While Johnson's military and congressional records were typical of prominent politicians of the era, his domestic arrangements were not. A slave owner, Johnson lived openly with Julia Chinn, a slave he had inherited from his father. He referred to her as his common-law wife and they had two daughters together, whom Johnson educated, raised as a family, and brought to Washington during part of his congressional career. After Julia Chinn's death in 1833, Johnson was known to have lived openly with other black and mixed-race women.[22] In the first half of the nineteenth century, this was not a private life that would attract southern votes, nor northern votes, in a national election. Despite this, Andrew Jackson wanted Johnson on the ticket with Van Buren in 1836 to attract western votes — and what Jackson wanted from the Democratic Party he usually got. For the Virginians, to have Rives pushed aside was one thing; to have Johnson as the replacement only rubbed salt into the wound.

Van Buren and his New York allies acquiesced in President Jackson's request — the Virginian, Rives, would be dumped as the vice presidential nominee and replaced with the Kentuckian, Johnson. The distasteful tasks of explaining this to the Virginians, and of getting enough votes to nominate Johnson, fell to Senator Silas Wright of New York, Van Buren's convention manager in Baltimore. Wright had the "unpleasant duty to inform the Virginians that the signals had changed without alienating them completely."[23] In rounding up the votes to get Johnson nominated, Wright stretched the bounds of political ethics. The failure of the Democratic Party of Tennessee, the home of the Andrew Jackson, to send any delegates to the convention was an embarrassment to the party. Factionalism in the Tennessee party between supporters of Jackson and of Hugh Lawson White resulted in no delegation at all from the Volunteer State being sent to Baltimore. To rectify this, Wright "acquiesced in a shabby scheme"[24] to get Tennessee's allotted fifteen Electoral College votes at the convention counted. Edward Rucker, a low-level Democratic politician from Tennessee, happened to be in Baltimore and was spotted in a local tavern as the convention began. He was approached and recruited by the operatives of the Little Magician to register as a delegate from Tennessee. Rucker agreed and, magically, he became the Tennessee delegation.[25] In a post-convention letter to the *Nashville Union* newspaper, Rucker explained:

> SIR: You will discover my name introduced into the proceedings of the Baltimore Convention. To prevent all misunderstanding, I make the following statement. I was not delegated to act in that convention. I happened to be in Baltimore at the time of its sitting, and after the delegations from the different states had their credentials examined by the Committees appointed for that purpose, there appeared to be no one present representing Tennessee. This circumstance seemed to be deeply regretted by many, and upon its being mentioned that I was there, and a Tennessean, it was suggested by some that I might vote, which I accordingly did.[26]

The Rives/Johnson matter and the Tennessee/Rucker matter were intertwined and more sleight of hand was used by the New Yorkers to keep the Virginians in Baltimore and to get Johnson nominated. The long recess requested by the Virginians on Friday morning was needed because they had threatened to bolt the convention entirely if Rives was not nominated for vice president. The New Yorkers had sent a man to Washington for consultation and his train had not yet arrived back in Baltimore at the time of the recess. When he returned, the New York delegation was told it had to support Johnson. Late in the morning, a deal was struck, whereby it was agreed that the two-thirds rule for nomination for president and vice president, which had been defeated by an amendment to the report of the Committee of Rules and Regulations earlier in the convention, would be reinstated. Based upon this, the Virginians agreed to stay, thinking that there was no way that Johnson could muster two-thirds of the votes needed for nomination. The Virginians were apparently unaware when they agreed to this deal that the New Yorkers had a card they had not yet played, in that they had recruited a single Tennessean, Rucker, to cast Tennessee's fifteen votes in the roll calls on the nominations.

When the convention reassembled at noon, the deal was formalized. The rule on the number of votes needed for nomination was reconsidered and the two-thirds rule was reinstated.[27] The Virginians stayed on the floor. The convention then proceeded to the uneventful process of nominating a presidential candidate. There was only one name placed in the nomination, Martin Van Buren, and he won all 265 votes cast. His total included fifteen votes from Tennessee, all of which were cast by Edward Rucker. The convention then moved to the

Known as the Little Magician, Martin Van Buren of New York eliminated all competitors in the Democratic Party and became Andrew Jackson's choice to succeed him in the presidency *(Library of Congress)*.

vice presidential selection. With a total of 265 votes, a two-thirds majority required 177 votes. Johnson received 178 votes, compared to 87 for Rives, just barely making it, by one vote, over the number required for nomination.[28] Johnson's total included fifteen votes from Tennessee, all of which were cast by Edward Rucker, the Tennessean who just happened to be in Baltimore during the week of the convention and who was recruited and certified by the Van Buren forces controlling the convention as the official Tennessee delegation. Without Rucker's fifteen votes, Johnson would not have prevailed on the first ballot and, quite likely, would have faded on subsequent ballots. Rives received all of the votes from Virginia, Maryland, North Carolina, Georgia, New Jersey, and Maine, as well as ten of fourteen votes from Massachusetts. When New York's votes were cast for Johnson, the Virginia delegation "hissed most ungraciously." At the conclusion of the roll call, an Ohio delegate noted that Massachusetts had cast votes for both Johnson and Rives and stated that seven members of his delegation had wanted to vote for Rives "but supposed they were not at liberty to do so." Under the unit rule used at Democratic conventions of the era, a state's delegation could split its votes, but only if this was permitted by the majority of that state's delegates, which was rarely granted. President Stevenson refused to permit any changes in votes and the contest was over. The other delegations that supported Rives later changed their votes and supported Johnson, but the Virginians did not go quietly. Their chairman announced to the convention that they would not support Johnson for vice president, that they had "no confidence in his principles, nor his character — they had already gone as far as possible in supporting Mr. Van Buren, and that they would go no farther."[29] A Kentucky delegate angrily responded that he "did not understand what the principles of Virginia were, but he was certain that Mr. Johnson had killed Tecumseh and, therefore, he ought to be made vice president."[30]

The New Yorkers had one more payback to accomplish before the convention concluded. A resolution was offered, and approved by a vote of 154 yeas and 77 nays: "States are encouraged to form electoral tickets ... so that the greatest possible effect may be given to nominations made by the convention" and to avoid the election being thrown to the House of Representatives.[31] This was done to appease the Muhlenberg faction in Pennsylvania, which had caved to the Van Buren forces and supported Johnson for vice president, while the competing Wolf faction had not.[32] Both factions would now be able to place their own slate of electors on the 1836 ballot for Van Buren and Johnson.

For all practical purposes, the 1835 convention in Baltimore was not a successful one for the Democrats. As one commentator noted, "the meeting was a most exciting one, and did not promise much for the harmony of the party in the election."[33] Fortunately for the Democrats, they still had a year and a half until the election. Immediately after the convention, the Whig press denounced the proceedings. The *Baltimore Patriot* observed that "we little dreamt that there would be so much strife, bickering, ill feeling and management here displayed, as which we witnessed." It also commented that "the Virginians were laughed at, derided and insulted. The New York delegation found the New Jersey, Massachusetts and Maine Jacksonism so pliable it could be moulded as New York pleased, and they snapped their fingers to the entire south, if it chose to desert them."[34] The *Patriot* predicted that, as a result of the convention, the Democrats would lose Pennsylvania, Virginia, and most of the South and Southwest. The *Maryland Republican* decried "the managing, time serving politicians of New York ... [whose] artifices were discovered, and their despicable schemes exposed."[35] Much of the commentary on the convention focused on the recruitment of Rucker and his certification as the entire Tennessee delegation: "Some anxiety has been expended to know who was the Mr. Rucker that represented the State of Tennessee in the late Baltimore convention, how he was appointed and whom he represented ... 'fresh from the people' of that state!"[36] To most outside observers, the Rucker matter was not only not fresh, it stunk. The name of the Tennessean even entered the American vocabulary for a few generations, as the term "ruckerize" came to be defined as assuming a position without authority, or, more broadly, as a synonym for political skullduggery.[37]

Whig Non-Convention

Having been badly beaten in the election of 1832, the National Republicans became discredited and ceased to function as the primary anti–Jackson force in American politics. Henry Clay, the party's standard-bearer in 1832, began to organize, in 1833 and 1834, a broader coalition, including southern state's-rights members of Congress, Anti-Masons, National Republicans, and anyone else opposed to President Jackson and his heir apparent, Martin Van Buren. Focusing on the alleged executive tyranny of the Jackson administration, this broader anti–Jackson coalition adopted the name Whigs, emulating the English political party that was opposed to the excessive power of the British monarch. Thus, the Whig Party in America was born. As one commentator has noted: "By itself the name helped to erase the stigma of anti-republican elites that had stunted the growth of its predecessor and to supply the credible appeal to republican values necessary for any party that hoped to compete successfully with the Jacksonian Democrats. Through this party, it promised voters, you can perform your duty to preserve the fruits of the revolution."[38]

The newborn political party was unable to agree upon a single candidate to challenge Van Buren in the 1836 election: "Not one of their leaders would defer to the other."[39] In such an environment, it was feared that holding a national presidential nominating convention would only lead to disaster. Thus, "by the end of 1834 most Whigs forlornly admitted that they could not hold a national convention without blowing apart."[40] The decision was made not to have a convention. The disastrous outcome of this approach can be seen from the outcome of the 1836 election and the fact that no major American political party has ever again gone into a presidential election without first holding a national nominating convention. After 1836, nominating conventions became required rituals in the process of electing a president.

Instead of holding a convention, the Whigs reverted to the prior system used by Jackson in the 1820s of having various state legislatures make nominations for the party's presidential standard-bearers. It was "hoped that one state's favorite would catch fire elsewhere and that anti–Jacksonians through the country would then concentrate behind him."[41] Absent this, some thought that multiple Whig candidates could each run well in their own region, perhaps denying Van Buren an Electoral College majority, and thus throwing the outcome of the contest into the House of Representatives. This is exactly what had happened in 1824, when Jackson had won the popular vote, but not an Electoral College majority, and the House of Representatives named John Quincy Adams the nation's sixth president. Henry Clay sat out the 1836 race, due in part to mourning the death of his last surviving daughter in late 1835.

Three candidates emerged from the haphazard process. First among these was William Henry Harrison, a former general and Indian fighter, whose résumé was very similar to that of Andrew Jackson. Although he had been born into a Virginia aristocratic family, Harrison made his home and his reputation in the West. In 1800, President John Adams appointed him governor of the Indiana Territory, a post he held for twelve years under three presidents. He was also a general and was the victor over the Shawnee Indians and their allies in the Battle of Tippecanoe, which was fought in 1811. During the War of 1812, his troops were again the victors over the Indians, and their British allies, in the 1813 Battle of Thames. After the war, Harrison served in the Ohio Senate, as minister to Colombia, and as a senator from Ohio.[42] After Harrison secured the nomination of the Anti-Masons in Pennsylvania in December 1835, many Whig parties in northern states jumped on his bandwagon.

Anti–Jackson southerners, however, had another candidate in mind. Hugh Lawson White was born in North Carolina in 1773 and moved to Tennessee as a child. His father was a founder of Knoxville. He studied law in Pennsylvania, returned to Tennessee to practice, and held various state offices, including judge and state senator. When Andrew Jackson resigned from the United States Senate in 1825, the Tennessee legislature selected White to fill the seat, where he remained for fifteen years. Initially, he was a strong supporter of the administration of his fellow Tennessean Jackson, but he broke with the president over the removal of deposits from the Bank of the United States. White was no fan of Van Buren and did not want to see him installed as Jackson's successor. White was first nominated by a caucus of the Alabama legislature in January 1835, and the Tennessee legislature soon followed. Passion for White, a slaveholder, spread throughout the South.[43]

The third Whig candidate in the race was Senator Daniel Webster of Massachusetts. Born and raised in New Hampshire, Webster had attended Dartmouth College and became a lawyer. He was originally elected to Congress in 1812 as a New Hampshire Federalist and was a vocal opponent of the War of 1812. He served two terms, was defeated, and then moved to Boston to advance his legal career. Representing business interests, he became known as one of the best attorneys in the United States, arguing several landmark cases before the Supreme Court. In 1822, he returned to Washington, this time as a congressman from Massachusetts. He moved to the Senate in 1827. Nicknamed "Black Dan," in part due to his dark complexion and in part to his disposition, Webster was a man of excesses. He made and spent large sums of money and, as a result, was constantly in debt to his wealthy political supporters. Like Henry Clay, he was rumored throughout his career to be a heavy drinker and a philanderer. He had a huge ego, was aloof, and could be condescending to others. In 1830, on the floor of the Senate, during the Nullification Crisis, it was Webster who famously debated South Carolina senator Robert Hayne over the issue of whether a state could repudiate a federal law, ending his remarks with the famous line, "Liberty and union, now and forever, one and inseparable." As a result, Webster became a national political figure. When the Whig Party was formed, Webster became one of its leaders. He had a serious case of "Potomac Fever" and believed that he was destined to be president of the United States. The 1836 race was the first of several presidential attempts that Webster would make during his career and, in all, he would be, at best, only a regional New England candidate. He never succeeded in obtaining his party's nomination, much less the presidency.[44]

The Campaign and Election

Rather than being a single national election, the campaign of 1836 was more like three regional contests, with Van Buren squaring off against his three opponents — Harrison in the North and West, White in the South, and Webster in New England. With the economy in good shape and with no international issues, the opposition focused its campaign on the alleged executive tyranny of Jackson and his attempt to impose his handpicked successor on the nation, which would, it was argued, be giving Old Hickory a third term. After Harrison received the nomination of the convention of the Anti-Mason Party in Pennsylvania (about the only place that this movement continued to have any strength), he picked up more support throughout the North, at Webster's expense. White ran more as a disgruntled anti–Jackson Democrat than as a candidate of the new Whig Party. Democrats in the South remained suspicious of Van Buren over the slavery issue. To limit any defection of southern Democrats, Van Buren came out publicly against the abolition of slavery in the District of Columbia and supported a gag rule in the House of Representatives, whereby discussion of abolitionist petitions in that body was prevented.[45] Van Buren's hometown of Kinderhook, New York, became the source of a nickname during the campaign. He became known as "Old Kinderhook," which became shortened to "O.K.," as in the slogan, "Martin Van Buren, He's O.K." This is thought to be the origin of the colloquialism that is still widely used today.[46]

Voting in the nineteenth century could be an intimidating process. There were no secret ballots. Often, one's vote had to be stated orally in front of the entire polling place or, where paper ballots were used, the ballots were printed by the rival political parties on colored paper of their own choice, so all present could easily see who took and cast a ballot for which party. The process encouraged straight party line voting, since voting for a candidate of another party required striking out one name on the ballot and writing in another. Voter intimidation was real. So was fraud. The expansion of the franchise to eliminate property and other requirements occurred before the mass influx of immigrants to the United States in the mid–nineteenth century who, as voters, were often intimidated or bribed. As one commentator has noted, "The typical antebellum American polling place displayed many of the worst features of all-male society: rowdy behavior, heavy drinking, coarse language, and occasional violence."[47]

When the votes in the election of 1836 were counted, Van Buren emerged the victor with almost fifty-one percent of the votes cast nationally, which was approximately 28,000 more than the combined total of his three opponents. He also secured, barely, a majority of the votes in the Electoral College, with 170 compared to 124 for his combined opponents. Harrison won seven states: Delaware, Maryland, Kentucky, Vermont, New Jersey, Indiana, and Ohio. White carried Tennessee and Georgia, while Webster won only his home state of Massachusetts. South Carolina, which in this era always marched to the beat of its own drummer in presidential contests, and whose electoral votes were decided by its legislature, cast its votes for Willie Mangum of North Carolina, a former member of the Senate who had supported nullification. Van Buren carried the rest: New York, Pennsylvania, Illinois, Virginia, Missouri, Louisiana, Mississippi, Alabama, North Carolina, Connecticut, Maine, New Hampshire, Rhode Island, Arkansas, and Michigan. By winning states in the North, the South, and the West, Van Buren succeeded in holding the old Jackson coalition together, and partisanship had triumphed over sectionalism. But there were warning signs for the Democrats — the Whig coalition of three candidates had run much better than Clay had run in 1832 as a National Republican. Van Buren's margins in several states were very small and a shift of a few thousand votes would have put the contest in the House of Representatives. The Democrats carried Pennsylvania by only 4,000 votes, Illinois by only 3,000 and Louisiana and Mississippi by only 300 each.[48] If this new Whig coalition could unite behind a single candidate, the presidency could be won in 1840.

Though the 1836 election decided the presidency, as it turned out, it did not decide the vice presidency. The sealed electoral votes from each state were formally received by Congress in a joint session held on February 8, 1837. The bitterness from the Democratic convention in Baltimore over the last-minute choice of Richard Johnson of Kentucky, who defeated Virginia's Senator Rives, continued in the Electoral College. Although Van Buren won Virginia and the Old Dominion's electors cast their twenty-three electoral votes for him, they refused to vote for Johnson and, instead, cast their vice presidential electoral votes for William Smith of Alabama. This left the Electoral College tally at 147 for Johnson and 147 for his combined opponents, leaving Johnson short of the majority necessary for election. Under the Constitution, the contest for vice president had to be decided by the United States Senate.[49] The

Senate then retired to its own chamber and the matter of the vice presidency was decided. The issue was handled quickly and without debate. Each senator received one vote. The Democrats controlled the Senate and Johnson received thirty-three of the fifty-two votes, and was elected vice president.[50] It was the only time in American history that the constitutional provisions for Senate election of the vice president were invoked.

CHAPTER 5

1840: Keep the Ball Rolling

What has caused this great commotion, motion motion,
Our country through.

It is the ball a-rolling on, for Tippecanoe and Tyler Too,
Tippecanoe and Tyler Too.

And with them we'll beat little Van, Van, Van is a used up man;
And with them we'll beat little Van.[1]

Whig campaign song, 1840

The campaign of 1840 was the first in American history marked by the hoopla generally associated with a modern presidential election. The Whigs, who were formed as a political party in opposition to Andrew Jackson, a general and former Indian fighter who hailed from the West, nominated as their standard-bearer William Henry Harrison, a general and former Indian fighter who hailed from the West. As a Democratic publication noted with disgust, as the election neared, the opposition had "at last learned from defeat the art of victory. We have taught them how to conquer us!"[2]

Whig Convention

The Whigs were determined not to have their votes split, as in 1836, and decided to hold a nominating convention to unite behind one candidate. The call for the convention came in May 1838 from a caucus of the Whig members of Congress. The month set for the gathering was December 1839 and the city selected to host the convention was Harrisburg, the capital of Pennsylvania. In addition to its central location, Harrisburg was likely chosen because of the importance of Pennsylvania to the Whigs in the election and the need to blunt the continuing strength of the Anti-Masons there. The Whigs knew that a convention of Anti-Masons would be meeting in Philadelphia in November 1838. That convention did meet, but had delegates from only six states (one-quarter of them from Pennsylvania) and it was viewed more as a regional, rather than a national, gathering. On a voice vote, the Anti-Masons at their Philadelphia gathering nominated Harrison as their candidate for president and Webster for vice president. Attempting to downplay the impact the importance of the Anti-Mason nomination of his Whig Party rival, Harrison, Clay wrote that it was a "mock nomination ... [which] has fallen still born."[3]

The first presidential nominating convention of the Whig Party began on December 4, 1839. The Whigs selected the newly reconstructed Zion Lutheran Church, located on South Fourth Street in Harrisburg, for their meeting.[4] The church was hoping for some help from the convention to pay for the structure, as a letter was read to the delegates at the convention pleading "that the congregation were in debt and would be very willing to receive any contributions that might be made by the delegates."[5] This was the first convention in American history where a party's nomination for the presidency was contested and where strategy and events during the convention itself would determine the outcome the nominee for the top of the ticket. As one commentator has noted, "never before or since has a house of God been made the scene of so adroit political maneuvering as went on there."[6] The delegates chose James Barbour, former governor of Virginia, as the convention's president, the same man who had presided over the National Republican Party's 1831 convention held in Baltimore.[7]

It was a three man contest for the 1840 Whig nomination. The Whigs' top vote getter in 1836, William Henry Harrison, was again in the race. He hoped to use his strong showing in the last election, his base of support in the West, and his support from the Anti-Masons to secure the Whig Party's nomination in 1840. Henry Clay, after having sat out the 1836 race, threw his hat once more into the ring. Clay was determined have a more national base of support this time than in the past. In an effort to accomplish this, he made a major speech in the Senate in February 1839 outlining his views on slavery. Like Thomas Jefferson before him, Clay wrestled with slavery, and he publicly called it an evil institution and the "darkest spot" on the nation's mantle. Trying to steer a middle course, Clay, who was a slaveholder himself, denounced both abolitionists in the North and extremists in the South. His solution was for a system of gradual emancipation of slaves, with provisions for compensation of slave owners and for the transport of freed slaves to Africa. When told by a Senate colleague that this speech hurt his chances in the election and would expose him to attack by extremists on both sides of the slavery issue, Clay uttered what would be his most famous line: "I had rather be right than be president."[8] The third candidate in the race, Winfield Scott, another general, was a newcomer to the presidential sweepstakes. A Virginian,

Zion Lutheran Church, which still stands, in Harrisburg, Pennsylvania, was the site of the first nominating convention of the Whig Party in December 1839. The ticket nominated at this convention led to one of the most famous campaign slogans in American history: "Tippecanoe and Tyler, Too!"

Scott had become a national military hero with his victory over the British in the Battle of Chippewa during the War of 1812. His greatest military success, however, still lay in the future, and would come during the Mexican War. Harrison's base of support was in the West, Clay's in the South, and Scott's was primarily in New York, where the Whig political boss, Thurlow Weed, had secured a majority of the Empire State's votes for him. Weed, believing that Clay's baggage as a slaveholder, a Mason, and as a two-time loser in past elections meant he could carry neither New York nor Pennsylvania in the election and, therefore, could not win. Some believed that Weed was using Scott as a stalking horse, his real candidate being Harrison.[9]

Approximately 250 delegates from twenty-two states attended the Whig convention in Harrisburg, with Arkansas, Georgia, South Carolina, and Tennessee sending no representatives.[10] The absence of these four southern states no doubt hurt Clay's prospects. Although Clay likely had more delegates at the convention supporting him, he lost the nomination to Harrison. Weed and his cohorts devised a plan to block Clay's nomination. They proposed, and succeeded, in having the convention adopt a rule on voting procedures that was a modified version of the "unit rule" used by Democrats at their conventions. This rule provided that committees of three delegates from each state would poll their delegations informally and continue until a majority of votes was obtained by one candidate. The state's entire vote would then be cast for the candidate who had the majority support.[11] It was argued that the delegates should adopt this rule because "the proper place to settle sectional differences of opinion was to do it among themselves, that each state might present an undivided front."[12] The unit rule was always used in Democratic Party conventions of the era, but not by the opposition party. Realizing too late the effect of the rule on their candidate, Clay's supporters were unable to get it reversed. Clay had support among some delegates from large northern states, but their votes were silenced under the rule adopted by the convention. On the first ballot, which was referred to as an informal ballot, Clay led with 103 of the 128 votes needed for nomination. Harrison had 91 first ballot votes, while Scott had 57. As one commentator has noted of Clay, "had State delegations been allowed to split their votes, his support in Ohio, New York, and Pennsylvania might have pushed him so close to the necessary 128 votes on the first ballot that he would have been impossible to stop."[13] Moreover, had the four southern states that failed to send delegates to the convention been present, most would likely have supported Clay and put him over the top. Clay's support then diminished on the second ballot, dropping to 95 votes, with Harrison staying at 91 and Scott moving up to 68 votes. On the third ballot, Harrison won the nomination with 148 votes to Clay's 90 votes and Scott dropping to a meager 16 votes.[14] No formal platform was adopted by the party.

The dramatic drop in Scott's support between the second and third ballots likely resulted from what has been called "the decisive maneuver of the convention,"[15] which doomed Scott's chances. With Scott having picked up eleven votes after the first ballot, there was some momentum in his direction. Prior to the convention, many had viewed him as a possible compromise candidate over Harrison and Clay. Scott, a native Virginian, would have been acceptable to the South, since it was assumed that he would not interfere with his home region's "peculiar institution" of slavery. His military hero status made him attractive in the North and the West. However, Thaddeus Stevens, a Pennsylvanian and an Anti-Mason, who was not a delegate to the Whig convention, was in Harrisburg and, along with Thurlow Weed of New York, "met with delegates in lobbies, bars and ... smoke-filled hotel rooms" to argue that Clay could not win the election and to urge the nomination of an alternative candidate. Stevens had obtained a letter that Scott had written to a New York delegate courting his vote and expressing his anti-slavery views. It is not known how Stevens obtained this letter, but it is known that he placed it on the floor of the headquarters of the Virginia delegation after meeting with them, where, as intended, it was discovered and read. Any hope of Virginia's, or other southern votes, switching to Scott was quickly extinguished and, with Clay's strength fading, Harrison picked up his votes in the South and became the nominee.[16] In the first contested convention for a presidential nomination, it was not the regular Whigs but the Anti-Masons who had been the shrewdest card players and who had swung the nomination to their favorite, Harrison. The outcome in Harrisburg led former President John Quincy Adams to comment that the results were a "triumph of Anti-Masonry."[17] The 1839 Whig convention would prove to be the first of many in the mid–nineteenth century where quick thinking and strategy during the convention, as well as some questionable actions, would determine the victor in the contest for a party's nomination for the presidency.

Clay was at Brown's Hotel in Washington drinking with friends when he received the news from Harrisburg. According to accounts written years later, and which are questioned by some historians, Clay was devastated and for one of the few times in his life, he lost his composure in public. He was "openly and exceedingly profane in his denunciations of the intriguers against his nomination." Observing the scene, two strangers in the room "stared at each other in disbelief. Could this be the great Harry of the West, the Great Compromiser, Prince Hal?" Clay then poured them a drink, apologized for his behavior, and walked across Pennsylvania Avenue to his boardinghouse. As short while later, some of his supporters from the convention arrived by train from Harrisburg and went to see him. Still enraged over his convention managers being outmaneuvered, he lamented, "My friends are not worth the powder and shot it would take to kill them!"[18]

William Henry Harrison's popularity as a military hero from an Indian battle at Tippecanoe, fought before the War of 1812, propelled him to the Whig Party's nomination and into the presidency in 1840 (*Library of Congress*).

It was the Whigs' choice of their vice presidential candidate in 1840 that would prove to be, in the long term, disastrous for the party. In an attempt to secure southern votes to balance Harrison and his western base, the convention unanimously nominated John Tyler of Virginia for the second spot on the ticket, but only after other southerners, angry over the defeat of

Clay, declined to be considered.[19] Tyler, who was a delegate to the convention and a Clay supporter, was an interesting choice. Born into an aristocratic Virginia family, he graduated from the College of William & Mary, became a lawyer in Richmond, and entered politics. He served in the House of Representatives and the Senate from Virginia and was a Democrat and a supporter of Andrew Jackson until early in Jackson's second term when he broke with Jackson over the president's bullying of South Carolina during the nullification crisis. Tyler's anti–Jackson views caused him to gravitate to the Whigs. In the nullification controversy and in all of his political views, Tyler was a supporter of state's rights and of strict limits on the authority of the federal government, which put him out of step with the leadership and mainstream of the Whig Party. Despite this, it was thought, what harm could there be from placing him on the ticket? After all, no president had ever died in office. It would turn out to be one the biggest nominating mistakes ever made by a political party. The addition of Tyler to the ticket did give the country what was perhaps the most famous campaign slogan in American history. Paired with William Henry Harrison, the hero of the Indian battle of Tippecanoe, the Whigs offered their ticket to the country under the banner of "Tippecanoe and Tyler, Too!" As one Whig, Philip Hone, later remarked, "there was rhyme but no reason to it."[20]

What would go down in history as the "Log Cabin and Hard Cider" campaign gained its name from an article in a Baltimore newspaper. Shortly after the convention ended, a supporter of Henry Clay, bitter over his candidate's loss, speculated with a reporter for the *Baltimore Republican* as to how Harrison could be removed from the campaign after having won the nomination. In his published answer to this question, the reporter wrote in an editorial that Harrison was rather common and unqualified for the presidency: "Give him a barrel of hard cider and a pension of two thousand a year and, my word for it, he will sit the remainder of his days in a log cabin, by the side of a … fire and study moral philosophy."[21] Untruths abound in this characterization of Harrison and how it was reported. Harrison had been born into an aristocratic Virginia family and his father, Benjamin Harrison, was one of the Old Dominion's signers of the Declaration of Independence. At the time of the campaign, he lived in a large house overlooking a scenic bend in the Ohio River that was decidedly not a log cabin. Yet, Whig Party leaders took a sneering comment, turned it on the Democrats, and made it the theme of their campaign. Harrison became the common man (à la Andrew Jackson), one who could be comfortable sitting in a log cabin and drinking hard cider, in contrast to the incumbent president, Martin Van Buren, whom the Whigs portrayed as an elitist who was living a pampered life in the White House.[22] Amazingly, with virtually no truth to support it, the Whig campaign theme worked.

In one of its last acts in Harrisburg, the Whig convention adopted a resolution, shortly before adjourning, "that this convention recommend to the Whig Young Men of the several states to appoint delegates from their respective states, to assemble in Convention at the city of Baltimore, on the first Monday of May next, to take such measures as will most effectually aid the advancement of the Whig cause and sound principles."[23] Baltimore may have lost out to Harrisburg for the Whig nominating convention in the campaign of 1840, but, in the first great counter-scheduling maneuver of American politics, it would host a political rally for the Whig ticket that would attract national attention. It was no coincidence that the Whigs selected the date of May 4, 1840, for their Baltimore rally, for that was the day before the Democratic Party was scheduled to open its nominating convention in Baltimore to renominate Martin Van Buren for the presidency. The Young Men's Whig Convention was the largest political gathering up to that date in the history of the United States and would prove to be one of the most colorful rallies of a campaign the likes of which the country had never before seen. An estimated 100,000 marchers and onlookers participated in a procession through the heart of Baltimore and to a rally at an abandoned horse racing track in nearby Canton.

After a rainy Sunday evening, the clouds broke and the sun came out on Monday, May 4, 1840, an early spring morning in Baltimore. Very little business would be done in the city this day. The streets began filling up shortly after dawn with thousands of Whigs. The gathering was officially named the Young Men's Whig Ratification Convention. Its schedule called for a two-mile march beginning near Cove Street, near what is now Martin Luther King, Jr., Boulevard. Thousands of marchers, organized by state, lined up in their staging areas on the streets intersecting Baltimore Street and then flowed onto the main route, where a grand parade moved eastward through the city and ended at the Canton Race Track, located at the intersection of Boston and Clinton Streets, for a huge ratification convention and rally.[24] Along the way, the Whigs would march within a block of the Assembly Rooms (near Baltimore's present-day City Hall) where the Democrats were making final plans for the opening of their convention the next day. The "Log Cabin and Hard Cider" campaign of 1840 officially stepped off in the streets of Baltimore promptly at 9:30 A.M. with the firing of a cannon. The Philadelphia contingent, arriving late, hurried, luggage in hand, to their assembly area as the grand procession got under way.[25]

A multitude of spectators lined the sidewalks of Baltimore Street, with hundreds of people on rooftops and balconies and with the "bright-eyed beautiful ladies of Baltimore" perched in front of every window along the parade route.[26] Along the way, "[s]treets and shops were decorated with flags and bunting, portraits of Harrison.... Spectators clung perilously to roof gables and leaned from balconies and windows, shouting, cheering, and waving flags as the parade of dignitaries and state delegations threaded its way slowly through the crowd."[27] Chief Marshal James O. Law led the procession, followed by officials of the hosting Baltimore City delegation and then by barouches carrying distinguished invited guests, including Senator Daniel Webster and Baltimore mayor Sheppard C. Leakin. Henry Clay, a featured speaker at the rally, was absent from the procession, leading to speculation by Democratic newspapers that he had refused to ride with his Whig Party rival, Webster.[28] The first large delegation to march in the procession was from Massachusetts, boasting more than a thousand participants and accompanied by a band and multiple banners. The Massachusetts contingent featured the Boston Brigade Band, which played a lively marching tune. The song was later arranged for the pianoforte and sheet music was sold under the name of "The Baltimore Whig Convention Quick Step."[29] In the even larger Pennsylvania delegation that followed, a group from one Keystone State county held aloft a huge banner on black satin with "a log cabin, in gilt, surrounded by thirteen stars ... attached to the cabin was a barrel of hard cider" along with gilt banners proclaiming "Harrison, Tyler and True Democracy" and "The Ball Is Rolling." The Fayette County contingent from Pennsylvania displayed a complete log cabin, on wheels, with several people inside, and drawn by six horses. The cabin was adorned on its sides with deer and fox skins, buckhorns, farming tools, and with the obligatory barrel of hard cider at its rear. Delaware delegates marched under a banner proclaiming "The First to Adopt — The Last to Abandon the Constitution."[30] The official beverage of the Whig campaign, and patriotism, were in abundant supply: "Hard cider appeared to flow freely and bunting shirts were all the go."[31]

The largest delegation was from Maryland. No less than four separate log cabins made their way down Baltimore Street as part of the Old Line State's delegation. Leading off the

At the Whig Party's ratification convention held in Baltimore in 1840, this huge ball, emblazoned with party slogans, was rolled through the streets of the city. The ball, and others used during the campaign, became the inspiration for the phrase "Keep the ball rolling."

Allegany County group was a flag announcing "Allegany Is Coming," followed by "a huge ball, about ten feet in diameter, which was rolled along by a number of the members of the delegation; the ball was apparently a wooden frame covered with linen painted divers colors, and bearing a multitude of inscriptions, apt quotations, original stanzas and pithy sentences, which it was impossible to collect in consequence of the motion of the ball."[32] The ball was said to have been rolled all the way from Clay's home state of Kentucky to Baltimore for the rally.[33] Variations of the rolling Whig ball would appear at rallies throughout the 1840 campaign and the phrase "Keep the ball rolling" became a Whig campaign slogan and a permanent part of the American lexicon.[34] The large Virginia delegation followed, proudly announcing the Old Dominion as the birthplace of the Whig standard-bearer, Harrison, and the home of the party's vice presidential nominee, Tyler. As one reporter noted, there was more than just politics on the minds of the young Whig male politicos in the procession and of the maidens of Baltimore cheering them on: "The most striking and interesting sight was the display of beauty in the windows, from the first to the fourth story of the stores and dwelling houses on either side of the street. Thousands of bright eyes beamed eloquently on the 'young men' as they marched on, and cheer upon cheer followed the graceful salutation of the fair ones, the waving of scarfs and handkerchiefs. The young men from the 'Old Dominion' appeared to be more enthusiastic than all the rest, when beauty was in question."[35] Ohio's contingent, representing the home of Old Tippecanoe at the time of the campaign, marched under a banner proclaiming, "She Offers Her Cincinnatus to Redeem the Republic." The Tennessee delegation was more subdued, wearing black armbands and mourning the recent death of its former senator and Whig presidential candidate in 1836, Hugh Lawton White.[36]

As the great procession reached a slightly elevated bridge on Baltimore Street, spectators looking westward saw a mile-long sea of humanity, with Whigs from the entire country marching up to ten abreast, tipping their hats to thousands of spectators cheering them on, who waved white handkerchiefs as they passed by.[37] Some estimate that there were 125,000 people in the streets of Baltimore that day, either as marchers or onlookers.[38] The *Baltimore Patriot*, a Whig newspaper, described the scene, no doubt with some exaggeration, as follows:

> Never before was seen such an assemblage of people.... It is impossible to convey the slightest idea of the sublime spectacle presented by the procession as it moved through the city.... In no country, in no time, never before in the history of man was there a spectacle so full of "natural glory...." Standing on an eminence commanding a view of the line of the procession on the whole extent of Baltimore Street, you beheld a moving mass of human beings. A thousand banners, burnished by the sun, floating in the breeze, ten thousand handkerchiefs waved by the fair daughters of the city, gave seeming life and motion to the very air. A hundred thousand faces were before you,— age, manhood, youth, and beauty filled every place where a foothold could be got, or any portion of the procession seen.... The free men of the land were there,— the fiery son of the South, the substantial citizen of the East, the hardy pioneer of the West, all were there.[39]

The grand event was not without tragedy. As the front of the procession approached Howard Street, heading east, a gang of about forty or fifty young men, apparently supporters of the Democrats, approached from the opposite direction, holding aloft a pole with a stuffed figure on its top, wearing a petticoat. In the campaign, the Democrats had begun to criticize the aging William Henry Harrison as a doddering old imbecile who was not up to the presidency. The fact that Whig Party leaders answered all of Harrison's correspondence for him gave credence to this line of attack.[40] Because the opposition ridiculed Harrison as "Old Granny" and the "Petticoat General," there was no doubt whom the "effigy with a red petticoat on" at the top of the pole was intended to represent. A confrontation ensued. The figure was ripped from the pole, whereupon one of the parade crashers struck a Whig marshal, Thomas Laughlin, over the head with the pole, a blow that "so staggered him that he fell backward and struck his head against the curb-stone, thereby fracturing his skull, which caused his death in a few minutes." In the confusion and mass of people, the perpetrators escaped into the crowd and were apparently never prosecuted.[41] The procession marched on.

By noon, approximately 25,000 marching delegates and onlookers reached the racetrack at Canton. The track was located on the south side of the intersection of Boston and Clinton Streets. Formerly farmland and it had opened for racing in 1823, and was known originally as Potter's Course and, later, as the Kendall Track.[42] By 1840, it was no longer being used for horse racing and, as a large open field close to Baltimore, it was the perfect site for the mass political gathering of the Whigs. The throng entered the grounds through an archway decorated with laurels and the American flag. A full-sized log cabin greeted them to the right. Across the track stood a scale model of Fort Meigs (the site of one of General Harrison's victories in the War of 1812), complete with gun portholes and topped by the American flag.[43] The invited guests then took the stage, including several veterans of the Revolutionary War. With all assembled, the ratification convention began. John V. L. McMahon was elected president of the proceeding and various resolutions were quickly proposed and approved. The choice of the Whig nominating convention in Harrisburg the previous December was ratified and the Tippecanoe and Tyler ticket was heartily recommended to the country. The speeches then began. The crowd called for Virginia's leading Whig, Governor Henry Wise, but he begged off for health reasons, castigating the Democrats who were then in power in Washington and stating, "I have been speaking for so long against this wicked and corrupt administration, that I have worn out the best pair of lungs ever given to man."[44]

The great Whig orators of the era, Henry Clay and Daniel Webster, then addressed the throng. Although both had been sorely disappointed when the party turned to Harrison, a military man who they considered intellectually and politically inferior, they toed the party line. Clay spoke first, stating his "hearty concurrence" with the party's choice for its nominee and declaring: "We are all Whigs. We are all Harrison men. We are united. We must triumph!" Warning against the complacency that comes with too much confidence, Clay despaired that, if Van Buren was reelected, "the struggle of restoring the country to its former glory would be almost a hopeless one."[45] Daniel Webster spoke next and, noting the windy day, told the crowd that "Every breeze says change, every interest of the country demands it.... We have fallen, gentlemen, upon hard times, and the remedy seems to be HARD CIDER."[46] Other speakers followed and the ratification convention continued until 4:00 P.M.

Not having had enough of political oratory, the Whigs resolved to meet again at nine o'clock the following morning, this time at Monument Square in the heart of Baltimore. Not coincidentally, this was within a couple of blocks of where the Democrats would be opening their convention that day to nominate Van Buren for the presidency. So, the next morning, once again, thousands of Whigs assembled to hear their leaders exhort them on to victory. On a somber note, each state delegation was asked to solicit contributions from their members of up to one dollar each for the widow and children of Thomas Laughlin, the Whig marshal who had been killed in the previous day's procession. After a day of speeches, the gathering adjourned at 4:00 P.M. and many of the Whigs then went to the home of Laughlin, a carpenter who had lived in the Federal Hill section of Baltimore, and to attend his funeral at a nearby church. Following the funeral, it was back to Monument Square for more speeches, which lasted well into the evening and finally ended around 11:00 P.M. with a closing speech by one of Maryland's most prominent attorneys and a leading Whig, Reverdy Johnson. He did not have far to go after the end of a long day. Johnson's elegant home was located on Monument Square, just to the west of the Battle Monument, at northwest corner of Calvert and Fayette Streets. Over the course of his long career, Johnson would move from the Whigs to the Democrats, and would serve as a United States senator from Maryland, as attorney general of the United States, and as minister to Great Britain. From the portico of his home, he had a front row seat to the activities in Monument Square during Baltimore's political conventions, and he actively participated in many of the conventions.[47]

Democratic Convention

Like John Adams before him, Martin Van Buren found that following a legend in the White House was no easy task. In his first few months in office, the American economy experienced its worst collapse since the founding of the republic. The Panic of 1837, which many believe was caused or exacerbated by the financial policies of his predecessor, Jackson, and which others believe was caused more by international economic factors, made Van Buren an unpopular president. Banks and businesses failed, capital dried up, jobs were lost, and the nation's finances were paralyzed. A second economic downturn in 1839 only extended the hard times. Whatever the reasons, the economy tanked and it occurred on Van Buren's watch.

The Whigs nicknamed the president "Martin Van Ruin," and it stuck.[48] Van Buren, however, had risen to the top through his consummate political skills and, despite the economic downturn, he maintained tight control over the Democratic Party that he had spent most of his adult life molding and shaping into the most dominant political force in the United States.

Once again, for the third consecutive time since their inaugural convention of 1832, the Democrats chose Baltimore as the site of their 1840 presidential nominating convention. With political gatherings no longer welcome at Baltimore's First Presbyterian Church, the site of their last gathering, the Democrats chose to convene in the Assembly Rooms. This structure two stories tall, located at the northeast corner of Fayette and Holliday Streets, had been around since 1797. The second floor consisted of a large room used as a dance hall for Baltimore society.[49] The building also housed the Baltimore Library Company on its first floor. Fronting on Fayette Street, the structure was described by an 1830s visitor as a "handsome house."[50] Complementing its "very elegant" exterior, the interior was equally impressive with a "suite of dancing and refreshment rooms, in which the regular winter balls are held, [that] are not surpassed in beauty by any in Europe."[51]

No dancing, nor fancy footwork, was required of Martin Van Buren at the Assembly Rooms to secure his party's nomination for a second term. He controlled the machinery of the party and no serious opposition arose. The convention opened at noon on Tuesday, May 5, 1840. Former governor Isaac Hill of New Hampshire served as the temporary president of the gathering. Delegates from twenty-one states were present. A committee consisting of one member from each state was appointed to recommend permanent officers. In a somewhat unusual move, a credentials committee was appointed with only nine members, who were selected by Governor Hill, rather than the typical committee composition of one member from each state. The convention then adjourned until late afternoon.[52]

When the gathering resumed, delegate Felix Grundy of Tennessee spoke of the absence of a legitimate delegation from his state at the previous Democratic convention in 1835 and urged "a strict scrutiny being instituted into the rights and qualifications of gentlemen presenting themselves here as delegates ... in order to prevent injustice being done to the party, as had been the case four years ago, in regard to Tennessee ... there are no Rucker delegates among us."[53] In other words, any visitors to Baltimore who might be hanging out in local taverns with the hope that Democratic Party leaders were going to tap them on the shoulder and ask them to become delegates and, perhaps, cast the deciding votes for the vice presidential nomination were going to be sorely disappointed this time around. Grundy then launched into an attack on William Henry Harrison, the Whig Party candidate, who had been nominated by his party at its convention held in Harrisburg six months earlier, in December 1839. Since then, it had become known that Whig Party leaders had muzzled Harrison and had formed a committee to review correspondence sent to him and to prepare responses. Noting Harrison's most recent job, which was that of a relatively low-level courtroom clerk in Ohio, Grundy complained that the Whigs:

> have a candidate whom they want to make president, and of whom four years ago very little was heard; but within the last few months, no mortal man has ever grown so vastly as he, from a plain honest clerk of a county court ... he has grown to be an astonishingly great man, destined in their opinion to carry all before him. But notwithstanding all this, no one can, by any possibility, come at his opinions on any of the great questions interesting to the country.... What have his friends done in regard to him?... They have shut him up (I will not say in a cage, but he might as well be in one), and will not let him have the use of pen,

ink and paper, while his conscience keepers say that he shall neither speak nor write....
Now I ask this convention of sober, reflecting men, if this is the way to make the president
for the people of the Unites States?[54]

After hearing the speech of Grundy, a Tennessean, the Committee on Permanent Officers
presented its report and nominated Governor William Carroll of the Volunteer State as permanent president of the convention, which was approved. It seems as though the Democrats,
this time around, wanted the presence of *legitimate* Tennessee delegates to be in the headlines.
Carroll then gave an opening address advising the delegates that he had "spent twenty years
of my life in the service of my country in peace and in war," but he had never been part of
a deliberative body and knew nothing of the rules and procedures for conventions. He hoped
that there would be "nothing but unanimity in our proceedings" and, therefore, "very little
demand for anything like talent in the presiding officer."[55] With this not-so-steady hand at
its helm, the convention then moved on with its business. The report of the Committee on
Credentials was received. There was great variation in the size of the delegations — New Jersey
had fifty-nine delegates present, but there were only three from Kentucky, Alabama, Louisiana,
and Michigan, two from Georgia, and only one delegate each from Massachusetts and
Arkansas. Virginia, apparently still resentful of the nomination (over its strong objection) of
Richard M. Johnson for vice president at the last convention, sent no delegates. As usual,
South Carolina was absent.[56] The convention then appointed three more committees with
one member from each of the twenty-one states present: one to prepare a platform for the
party, another to prepare an address for the American people, and a third to make nominations
for president and vice president. With that, the delegates called for speeches from some of
the leading Democrats present as delegates, and those delegates gladly complied.

Tilghman Howard, a congressman from Indiana, was the first to address the convention.
He noted that this was a gathering of Democrats who were "plain and honest," who loved "equality and simplicity," and who did not need "any badge about them, with a piece of blue ribbon,
and a pewter medal around their necks, like school boys." Mocking the symbol of "hard cider"
that the opposing Whigs had adopted as their campaign theme, Howard noted that the term
"'Whig' now means 'hard cider.'... It was a little acidulous at the commencement of the campaign
and would be very, very sour at the end of it in November." The Hoosier closed his remarks by
stating that he wanted to go out and be a tourist in Baltimore, "to visit every part of the monumental city and to see her improvements, and the monuments which she has raised to the valor
of her own sons, and to the fame of the great leader of the revolution."[57]

After loud calls for remarks from Alexander Duncan, a congressman and delegate from
Ohio, he also addressed the cheering convention. He said that he, en route to Baltimore, had
seen an old man walking along the side of the road with an axe on his shoulder. When Duncan
asked the old man where he was going, he replied that he was "going to hew wooden razors
to shave the dead Whigs with next fall." When asked about the poor economy, the old man
responded "D — — — d the panic ... if you would all work as I do you would have no panic."
Duncan then regaled the convention with his interpretation of the grand Whig procession
through the streets of Baltimore the previous day: "What was the animal show we had yesterday," he asked? Noting the proliferation of log cabins going down Baltimore Street, he
stated that a friend of his went to watch the show and swore that there were less than 8,000
people present, and:

> If we deducted all bank presidents, bank lounging loafers, and all the idle dogs that paraded the
> streets on the occasion, how many log cabin men would there be left? He [Duncan's friend] had
> endeavored to get an introduction to some of these gentry for the purpose of feeling their soft

delicate hands. As soon as he had taken hold of them he was pretty careful to put his hand on his purse.... They would rob you if they had the opportunity.... You are contending with a foul faction under various claims and under various banners, but whose principal banner is that of federalism. The contest, then, is federalism against democracy.[58]

The delegates, having been fed their red meat, adjourned for the day and descended upon the streets, hotels, and taverns of Baltimore.

The controversy at the convention, as it had in 1835, centered on the vice presidential spot on the Democratic ticket. The incumbent vice president, Richard M. Johnson of Kentucky, wanted to be renominated. Having been forced on Van Buren, primarily at the urging of Andrew Jackson, Johnson was never an integral part of the administration. As with most vice presidents of the era and, indeed, until the late twentieth century, he had been chosen to provide regional balance to the ticket and was there to fill the constitutional role of succession in the event of a tragedy, to break tie votes in the Senate, and to do little else. By 1840, however, knowledge of Johnson's unusual domestic arrangements (living openly with black and mixed-race women who had been his slaves) had become more widespread. Even Old Hickory was now urging Van Buren to dump Johnson in 1840. Van Buren was indecisive, was unwilling to offend the constituencies that Johnson represented (the West and veterans), and refused to openly endorse or oppose Johnson, or any other potential running mate.[59] As the Democrats gathered in Baltimore in early May, it was an open question as to whether the purported killer of Tecumseh would himself survive as vice president or not.

When the convention opened for its second day of proceedings on Wednesday, May 6, 1840, the delegates heard the report from its platform committee. There were no surprises. The Democratic Party's philosophy of a non-activist federal government and the protection of slavery were the major themes. The platform provided that the federal government is one of limited powers, that there is no constitutional basis for a general system of internal improvements, no government help to foster one branch of industry over another, economy in government, no power of Congress to charter a national bank, separation of the money of the government from banking institutions, and no power of Congress to "interfere with or control the domestic institutions of the several states, and ... that all efforts of the abolitionists or others ... are calculated to lead to the most alarming and dangerous consequences ... and endanger the stability and permanency of the union, and ought not to be countenanced by any friend of our political institutions."[60] Each plank of the platform was approved unanimously.

Next, President Hill called for the report from the committee assigned the task of preparing an address to the American people. Some delegates, anxious to move on to the nomination process and curious as to what would be done with the vice presidency, wanted to dispense with the reading of the address, to simply approve it, and have it printed after the convention. Delegate Grundy of Tennessee objected, noting that the delegates had come to Baltimore, "some of us from a distance of 1,000 miles to deliberate on the important concerns of the nation ... I will never vote for a paper till I hear it read. Let us hear what it is, and let me give it the sanction of my understanding as well as my heart."[61] Grundy's view carried the day. The lengthy, indeed very lengthy, address was then read, word for word, to the delegates, taking up nine full pages in the official proceedings, almost one half of the total pages recorded for the entire convention.[62] Unfortunately for the delegates, crossword puzzles, laptop computers, and other modern methods of coping with boredom had not yet been invented. After being read in its entirety, the address to the American people was approved.

The convention then heard the report from its nominating committee. As expected, the incumbent president, Martin Van Buren, was renominated for a second term. The incumbent vice president, Richard M. Johnson, did not fare so well. Noting that "different individuals" had been mentioned as potential candidates, the committee proposed the adoption of a resolution stating that "the Convention deems it expedient at the present time not to choose between the individuals in nomination, but to leave the decision to their republican fellow-citizens in the several states, trusting that before the election shall take place, their opinions shall become so concentrated as to secure the choice of a vice president by the electoral colleges."[63] This compromise strategy, not totally dumping Johnson but not renominating him, was apparently discussed in advance of the convention and was likely conveyed to him. After the nominating committee's report was given to the convention, a letter from Johnson, dated April 25, 1840, was read to the convention. In it, Johnson said of the delegates:

> If, in their opinion, the great principles for which we contend, will be more likely secured by the use of my name, they will use it — if, in their opinion, another selection will be more likely to ensure success, they will make another selection. If, in their opinion to make no nomination of a Vice-President, and to leave the selection to the pleasure and preference of the Republicans of the several states, will give the most strength to our friends, the convention will take that course.... I hope my friends will feel a perfect freedom of action in the Convention.[64]

After much debate on whether to take a roll call vote of the states on the vice presidential nomination (some delegates had come to the convention with instructions from their state party to vote for Johnson), it was finally decided to just have a voice vote on the nominating committee's report, which was done and which was approved by acclamation.[65]

The convention then took a recess and resumed in mid–afternoon, at which time the delegates adopted a resolution thanking the "central committee of the city of Baltimore, for the commodious and appropriate arrangements made by them," heard a few more speeches, a closing prayer, and then adjourned *sine die*.[66] For the first (and to date, the only) time, a major American political party had failed to nominate a candidate for the vice presidency at its convention.

By the early 1840s, cities began to realize the advantages that hosting conventions could bring, both from an economic standpoint and in terms of civic pride and prestige. In addition to hosting the Whig rally and the Democratic convention in the first week of May 1840, Baltimore also hosted two religious conventions that week, the Methodist Conference and the Convention of Bishops of the Catholic Church. In words that could be improved upon by neither a modern municipal chamber of commerce nor convention bureau, one Baltimore newspaper commented on the economic benefits to the city from all of the conventions:

> For the last week our city has been all life and animation. A dense crowd of strangers, from different sections of the country, of all classes, parties and denominations thronged our streets.... Men of talent and distinction in both political parties, as well as the most celebrated divines, have given the people an opportunity of hearing a display of their transcendent oratorical powers ... we are made, as it were, the great centre of a nation. Our thousand advantages and attractions are shown off to the best advantage — an impression is produced upon the minds of those who sojourn with us most favorable — they see every thing lively and flourishing — they have an opportunity of trying and reciprocating our good feeling — they learn by personal observation, that Baltimore is not behind her sister cities in point of energy, perseverance, commerce, and all the advantages pertaining to a seaport. With these impressions, they return home, tell the story of their adventures to their

children, their friends and acquaintances. Thus, they in turn become fascinated with the recital of that so attractive to others, and determine in [the] future to see the place, of which they have heard so much spoken.[67]

The Campaign and Election

The campaign of 1840 was like no other prior presidential canvas. The Whigs held massive campaign events throughout the country. It seemed as though half the country took a few months off from the daily routine of life to attend political parades, rallies, and picnics, to build log cabins, and to drink hard cider. For the Democrats, Van Buren campaigned in the traditional manner, primarily by staying in the White House and writing letters to friends and to newspapers outlining his positions. Harrison, against the advice of Whig Party leaders, actually actively campaigned, a first in American history. In response to Democratic attacks that he was too old and feeble to assume the office of the presidency, Harrison went on trips through Ohio and Indiana in June, and again in September. The June trip was to attend a celebration of the anniversary of his War of 1812 victory at Fort Meigs in northwestern Ohio, and he made more than twenty speeches during his journey.[68] His purpose was to show the people, as he explained, "I am not the old man on crutches," and he generally told stories of his battlefield experiences of days gone by, rather than address any current policy issues, which would have been deemed unseemly. He did denounce a powerful executive as a danger to the country and pledged, if elected, that he would serve only one term.[69] As one author noted, Harrison "campaigned against campaigning while campaigning."[70] In contrast, Van Buren stayed in Washington during most of the campaign, attending to "public duties," and followed what would be called today a "Rose Garden strategy" for reelection, long before there was a rose garden on the grounds of the White House. He did reply to many letters addressed to him on various issues with "long, thoughtful responses" that he intended and expected would end up in newspapers.[71] While history remembers the campaign of 1840 for its "log cabin and hard cider" hoopla, there were issues in the campaign. The Whigs favored government intervention in the economy and opposed the increased use of presidential power under Jackson and Van Buren. They denounced the condition of the economy, pointing to the Panic of 1837 and another downturn in 1839, which continued during the election year. The Democrats campaigned against the constitutionality of federal power to promote internal improvements or to interfere with slavery, promoted the separation of banks from government, and pledged economy in government.[72] Although Richard Johnson had not been formally renominated by the Democratic convention, no candidate within the Democratic Party arose to oppose him for vice president after the convention, and he remained the party's candidate and was on the ballot in all states for the second spot.[73]

The election took place in the various states during the two-week time span from October 30 until November 12. When the votes were counted, Harrison was the victor. As has been the case in many subsequent elections, the party in power during bad economic times suffered the wrath of the voters. An astonishing eighty percent of eligible voters cast ballots, a dramatic increase from the fifty-seven percent turnout in the 1836 election and, up to the present time, a turnout level matched by only two other elections, those of 1860 and 1876.[74] In the popular vote, Harrison won by about 150,000, with 1,275,016, compared to Van Buren's 1,129,012, a margin of roughly fifty-three percent to forty-seven percent. Interestingly, with the large turnout, Van Buren had 400,000 more votes in losing in 1840 than he had in winning in

1836. In the Electoral College, however, it was a Whig landslide, with the party earning 234 electoral votes, compared to only 60 for the Democrats. The Little Magician had lost his charm, carrying only seven of the twenty-six states — New Hampshire, Illinois, Missouri, Arkansas, Alabama, Virginia, and South Carolina.[75] The vote tally in several states was very close, with the Whigs gaining narrow majorities in Pennsylvania, New York and Maine, and with Democrats barely winning Virginia and Illinois.[76] For the third time in American history, as in 1800 and in 1828, the party in power had been turned out of the presidency. The Whig Party, by holding its first nominating convention to consolidate its support behind one candidate, and by nominating a military hero, had indeed learned from its past mistakes and, only six years after its founding in 1834, had succeeded in winning the top prize in American politics.

CHAPTER 6

1844: Texas Two-Step

His choice occasioned some surprise. Good democrats rolled up their eyes.
Oh, asking, "Tell us, who is he, James K. Polk of Tennessee?"

Hark, the people rising say, He's the man to cope with Clay.
Ha ha, such a nominee, Jimmy Polk of Tennessee!

But soon the vast excitement o'er, they see what ne'er was seen before.
The best selection that could be, Ex-Speaker Polk of Tennessee![1]

Democratic campaign song, 1844

If the turn of events from 1841 to 1844 had not been so unfortunate and tragic for the Whig Party, they would have been comical. After having endured twelve years of their nemesis, Andrew Jackson, and his hand-picked successor, Martin Van Buren, in the White House, the Whigs controlled all the levers of power in Washington after the election of 1840. Not only had the first Whig president, William Henry Harrison, and his vice president, John Tyler, won a resounding victory, but the Whigs controlled both houses of Congress in the session beginning in 1841. If there was a signature issue for the Whig Party, it was the reestablishment of a national bank, its rechartering having been vetoed by Andrew Jackson in 1832. As 1841 began, the Whigs were on the threshold of enacting this key item, as well as the rest of their agenda.

It was not to be. Every schoolchild in America has been taught the story. William Henry Harrison, at age sixty-nine, was the oldest man, at the time, to have been elected to the presidency. On a cold and rainy inauguration day, March 4, 1841, he stood on the steps of the Capitol, without an overcoat, and gave the longest inaugural address in American history, lasting one and one-half hours. Harrison caught a cold that developed into pneumonia and, within a month, became the first president to die in office. His vice president, John Tyler of Virginia, who had been nominated and elected as a Whig by the Whig Party, then assumed the presidency. Tyler, a former Democrat with strong beliefs in state's rights, had soured on the Jackson administration and had aligned himself with the Whigs in the 1830s.

The Whigs in Congress promptly passed their signature piece of legislation, the rechartering of a national bank, and sent it to their Whig president, Tyler, for his signature. To their dismay, he vetoed the bill, stating that it infringed on state's rights. The Whigs, lacking the two-thirds vote required in Congress to override the veto, made some revisions to the proposed law, seeking to alleviate Tyler's concerns as expressed in his veto message, and sent a second bank bill to the president's desk for his signature. He also vetoed that one. Again, the veto was not overridden. For the first time in American history, there was open political warfare between congressional leaders and a president of the same party. In fall 1841, the entire Whig cabinet, with the exception of Secretary of State Daniel Webster, resigned from the administration. Tyler was excommunicated from the party by congressional Whigs.[2] The stalemate continued for the remainder of Tyler's term.

By the time the 1844 campaign season arrived, Tyler was a president without a party. Desperately wanting to be elected to a term of his own, the president had been courting conservative Democrats since 1841 and had named many of them to public offices. He had even privately offered an appointment to the Supreme Court to the likely 1844 Democratic nominee, former president Van Buren, to get him out of the race. The offer was flatly rejected.[3] The Tyler strategy for retaining the presidency in 1844 was two pronged. First, use the power and patronage of the presidency to create a viable third party with Tyler at its head. Second, use the third-party threat as leverage to persuade the Democrats to nominate Tyler as their presidential candidate in 1844. The key to all of this was the annexation of Texas.

In 1844, there were twenty-six states in the Union, thirteen free and thirteen with slavery. The Missouri Compromise had succeeded in keeping the slavery issue on the back burner of the political stove during the quarter-century since its enactment in 1820. As the 1844 campaign season began, there was one issue that had the potential to upset the sectional balance and to dominate the presidential contest — Texas. Texans, most of whom had come to that region from the United States, had defeated the Mexican army at the Battle of San Jacinto in 1836 and had established their own country, the Republic of Texas, that same year. While the shooting had stopped, technically, in 1844, there still existed a state of war between Mexico and Texas. While many Texans favored joining the United States, and while many Americans favored bringing Texas into the Union, any annexation of Texas would almost certainly provoke a war between the United States and Mexico.

The issue of Texas annexation was accelerated by a tragic accident. On the last day of February in 1844, the political and social elite of the American government gathered on the nation's newest warship, the U.S.S. *Princeton*, for a cruise down the Potomac River and a mid–nineteenth century demonstration of the American military's "shock and awe." The *Princeton* was equipped with two twelve-inch guns, nicknamed the Oregon and the Peacemaker, each capable of firing a shot of over two hundred pounds for more than three miles. Among the distinguished guests on the ship on this clear late winter day were President John Tyler, Secretary of State Abel Upshur, Secretary of the Navy Thomas Gilmer, several members of Congress, and the cream of Washington society, including former first lady Dolly Madison. The ship's commanding officer, Captain Robert F. Stockton, had his sailors fire two shots from the Peacemaker for the enthralled crowd and the massive gun performed flawlessly. As the gleaming new warship plied the Potomac below Mount Vernon and prepared for its return trip to Washington, Secretary Gilmer asked Captain Stockton for one more demonstration of the ship's firepower. Concerned that the guns were overheated, the captain at first balked, but the insistent secretary of the navy was then granted what would be his last wish. As the Peacemaker was fired again, it exploded and huge slabs of iron were thrown across the deck. Eight onlookers were killed instantly, including Secretary of State Upshur and Secretary of the Navy Gilmer. President Tyler was below deck at the time of the explosion, sipping champagne with twenty-four-year-old Julia Gardiner, a New York socialite whom the fifty-four year old widowed president would marry within a few weeks.[4] Her father, David Gardiner, had the misfortune to be on the deck and was one of the fatalities.[5]

In the aftermath of the *Princeton* tragedy, the president had to replace his deceased secretary of state, Upshur, and, in doing so, advanced his strategy of using the annexation of Texas to retain the White House in the election of 1844. By mid–March, he nominated John C. Calhoun, an ardently pro-slavery South Carolinian, Democrat and former vice president and senator, to be his new secretary of state and the two moved the annexation of Texas to the front burner of American politics. Quickly confirmed by the Senate, Calhoun completed, in a matter of a few weeks, negotiations that his deceased predecessor, Upshur, had been having with the Republic of Texas, headed by President Sam Houston. By mid–April, a secret treaty for the annexation of Texas into the Union was submitted to the Senate. Accompanying the treaty was a letter, also confidential, that Calhoun had written to the British foreign minister, wherein he justified the annexation as necessary to block a suspected British offer to provide financial assistance to the Texans in exchange for their agreement to ban slavery in the Republic of Texas.[6] Tyler, with no political party to call his own, renounced by the Whigs and considered a turncoat to the Democrats, had thrown down the gauntlet of Texas into the 1844 presidential campaign.[7]

The leading presidential candidates of the two major parties, former president Martin Van Buren for the Democrats and Senator Henry Clay for the Whigs, were bewildered by this turn of events. Each needed to draw support from both the North and the South to win the election and making immediate annexation of Texas the focal issue of the campaign spelled disaster for them. Most southerners favored annexation and slavery in Texas, while most northerners did not. Tyler's secret treaty for the annexation of Texas was sent to the United States Senate for ratification on April 22, 1844. Within days of its being submitted to the Senate, an anti-slavery senator from Ohio leaked the treaty's terms to a newspaper, along with Calhoun's letter to the British stating that a primary motive for annexation was the protection of slavery in Texas.[8] Then, within a week, on April 27, 1844, in a stunning coincidence or a choreographed exercise, both Van Buren and Clay had lengthy letters published in newspapers stating that they did not favor the annexation of Texas at that time under the circumstances then existing. Van Buren's lengthy letter was written in response to an inquiry on Texas from Congressman William Hammet of Mississippi, who was an uncommitted delegate to the upcoming Democratic convention.[9] Published in Washington's Democratic newspaper *The Globe*, the Hammet letter held out the hope of an eventual peaceful resolution of the Texas issue. In time, Van Buren argued, Mexico would drop its claim to Texas and the ultimate goal could be accomplished without abrogating existing treaties with Mexico and without provoking a war.[10] Clay's letter, referred to by historians as his Raleigh letter, because it was written by Clay during a political trip to the North Carolina capital city, was published the same day in the Whigs' Washington paper *The Intelligencer*, and expressed basically the same anti-annexation views as Van Buren. The lengthy letter ended with Clay's statement "that I consider the annexation of Texas, at this time, without the consent of Mexico as a measure compromising the national character, involving us certainly in war with Mexico, probably with other foreign powers, dangerous to the integrity of the union, inexpedient in the present financial condition of the country, and not called for by any general expression of public opinion."[11] Historians differ as to whether Van Buren and Clay conspired in an effort to keep the issue of Texas annexation out of the 1844 campaign. Arch political rivals, the two had been together for a week in May 1842 when Van Buren visited Clay's Kentucky home, Ashland, while on a political tour of the South. Both adamantly denied that any deal was struck, proclaimed that their letters were independent of each other, and that the timing of publication on the same day was purely coincidental.[12] Van Buren and Clay both lobbied their friends in their respective parties in the Senate to defeat the Tyler treaty, and this was done on June 8, 1844, by a vote of 35 to 16.[13] Whigs from both the North and the South overwhelming opposed the treaty, Democrats from the South unanimously supported it, and Democrats in the North split almost evenly.[14] Whether by plan or by happenstance, both former president Van Buren and potential president Clay misread the mood of the country on the Texas issue. Their allied stance against immediate annexation of Texas would cost Van Buren his party's nomination and Clay his last realistic chance of winning the presidency.

Another former president was a more accurate reader of the political winds. Andrew Jackson, the man who had handpicked Martin Van Buren as his successor in the president's chair, betrayed his friend over the Texas issue and orchestrated a campaign behind the scenes to deny his former mentee the Democratic nomination in 1844. Eight years into his retirement from the presidency, Old Hickory called a meeting at his home, the Hermitage, near Nashville, on May 13, two weeks after publication of Van Buren's Hammet letter and only two weeks before the opening of the Democratic convention. Present with the old man was Andrew Jackson Donelson, his nephew; Robert Armstrong, United States postmaster for Nashville; and James K. Polk, a Tennessean who had been spreading the word that he wanted to be the vice presidential nominee on a Van Buren–led ticket. Polk was not a national political figure. Born in North Carolina, he had moved with his family to Tennessee as a child. He became a lawyer and was a chief lieutenant in Jackson's Democratic Party political machine in Tennessee. Elected to Congress in 1825, Polk became more powerful after his friend and ally Jackson became president in 1829. Polk served as speaker of the House of Representatives from 1835 to 1839, but resigned from Congress and returned home to Tennessee during Van Buren's administration. There, he was elected governor in 1839, but lost his bid for a second term in 1841 and, again, lost an election for the Volunteer State's governorship in 1843.[15] Having been rejected by the voters in his home state the last two times that he stood for election, Polk's political star was not exactly on the rise in 1844. Much to Polk's surprise, however, Jackson announced at the Hermitage meeting that, if Van Buren did not change his position on the annexation of Texas before the convention, then Polk himself must seize the presidential nomination.[16]

A shocked Polk wrote to his Tennessee friend and political ally Cave Johnson advising him of the plan:

> General Jackson says the candidate for the first office should be an annexation man, and from the Southwest, and he and other friends here urge that my friends should insist upon that point. I tell them, and it is true, that I have never aspired so high and that in all probability the attempt to place me in the first position would be utterly abortive. In the confusion that will prevail ... there is no telling what will occur.[17]

It was against this backdrop — the *Princeton* tragedy, the naming of Calhoun as secretary of state, the completion and submission of the Texas annexation treaty to the Senate, the publication of the Van Buren and Clay letters, and the beginning of the plot to make Polk the Democratic nominee — that the nation's attention would once again focus on Baltimore in May 1844 for the presidential nominating conventions. Three conventions would be held that month in the Monumental City — by the Whigs, by the Tyler third-party movement, and by the Democrats. With all three groups meeting in Baltimore in the same month, "it was feared at one time that the means of accommodation would be inadequate for so vast a number. But like the magic tent of the Arabian story, the city's capacity to entertain seemed to enlarge in proportion as the number of the guests increased."[18]

Whig Convention

In 1844, the Whig Party returned to its first love, to its ideological roots, and to its founder and best-known national figure. The party had rebuffed Henry Clay in 1840 for a man in uniform, William Henry Harrison, and had a successful campaign with him, only to have him die after one month in office. His death had resulted in the now hated Tyler becoming president and the Whigs were ready to put their trust again in a familiar face. Rarely in American history has a party that was not nominating an incumbent president been so united behind a candidate as were the Whigs in 1844. No party challengers arose to Henry Clay and the nominating process was more of a coronation, rather than a nominating convention. After having met in Harrisburg for their first convention in 1839, the Whigs came to Baltimore in 1844 for their second nominating convention and the opening date was set for May 1. One contemporary observer recorded the atmosphere on the weekend prior to the opening of the convention:

> The city pulsated with excitement.... People crowded the sidewalks, clustered near hotels, and chatted, laughed, and cried huzza. As each new delegation arrived in town, banners appeared, music sounded, parades formed. All the hotels and boardinghouses were filled to capacity. Even private homes were thrown open to accommodate the swelling numbers of politicians and their followers....
>
> Clay badges hung conspicuously from every buttonhole. Clay portraits, Clay ribbons, Clay hats, Clay cigars, Clay banners, Clay songs, Clay marches, Clay quicksteps, Clay caricatures enveloped the city. "Oh, the rushing, the driving, the noise, the excitement!" To see it and hear it and feel it was sheer ecstacy [sic].[19]

May 1 would be not only the opening date but also the closing date for the 1844 Whig convention, the shortest in American political history. The opening gavel fell at 11:00 A.M., the closing gavel came at 5:00 P.M., and in the intervening six hours, the party nominated its candidates for the presidency and vice presidency. In their haste to get their work done, they worked through lunch without a recess.

The convention met in the Universalist Church building located on the northeast corner of Calvert Street and Pleasant Street in Baltimore, about three blocks north of Monument Square. The church was built in 1837, but it served as a sanctuary for only a short time. In 1839, creditors who were owed money by the congregation for unpaid construction costs sold the building and it was then used primarily as a lecture hall and for public meetings. Years later, during the Civil War, in 1863, the building was purchased by the Catholic Church and became St. Francis Xavier Colored Catholic Church, the first African American Catholic parish in Baltimore.[20]

The outcome not in doubt, Maryland Whig Reverdy Johnson of Baltimore conducted an opening roll call. Two hundred seventy-five delegates were present, with representatives from all twenty-six states. As there was no dispute or controversy as to the outcome of the convention, there was no credentials committee appointed to certify delegates, nor any rules committee appointed. Arthur Hopkins of Alabama was named the temporary president of the convention. The opening prayers were longer than in other conventions of the era. Two different Baltimore ministers led the delegates in the Lord's Prayer, various Episcopal service prayers, and a prayer that had been recited at the Continental Congress, followed by readings from passages of the Bible.[21] The event having been more than sufficiently blessed, Johnson announced that a Committee on Permanent Officers, consisting of two members from each

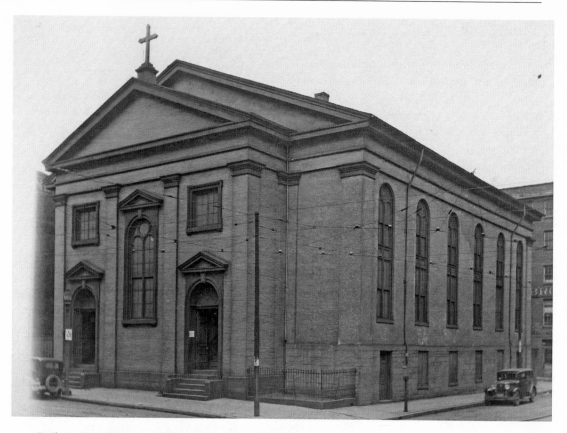

Built in 1837, Baltimore's Universalist Church building was used as a church for only a short time and then became a place for public meetings. It was the site of the 1844 Whig convention that nominated Henry Clay and of the 1848 Democratic convention that nominated Lewis Cass *(Enoch Pratt Free Library)*.

state, and which had been appointed on the eve of the convention, was ready to report. The committee's report was then read. It recommended Ambrose Spencer of New York as the president of the convention and named a vice president from each state and four secretaries. These recommendations were unanimously approved, and a committee of two, Archer of Virginia and Johnson of Maryland, escorted the officers to the platform. Spencer gave a lengthy speech criticizing the Tyler administration and decrying the sad state of the country since the untimely and unfortunate death of President Harrison in 1841.

The convention president then recognized delegate Leigh of Virginia, who offered a resolution that the normal roll call of the states for nomination of a presidential candidate be waived and that, instead, a resolution be adopted announcing to the country that "Henry Clay of Kentucky [is] to be unanimously chosen as the Whig candidate for the presidency of the United States, and that he be recommended to the people as such." This resolution was adopted by acclamation and there followed a demonstration that shook the rafters and rattled the building. The reporter present from the *Baltimore Sun* described the scene:

> Every delegate in the house, with the crowds of spectators in the gallery arose upon the instant, many getting up on benches, as cheer succeeded cheer, with deafening exclamations, bravos and hurrahs and the waving of hats and handkerchiefs, a scene was presented that baffles description. It subsided at length after three distinct cheers "for Henry Clay."[22]

A committee of five members was chosen to advise the senator from Kentucky, who was in nearby Washington, of his nomination. There then arose an interesting exchange that solidified the tradition that nominated candidates would not personally address their conventions, a tradition that would last until Franklin D. Roosevelt delivered his acceptance of his nomination in a speech before the Democratic Convention in Chicago in 1932. A motion was made that Mr. Clay appear before the convention two days hence, on Thursday, and deliver his reply to the nomination. Having apparently been warned in advance that such an invitation may be offered, Reverdy Johnson of Maryland quickly took the floor and read a letter from Clay declining to personally appear as "he could not reconcile it with his sense of delicacy and propriety to attend the convention."[23] In an era when open campaigning by a presidential candidate was frowned upon, Clay felt that addressing the nominating convention in person was crossing over the line of acceptable behavior. The convention acceded to the nominee's wishes and the motion was withdrawn.

The convention then moved to its second task, the nomination of a vice presidential candidate, and, as a letter was being read from John Clayton of Delaware announcing that he declined to be nominated for the second spot on the ticket, chaos erupted in the Universalist Church building. A loud noise was heard in the southwest corner of the gallery located above the convention floor. Hundreds of people both on the floor and in the gallery panicked and rushed for the doors amid cries of "the gallery is giving way." More than a few leaped from the side windows of the building in their haste to flee what was thought to be imminent collapse. After a few minutes, calm was restored, the gallery did not collapse, and the convention resumed, albeit with very few people seated in the southwest gallery or under it. No physical damage to the building was discovered. Most likely, the stomping of feet and the jumping of the delegates in the gallery during the post-

Henry Clay of Kentucky ran for president in almost every election between 1824 and 1848. In 1844, he was the consensus choice of the Whigs to be their nominee and Theodore Frelinghuysen of New Jersey was selected to be his running mate *(Library of Congress)*.

nomination demonstration a few minutes earlier had caused a settling of the building and led to a loud noise.[24]

The nomination of a candidate for the bottom of the ticket, unlike the top, was not pre-ordained. Since there had been no roll call of votes for president, the rules had to be decided. It was decided that a majority vote was needed for nomination and that each state would cast the number of votes it had in the Electoral College, which had by then become the standard formula used in conventions of the era. Since there was a total of 275 delegates, a simple majority of 138 votes was needed for nomination. Four names were placed in nomination and, to provide regional balance with the Kentuckian Clay, all were northerners: John Sargent of Pennsylvania, Millard Fillmore of New York, John Davis of Massachusetts, and Theodore Frelinghuysen of New Jersey. Frelinghuysen led on the first ballot with 101 votes. There were 83 for Davis, 53 for Fillmore, and 38 for Sargent. Frelinghuysen picked up 17 votes on the second ballot, mostly at the expense of Davis. On the third ballot, the delegates from Pennsylvania switched from their native son, Sargent, to the candidate from neighboring New Jersey, and Frelinghuysen was nominated with 155 votes, compared to 78 for Davis, 40 for Fillmore, and one die-hard for Sargent.[25]

The winning candidate, Frelinghuysen, was a lawyer in Newark who had previously served as attorney general of New Jersey and in the United States Senate. Frelinghuysen's most famous speech in the Senate was a moral diatribe delivered in the early 1830s opposing President Jackson's forced removal of the Cherokee and Creek Indians westward from their ancestral land in Georgia. A devout Christian, Frelinghuysen had served as president of the American Bible Society and of other religious and charitable associations. His moral qualities were no doubt seen as a balance to Clay, who was frequently portrayed by the opposition (with some truth) as a gambler, a drinker, and a womanizer.[26]

After a brief speech by a New Jersey delegate extolling the virtues of the vice presidential candidate, the second convention of the Whig Party was over, exactly six hours after it had begun. But for the false alarm of the collapsing gallery, they could have done it in five. No platform was adopted. There were no disputes over the seating of delegates, nor over rules and procedures. It was a harmonious affair and the party presented a united face to the country, confident of victory. The issue that would ultimately dominate to campaign in the fall of 1844 — the annexation of Texas — was never mentioned from the floor of the convention. Having made political history in 1840 with the catchy slogan of "Tippecanoe and Tyler, Too!," the Whigs in 1844 presented a new, if less memorable, slogan to the nation: "The Country Is Rising, for Clay and Frelinghuysen!"[27]

The convention over, the Whig festivities in Baltimore were not. It had become the custom in the days and weeks following the national nominating conventions of both major parties for "ratification conventions" to be held around the country. These were huge political rallies held to publicize the outcome of the nominating conventions, generally accompanied by speeches from local party leaders and, on occasion, from national party leaders, but never from the nominated candidates. As noted in the previous chapter, the Whigs had staged a well-attended ratification convention in Baltimore four years earlier, in May 1840, which had been strategically timed to coincide with the Democratic presidential nominating convention being held in Baltimore the same week. In 1844, however, the Whigs scheduled their primary ratification convention on the day after their own nominating convention and in the same city. Thousands of Whigs descended on Baltimore for a reprise of the 1840 event and a march down Baltimore Street to the Canton Race Track and a grand political rally.

The morning of May 2, 1844, dawned with overcast skies in Baltimore, but, thankfully for the Whigs, there was no rain. Organized in five divisions based upon the geographic regions of the country, the marchers assembled on the west side of Baltimore on the same side streets adjacent to Baltimore Street, and followed the same route as they had done in 1840. Prior to the beginning of the procession, participants from each state were counted in the staging areas, with a large banner to be presented to the state with the most participants. It was a two-mile march to Canton. There were two large arches covered in evergreens spanning Baltimore Street along the way. One was at Hanover Street and displayed the names of all of the prior presidents (only ten as of that time), and the second was located at Calvert Street and displayed the names of the twenty-six states, as well as Whig Party slogans. At the Canton Race Track, a large platform had been erected in the track's infield.

At 10:00 A.M., the grand procession began, with the First Division being led by the Whig Mayor of Baltimore, James O. Law, and the delegates to the nominating convention held the previous day, some in open barouches pulled by horses, but most on foot. The banner to be awarded to the state with the most participants was mounted on a cart. The march of the states began with the Second Division, led by New Hampshire. Each state's delegation was led by a banner with that state's seal or motto, followed by multiple banners, brass bands, and an occasional caged raccoon. The "coon" had become the symbol of the Whig Party (stemming from the 1840 "log cabin" campaign, during which Whigs often wore coonskin clothing and caps), much as today the donkey is the symbol of the Democratic Party and the elephant is of the Republican Party. Some of the banners were catchy and clever, some not so. More than a few had been used in the 1840 march in Baltimore and were modified, as appropriate, to fit the new campaign in 1844. The Massachusetts marchers displayed a banner touting their state as "Home of Paul Revere," and a longer slogan proclaimed, "The rulers of the Republic are selected to serve, not to tyrannize over the people." New York's marchers displayed a banner of one of Henry Clay's famous sayings: "I had rather be right than be president" (to which a clever Democrat had once responded that Clay would never be either). On what must have been a very large banner (or one with very small writing), New Jersey's marchers proclaimed: "Henry Clay; he is honest, he is capable; for his patriotism and talents, we honor him, for his virtues and his worth, we will elevate him." A Pennsylvania banner referred to the party's jilting of Clay in 1840 for Harrison and announced: "Betrayed but not dismayed — Justice to Henry Clay." The Keystone State also brought along a caged raccoon held aloft and housed in a "rustic observatory, from which he surveyed the scene below, with wonderful interest." Delaware's marchers, having retrieved their banner used in the 1840 procession, again declared that their state was "The first to adopt the Constitution, the last to abandon it." Several banners referred to Clay, a Kentuckian, as the "Star of the West" and to his long presence on the political scene: "Clay: We Know the Man."

The Third Division of the grand procession was led by the hometown contingent from the Old Line State. Marchers from Baltimore County went for a symbolic message: a painted figure of the mythical Hope, with an American flag draped over her shoulders and with her hand pointing to the East, under which was written "The day has dawned where that magnificent planet of the West will be seen to rise in greater brilliancy in the East." Recognizing the appeal of a rhyme, a Somerset County marcher held a banner announcing "Henry Clay, Our Nation's Stay." In what appears to have been a forerunner of the floats seen in modern parades, a group of factory workers from Laurel had six white horses, all trimmed in red, white and blue muslin, pulling a fifteen-foot wagon. In the wagon, there was a large spinning and weaving machine, which operated along the route through bands attached to the wagon's wheels. A contingent from Hagerstown was dressed entirely in coonskins, accompanied by several live raccoons. The highlight of the Maryland contingent, however, was the resurrection of the Whig rolling ball from the 1840 campaign. This one was even bigger, fifteen feet in diameter, and was red, white and blue, with stars at each axis. Painted on it were slogans supporting various Whig issues (a national bank, distribution, a uniform currency, and so on) and couplets from Whig campaign songs. The ball was rolled along the route by fifty men from Allegany County, who succeeded in keeping it on the parade route until Canton was reached.

The Fourth Division consisted mainly of southern states, although Vermont was curiously in the mix, perhaps due to a late arrival in the staging area. A Virginia banner declared, "Virginia honors her son — Whig principles forever," as Clay had been born in the Old Dominion. South Carolina's Whigs proclaimed, "As in '76, so in '44, few but firm and faithful," while those from the Green Mountain Sate announced that "Vermont is rising for Clay and Frelinghuysen."

The Fifth Division, the last one in the long procession, consisted of a mixture of western and southern states. Mississippi expressed the hope that "the laurels of 1840, will bloom afresh in 1844." A defiant Alabama banner proclaimed "Fail. There is no such word as fail." The massive throng of Whig marchers, observed by thousands of onlookers, made its way through the streets of Baltimore to Canton. A reporter for the *Baltimore Sun* noted that it took one hour and twenty-five minutes for the entire procession to pass by the newspaper's Sun Iron Building, located at Baltimore and South Streets. It was estimated that the crowd was larger than the Whig rally in 1840. The pro–Whig Annapolis paper, the *Maryland Republican*, offered a perhaps biased observation of the Whig participants: "No observer of the procession could fail to notice the fine looking appearance of the men composing the various Delegations. The substantial population of the union, the men of industry, enterprise, intelligence and respectability, constituting the real conservative elements of the Republic — farmers, planters, manufacturers, mechanics."[28]

As the marchers reached Canton, they went through a large archway and gathered around the platform in the infield of the track. There the formal ratification convention began. John Clayton of Delaware was named the president of the proceedings and several vice presidents were named. The prize banner was presented; it went to Delaware, with 992 participants. Under the

This campaign ribbon honoring Henry Clay is from the 1844 Young Men's Whig National Convention held in Baltimore to ratify the Whig ticket, which had just been nominated in the city the day before *(Library of Congress)*.

announced rules, the count was made at a designated time in the parade staging area and Delaware had the most at that time. By the end of the procession, however, Delaware had been surpassed by Pennsylvania, with an estimated 2,700 participants, and by Virginia, with an estimated 1,240 marchers. The nominated Whig ticket of Clay and Frelinghuysen was announced to the gathering, which unanimously ratified the choice. A letter was read from Henry Clay, dated that morning and written in Washington, stating of his nomination the previous day: "I accept it, from a high sense of duty, and with feelings of profound gratitude." With that, the speeches began. The featured speaker was the great Whig orator Daniel Webster of Massachusetts, once and future senator and secretary of state, and himself a lifelong aspirant to the Whig nomination and to the presidency. Webster and Clay had long been intra-party rivals, but Webster noted that their differences were over minor issues, that they agreed on the great issues of the day, and that they always had mutual respect and esteem. Webster's lengthy speech was followed by three much shorter orations by Whigs from Delaware, Kentucky, and Ohio. In a sign that perhaps the Almighty favored the Whigs, the overcast day remained dry until the end of the speeches, at which time the heavens opened, the rain began, and the great throng made its way back to Baltimore.[29]

The Whigs left Baltimore more united than they had ever been, and they were confident of victory in the election. The man they loved to hate, Martin Van Buren, was their likely opponent in the fall. They had beaten him soundly in 1840 and felt sure that they could do so again in 1844. Their optimism would have to be revised, however, after a surprising turn of events that would occur at the Democratic presidential nominating convention, scheduled to begin in the same city only three weeks hence.

Tyler Convention

The one and only Democratic National Tyler Convention opened in Baltimore on May 27, 1844, at Calvert Hall in Baltimore, located on Saratoga Street just west of Charles Street. This new structure was built as a school for boys of the Cathedral parish of Baltimore, and would not formally open as a school until the fall of 1845.[30] The timing of the convention was not chosen at random. The presidential nominating convention of the Democratic Party also opened on May 27 and was being held just a few blocks away at Odd Fellows Hall. The opening gavel for both conventions was scheduled for noon. Once again, as in 1840, the hotels, restaurants, and streets of Baltimore overflowed with people as rival political gatherings congregated in the city at the same time. The Tyler convention had been called for only one month earlier, in April, when a "large number of republicans, who had been called to Washington from various quarters of the Union by other duties, spontaneously assembled" and sent out a letter to "Democratic republicans" throughout the country to assemble for a convention in Baltimore on the fourth Monday in May to nominate Tyler for the presidency.[31]

Estimates of the strength of the Tyler movement varied. On the eve of the convention, the *Baltimore Sun* noted, "It was once said that all the friends of Mr. Tyler would only make a cab load," yet it was estimated that 2,000 delegates and friends of Tyler were in Baltimore for the convention. A Saturday evening pre-convention meeting had to be adjourned because the room overflowed with people. The exact number of delegates was not recorded, since no roll call votes were taken. One estimate was that there were 1,000 delegates, but an anti–Tyler newspaper alleged that the "room was not crowded and a large portion of the persons within were spectators."[32] The event had a Lone Star theme, with the delegates strolling the streets of Baltimore sporting yellow buttons adorned with a single star, the symbol of Texas. The only decoration inside Calvert Hall was a "plain, home-spun" banner with a single star at its center and the seal of the United States on the sides. Above the star was written "Re-Annexation of Texas" and below it was written "Postponement Is Rejection." A "very excellent band" was also in the hall, which entertained the crowd with patriotic songs during recesses.[33]

As the convention opened, the temporary president, William Shaler, an alderman from New York, addressed the gathering and told the delegates that their purpose was "to do justice to John Tyler." A preliminary motion by a Michigan delegate to reserve on any presidential nomination until it was known whom the Democratic convention, meeting a few blocks away, had nominated, was overwhelmingly rejected in a voice vote. Delegates from nineteen of the twenty-six states in the Union were present. A committee of two delegates from each state was named to decide upon the rules of the convention, while a committee of one from each state was named to select permanent officers. There was no committee for credentials, as apparently anyone who showed up and wanted to be a delegate became one. After a brief fifteen-minute recess, the committees reported back that the procedural rules of Congress would govern the convention and that the permanent president would be Judge Joel W. White of Connecticut, along with a vice president from each of the states represented.

The opening address of President White emphasized the Democratic Party roots of most of those assembled: "I am surrounded by men who have long been identified with Jeffersonian Democracy ... men who have grown grey in that glorious cause." The incumbent president and proposed nominee of the convention, who had been elected on the Whig ticket four years earlier, was described as the savior of the Democratic Party. White proclaimed that John Tyler was "the man who so nobly stood by the Constitution of his country ... who has saved the democratic party, and raised it up from the prostrate condition in which it was left at the close of the campaign of 1840, as the *only* man whose name has been placed in our hands by the *people*."[34]

A nominating speech by delegate Smith of Ohio decried any notion of waiting to see what the Democratic Party would do at its convention: "No, ... we will not wait, we will not allow any other body of men to steal our thunder.... They shall not take our vetoes; neither shall they appropriate Texas to their own party uses." The resolution nominating Tyler as the convention's candidate for the presidency was approved by acclamation, followed by several minutes of enthusiastic cheers for "Tyler and Texas!"[35]

Enthusiasm soon gave way to division when a literal floor fight broke out after delegate Eddy from New York proposed that a committee of twenty-five be named to "confer" with the "other Democratic convention" then meeting in Baltimore. When the motion was tabled, Eddy got into an argument with the Virginia delegation. Another New York delegate, enraged at his Empire State colleague, "denounced, in no measured terms, and in a very special and particular manner," persons from New York who passed themselves off as delegates without proper credentials. With blows apparently about to be exchanged, the delegate was restrained and was "withdrawn by his friends from the area of debate."[36] The convention's opening day ended with the appointment of three more committees: a committee of five to notify President Tyler of his nomination, a committee of nine to draft an address from the convention to the people of the United States, and a committee of one from each state to name a vice presidential nominee.

When the convention reconvened on Tuesday, May 28, it was announced that the Baltimore & Ohio Railroad was offering half-fare tickets for any delegates who wanted to take a round trip on one of its trains from Baltimore to Washington. More speeches followed and then a curious report was received from the vice presidential nominating committee. Basically, the committee declined to do what was asked of it by the convention and, instead, proposed that the president of the convention name a seven member National Nominating Committee for vice president and that the name of the nominee be circulated by newspapers after this proposed committee met. It was suggested that the proposed committee meet "as soon as practicable ... and that this committee be discharged from further duties." The convention agreed, most likely with the slim hope that the Democratic Party convention could be persuaded to also nominate Tyler for president and this strategy would leave open the choice of the second spot on the ticket. With that, one of the strangest political conventions in American history adjourned with nine cheers for "Tyler and Texas!" and an announcement that the delegates were to meet that evening for a rally.[37]

For unknown reasons, the location of the evening rally was not properly conveyed — part of the Tyler delegates and supporters met outside the convention site, Calvert Hall, while others met at Monument Square, a few blocks away. The group at Calvert Hall decided to move on to Monument Square, only to arrive there to find the Democratic Party delegates, also in town, holding their own night rally. The Democratic speakers were located in the courthouse, on the west side of the square and north of Baltimore Street. The Tyler group joined their colleagues already gathered on the steps of Barnum's City Hotel, also located on the square, just to the south of Baltimore Street. Dueling political speeches then began. As the *Baltimore Sun* reported, "This commingling of discordant elements ... produced much confusion." The Democrats won the battle of dueling speakers. After one of their speakers appeared next to a Tyler orator on the steps of Barnum's, the Tyler group, overpowered by numbers, withdrew from the square and rallied elsewhere. The Democrats had won the first skirmish of the 1844 campaign.[38]

The Tyler convention's vice presidential candidate would never be named. With the nomination of a pro–Texas annexation candidate, James K. Polk, later that week by the Democrats, the thunder of Texas was stolen from the Tylerites. Still, with Tyler in the race and both Tyler and Polk seeking votes from the same pro–Texas constituency, worried Democratic Party leaders feared that a split of these votes would hand the election to the united Whigs and Henry Clay. Old Hickory himself, Andrew Jackson, then eight years out of the presidency and in retirement at the Hermitage near Nashville, was enlisted in the cause to deny his old nemesis, Clay, the presidency once again. Jackson wrote a letter to Major Lewis, a mutual friend of Jackson and Tyler, urging Tyler to withdraw from the contest. Lewis shared the letter with Tyler, who acquiesced, and announced, on August 20, 1844, his formal withdrawal from the race.[39] Tyler claimed, years later, that he really never wanted a term in the White House of his own, but that he only wanted to force the Democrats to endorse a pro–Texas annexation candidate:

> I chose to ... raise the banner of Texas, and convoke my friends to sustain it. Many [of the Tyler convention's delegates] called on me on their way to Baltimore to receive my views. My instructions were, "Go to Baltimore, make your nomination, and then go home, and leave the thing to work out its results." I said no more, and was obeyed. The democratic convention felt the move. A Texas man or defeat was the choice left, — and they chose the Texas man. My withdrawal at the suitable time took place, and the result was soon before the world. I acted to insure the success of a great measure, and I acted not altogether without effect. In doing so I kept my own secrets; to divulge my purposes would have been to defeat them.[40]

In what would turn out to be an extremely close election, Tyler's withdrawal as a third-party candidate undoubtedly determined the outcome of the contest and led to the election of Polk.

Democratic Convention

The Nashville plot to nominate Polk instead of Van Buren, hatched on May 13, 1844, at the instigation of former President Andrew Jackson, because of Van Buren's opposition to the annexation of Texas, quickly picked up steam. Polk's former law partner, Gideon Pillow, his Tennessee friend Cave Johnson, and Samuel Laughlin, the editor of the *Nashville Union* newspaper, as well as others, were brought in on the plan. The device that would be employed to defeat Van Buren would be insistence at the convention on the Democrats' two-thirds rule for nomination, a rule that Jackson had forced on the Democratic Party in 1832 to show support for Van Buren as his vice presidential choice. As was typical of most of the conventions of the era, many of the delegates, especially from the South, stopped in Washington on their way to Baltimore for last-minute meetings with members of Congress and party leaders. The Tennesseans — Pillow, Johnson, and Laughlin — were there to greet them and to plant the seed in their minds of a Polk "dark horse" candidacy. Most of the delegates had been selected prior to the publication of Van Buren's Hammet letter and a majority of them were under instructions from their state party to vote for Van Buren in Baltimore, at least on the first ballot. After the Hammet letter became public, however, some began to desert the former president. The central committee of the Virginia Democratic Party went so far as to pass a resolution releasing its delegates from their prior instructions to support Van Buren.[41]

The delegates arriving in Washington were told by Pillow, Johnson, and Laughlin that Van Buren could not possibly win the election and that an alternative pro–Texas candidate, perhaps Polk, should be chosen. Polk had detailed the strategy in a letter written to Johnson:

> I have hope that the Delegates "fresh from the people" — who are not members of Congress — and have not been so much excited can be brought together. Let a strong appeal be made to the Delegates as fast as they come in, to take the matter into their own hands, to control and overrule their leaders at Washington, who have already produced such distraction, and thus save the party. The Delegates from a distance can alone do this. I suggest as a practical plan to bring them to act, — to get one Delegate from each State who may be in attendance to meet in a room at Brown's hotel or somewhere else, and to consult together to see if they cannot hit upon a plan to save the party. If you will quietly and without announcing to the public what you are at, undertake this with energy and prosecute it with vigor, the plan is feasible and it will succeed.[42]

Andrew Jackson had made his Texas views known publicly in a pro-annexation letter published in the *Nashville Union* on May 13. In addition, he also wrote a private letter to Benjamin F. Butler, who was going to be Van Buren's top operative at the upcoming Baltimore convention, expressing the opinion that, unless Van Buren changed his position, his candidacy was doomed because "you might as well, it appears to me, attempt to turn the current of the Missipi [sic] as to turn the democracy from the annexation of Texas to the United States."[43]

The fourth presidential nominating convention of the Democratic Party opened in Baltimore on May 27, 1844, in the Odd Fellows Hall, located on the west side of Gay Street between Fayette and Saratoga Streets. This structure was originally dedicated on April 26, 1831, and was expanded over the years. The Odd Fellows were, and still are, a fraternal organization that originated in England in the seventeenth century, dedicated to charitable and philanthropic causes. The organization emerged in the United States in 1819, with the first lodge established in Baltimore. The Odd Fellows grew rapidly in Maryland and in other states. By 1831, the hall on Gay Street was built to house all of the Baltimore area lodges. The building

Odd Fellows Hall, the Baltimore headquarters of the fraternal organization of the same name, hosted the 1844 Democratic convention, where the first "dark horse" candidate for the presidency, James K. Polk, was nominated (*Enoch Pratt Free Library*).

was described in the 1830s as a "new and handsome brick house ... appropriately arranged for the purpose intended, which was the accommodation of the several lodges of the city." There were thirteen local lodges that met weekly in the building, with meetings of the Grand Lodge held quarterly.[44] It housed an extensive library and was "complete with every convenience."[45] The grand upstairs ballroom, known as the Egyptian Saloon, was the meeting place for the Democratic Party's delegates. It was appropriately named, for it was there that Martin Van Buren was about to be mummified. There were 266 delegates from every state except South Carolina. As the gavel fell at noon, a reporter for the *Baltimore Sun* commented on the national leaders in the crowd: "The familiar faces of honorable gentlemen, whose talents, elevated position and popular character have made their names and fame household words throughout the country, were encountered at every glance."[46]

Although it was the largest meeting room in Baltimore at the time, the choice of Odd Fellows Hall for the convention proved to be a poor one. The delegates, politicians, and spectators crammed into the room with confusion, the acoustics were terrible, and tempers were on edge. The gallery for spectators was small and dark and was described by one onlooker "as black as the hole of Calcutta."[47] Adding to the mass of humanity were delegates and supporters of the Tyler presidential nominating convention, meeting just a few blocks away at Calvert Hall, who wandered about proudly displaying their yellow Texas Lone Star buttons and handing out pro-annexation political leaflets.[48]

It was clear to all that the outcome of the convention would turn on the opening session and the adoption of the rules to be used at the convention. If the two-thirds rule for nomination was adopted, Van Buren was likely doomed; if not, he would be the victor. Prior to the convention, the primary opposition to Van Buren was thought to be Michigan senator Lewis Cass, who was in favor of Texas annexation. No one was mentioning, at least publicly, the name of James K. Polk. The strategy of the anti–Van Buren forces was to nominate as the temporary and permanent presiding officers of the convention obscure pro–Texas men, who would not raise the suspicions to the Van Buren floor managers, and then force the two-thirds rule through on a voice vote while the New Yorkers were still looking for their seats and unable to hear what was going on. The Van Buren forces were led on the floor by Benjamin F. Butler.[49]

As soon as the opening gavel fell, Romulus Sanders, described as "a bearish man with a loud voice and an overbearing manner," fought his way through the crowd, mounted the stage, and nominated Hendrick B. Wright of Pennsylvania as the convention's temporary chair. Wright was not a well-known figure, and the Van Buren managers went along, not wanting to offend the Pennsylvania delegation, whose support they would need to nominate Van Buren. Sanders, from North Carolina, who was a delegate pledged to Cass, had seized the rostrum at the request of Senator Robert John Walker of Mississippi, a leader of the anti–Van Buren faction who was operating totally independent of the Tennesseans plotting to steer the nomination to Polk.

As soon as Wright took the rostrum as temporary convention president, the vocal Sanders again took the floor and quickly moved for adoption of the two-thirds rule for nomination, citing as precedent the use of the rule at prior Democratic conventions. The Cass supporters were trying to steamroll such a vote through in the opening minutes of the convention. The wily Tennesseans realized that there was no need for them to openly offend the Van Buren forces, who considered Cass to be their main challenger. Tennessee Congressman Cave Johnson stood in his chair and objected to any further votes being held in the unruly hall until a Committee on Credentials was appointed by the chair and reported back as to exactly who was properly certified as a delegate and entitled to vote. In so doing, Johnson led Butler and the other Van Buren floor managers to believe that the Tennesseans were looking after their man. Johnson's request was granted and temporary president Wright himself selected a credentials committee, with one member from each state.[50]

The noise and confusion in the hall continued. One delegate, describing himself as a "plain farmer," took the floor and asked that a larger room in Baltimore be located for the convention. This was seconded by others, but members of the organizing committee of the convention responded that there was no more suitable site in Baltimore for accommodating the convention.[51] The Democrats would continue to select their nominee amid the depictions of the pharaohs and ancient Nile River culture adorning the Egyptian Saloon. After ninety minutes of confusion and excitement, the convention adjourned at 1:30 P.M., scheduled to resume at 4:00 P.M.

The convention's second opening day session consisted of more debates over committees and rules. The Credentials Committee reported that there were no disputes as to certification of delegations. It was agreed that Louisiana's two delegates could cast the state's allotted six electoral votes. A Committee on Permanent Officers was appointed, with one member from each state. Butler, the Van Buren floor manager, then rose and proposed that a Committee on Rules be appointed to determine whether to adopt the two-thirds rule or not. Senator Walker of Mississippi and Butler then debated the two-thirds rule. Walker argued that the precedent of past Democratic conventions in 1832, 1836, and 1840 had to be respected and that any departure now would be "an abandonment of democratic principles" and "would resign all the hopes and prospects of the party to the control of a minority." Butler responded and asked where support was found for a two-thirds rule in the Declaration of Independence or in the United States Constitution. Had not the great Jefferson, the founder of the Democratic Party, stood for the principle that the will of a simple majority was the bedrock of American political beliefs? The American system was based on majority rule, not super-majority rule. Referring to Walker's use of the year 1840 as a precedent, Butler brought needed laughter to the hall by stating that 1840 had unfortunately been a year "when reason had been debauched amid log cabins, hard cider and coon skins."[52] Three times during his oration, the emotional Butler leaped into the air to emphasize his points, exciting the crowd.[53] In what would prove to be a strategic error, Butler, who seemed to have the crowd on his side after his speech, then permitted an adjournment for the day without requiring a vote on the adoption or rejection of the two-thirds rule. Before adjournment, the Committee on Permanent Officers reported to the convention its recommendations that Hendrick Wright of Pennsylvania, the temporary chair, also be the permanent chair of the convention, along with twenty-five vice presidents (one from each state present), which were adopted by acclamation.

When the second day of the convention opened on the morning of May 28, 1844, convention president Wright delivered his opening address and stressed the need for unity and for the delegates to surrender their individual preferences for the common good of the party and of the country. The debate over the two-thirds rule continued, with Senator Walker of Mississippi responding to Butler's speech from the previous evening. Walker felt that Butler's "long intimate friendship" with Van Buren "had blinded his judgment" and that established precedent should not be discarded "to secure the empty glory of a nomination by a mere majority." During the debate, a "splendid bouquet" was delivered by a gentleman to convention president Wright from "a Democratic lady from this city." Noting that "the lady who presented them was fairer than the flowers," Wright gladly accepted the bouquet.[54]

The roll call on the motion to adopt the two-thirds rule then began, starting with the delegation from the state of Maine, proceeding down the East Coast, and then westward. It was clear by the time the voting reached the Mason-Dixon line that Van Buren–pledged delegates in the North were abandoning the New Yorker and supporting the two-thirds rule, effectively killing Van Buren's chances for the nomination. Massachusetts cast seven of its twelve votes for the rule, with eight more votes coming from Vermont, Rhode Island and Connecticut, and then New Jersey and Pennsylvania casting split votes. The final tally was 148 votes in favor of the rule and 116 against, with two delegates not voting.[55] The forces of the Little Magician now really needed to work their magic wands, for 178 votes were now needed for nomination, not just a 134 majority. With the two-thirds rule now formally adopted, the convention's morning session ended.

When the afternoon session began, the convention got down to the business of nominating a presidential candidate. On the first ballot, Van Buren led with 146 votes, to 83 for Cass of Michigan, 24 for Van Buren's former vice president, Richard M. Johnson of Kentucky, and 13 scattered votes for others. There was a clear majority for Van Buren, but his tally was short of the two-thirds count of 178 needed for the nomination. Seven ballots were cast that afternoon, and Van Buren's support gradually decreased while Cass's gradually increased. When the convention adjourned for the day at 7:00 P.M., the relative strength of the two front runners had switched, with Cass having 123 votes and Van Buren at 99.[56] The "dark horse," James K. Polk, was still in the stable, his name not having been mentioned from the floor of the convention and no votes having been cast for him. For the Tennesseans, everything was going according to plan.

That evening, serious politicking took place in the hotels and taverns of Baltimore. The Cass managers tried to strike a deal securing the supporters of Johnson of Kentucky and Buchanan of Pennsylvania, who together had 43 votes on the last ballot of the day, but were rebuffed by the representatives of those two candidates. Van Buren's manager, Butler, devised a strategy to keep a New Yorker and an opponent of Texas annexation at the top of the ticket. Before the convention, Van Buren had written a letter to Butler advising him, if it appeared in the midst of the convention that Van Buren could not be nominated, then Butler was to persuade Van Buren's good friend and colleague, New York senator Silas Wright, who was also against annexation of Texas, to permit his name to be offered as the nominee and Butler was to lead the effort for Wright before the convention.[57] Wright somehow heard of this fallback strategy before the convention and, as a true loyalist to Van Buren, was adamantly against permitting his name to be substituted for Van Buren. Wright wrote and delivered a letter of his own to another New York delegate, Judge Fine, forbidding his name from being placed in nomination at the convention and instructing Fine, if necessary, to read the letter to the convention.[58] Unaware of Wright's position, Butler spent the evening caucusing with Van Buren delegates from various states and securing an agreement from many of them to support Wright and to withdraw Van Buren's name the following morning. Maybe the Democrats would nominate an anti–Texas candidate after all.

Early the next morning, May 29, Butler met with the entire New York delegation at 8:00 A.M. at Barnum's Hotel, near Monument Square, a few blocks from the convention site. He read to them Van Buren's letter offering to withdraw in favor of his New York colleague, Silas Wright, and gained their support for the plan. One man, however, stopped the plan dead in its tracks. Judge Fine, who possessed Wright's letter to him declining in no uncertain terms to have his name placed in nomination, threatened, if Butler persisted, to read the letter from the floor of the convention. A dejected Butler then admitted defeat, told the other state delegations that he had met with the previous evening that the Wright plan was dead, and requested that they stick with Van Buren as long as his name was before the convention.[59]

Meanwhile, the previous evening, the Tennesseans had been busy. Pillow, Polk's former law partner, worked on finding northern allies. He found a friend in Massachusetts delegate George Bancroft, a noted historian who was a Van Buren supporter and strongly opposed to Cass receiving the nomination. Bancroft and Pillow spent the evening with key members of Ohio and New York delegations, until well past midnight, urging them to support Polk. To have any chance of success, they believed that a movement for Polk had to start with a northern state. *Nashville Union* editor Laughlin later told Polk that it was Bancroft and his Bay State colleague, Marcus Morton, who "were mainly responsible for wheeling the 'Yankee States' into the line."[60]

It was agreed that, when the voting started with the eighth ballot on the morning of May 29, New Hampshire would be the first to cast votes for Polk. Massachusetts, Tennessee, Louisiana, and Alabama followed, and Polk went from nowhere to having 44 votes, compared to 114 for Cass and 104 for Van Buren. The Polk bandwagon now began to roll. The large

Opposite: Former president Andrew Jackson engineered the surprise nomination of his fellow Tennessean, James K. Polk, by the Democrats in 1844 because the favorite for the nomination, former president Martin Van Buren, came out in opposition to the annexation of Texas. Polk's running mate was George Dallas of Pennsylvania *(Library of Congress).*

J.K.POLK.

G.M.DALLAS.

Entered according to Act of Congress in the Year 1844 by J. Baillie in the Clerks Office in the Dt Court of the Sn Dt of N.Y.

GRAND DEMOCRATIC BANNER.

Lithd & Publd by J. Baillie 113 Nassau St N.Y.

delegations from New York and Virginia withdrew to caucus. Virginia returned and, on the ninth ballot, switched its votes from Cass to Polk. Butler then withdrew Van Buren's name, and New York cast thirty-four of its thirty-five votes for Polk. By the end of the ninth ballot, Polk was nominated by acclamation.[61] For the first time in American history, a major political party had nominated a relative unknown for the presidency. Back at the Hermitage, the seventy-eight-year-old Andrew Jackson, who had hatched the Polk nomination plot only two weeks earlier, was undoubtedly smiling. If Polk won the election, Jackson would have hand-picked two of his successors in the presidency. Judas-like, it was through betrayal of the first, Van Buren, that he anointed the second, Polk.

The selection of an unknown as the presidential nominee did not end the excitement. The Democratic convention of 1844 is remembered for another Baltimore connection — literally. New technology used for the first time in May 1844 would forever change political conventions and the manner in which they were reported to the American people. Samuel F. B. Morse, a professor at New York University, had been working since the mid–1830s on a system to send signals through wire by use of an electromagnet. Using distinctive pulses of current to identify different letters and numbers, Morse's code and the telegraph would revolutionize communication. Although Morse had demonstrated the use of the technology by 1838, there was no perceived market for it and, thus, no investors. Recognizing the public interest involved, a Whig congressman, John Pendleton Kennedy from Maryland, was instrumental in moving a bill through Congress to appropriate $30,000 for the construction of a telegraph line covering the forty miles between Washington and Baltimore. The bill finally passed in March 1843. At first, the telegraph wire was put in insulated pipes and laid underground, but the insulation proved to be ineffective and no electronic pulse could be carried within it over long distances. The wire was then strung on chestnut poles, with cross-arms, which were planted parallel to the route of the B & O Railroad between Washington and Baltimore. The construction started in Washington and had reached northward twenty-two miles by early May 1844. On May 1, a southbound B & O train stopped at Annapolis Junction, where the line then ended, and telegraphed a message to Washington that Clay and Frelinghuysen had just been nominated at the Whig convention in Baltimore. During the next three weeks, the project was completed and telegraph recording instruments were set up at each end of the line — at the B & O's Mount Clare Station in Baltimore and in the chamber of the Supreme Court in the Capitol building in Washington. On May 24, the Saturday before the opening of the Democratic convention, the famous message "WHAT HATH GOD WROUGHT" was transmitted by telegraph between the two cities.[62]

The telegraph was quickly put into use the following week to report the events of the Democratic convention. During the days of the Democratic convention, and the simultaneously held Tyler convention in Baltimore, crowds gathered on the north front of the Capitol building to receive updated news on the progress of the conventions. When the news of the surprise nomination of Polk was announced, "it was heard by all the faithful with speechless amazement."[63] The Washington insiders quickly got over their shock and, within an hour of the nomination of Polk, a telegraphic response was received from the Federal City and read to the Baltimore convention: "The democratic members of Congress, to their democratic brethren in convention assembled, send greetings, three cheers for James K. Polk."[64] Confidence in the accuracy of the new-fangled telegraph, however, was not universal.

With Polk nominated by acclamation, the convention broke for lunch and resumed at 1:00 P.M. for its afternoon session, in order to begin the process of nominating a vice presidential candidate. There was a consensus that New York, with Van Buren having lost the top spot in the ticket, had to be appeased. Senator Walker of Mississippi, the nemesis of Van Buren who had led the successful fight for adoption of the two-thirds rule, took to the floor and nominated Silas Wright, New York senator and close friend and colleague of Van Buren, for vice president. Said Walker, "New York has made a noble sacrifice." The Kentuckians had been promoting Richard M. Johnson for his old job again, but the head of the Kentucky delegation withdrew Johnson's name, after being assured by a New York delegate, he joked, that Senator Wright was a good rifleman. Not missing on opportunity to skewer the opposition party, he added that everyone knew that "the Whigs are not good at shooting of any kind, unless it is on the dueling field."[65] Wright received 238 votes on the first ballot, well over the two-thirds required, and was nominated. The only other candidate to receive any votes was Senator Levi Woodbury of New Hampshire with eight votes, curiously, from the Georgia delegation. In lieu of a formal platform being adopted by the convention, a committee of twenty-six members, one from each state (an unofficial delegate from South Carolinian had shown up and was included), to prepare an address to the American people from the convention and the Democratic Party. A committee of five was also named to notify the nominees of their selection as standard-bearers by the convention. The meeting then adjourned for the day, to resume the following morning at 7:30 A.M. for a brief closing meeting and then final adjournment. As it turned out, there would be more work than that to be done.

The telegraph was a wonderful device. It conveyed information from the Democratic convention in Baltimore to Washington within a matter of minutes. The two major news events on May 28 — the nomination of Polk for president in the morning and the nomination of Wright for vice president in the afternoon — spread like wildfire through Washington. In Washington, Senator Wright, a close friend of Van Buren, who had refused to permit Van Buren's convention managers in Baltimore to substitute his name for Van Buren's for the presidential nomination, was devastated and angry when he received the news in the morning, via telegraph, of Van Buren's defeat and Polk's nomination. When the clatter of the telegraph machine in the Supreme Court Chamber in the Capitol brought the news in the afternoon of his own nomination for the vice presidency, Wright, still in a rage, immediately had a telegraphic response sent back to Baltimore declining the nomination. No one had ever rejected the nomination of a major party for the presidency or vice presidency. Dumbfounded, and thinking the response from this new gadget was an error, the leaders of the Baltimore convention sent a second telegraphic message to Wright, again notifying him of his nomination. A quick reply was received: "NO, under no circumstances." Wright then penned a short letter to Benjamin Butler, Van Buren's floor manager at the convention, confirming his denial and sent the letter off by train to Baltimore, also apparently questioning the accuracy of the news:

> MY DEAR SIR — Being advised that the convention of which you are a member has conferred upon me the unmerited honor of nominating me as a candidate for the office of Vice-President, will you, if this information is correct, present my profound thanks to the convention for this mark of confidence and favor; and say for me that circumstances, which I do not think it necessary to detail ... render it impossible that I should, consistently with my sense of public duty and private obligations, accept this nomination.
>
> I am with great respect,
> Your obedient servant,
> Silas Wright[66]

A total of four telegraphic messages were sent from Mount Clare Station in Baltimore to Wright that afternoon and, from the Supreme Court Chamber in the Capitol, with Samuel F. B. Morse himself at the telegraph, the response to each was "No."[67]

The recipients of the negative responses in Baltimore felt sure that the telegraph was defective and immediately dispatched several delegates by train to Washington to hear from Senator Wright personally. The story was related several years later in a letter written by Hendrick B. Wright (no relation to Silas Wright), who was the president of the convention:

> I wish to state to you an anecdote concerning the telegraph. At this date ... the only telegraph in the United States was between Baltimore and Washington. I was the president of the convention. We nominated Silas Wright for Vice-President of the United States, and the convention directed me to notify him of his nomination and learn if he would accept it. I sent a dispatch, and he answered immediately that he declined the nomination. The convention, however, refused to consider the information as authentic. They could not be made to understand this way of communication, and adjourned the convention over to the next day to enable a committee to go to Washington by rail where Mr. Wright was, and get at the truth of the act. So we adjourned over, and on the next day the committee came back with the same answer that we had received by the wire. And so incredulous were the great majority of the body that after the final adjournment most of us went to the telegraph office to see the wonderful invention, and even when the wires were put in motion at our suggestion many of the delegates shook their heads and could not but think the whole thing a deception.[68]

Rumors of Wright's rejection of the nomination spread through the convention, but nothing was formally announced until the body reassembled at 7:30 A.M. on the morning of May 29. Butler read Wright's rejection letter, which had by then been received in Baltimore, to an astonished crowd. The delegates then proceeded, for the second time, to nominate a vice presidential candidate. On the first ballot, the field was wide open —107 votes for Fairfield of Maine, 39 votes for Cass of Michigan, 26 for Johnson of Kentucky, 44 for Woodbury of New Hampshire, 23 for Stewart of Pennsylvania, 13 for Dallas of Pennsylvania, and 5 for Marcy of New York. On the second ballot, the delegates decided that, lacking a New Yorker on the ticket, they needed to nominate a candidate from another large northern state and most votes shifted to George M. Dallas of the Keystone State who was a leader of one of the Democratic Party factions in that state, and who had previously served as the American Minister to Russia, Mayor of Philadelphia, Attorney General of Pennsylvania and as a United States senator from Pennsylvania. He was declared the nominee with 219 second ballot votes, compared to 38 for Fairfield and 8 for Woodbury.[69]

There being no telegraph lines to Philadelphia, where Dallas lived, notification was made to him by the more traditional method. It was decided that several of the delegates from the eastern states, accompanied by Senator Walker of Mississippi (a personal friend of Dallas), would stop by Dallas' home on their way home from the convention. About sixty delegates arrived at the Dallas house at 5:00 A.M. on the morning of Friday, May 30. Walker rapped on the door and Mrs. Dallas poked out her head from an upstairs window. She awakened her husband, who rushed downstairs, half-dressed and barefoot, and opened the door. In walked more than fifty men shouting three loud cheers for "Polk and Dallas!" With the disheveled Dallas still not understanding what was going on, Governor Fairfield of Maine explained to him that he was the nominee of the Democratic Party for vice president of the United States. More cheers ensued, all of which awakened the neighbors, who then also joined in the early morning celebration.[70] The official notification to Polk was more subdued. Playing the "dark horse" role to its best effect, in his written response to the nomination, Polk accepted and declared that: "The office of president of the United States should never be sought nor declined. I have never sought it, nor shall I feel at liberty to decline it."[71]

The Campaign and Election

At the outset of the campaign, the Whigs could not believe their good fortune. How could the Democrats nominate an unknown for the presidency? "Who is James K. Polk?" went the battle cry. "Are our Democratic friends serious?... We must beat them with ease if we do one half of our duty," wrote the Whig nominee, Henry Clay, to a friend.[72] Another version of Clay's reaction to the Polk nomination, probably apocryphal, is very different. In Kentucky, upon hearing the news from his son that the Democrats had a nominee, "Harry of the West" purportedly asked if it was "Matty? Cass? Buchanan?" and upon being told no to each inquiry, he then laughed and said "Don't tell me they've been such fools as to take Calhoun or Johnson!" When finally told that it was Polk, Clay is said to have poured himself a drink, sat in his chair, and muttered "Beat again, by God!"[73] Despite this version of Clay's reaction to the Polk nomination, the facts that the Democrats had been badly split at their convention, that the Whigs were united, and that the incumbent president, John Tyler, was in the race as a third-party candidate and would siphon off Democratic votes, were all seen as harbingers of a Whig victory in the fall.

It was not to be. As usual, by tradition, the nominees themselves did no active campaigning, which was left to surrogates. Cave Johnson, Polk's Tennessee friend and colleague, told him, "If you could avoid reading or speaking or writing from now until the election, our success would be certain."[74] Young Hickory, as Polk came to be called (a nickname that sought to favorably compare him with his mentor Andrew Jackson, who was known as Old Hickory), generally avoided all speaking requests during the campaign, although he did appear at one large Democratic rally in Nashville. His silence caused the Whig governor of Tennessee, James P. Jones, to comment: "Why are his lips sealed as with the stillness of death?"[75]

It was advice that Polk's opponent, Clay, should have heeded. By summer, when it appeared as though the Texas issue was gaining a foothold with the electorate, Clay attempted to soften the anti-annexation stance that he had outlined in his Raleigh letter, written in April. In July, he wrote two letters to Alabama newspapers (referred to as the Alabama letters by historians), wherein he softened his position. In the second Alabama letter, he stated that he was not personally opposed to the annexation of Texas, or to slavery there if it became a state, if it could be done consistent with the nation's treaty obligations and without causing a war with Mexico. Said Clay of annexation, "[I] would be glad to see it, without dishonor, without war, and with the common consent of the Union, and upon fair and just terms."[76] This was heresy to many in the North, who opposed annexation of Texas solely because it would be an expansion of slavery in the Union, not because of fears of broken diplomatic relations and possible war with Mexico. The general consensus among historians is that Clay's backtracking on the annexation issue looked like pandering and that it probably cost him more votes in the North than it gained him in the South. In an era when presidential candidates were told by their party leaders to keep quiet and say and write as little as possible, one commentator, in a play on words on Clay's famous statement "I had rather be right than be president," concluded that the Alabama letters showed, instead, "If you want to be president, don't write."[77]

In addition to Texas, the Democrats had shrewdly included in their platform a call for acquiring Oregon from the British, by force or otherwise. This allowed the party to couple Texas and Oregon under the campaign slogan "All of Texas, All of Oregon" and, since Oregon would likely be free territory, focused attention in the North more on the "manifest destiny" of a continental nation, rather than solely on the expansion of slavery into Texas.

There were more problems for the Whigs. The intra-party wounds of the Democrats healed. The Van Buren faction of the party, which had viewed Michigan's Cass as their main opponent and which were not aware of the Tennesseans' plotting to deny Van Buren the nomination, generally toed the party line and supported Polk. By August, President Tyler acceded to Democratic wishes and dropped out of the race. His third-party movement ended and his supporters naturally went to the pro–Texas annexation candidate, Polk. Complicating matters for the Whigs was another third-party candidate, who was in the race to stay. The Liberal Party nominated James G. Birney of New York, an abolitionist, as their candidate for president, and he drew northern anti-slavery votes away from Clay. But the factor that may well have been the final nail in Clay's coffin in 1844 was immigration. A massive number of immigrants had come to the United States in the early 1840s. Most immigrants were Catholic and they tended to vote overwhelmingly Democratic. The presence of Theodore Frelinghuysen, who was a leader of many zealous Protestant organizations, as the vice presidential nominee on the Whig ticket no doubt added to the woes of the Whigs with the newest Americans.[78] Democratic officeholders in many northern states and cities had succeeded in liberalizing citizenship requirements and, as a result, thousands upon thousands of immigrants were naturalized in the weeks before the 1844 election. As a result, many of them became voters and they generally voted Democratic.

When all the votes were counted, the 1844 election turned out to be one of the closest in American history. Polk won the popular vote by only 38,000 out of 2,700,000 cast, receiving 1,337,243 votes, compared to Clay's tally of 1,299,062.[79] David G. Birney, the candidate of a small abolitionist third party, the Liberal Party, received 62,000 votes nationally, with almost 16,000 of those coming from New York. Clay lost New York's massive 36 electoral votes by only 5,000 ballots. If he had won New York, he would have been president. Several other states were exceedingly close, with Clay losing Louisiana by only 700 votes, Indiana and Georgia by about 2,000 votes each, and Michigan by about 3,500 votes. It is generally agreed that the Democrats won Louisiana only by voter fraud, as the vote totals in at least one parish doubled the white male population there.[80] The Electoral College count was more impressive for Polk, with 170 electors to Clay's 105, but the switch of a few thousand votes in New York, or of a similar shift in a few other states, would have changed the outcome of the election.[81]

Elections have consequences. Viewing the results as a mandate for Texas annexation, President Tyler, in his last act in office, pushed a joint resolution through Congress that he signed into law on March 1, 1845, offering to make the Lone Star Republic the nation's twenty-eighth state.[82] This was a sly procedural move that required only a majority vote in each house, as opposed to the two-thirds vote in the Senate that would have been required if the deed had been done by a treaty. After approval by the voters of Texas in October 1845 (along with a state constitution approving slavery), Texas officially entered the Union in December 1845. Within five months, by May 1846, the United States and Mexico would be at war.

CHAPTER 7

1848: New York, New York

We've got Old Zack upon the track,
He'll soon put Lewis on his back.

In Mexico, he whipped a nation—
November next he'll thrash creation.

Get out of the way for Rough and Ready.
The country needs an arm that's steady.[1]

Whig campaign song, 1848

By 1848, nominating conventions had become the established method for American political parties to nominate their presidential candidates. Delegates to conventions in the mid–nineteenth century were similar to delegates of the modern era. Then, as now, delegates were party activists, with the party's elected officeholders, lowly and not so lowly, comprising a large percentage of the delegations from many states. The lists of delegates from the era reveal sitting and former governors, senators, and members of the House of Representatives, as well as state legislators. Still, there were numerous non-elected officeholders among the delegates, who represented the majority of the delegates at most of the conventions. More than a few held government jobs given to them through political patronage. The procedure for selecting delegates became standardized by both major parties shortly after the first conventions were held. Following the procedure first established by the Anti-Masons in 1832, each state was generally allotted at conventions the number of delegates equal to its total number of votes in the Electoral College, meaning one delegate for each congressional district and two additional allotted to each state for its two senators. While the methods sometimes varied, delegates to a party's national convention were generally selected at the party's local conventions, which were held at the congressional district level. The two additional delegates allotted would usually be selected at a statewide convention. Alternate delegates began to be selected fairly early on in the process, no doubt as a way to reward more party activists. With only a few exceptions, political conventions in the mid–nineteenth century were held in the late spring of presidential election years. Weather was an important factor in the timing. With conventions generally being held in a centrally located East Coast city, the weather made extended travel impossible for many coming from northern and western states during the winter and early spring. Similarly, no one wanted to sit in a convention in a major city during the heat and humidity of summer.

America changed between 1844 and 1848. The fears of those who had opposed annexation of Texas in 1844 had been realized by 1848. The addition the Lone Star State to the Union did lead to war with Mexico. Victory in the war led to acquisition by the United States of the territories of California and New Mexico from Mexico (at a price of $15,000,000) and the inevitable question of whether the new territories would be slave or free. Sectional hostilities were increased early in the Mexican War, in fall 1846, when a little known Democratic congressman from Pennsylvania, David Wilmot, successfully inserted into an appropriations bill for the war in the House of Representatives an amendment barring slavery in any territory obtained by the United States from Mexico as a result of the hostilities. Known to history as the Wilmot Proviso, this prohibition passed the House in successive sessions, but failed in the Senate, where the South had more power. For a generation, the Missouri Compromise of 1820 had kept a lid on the issue of expansion of slavery by permitting it (except for Missouri) only south of the 36 degree, 30 minute north latitude. Old wounds were opened by the proviso. Northerners favored the prohibition of slavery in any newly acquired lands, while southerners opposed it. Support for or opposition to the Wilmot Proviso, or coming up with an alternative, became the hot button issue in the campaign for the presidency in 1848.

Democratic Convention

Modern politics lacks the colorful and descriptive party and faction names of the past. The nineteenth-century gave us Locofocos, Bucktails, Wide Awakes, Hard Shells, Soft Shells, Carpetbaggers, Doughfaces, Swallow-Tails, Butternuts, Fire-Eaters, Copperheads, Barnburners, Hunkers, Short-Hairs, Woolly Heads, Stalwarts, Mugwumps, Know-Nothings, Silver-Grays, and Scalawags.[2] Many of these names derived from the byzantine world of political factions in New York State. In 1848, the New York Democratic Party split into two groups, known as the Barnburners and the Hunkers, and the battle between them would dominate the party's nominating convention and, ultimately, the outcome of the presidential election. The Barnburners earned their nickname from an old story about a rodent-hating Dutch farmer who burned down his own barn to get rid of pesky rats. He accomplished his goal, but at a great cost. The Barnburners were strong supporters of the Wilmot Proviso. The Hunkers, who opposed the proviso, were the more conservative of the two New York factions and were so-called because they sought, or hunkered for, all of the political patronage jobs available to the party and its faithful.

The incumbent president, James K. Polk, had made a pledge at the outset of his administration to serve only one term and it was a pledge that the Tennessean kept. Exhausted and unpopular by the end of his term, Polk would die in June 1849 at the young age of fifty-three, only three months after leaving the White House. Without an incumbent in the race, the battle for the 1848 Democratic nomination was wide open. In the weeks leading up to the convention, the names of several candidates were being promoted by their supporters. The two perceived leading contenders were Lewis Cass and James Buchanan.

Cass, a senator from Michigan, was sixty-six years old in 1848, had been a brigadier general in the War of 1812, was a longtime governor of the Michigan Territory, and served as secretary of war under Andrew Jackson, during which time he vigorously enforced Jackson's removal of Indian tribes to lands west of the Mississippi River. He served as Van Buren's minister to France and was a vocal proponent of manifest destiny. Cass developed a reputation of being a calculating politician. He incurred the wrath of many northern Democrats when he opposed Van Buren for the nomination in 1844 and joined with the Polk forces in denying the nomination to the Little Magician. On the key issue of the day in 1848, the Wilmot Proviso, Cass had initially supported it, but then backed away from that position and opposed it, which resulted in many northerners opposing his nomination. Cass became a leading proponent of the doctrine of "popular sovereignty," which held that the people of a state should be able to decide whether to have slavery or not at the time statehood was granted, through the drafting of their state constitution. On the question of whether the people of a territory, prior to statehood, could restrict or prohibit slavery through their territorial legislatures, Cass was deliberately vague.[3]

Buchanan, of Pennsylvania, also had a distinguished resume. Fifty-seven years old in 1848, he was a lawyer and had served in the Pennsylvania legislature and as a congressman during the 1820s. He was Jackson's minister to Russia and served for more than a decade in the Senate before becoming Polk's secretary of state in 1845. Known as "Old Buck," Buchanan was still serving as the nation's top diplomat at the time of the 1848 campaign and hoped to use that position as a stepping-stone to the White House, as many of his predecessors had done before him. Buchanan also opposed the Wilmot Proviso and, instead of a total prohibition on slavery in any new territories, he favored extending the Missouri Compromise dividing line of 36 degree, 30 minute north latitude between free and slave land all the way to the Pacific Ocean.[4]

There were other, lesser candidates in the mix for the 1848 Democratic nomination. Buchanan's Pennsylvania party rival, George Dallas, the incumbent vice president, hoped to move up to the top job, but had little realistic hope of doing so with support in his own state divided and with many Pennsylvanians supporting Buchanan. Supreme Court Justice Levi Woodbury, of New Hampshire, also let it be known that he would be interested in the nomination. Despite the president's stated wishes to the contrary, friends of Polk were still hoping for an opportunity to put his name forward as a draft candidate, if a consensus did not develop before or at the convention for any of the contenders. No mid–nineteenth century presidential race would be complete without a military man in the mix and General William J. Worth,[5] a Democrat and a New Yorker who had served with distinction in the Mexican War, had written a letter on the eve of the convention positioning himself as a potential candidate.[6]

For the fifth time in a row, in 1848, the Democrats selected Baltimore as the site for their convention. The month of May was chosen for the gathering and the location was the Universalist Church on the northeast corner of Calvert and Pleasant Streets, the same building where, just four years earlier in 1844, the Whigs had nominated Henry Clay for the presidency. In the weeks prior to the convention, all attention focused on New York. It was known that the Empire State would be sending two competing delegations to Baltimore, thirty-six pro–Wilmot Proviso Barnburners, and an equal number of anti–Wilmot Proviso Hunkers, each group selected at separate state conventions.[7] Like Yankees fans at a modern Baltimore Orioles home baseball game, New Yorkers would be flooding into the Monumental City for the convention. The Barnburners were in no mood for compromise. Prior to the convention, one of their leaders declared: "Unless recognized as the true and the only representatives of the New York party, our delegates will regard any proposal by the convention for admission of both sets of delegates or for the admission of one half of each set ... as equivalent of rejection — indeed more distasteful than the out and out admission of [the Hunkers]."[8] As typical of the conventions of the era, many of the delegates, especially from the South, stopped in Washington for a couple of days, while en route to Baltimore, to "ascertain, if possible, the direction of the wind."[9] The politicians in Washington were also planning to head to Baltimore, with the Senate voting to adjourn from Monday to Thursday of convention week and the House of

Representatives holding only a brief Monday morning session and then adjourning so its members could board a B & O train to Baltimore.[10] On the weekend before the convention's opening, the *Baltimore Sun* reported, "Every conveyance of travel to our city brought in crowds of delegates and strangers, filling the principal hotels, and causing a general opening of private homes to accommodate the vast assemblage."[11]

When the opening gavel fell at noon on Tuesday, May 22, 1848, more than 250 delegates, plus alternates, from all thirty states in the Union, many of the Democratic Party's leading figures, politicos, reporters, and hundreds more onlookers and the curious gathered in and around the Universalist Church. A *Baltimore Sun* reporter witnessing the scene was either lazy, or just appreciated a good description, writing that "the familiar faces of honorable gentlemen, whose talents, elevated position, and popular character, have made their names and fame as familiar as household words throughout the country, were encountered at every glance of the eye."[12] If this lofty depiction of the scene inside the church sounds familiar, it should, since the exact same phrases were used by the *Sun*'s reporter in describing the opening session four years earlier inside Odd Fellows Hall at the 1844 Democratic convention.[13] In an age before photocopying and the internet, it is unlikely that anyone noticed the repetition. The convention's opening session was taken up with the organizational activities that, by then, had become standard. Judge J. S. Byrne of Louisiana was named temporary president and he advised the delegates that he hoped the proceedings would be characterized by "order, Heaven's first law." A Baltimore clergyman gave an opening prayer. A Committee on Credentials was appointed, consisting of one member from each state, with New York excluded, since it had competing delegations. A proposal to give two committee votes to the New Yorkers, one for each faction, was not approved. The committee was given the power to fully investigate the claims of two New York factions and to make a recommendation. The Florida delegate named to the committee asked to be excused and confessed "in this house of God" that he could not be a fair judge of the credentials of the Barnburners, since he was opposed to all that they stood for. Like a judge dealing with a recalcitrant juror, however, the convention made him serve anyway. With that, the convention adjourned its opening Tuesday morning session.[14]

When the gathering resumed for its second session of the day at 5:00 P.M., the gallery in the church was overflowing "notwithstanding the excessive heat of the weather." A Committee on Permanent Officers was named, again with one member from each state except New York, and they retired to the basement of the building to begin their deliberations. Senator Edward A. Hannegan of Indiana, a delegate, urged the Barnburners and the Hunkers to bury their differences for the "good of their country, their party and their principles" and to "come, and lay down all your animosities and petty disputes on the altar of your country." An Alabama delegate, William L. Yancey, an outspoken advocate of slavery who would be frequently heard from at this gathering, then gave a twenty-minute oration "in a strain of eloquence that drew forth the most enthusiastic expression of delight," followed by remarks from delegate Sam Houston of Texas, who, not surprisingly, spoke glowingly of the Polk administration and its prosecution of the Mexican War. By this time, the Committee on Credentials had returned with its report, or at least a partial report. There was a dispute over South Carolina. In somewhat of a rarity, South Carolina had actually sent a delegate to the convention, a single delegate, but a delegate nonetheless.[15] The committee recommended that this single delegate be entitled to cast all of South Carolina's allotted nine votes at the convention, which was challenged on the floor of the convention. There were echoes of the Edward Rucker fiasco from the 1835 convention. The convention affirmed the committee and permitted the sole South Carolina delegate to cast the Palmetto State's full nine votes.[16] The committee announced that it still had not reached a decision on the competing New York delegations and that it would be meeting that evening to deliberate further. The Committee on Permanent Organization then returned and nominated Andrew Stevenson of Virginia as the convention's permanent president, along with a vice president from every state (except New York), and nine secretaries. Thus ended the first day's proceedings.[17]

When the convention resumed on the second day on Wednesday, May 23, the gallery was packed with people, as was the street in front of the church. The delegates first heard remarks from President Stevenson who, in what we would today call a keynote speech, extolled the virtues of nominating conventions and pleaded for compromise and unity:

> The destiny of our country — its peace, prosperity and happiness — may depend on the approaching Presidential election. To secure the election and to guard against the evil of one by the House of Representatives, national conventions have been looked to as the only practicable mode of securing these blessings to us and to our posterity. Is there any one who can believe that this duty can be discharged properly except by compromise and by concession — by mutual and united counsels? ... We come as brethren ... to unite in the great act of selecting the individual most worthy to fill the Executive chair.... Let not your deliberations be threatened, nor your councils divided. But let the spirit of peace, harmony, and brotherly affection shed its holy and blessed influence around us.[18]

Following Stevenson's remarks, the vice presidents took the stage and the opening prayer was delivered. The convention then took up the two controversial rules that were debated at every Democratic convention of the era, the unit rule and the two-thirds rule. Under the unit rule, each state's votes would be cast unanimously, unless a majority of that state's delegation decided otherwise. The two-thirds rule, of course, required the vote of two-thirds of the delegates to secure the nomination. A Louisiana delegate spoke in opposition to the rule, arguing, "If then, you do in 1848 what you did in 1844, some 'outsider' — some hero from Mexico, perhaps, but who has not been indicated by the people — will be nominated and the people of the United States will regard you with distrust, and Democratic conventions will be made odious in the eyes of the people." An Alabama delegate quickly jumped to his feet proclaiming that his "ear was struck with surprise" by the 1844 reference and the characterization of the party's incumbent president as an "outsider." He responded to the perceived slight: "If Mr. Polk be an 'outsider,' who, I ask, is an insider? Sir, when millions of men who have figured in history may have been forgotten, and even their names no longer recollected, you will hear the Democrats from the lakes to the Gulf of Mexico, and from the Atlantic to the Pacific ocean, shouting, as the watchword of victory, the names of Jefferson, Jackson, and Polk."[19] Delegate Hannibal Hamlin[20] of Maine argued that many believed that the two-thirds rule was adopted in 1844 solely for the purpose of defeating Van Buren and, if it were abandoned now, "Would we not confirm the impression?" A Maryland delegate, Humphreys, moved for a majority rule and spoke glowingly of his candidate, Cass, and of Cass' distinguished resume, and feared that like Van Buren, he "would also be decapitated" under the two-thirds rule.[21]

While President Stevenson was moderating this debate, there came that inevitable moment that seems to have occurred in many Baltimore conventions — the crash. As reported by the *Baltimore Sun*, "a scene of consternation arose, from a crash thought to be from sinking of the gallery on the south side of the church. The members under the gallery made their escape out of the windows, whilst there was a general rush from the lower part of the church to the doors. Those in the galleries being wedged together in an almost immovable mass, were generally compelled to retain their position, though a considerable number of the more timid slid down the pillars and gas pipes to the lower floor." The convention, surprisingly, at first tried to carry on amid the confusion. When one delegate complained of the commotion coming for the Baltimoreans in the gallery, a Maryland delegate, a congressman from Baltimore, responded, "There was no class of people more orderly than the constituents he had the honor to represent ... [and] they had been as orderly and as quiet as could be desired." The convention did finally agree to take a recess of one-half hour to clear the galleries, and it was thought that the southeast corner of the balcony had settled about two inches, causing the commotion. When some argued that a new site should be sought for the proceedings, delegate Yancey of Alabama rose and said he saw no danger, as the Whig Party had met in this building in 1844 to nominate Henry Clay "and had been permitted by Providence to depart in safety to receive a severe whipping" from the Democrats. The convention continued following the brief recess, but with the galleries closed for the rest of the day.[22] The vote on the two-thirds rule was then taken and the rule was adopted with 175 yeas and 78 nays, with most of the opposition to the rule coming from Ohio and Pennsylvania. The morning session then adjourned.[23]

When the convention resumed for its evening session, the chairman of the Committee on Credentials, delegate Howard of Maryland, advised that the committee had decided not to consider the credentials of the competing New York delegations until each faction declared its willingness to support the nominee of the convention. Since the New Yorkers were not yet official delegates, they were not in the convention hall. The Hunkers sent word from the Exchange Hotel, where they were staying, that they would "cheerfully acquiesce" in the proposed loyalty oath as a prerequisite for admission as delegates. The Barnburners, in contrast, advised that they would not agree to the committee's request and demanded to be seated "unconditionally, or not at all." Reportedly, the loyalty oath requirement passed the committee by only a single vote.[24] The convention then debated the committee's recommendation. Delegate Tousey of Connecticut objected to the proposal, noting that the same oath was not being required of all of the delegates: "But I tell you, sir, that if when I presented myself at the door of this convention, a pledge of that kind had been demanded of me, I should have buttoned my coat, taken my hat, and walked home." The Barnburners had an unlikely ally in delegate Yancey of Alabama, who stated, "Far be it from me to sympathize with the principles of the barn-burners of New York," but he felt that the committee had exceeded its authority. When a fellow southerner, Forman of Georgia, commented that Yancey was "fond of hearing himself make speeches," the Alabaman responded with some wit and some arrogance: "I do not, let me assure the gentleman from Georgia, desire to hear myself talk; although if I speak more intelligently than some, I should prefer listening to myself." The two exchanged more comments and had to be called to order by President Stevenson. The result of the debate was that the committee's loyalty oath proposal was laid on the table and, instead, the convention passed a resolution to have representatives of the two New York factions address the full convention for one hour each the following day and for each to present their argument why they should be recognized as the true and legitimate delegates of the New York Democratic Party. With that, the convention adjourned for the day.[25] As with previous Baltimore conventions, the 1848 Democratic convention was not without its share of evening festivities. Throughout the week, the city was "kept lively by the nightlong high jinks of celebrants who use songs, libations and heated arguments to prove their fealty to party and candidates."[26]

The convention's third day, Thursday, May 24, 1848, was showdown day for the New Yorkers. The Hunkers were first up and their spokesman was Senator Daniel Dickinson. His group, he argued, "represented the regularly organized democracy of New York." Responding to charges that the Hunkers had "degraded" themselves by agreeing to a loyalty oath to support the nominee as proposed by the Committee on Credentials, he wished, "Would to God that all Democrats might even be so degraded." When the regular convention of the state party had met in Syracuse, Dickinson pointed out that the majority of that body had rejected proposals from the Barnburners that contained "strong and emphatic terms against any extension or introduction of slavery in any territory," and that the Barnburners were, in effect, just sore losers and were now being bullies by trying to steal the seats of the Hunkers at the party's national convention.[27]

When the Barnburners had their turn at the podium, it was obvious that the hostility between the two groups was personal, as well as political. Their speaker, J. C. Smith, responded to Dickinson's comment about being degraded and stated that he "doubted Mr. D. had sufficient moral sense to discern what the degradation was." According to Smith, it was the Hunkers who started the New York factionalism by their efforts "to secure and retain all the offices at the expense and to the detriment of the credit of the State." Regarding the Syracuse convention, the Hunkers had "obtained by fraud a working majority in that convention, disregarded in every respect the rights of the minority and the usages of the Democracy and thus accomplished their designs." Following a separate meeting held at Herkimer, the Barnburners called for another state party convention at Utica, which "was offered as a conciliatory movement in conformity with the party usages," and the Barnburner delegation present in Baltimore was duly appointed at that convention. The Barnburners, Smith argued, were not abolitionists but, rather, stood with the founder of the Democratic Party, Thomas Jefferson, who had, in part, drafted the Northwest Ordinance of 1787, which excluded slavery from the Northwest Territory.[28] So it should be with new territories won in the Mexican War. A second Barnburner speaker, Preston King, declared that, if the Barnburners were excluded from the convention because they supported the Wilmot Proviso, then "there would be an end of the Democratic party, it would be disbanded. The Democracy of New York would never submit that the party should be made the carrier of slavery throughout the land."[29]

The remarks of the Barnburners' speakers "caused great excitement" among the delegates. Yancey of Alabama, who had the previous day spoken opposing the proposal that the Barnburners should agree to a loyalty oath, now spoke against them being seated as delegates. By their own words, the silver-tongued Alabaman argued, the Barnburners "have shown themselves to be Whigs in disguise and Abolitionists." According to Yancey, the Wilmot Proviso was unconstitutional because "the General Government had no right to establish or abolish slavery anywhere — it was for the States alone to decide." After hearing from the cantankerous New Yorkers, the *Baltimore Sun* commented, "The Convention had the felicity of listening to all the details of as petty a family quarrel as ever entertained an assembly.... It is a misfortune that the vote of the State of New York is so large, and consequently important and influential in the contest."[30] With the New York matter still unresolved, the convention ended its morning session.[31]

At 5:00 P.M., the business of the convention resumed and it was decision time. The report of the Committee on Credentials requiring a loyalty oath of any admitted New York delegates was brought to a vote and was defeated with 51 yeas and 201 nays. The convention then narrowly approved, by a vote of 126 yeas to 125 nays, a resolution to admit both New York delegations with the two factions equally splitting New York's 36 votes at the convention. The gathering thus ended for the day and it remained to be seen whether this Solomonic action would please everyone or please no one.[32]

When the convention met for its fourth day, May 25, 1848, it finally got down to the business of nominating a candidate for the presidency. On a positive note, both New York delegations showed up, but neither looked very happy about the admission of the other. In order to forestall any draft Polk movement, a letter was read from the president, which was written in Washington in May 20, and which was said to reveal his "true position" as to renomination. In it, Polk flatly declared, "I am not a candidate for the nomination," and warned that any attempt to place his name before the convention "is without any agency or desire on my part." The reading of the letter was followed by much applause in honor of the sitting Democratic president. In a sign of potential trouble, the New York Barnburners requested permission to withdraw for consultation, which was granted. Yancey of Alabama again took to the floor and moved that the convention adopt a platform first, before considering a presidential nominee. His motion was soundly defeated, with 21 yeas and 232 nays. Three names were then formally placed in nomination: Cass of Michigan, Buchanan of Pennsylvania, and Woodbury of New Hampshire. There were no nomination speeches and the voting quickly began. On the first ballot, Cass led with 125 votes, to 55 for Buchanan, 53 for Woodbury, 3 for Dallas, 6 for General Worth, and 9 for Calhoun (all cast by South Carolina's lone delegate). No votes were cast from New York and, for unknown reasons, Florida also did not vote. With 254 voting delegates, a two-thirds vote of 170 was needed to win the nomination. On the second ballot, Cass picked up a few additional votes to bring his total to 133, to 54 for Buchanan, 56 for Woodbury, 3 for Dallas, and 6 for Worth. On the third ballot, the senator from Michigan increased his total to 156 votes, but still short of the two-thirds needed. Finally, on the fourth ballot, Cass went over the top with 179 votes, compared to 33 for Buchanan and 38 for Woodbury. The usual switching of votes for all to jump on the winner's bandwagon then occurred, but the nomination was not unanimous. Yancey of Alabama refused to support Cass until he saw the party's platform. The Florida delegation took the same position. The convention then adjourned until its evening session.

When the proceedings resumed, the seats of the Barnburners were empty. Word was received that they had withdrawn from the convention. There were few regrets over their departure and a resolution was quickly passed naming the Hunkers as the sole New York delegation, with the right to cast New York's full 36 votes. A Platform Committee was named, with one member from each state. The business of filling the second spot on the ticket was then taken up. Six names were placed in nomination for the vice presidency: General William O. Butler of Kentucky, General John A. Quitman of Mississippi, Benjamin C. Howard of Maryland, John Y. Mason of Virginia, William R. King of Pennsylvania, and General James J. McKay of North Carolina. Many of these men were easterners and many thought that, with Cass from Michigan at the top of the ticket, an easterner was needed for regional balance. Howard, who was chair of the convention's controversial Committee on Credentials, apparently had had enough of politics for a while and asked that his name be withdrawn. On the first ballot, 252 votes were cast, with 114 going to Butler, 74 for Quitman, 24 for Mason, and 26 for King, with the remaining votes scattered among others. Based on the number of delegates voting and the two-thirds rule, 168 votes were needed for nomination. On the second ballot, Butler picked up significant additional support and won the contest with 169 votes, to 62 for Quitman, 11 for McKay, and the rest scattered in single digits for others.[33] With the ticket of Cass and Butler nominated, the convention adjourned for the day.

William O. Butler came from a military family and his father and uncles had served under George Washington during the American Revolution. During the War of 1812, he also became a soldier, and ended up serving under Andrew Jackson in Florida and in the Battle of New Orleans. His close association with Jackson made him a strong Democrat, but he returned home to Kentucky after the war's end and, other than brief service in the Kentucky

Lewis Cass of Michigan, a longtime governor of the Michigan territory before it became a state, was a leading proponent of "popular sovereignty" concerning slavery in new states. Cass won the 1848 Democratic nomination at a convention held in Baltimore and William Butler of Kentucky, a Mexican War general, was nominated to be his running mate (*Library of Congress*).

legislature, was not politically active. He practiced law for twenty years and was also an amateur poet. Persuaded by the Democratic Party in 1839 to seek a Kentucky congressional seat, he ran and he won, but disliked Washington and returned home after two terms. The Democrats in the Bluegrass State then nominated him for governor in 1844, an election that he lost. With the outbreak of the Mexican War in 1846, President Polk, looking for Democrats to serve in the Whig-laden officer corps of the United States Army, made Butler a major general. He was wounded in the knee during a battle, returned home to Kentucky for a while, and then went back to Mexico as the war was concluding. When General Winfield Scott returned to the United States after his successful capture of Mexico City, Butler became the commanding officer in the field as the peace treaty ending the conflict was announced.[34] Putting Butler on the ticket gave the Democrats leverage against either of the anticipated Whig nominees in 1848. His military credentials would balance those of General Zachary Taylor and his Kentucky connections could help in Henry Clay's home state.

When the Democratic convention of 1848 met for its fifth and final day on Saturday, May 26, the vice presidents of the convention were chosen as a committee to notify the two nominees of their selection. This convention became the first in American history to appoint a national committee of the party, with one member from each state, the purpose of which was to manage the campaign.[35] The only matter of substance left to perform was to receive the report from the Committee on Resolutions and to act on it. The proposed platform was standard fare for the Democratic conventions of the era: it proclaimed that the federal government was one of limited powers, that there was no federal power over internal improvements, that the federal government should not foster one industry over another, that there was no federal power to charter a national bank, that the government's money should not be kept in private banks, and that Congress has no power to "interfere with or control the domestic institutions of the several states." In an effort to attract support from the hundreds of thousands of immigrants who had come to the United States in the 1840s, most of whom supported the Democratic Party, the committee proposed that any attempts to abridge the privilege of immigrants becoming citizens should be resisted. The committee also proposed a resolution declaring the Mexican War "a just and necessary war" and threatening vigorous prosecution of the war if Mexico did not accept the "liberal" treaty terms that were then pending. Delegate Yancey of Alabama, who was his state's representative on the committee, offered a minority report of his own concerning slavery in the territories. Yancey proposed that the party go on record as declaring that "the doctrine of non-interference with the rights and property of any portion of the people of this Republic, in the States or Territories, is the true Republican doctrine." The rest of the platform was approved, while Yancey's proposed amendment went down to a resounding defeat by a vote of only 36 yeas to 216 nays.[36] An angry Yancey then attempted to persuade other Southern delegates to walk out of the convention with him. Only one followed his lead and the two of them left the Universalist Church in a huff and strutted out onto Calvert Street.[37] As will be seen later, it was not the last time that William Lowndes Yancey would walk out of a Democratic convention, but he would have considerably more company the next time around.

Whig Convention

The Mexican War, a war started by and brought to a conclusion by a Democratic president, Polk, had unintended political consequences. As with most wars, the Mexican War created military heroes. Unfortunately for the Democrats, the two most popular military leaders to come out of the war, General Zachary Taylor and General Winfield Scott, were not Democrats. Other than their opposition to the Polk administration and not being Democrats, Taylor and Scott could not have been more different in their personalities and even in their style of dress, which earned them their nicknames. Scott always dressed "like Mars going into battle" and became known as "Old Fuss and Feathers," a reference to the feathers worn, in that era, on the hats of generals. Taylor dressed like a private who had been in the field a bit too long and was referred to as "Old Rough and Ready."[38] As the minority party, the Whigs were desperate for any edge with voters that could help them win back the presidency. As Jackson and Harrison had shown in the past, military men were proven vote-getters. In the pre-convention maneuvering, there were four major candidates for the Whig nomination: the two Mexican War heroes, Taylor and Scott, and the party's two aging stalwarts, Daniel Webster and Henry Clay.

The apolitical Taylor proudly announced to the country that he had never before cast a vote for president, nor for any other office. Born in Virginia, raised in Kentucky, and a resident of Louisiana after the Mexican War, Taylor owned hundreds of slaves and was popular in the South. Despite this, his military hero status and his ambiguous stand on the Wilmot Proviso attracted some support in the North. His flirtations with the Whig Party were, at best, on a "take it or leave it" basis. Taylor's preference was to be drafted for the presidency by a national nonpartisan convention. In an attempt to get the general to publicly declare his support of Whiggery, three party leaders visited him at his Baton Rouge home over three days in April, bringing with them a draft of a letter they hoped to get him to sign in which Taylor would firmly declare himself a Whig. Taylor grudgingly complied, made suggestions for changes, but eventually agreed to write in longhand the revised letter and addressed it to Captain John A. Allison, his friend and brother-in-law. In this famous Allison letter, written on April 22, 1848, six weeks before the start of the Whig convention, Taylor wrote: "I repeat what I have often said ... I am a Whig, but not an ultra Whig ... I would not be the mere president of a party. I would endeavor to act independent of the party domination. I shall feel bound to administer the government untrammeled by party schemes." He also expressed his support for a limited role of the power of the presidency and for sparing use of the veto, if elected.[39] This lukewarm statement was not all that the Whig Party leaders had wanted, but, desperate for a winning candidate, they convinced themselves and others that Taylor and the Whigs were a match made in heaven.

Having lost the Whig nomination in the last two elections to Harrison and to Clay, Daniel Webster thought 1848 should be his year. He had, however, enemies within the Whig Party arising from his decision to remain as secretary of state under President Tyler, at the time when the rest of the Whigs in the cabinet resigned over Tyler's vetoes of the Whigs' national bank re-chartering bills. In all of his runs for the presidency, Webster never attracted any significant support outside of his New England base. Tact was not his forte. When a southern senator once complimented him during a toast as being a northern man with southern principles, Webster responded, "I am certainly a Northern man. As to my southern principles — Do I ever leave any whisky in my glass? Don't I love to play cards? Do I ever pay my debts? Am I fond of challenging men who won't fight?"[40] It was not a response, whether intended jokingly or not, that endeared him to southern hearts. Once again in 1848, Webster would be in the race, but not a top contender.

The other Whig stalwart, Henry Clay, in retirement since his unexpected 1844 defeat by Polk, delivered a major policy speech on November 13, 1847, in his home state of Kentucky, at Lexington, which was viewed as his unofficial entry into the 1848 race. In the speech, Clay denounced the Mexican War as having been unnecessary and offensive in nature, and he pledged to take no additional territory from Mexico as a result of the conflict. This key issue of his candidacy was undercut and rendered moot a few months later when the Treaty of Guadalupe Hidalgo was ratified by the Senate in March 1848, gaining for the United States the vast new territories of California and New Mexico.[41] Many Whigs believed that the party needed a new face to present to the country in 1848. When the state Whig convention in Kentucky met in February and elected a slate of delegates to the national convention that was uncommitted to any candidate, any momentum that Clay may have had was halted.[42] Despite this, Clay formally announced his candidacy on April 10, which did nothing to turn around the lackluster response he had been receiving since November. Jealous of two of his opponents' popularity as war heroes, Clay purportedly said "I wish I could slay a Mexican."[43]

Of the other candidates, General Winfield Scott was waiting in the wings, more of a compromise candidate than a real contender for the nomination. Once again, a trial balloon had been floated for Justice John McLean of Ohio, this time by Horace Greeley of the *New York Tribune*, but, like all potential McLean candidacies, it quickly fizzled.[44]

The third presidential nominating convention of the Whig Party was held in Philadelphia from June 7 to 9, 1948. The site was the Chinese Museum, which was a misnomer, as the meeting room was the spacious first floor of the Philadelphia Museum, located at Ninth and Sansom Streets. Opened in 1838, the room had originally housed a grand exhibit of Chinese clothing and life, complete with representations of Chinese streets, parlors, and temples. In the early 1840s, the Chinese exhibit was removed, but the name stuck. The room then became one of Philadelphia's most popular sites for large public balls and meetings.[45] All states were represented at the convention, except Texas and South Carolina. A young Whig congressman from Illinois, Abraham Lincoln, traveled from Washington to Philadelphia to observe the proceedings. Although he had been a longtime supporter of Henry Clay, Lincoln, who was not a delegate to the convention, had become convinced that Zachary Taylor was the best choice for the party in 1848.[46]

On the convention's first day, the Philadelphia crowd in the galleries made Baltimore onlookers at past conventions look dignified in comparison. The local crowd "tended to be unruly. They widely applauded or hissed and booed speakers and generally made a nuisance of themselves."[47] Distribution of gallery tickets was more tightly controlled on the second day, when the nomination process began. On the first ballot, Taylor led with 111 votes, compared to 97 for Clay, 43 for Scott, 22 for Webster, and 6 votes scattered among others. A majority vote of 140 was necessary for nomination. It was a stronger showing for Clay than many had anticipated. Taylor's support was mainly from the south, Clay's from the north, Scott's from Ohio, and Webster's from New England. On the second ballot, Taylor picked up 7 votes, for a total of 118, while Clay dropped by 10 votes to 87. The convention adjourned for the evening, and overnight efforts by Clay's managers to stop the hemorrhaging were not successful. On the third ballot, Taylor rose to 133, while Clay dropped to 74. The inevitable outcome occurred the following morning, June 9, on the fourth ballot, with Taylor going over the top with 171 votes, and Clay dropping into third place, with only 35 votes, and finishing behind Scott's 60 votes. The Taylor victory was viewed as a victory for southerners, which was evident when a motion to make the nomination unanimous was opposed by the Massachusetts delegation.[48]

The vice presidential nomination was wide open, and fourteen names were placed in nomination. From this logjam of candidates, Millard Fillmore of New York emerged as the victor on the second ballot. Born into an upstate New York family of modest means, Fillmore had no formal education until the age of fourteen and he did not attend college. Despite these obstacles, he became an attorney and a political leader in Buffalo, serving in the New York legislature and then in Congress. His nomination was a somewhat surprising choice, since Fillmore was not part of the Weed-Seward faction that dominated the Whig Party in the Empire State. Although he had served several years as a congressman from New York, first elected as an Anti-Mason in 1832, then as a Whig, and had risen to become chairman of the Ways and Means Committee, Fillmore voluntarily left Congress in 1842 and then lost a race for the New York governorship in 1844. It was a career path not unlike that of the Democrat James K. Polk a few years earlier in Tennessee — a successful election to the House of Representatives with a leadership position there, then defeat at home for governor, only to be plucked from seeming oblivion and placed on his party's national ticket. As a northerner, Fillmore was viewed as a balance to Taylor, a southerner. He was also thought to be a strong Clay man (although in reality he was not), which placated the supporters of the defeated Kentuckian.[49]

On the evening of the convention's conclusion, a large ratification rally was held on the grounds of Philadelphia's Independence Hall. A main platform was constructed at the south portion of the building in which the founding fathers had debated and approved the

FOR PRESIDENT OF THE PEOPLE

ZACHARY TAYLOR

About party creeds let party zealots fight
He cant be wrong whose life is in the right.—

The apolitical Zachary Taylor, a hero from the Mexican War, was nominated by the Whigs in 1848 at their convention held in Philadelphia. Taylor not only won the nomination, he was also elected to the presidency *(Library of Congress).*

Declaration of Independence and the Constitution. Rising twenty feet above the ground, the platform was decorated with bunting and was illuminated with eighteen large glass lamps. At its front, an eagle held a ribbon in its beak emblazoned with the names of Taylor and Fillmore. Above the rear of the platform, a transparent banner proclaiming "Democratic Whig Nomination — Zachary Taylor for President — Millard Fillmore for Vice President of the United States," glowed from the flicker of gaslights. Six speakers at the main platform addressed the enthusiastic crowd of thousands and extolled the virtues of the just nominated ticket, while additional speakers addressed the throng from two other smaller platforms elsewhere on the grounds of Independence Hall. A reporter for *Cummings' Evening Telegraphic Bulletin* described the scene:

> It is now half-past eight o'clock, the yard is full — every street presents a moving mass of human beings — music comes from every quarter — tremendous cheers from the State House yard rend the air, and fairly strip the foliage from the trees — cannon are fired at intervals from the main staging — the boys following suit, are firing off crackers a la Fourth of July — cheer after cheer ascends for old Rough and Ready, Palo Alto, Buena Vista ... three Drummond lights are just started, two facing the north and one the south, their rays passing over the immense multitude, induce applause.[50]

Whig newspaper editor Horace Greeley called the 1848 Whig convention the "slaughter-house" convention, because, in nominating Taylor, it slaughtered Whig principles. As seeming confirmation of this, the convention did not adopt a formal platform and, thus, like its nominee, there was no record of what the party proposed or stood for. As it had done in 1840, the party, looking for a victory in November, went for "a little gunpowder" and nominated another military leader as its candidate. Clay and Webster both initially refused to endorse the nomination of Taylor, although they did not work against or openly oppose him during the campaign. Both were bitter. Clay noted, "Magnanimity is a noble virtue, and I have always tried to practice it, but it has its limits." Webster commented on Taylor's convention victory by saying, "Such a nomination was not fit to be made." Both did finally endorse Taylor late in the campaign, in September, three months after the convention.[51] With his loss of the 1848 Whig nomination, all knew that the seventy-one-year-old Clay would never attain the presidency, an office he had sought for a quarter of a century. One Alabama delegate to the convention, who had left home with the intention of supporting Clay and ended up voting for Taylor in Philadelphia, wrote of his guilt shortly after the convention: "As I write these words, a feeling of sadness steals over me. I grieve to think that the last hope of elevating that great man to the presidency — no — of elevating the presidency to that great man, is extinguished, and extinguished by the hands of his friends."[52]

Free Soil Convention

The nominations of Cass by the Democrats and of Taylor by the Whigs left those members of both parties who strongly opposed the extension of slavery into the territories with a choice — toe the party line and support their party's nominee, or form a third party. Some chose the latter course. The Barnburners of New York, who had bolted the Democratic convention in Baltimore in May after having been given only shared representation at the convention with their hated in-state rivals, the Hunkers, met for their own convention in Utica on June 21, 1848. John Van Buren, the son of former President Martin Van Buren, was one of their leaders. Against the elder Van Buren's stated wishes, he was nominated by this gathering as its candidate for president. Originally just a state movement in New York, this effort became national in scope when disaffected Whigs, abolitionists of the Liberal Party, and the Barnburners all agreed to meet in Buffalo on August 7, 1848, for a convention of what became a new third-party, the Free-Soil Party. This convention also nominated former President Martin Van Buren as its presidential candidate, and nominated Charles Francis Adams, the son of former President John Quincy Adams, for the vice presidency. It was an ironic pairing and showed how times and political coalitions had changed. Van Buren, Andrew Jackson's handpicked successor in the White House, was now paired on a third-party ticket with the son of Jackson's hated political rival, John Quincy Adams. The new party presented itself to the country with the catchy slogan of "Free Soil, Free Speech, Free Labor and Free Men!"[53]

The Campaign and Election

The campaign of 1848 was fairly low key, with the presidential candidates following the traditional pattern and staying at home, saying little, and writing only a few letters. The letters that Taylor did write got him into trouble with the Whigs. In his letter accepting the Whig nomination, he only pledged to serve honorably, if elected, and stated nothing about the party, nor his proposed policies once in office. In July, he wrote to a Philadelphia supporter, George Lippard, that he was "not a party candidate; and if elected cannot be president of a party, but the president of the whole people." Further, Taylor accepted a nomination given by a group of dissident Democrats from South Carolina, and wrote to a South Carolina newspaper that he would have accepted the nomination of the national Democratic Party, had it been offered to him.[54] So much for any differences on the issues, as seen by Taylor, between the two parties. In an effort at damage control, the Whig Party leaders got Taylor to sign another letter to Major Allison, which they wrote for him. In the September 4 letter, known as the Second Allison Letter, it was claimed that all of the doubt over Taylor being a Whig was just a misunderstanding. The letter stated that the officers who served under him in Mexico knew that he held Whig principles. His promises not to act as a partisan president, not to engage in wholesale patronage changes once in office, not to use the veto pen unless absolutely necessary, were all, in Taylor's view, an affirmation of basic Whig beliefs that a president should be the leader of all the people, not just of a party, and that the executive should not usurp power once in office.[55] This letter was just what the party leaders had wanted. Perhaps more importantly, they persuaded Taylor to put down his pen for the rest of the campaign.

In 1848, for the first time, a single fixed day for the presidential election was established by act of Congress. On November 7, 1848, Americans went to the polls and elected a new president. It took a week to count the ballots and Taylor emerged the victor. In the three-way contest, Taylor won a plurality of the 2,880,572 votes cast, with 1,360,099; to 1,220,544 for the Democrat Cass, and 291,263 for former president Van Buren, the candidate of the Free-Soil Party. The Free-Soilers had been on the ballot in seventeen of the thirty states. In the Electoral College, Taylor won 163 votes, compared to 127 for Cass and none for Van Buren. It was a national victory for Taylor, as Old Rough and Ready carried states in New England, in the Mid-Atlantic, in the border states, and in the South. Still, without New York's thirty-six electoral votes, Taylor would not have won the election, and the strong showing of New Yorker Van Buren in his home state, where he finished ahead of Cass, made the difference in the contest.[56] As in 1840, the Whigs had nominated a military hero and had succeeded in electing a president. But one lingering question remained — was Zachary Taylor really a Whig?

CHAPTER 8

1852: Frank and Fuss and Feathers

For Pierce and King we'll shout and sing while on our "winding way"
So "Coons" look out what you're about a win on election day.

Yes, come next March, we'll take the starch out of Fillmore's collar
Old Scott we'll beat the very first heat and make the "Coons" all holler.

High Locos, ho Locos, listen while I sing
A song for you that's good and true about our Pierce and King.[1]

Democratic campaign song, 1852

Both major political parties returned to Baltimore for their presidential nominating conventions in 1852. In the heat and humidity of early summer in the Monumental City, the Democrats and the Whigs held conventions in June that stalemated for days over the selection of a presidential nominee. It was only after more than ninety ballots between them that the two parties chose their standard-bearers. The Democrats were unable to choose among their leading candidates and, for the second time in their history, nominated a man who was unknown nationally before the convention. The Whigs nominated another military hero for the third time in four of their conventions and, in doing so, rejected their own incumbent president. The story of the 1852 conventions is one of increasing sectionalism and of the efforts of each party to bridge the chasm between its northern and southern members.

The key political issue leading up to the 1852 conventions was the Compromise of 1850 or, more specifically, whether that legislation represented "finality" of the federal government's involvement in the slavery issue. The Compromise of 1850 was the end result of a series of measures introduced in January that year by seventy-three-year-old Senator Henry Clay of Kentucky, who was in the twilight of his life and who had been the personification of the Whig Party since its founding in the mid–1830s. In addition to Clay, the measures were pushed through Congress by the leadership of Democratic senator Stephen A. Douglas of Illinois. There were four elements of the compromise as passed by Congress and signed into law by President Millard Fillmore in autumn 1850. First, California was admitted to the Union as a free state. Second, the western boundary of Texas was established, and the remainder of the Mexican cession lands (currently the states of New Mexico, Arizona, Utah, and Nevada) would be organized as free or slave under the principle of popular sovereignty. Third, the trading of slaves (although not slavery itself) was outlawed in the District of Columbia.

Fourth, a fugitive slave law was enacted that made the federal government the enforcer of the recapture of runaway slaves, with federal marshals empowered to summons citizens to aid in the law's execution and with the establishment of court-appointed commissioners to decide the fate of alleged runaways. The political maneuvering leading up to the Compromise of 1850 and the story of how the legislation passed Congress and was signed into law by President Fillmore, who had only recently assumed office upon the sudden death of Zachary Taylor in July 1850[2] (Taylor had opposed the Compromise measures), are subjects beyond the scope of this book.[3] Each of the compromise measures was voted upon separately and passed with bipartisan votes, but with shifting coalitions on each bill, and with several coordinated abstentions. In general, both northerners and southerners felt that the other side had gotten the better part of the deal, but both were willing to compromise their beliefs for the continued preservation of the Union.

The Baltimore site for both conventions in 1852 was the newly opened hall of the Maryland Institute. The predecessor to the current Maryland Institute College of Art (MICA) the Maryland Institute was originally established in 1825 and was the brainchild of Baltimore's John H. B. Latrobe, a local lawyer, artist, and inventor.[4] Its purpose was the dissemination of "scientific information, connected with the mechanic arts, among the manufacturers, mechanics, and artisans of the city and state, by the establishment of popular lectures upon appropriate subjects, the price of admission to which should be fixed so low as to be within

HALL OF THE MARYLAND INSTITUTE, BALTIMORE.

Baltimore's Hall of the Maryland Institute was called the grandest meeting room in America when it opened in 1851. It hosted the 1852 Democratic and Whig conventions, the 1856 Whig convention, and the convention of Southern Democrats in 1860 (*Enoch Pratt Free Library*).

the means of all. It was also proposed to hold exhibitions of the products of domestic industry and to offer premiums for excellence in various branches."[5] The original Maryland Institute was housed in the first Athenaeum building located at St. Paul and Lexington Streets, which had been the site of all three inaugural presidential nominating conventions (Anti-Mason, National Republican, and Democratic) in 1831 and 1832. When the Athenaeum burned to the ground in 1835, however, the organization ceased to exist for several years. It was reorganized in 1849.[6] Known officially as the Maryland Institute for the Promotion of the Mechanical Arts, the reconstituted organization constructed a new building in which to hold its exhibitions and also to supply a place for public meetings in Baltimore. The building was erected over the site of an existing market, known as Center Market, fronted on Baltimore Street, and extended more than 350 feet to the south. Built in only seven months, the new Hall of the Maryland Institute was dedicated in October 1851. Shaped like a giant railroad car, the structure had a tower at both ends, the taller of the two being on its north side facing Baltimore Street. The first floor continued to house the open-air market that had previously existed on the property, with access provided through large archways. The great hall was on the second floor and had ten large windows on each side to let in light and air. It was 260 feet long and 60 feet wide, with a gallery located above. The hall could hold up to 6,000 people and was one of the largest rooms in the country.[7] A reporter attending one of the annual exhibitions described the hall as "finished in a neat and substantial manner, abundantly lighted in the day time by numerous large windows on each side, and brilliantly illuminated at night by means of chandeliers pending from the centre of the ceiling, and several hundred lesser lights arranged in a double row of bracket burners, tastefully displayed in groups along the front of a narrow gallery which hangs some fifteen feet above the main floor, and extends entirely around the hall."[8] The new Hall of the Maryland Institute quickly became the premier place for public meetings in Baltimore and was the logical site to host political conventions there.

Democratic Convention

In 1852, the Democratic Party of the United States held its sixth presidential nominating convention and, for the sixth straight time, the location was Baltimore. With the Whigs occupying the White House, there was no clear frontrunner for the nomination. Senator Lewis Cass of Michigan, the party's 1848 nominee, and his vice presidential running mate, General William O. Butler of Kentucky, were thought to be leading contenders going into the convention. Butler was being promoted as a moderate and, since he had few publicly stated comments on the issues of the day, his supporters tried to appeal to all people. When southerners accused him of being soft on the slavery issue, however, he responded with strong pro-slavery comments, effectively killing any chance he had of drawing northern support and of winning the nomination.[9] He was a better military man than a politician. Others known to want the nomination were Senator James Buchanan of Pennsylvania, who had been an 1848 contender, and newcomers Senator Stephen A. Douglas of Illinois, former secretary of war William L. Marcy of New York, and Sam Houston of Texas.[10]

As delegates descended on Baltimore in the days leading up to the convention, rumors swirled as to which candidate was moving up, or down. The *New York Times* noted, "Democratic Delegates and politicians have lighted upon this City like a swarm of bees" and opined that Buchanan and Cass were the frontrunners, followed by Douglas, Marcy, Houston and

Dickinson.[11] The *Baltimore Sun* noted on May 31 that the "rumors of the day ... are in favor of Mr. Douglas," and that there was strong demand in all quarters of the city for "the eatables, drinkables, sleepables and socialables of life."[12] Buchanan supporters from nearby Pennsylvania came to Baltimore in the largest numbers and made their headquarters at Carroll Hall. Located one block south of the Battle Monument at the southeast corner of Calvert and Baltimore Streets (currently the site of the Continental Trust Building), Carroll Hall was three stories tall and its large meeting room on the second floor was a favorite site for political meetings in the city.[13] The Buchananites who came to Baltimore were noted to "exhibit more energy and determination" and, at Carroll Hall, had "arranged for a bountiful supply of refreshments, to which several thousand tickets will be issued, to last good until adjournment."[14] Thus, the convention hospitality suite was born, with the Pennsylvanians hoping that food and alcohol would bring undecided delegates into Old Buck's camp.

As the convention opened at noon on Tuesday, June 1, 1852, the surrounding streets were mobbed with people. New York supporters of Senator Cass fired a cannon, which boomed with gun smoke several times, and which was accompanied by a brass band brought from New York for the occasion. The decorations inside the hall were highlighted by "a large undulating canopy of striped bunting, with the American flag displayed at each extremity."[15] Although immense in size, the floor of the hall was more than four times as long (260 feet) as it was wide (60 feet). The convention planners had constructed a large platform of about 75 feet at the southern end and, adjacent to it, a lower platform for secretaries and reporters. Local Baltimore boys were designated as pages, one for each state, to facilitate communication between the convention leaders on the platform and each state's delegation. As the convention began, it became clear that this design was poor from an acoustical standpoint. No one at the other end of the long and narrow room could hear anything being said from the platform. The convention floor was crowded with both delegates and nondelegates. Many states had sent more than their allotted number of delegates, which added to the confusion. The convention did manage during its opening morning session to elect a temporary president, General Romulus Sanders of North Carolina, who tried to quiet the unruly crowd by crying out that the disorder "was so serious as to embarrass the organization of the meeting." Over cries of "we can't hear a thing," the convention appointed a Committee on Organization, with one member from each state, to nominate permanent officers, as well as a Committee on Credentials, to decide disputed delegate seats. It then adjourned until the afternoon.[16]

The convention reassembled in the afternoon, at which time the commotion and confusion was no better. A motion to have the Committee on Organization decide upon the parliamentary rules to be used by the convention "was finally adopted, not half the convention seeming to understand its purport." A Connecticut delegate had enough of the confusion and moved for the appointment of a committee "to procure another room, where gentlemen can hear and understand what is going on." He did not want to "impute any want of hospitality to the citizens of Baltimore, but they have provided us with a hall that is quite too large." After some discussion, the motion was laid on the table with the promise of convention officials that a solution to the problem would be worked on at the conclusion of the day's proceedings.[17] The Committee on Organization reported its recommendation of John W. Davis of Indiana as the convention's president, along with thirty-one vice presidents, one from each state present. These recommendations were approved, but the vice presidents could hardly make it through the crowd to the platform. The committee further reported its recommendations that the rules of the House of Representatives be adopted, that a two-thirds vote be required for nomination for president and vice president (by now a sacrosanct Democratic Party tradition), and that each state be allotted a number of votes for the nominating process equal to its total number of electoral votes. All of these recommendations were adopted. In his opening address, convention president Davis reminded his audience of the old maxim that "order is heaven's first law," and then appointed a committee of five to try to find a better way to organize the hall. The convention then adjourned for the evening.[18]

When the convention reassembled on Wednesday morning, June 2, the president's chair had been moved from the southern end of the platform to the northeast corner, a portion of the floor previously reserved for alternate delegates and invited guests had been reassigned to some of the larger state delegations, and a new ticket policy for admission to the convention floor was introduced. The strict ticket policy worked a bit too well, for when a test roll call of the states was made, three states were missing from the floor, their members shouting down from the gallery that they had been denied admission. A North Carolina delegate spoke from the floor and alleged that members of his delegation had been denied access to the floor and "they had been insulted and violence offered to their persons." A motion to name a committee to draft the platform was made and then tabled, it being decided that the Committee on Credentials needed to report the names of the accredited delegates before further substantive business could be conducted. A resolution to support the finality of the Compromise of 1850 was also made, and was also tabled. The chaos on the floor continuing, "in order that the opportunity might be afforded to make better arrangements in the hall, the convention took a long recess for most of the afternoon."[19] Baltimore's new showplace arena was not off to a good start as a meeting place for political conventions.

When the convention resumed at 5:00 P.M., the old platform was gone and the president's chair had been moved to an elevated area in the middle of the east side of the hall. This seemed to solve many of the problems, since the presiding officers and speakers could now be heard more easily by all. Thus, after two days of moving around the furniture, the convention finally got down to its business. A Committee on Resolutions was appointed to draft a platform. A debate then ensued as to whether the party's platform should be adopted before or after the presidential nominating process. Prior Democratic conventions had always addressed the platform after the nominations and this procedure was again followed. The Committee on Credentials then gave its report. There were two rival delegations from Georgia present, one with twenty-one proposed delegates, the other with seventeen. The committee decided to seat both which, under the unit rule used at Democratic conventions, in effect gave the larger delegate group the right to cast all of Georgia's votes in the nominating process. The committee also excluded South Carolina's lone delegate, General James Commander (a fitting last name for a military man) for lack of proper credentials, over his strong objection and repeated pleas to be heard by the convention as a whole, which were rejected.[20]

The convention then proceeded to its primary business — the nomination of the Democratic Party's presidential candidate. The roll call of the states, again following the tradition of past conventions, began with Maine, in the northeastern corner of the country, proceeded down the eastern seaboard and then moved westward, with California being the last state called. On the first ballot, Cass of Michigan led with 116 votes, Buchanan of Pennsylvania had 93, Marcy of New York had 27, Douglas of Illinois had 20, and five other candidates split the remaining handful of votes. With a total of 288 delegate votes to be cast, the convention's two-thirds rule required 192 votes for victory. Thus, no candidate had even a majority vote of 145, much less the required two-thirds. Of the two leading first ballot contenders, most of Cass's votes came from the North, while most of Buchanan's came from the South. The young Douglas was viewed as a bit too brash and his critics charged that he "drank too heavily, lived too freely, and associated too much with corruptionists and looters."[21] The convention trudged through eight ballots in the morning session, with little movement among the candidates, and then adjourned for a few hours.[22]

When the gathering resumed in the late afternoon, the heat of an early summer day in Baltimore had added to the tension, as "palm leaf fans and iced water were liberally supplied, as a slight relief to the oppressive heat in the hall."[23] In the middle of the eleventh ballot, shortly after Missouri switched its nine votes from Cass to Douglas, a loud noise in the gallery caused a panic, and "the Convention was thrown into such a state of confusion as to render it impossible to proceed with any business for several minutes." Many believed the gallery supports were giving way and that Baltimore's grand new arena was falling to the ground. First the bad acoustics, and now this. After a few anxious minutes, it was determined that a bench in the gallery had broken, causing the noise. A New York delegate, speaking from the floor, assured the convention and the gallery "that there was not the least cause for apprehension, as the building, which was strongly constructed, stood upon the solid rock, and the galleries were sustained by iron bars, which could not give way."[24]

The excitement over, the balloting continued. After the twelfth ballot, the Committee on Credentials reported that it had decided to let a delegation from the District of Columbia (which had no electoral votes in that era) to be seated on the floor as "honorary" (non-voting) members of the convention.[25] During the twenty-first ballot, Maryland switched five of its eight votes from Buchanan to Cass, causing hisses and groans from the gallery. A North Carolina delegate then took the floor and proposed that the Democratic convention never be held in Baltimore again, due to the "corrupting influence of Washington City, and the bad treatment the Convention had received at the hands of its citizens," referring to the hissing coming from the gallery. Of course, the comment only increased the noise coming from the gallery. A Baltimore member of the Committee on Arrangements then appealed "to the Baltimoreans in the gallery to preserve order and decorum and not to interrupt the proceedings of the Convention," while also assuring the delegates that "the crowd was by no means composed entirely of citizens of Baltimore."[26] After a few more ballots, with little movement among the top contenders, the convention adjourned for the day.

When the convention resumed on Thursday, June 3, it was more of the same — another day of "fruitless balloting." By the end of the day, the states had been called, from Maine to California, a total of seventeen times, and the tally stood at 99 for Cass, 87 for Buchanan, and 50 for Douglas.[27] Friday, June 4, was a repeat of Thursday. Another sixteen ballots were cast and, still, no decision. When the convention called it a day on Friday evening, at the end of the thirty-third ballot, Cass had 123 votes, Buchanan 72, and Douglas was at 60 votes. No one was close to the two-thirds vote of 192 required to secure the nomination.[28] No votes on any ballot had been cast for Franklin Pierce of New Hampshire, but that was about to change.

In the weeks and months before the Democratic Party convention in Baltimore, Franklin Pierce went about his business in New Hampshire as a practicing trial attorney. A former congressman who had also served as a general in the Mexican War, Pierce was closely monitoring the latest news on the ups and downs of the various candidates. Even the darkest of dark horses does not achieve a presidential nomination without active planning and maneuvering to exploit an opportunity which may develop. Lightning had struck eight years earlier when a deadlocked Democratic convention in Baltimore had turned to the then nationally unknown James K. Polk. Not only had Polk won the nomination, he had also won the election. Could lightning strike again in Baltimore?

In January 1852, the New Hampshire State Democratic Party convention had, in effect, nominated Pierce as a favorite son candidate for the presidency. In an age when politicians did not want to be seen as craving or actively seeking high office, Pierce wrote to a New Hampshire political friend and a delegate to the Baltimore convention, Charles G. Atherton, stating that presenting his name as a candidate to the Baltimore convention would be "utterly repugnant to [his] tastes and wishes." The *Concord Patriot* newspaper published the letter, but editorialized, "We do not understand ... that he forbids the use of his name entirely ... or that he would decline a nomination tendered him by the great party to which he belongs."[29] Friends of Pierce in Washington began to quietly mention his name and his availability as a compromise candidate, if the convention were to deadlock. Two leading plotters were former General Gideon J. Pillow of Tennessee and Caleb Cushing of Massachusetts. Pillow had served with Pierce in the Mexican War and both he and Pierce had served in that conflict under General Winfield Scott, who was thought to be likely Whig nominee for the presidency in 1852. Pillow had a long-running feud with Scott after the latter had him tried by court-martial shortly after the Mexican War. The charges arose from Pillow's claims that he had been responsible for victories in battles for which Scott (rightfully so, according to most historians) had claimed credit.[30] A movement in the winter to nominate another Mexican War general, William O. Butler, had fizzled and Pierce's Washington supporters sought to fill the vacuum with their man.

Advised by his supporters in Washington in the early spring that the likelihood of a deadlocked convention was increasing, Pierce's interest in the nomination increased. He wrote to them that he would leave it up to their good judgment to determine "what is my duty and what may be the best interest of the party."[31] In other words, Pierce was telling them, "Go for it!" By mid–May, he wrote another letter, more explicitly stating his availability in the event of a deadlocked convention: "My name must in no event be used until all efforts to harmonize upon one the candidates already before the public shall have failed.... If, however, there shall arrive a time in the convention 'when ... the highways are broken up and the waters are out,'—then you will of course seek harmony at all events and take such measures as the interests of the party and the country demand."[32]

As the opening date of the convention neared, Pierce and his wife left Concord and went to Boston to stay with friends and await news from Baltimore. He had received a letter from a Richmond newspaper editor inquiring as to his position on the Compromise of 1850 and, in particular, whether he favored and any changes in the Fugitive Slave Law. He penned a response and addressed it to a Maine delegate to the convention, Major Lally, and had it delivered to Lally in Baltimore. It was a letter that placed the northerner Pierce squarely on the side of the South as to the finality of the Compromise of 1850: "If the compromise measures are not to be substantially and firmly maintained, the plain rights secured by the constitution will be trampled in the dust. What difference can it make to you or me, whether the outrage shall seem to fall on South Carolina, or Maine, or New Hampshire? Are not the rights of each equally dear to us all?"[33]

During the first week of June, Pierce received regular telegraphic reports of the proceedings of the convention, and of the support of the leading candidates fluctuating up and down on multiple ballots, but with none receiving a majority vote on any ballot, much less the two-thirds required for nomination. Everything was going according to plan. On Saturday morning, June 5, Pierce and his wife took a carriage ride from Boston to nearby Cambridge, seeking

Opposite: In 1852, Franklin Pierce of New Hampshire became the second "dark horse" candidate to be nominated by the Democratic Party at a convention held in Baltimore and to also go on and win the election. His running mate was William R. King of Alabama *(Library of Congress)*.

to avoid the tense atmosphere of just sitting and waiting. Around noon, as they were starting back toward Boston, they noticed a man on a horse galloping in their direction. They soon recognized the man as Isaac Barnes, a friend and New Hampshire politician, who shouted as he approached the carriage that Pierce was the nominee of the Democratic Party for the office of president of the United States. Pierce was speechless at the news. His wife fainted.[34] Lightning had indeed struck again in Baltimore and another political unknown was on his way to the highest office in the land.

Events had moved quickly that Saturday morning in Baltimore. On the first ballot of the day, the thirty-fourth overall, the Virginia delegation announced it was switching its votes from Buchanan to Daniel Dickinson of New York, who had not previously been in the race. This was a surprise to Dickinson, who was a New York delegate and who was present on the floor. As he began to speak in response to the action of the Virginians, Dickinson was showered with bouquets of flowers from ladies in the gallery above him. While he appreciated the respect and honor from the Virginians, Dickinson advised that he had been sent to the convention to vote for Lewis Cass for president and that he declined to have his name entered into the contest. By doing so, he said, "I will go home a prouder, if not better, man." On the next ballot, the thirty-fifth, the Virginians retired for consultation and, after returning, announced another surprise. The Old Dominion then cast all of its votes for Franklin Pierce of New Hampshire.[35] There was not an immediate bandwagon effect. After another quick eleven ballots, Pierce had moved up to only forty-one votes. On the forty-sixth ballot, the Kentucky delegation retired for consultation, returned, and cast its votes for Pierce. On the forty-ninth ballot, the logjam broke. North Carolina went for Pierce. Then Mississippi did, and then Tennessee. The large New York delegation withdrew for consultation. While the roll call continued, the Alabama, Vermont, New Jersey, Missouri, Arkansas, and Indiana delegations all joined the Pierce bandwagon. The chairman of the Florida delegation, in announcing his state's votes, proclaimed, "From the land of orange and vine — the land of everglades — we stretch our hands across the Union to the granite hills of New Hampshire in pledge of our fidelity to Franklin Pierce!" New York returned and went for Pierce as, finally, did Buchanan's home state of Pennsylvania. By the end of the forty-ninth ballot, Pierce had come from nowhere to having 282 votes and handily won the nomination.[36] Amid celebration with the boom of cannon outside the Maryland Institute, the convention then adjourned its morning session. After five days, the Democrats finally had a presidential nominee.

When the convention resumed for its Saturday afternoon, and final, session, telegraphic messages received from the losing candidates were read to the convention. Douglas congratulated the convention and predicted that his state of Illinois would give Pierce the largest majority in the election of any state in the union. Similar dispatches were received from Cass and Houston. There remained the issues of the vice presidential nomination and the platform, which were quickly resolved. Since a northerner had been given the top spot on the ticket, most felt that the second spot should go to a southerner. On the second ballot, Senator William R. King of Alabama received the nomination.[37] The platform was without controversy and was adopted, its most important plank being an endorsement of the finality of the Compromise of 1850 as to any issues involving slavery.[38]

Had the convention, in rushing to break its deadlock, nominated a man who was up to the job of the presidency? Shortly after the conclusion of the convention, an elderly acquaintance of Pierce from his hometown in New Hampshire was reported to have made comments that proved to be prophetic: "Well, well, dew tell! Frank Pierce for President! Neow Frank's a good fellow, I admit, and I wish him well, he made a good State's attorney, that's no doubt about that, and he made a fair Judge, thar's no denying that, and nobody kaint complain of him as a Congressman, but when it comes to the hull Yewnited States I dew say that in my judgment Frank Pierce is a-goin to be spread durned thin."[39]

Whig Convention

The three contenders for the Whig nomination in 1852 were Millard Fillmore of New York, the sitting president; Fillmore's own secretary of state, Daniel Webster of Massachusetts; and the highest-ranking military officer in the nation, General Winfield Scott of Virginia. Ironically, Fillmore, a northerner, had the support of most southern Whigs, while Scott, a southerner, was the preferred candidate of most northern Whigs. Webster had much less support, mostly concentrated in his native New England, but the pre-convention speculation was that his presence in the race could be sufficient to prevent either of the leading contenders from controlling a majority of the delegates and that he could be the kingmaker.

Winfield Scott was a true American hero. Already famous as a young man for his victories in the War of 1812, years later, in 1846, at the age of sixty, he led the American military campaign that captured Mexico City and ended the Mexican War. He was a master of organization, detail, and planning. Scott had a commanding presence, but was perceived as perhaps a bit too pompous in his constantly worn dress uniforms, earning the derogatory nickname of "Old Fuss and Feathers," a reference to the plume of feathers that then adorned the hats of generals. In a sense, he was the Democrats' worst nightmare. The Mexican War, started by President Polk, a Democrat, and opposed by the Whigs, had produced two famous military heroes, General Zachary Taylor and General Winfield Scott, both of whom were Whigs. Taylor had won the Whig nomination and had beaten the Democrats in the presidential election of 1848, and now Scott was vying to do the same thing in 1852.

A clear sign that the Whigs would be divided in 1852 came from the Whig caucus in Congress that met in April to select the site for the party's convention. Meeting in the Senate Chamber in the Capitol, the initial caucus on April 9 ended in heated exchanges between the supporters of the leading candidates over the issue of whether the caucus should go on record as supporting the finality of the Compromise of 1850 over all slavery-related issues. When the Whig caucus reconvened on April 20, attendance was sparse, with some southerners and some Webster supporters absent. At this second meeting, a Kentucky congressman again offered his resolution from the first caucus supporting the finality of the Compromise. The chairman of the caucus ruled it out of order. Of the fifty-eight members present, forty supported the chairman's decision and eighteen, mostly southerners, opposed. Several southern members then left the meeting in anger. By the time the site for the party's convention came to a vote, forty-nine members remained. The choice was between Baltimore and Pittsburgh, and Baltimore prevailed by a vote of 31 to 18.[40] Since the Democrats had already selected Baltimore as the location of their 1852 convention, the city would host both major party conventions, just as it had done in 1832 and in 1844.

Baltimoreans were justifiably proud of their city's selection by both parties. The *Baltimore Sun* noted that Baltimore will be "for the time being, the pulsating political center of the nation" and editorialized that the choice by both parties represented "a renewed recognition of the advantages of her position as the centre of an extended and convenient system of rapid and easy communication with every quarter of the country; and also of the healthful political influences by which she is surrounded in the conservative heart of old Maryland." The hometown newspaper boasted that the location of the convention is "a pleasing and flattering evidence of the estimation in which our citizens are held for hospitality and courtesy to strangers." Finally, noting the city's new exhibition facility, the newspaper concluded that "no city in the Union possesses a better and more extensive Hall for such assemblages ... than that of the Maryland Institute in Baltimore."[41]

In the two months between April, when the Whig caucus in Congress called for the convention, until the opening session in June, speculation focused on the whether the convention would adopt a platform supporting the finality of the Compromise of 1850, whether either leading candidate could achieve a majority of votes on the first ballot, and whether President Fillmore would even stay in the race until the convention. It was rumored that Fillmore, who as president had signed the Compromise of 1850 into law, had prepared a letter withdrawing his name if the convention did not support what he felt was the major accomplishment of his administration and adopt a pro-compromise platform.[42]

The Scott campaign was being spearheaded by Senator William Seward of New York, the leader of the New York Whig faction that opposed that state's faction led by President Fillmore. There was speculation that Seward wanted Fillmore to lose more than he wanted Scott to win. Some political observers thought that if Scott prevailed in the battle for the nomination, he would likely lose in the general election, and leave Seward as the frontrunner for the Whig nomination and the presidency in 1856. On the eve of the convention, Seward estimated that Scott would earn 149 first ballot votes (more than needed for the nomination), but that only 15 of these would come from the South.[43] A Philadelphia newspaper estimated that Fillmore would be the frontrunner with 144 votes, compared to 115 for Scott and 37 for Webster.[44] The *New York Tribune*, whose editor, Horace Greeley, was a staunch Whig, considered Scott a "pompous fool" and complained, "We must run Scott for President and I hate it."[45] Greeley estimated 141 first ballot votes for Scott, 118 for Fillmore, 26 for Webster, and 8 votes uncertain.[46]

During the second week of June, the Whig delegates throughout the country began their travels to Baltimore. En route, some of the delegations met regionally in large East Coast cities to plot their convention strategy. New York delegates met for a dinner at the Astor House in New York City and favored the nomination of Scott, if it was "untrammeled by letters or resolutions," that is, if Scott did not fully endorse, or was not forced to endorse, the finality of the Compromise of 1850 over the slavery issue. The New York Whig delegation was of the belief that if "either the convention or nominee should recognize the compromise, then they would be done with them and him."[47] In Philadelphia, delegates from Pennsylvania, Ohio, and New York met and decided to oppose the adoption of a convention platform until after the presidential nominee was selected.[48] In the City of Brotherly Love, on the eve of the convention, it was reported that "every train that arrives from the East or interior contains hundreds bound for the Whig Convention, either as delegates or lookers on." Delegates from Philadelphia, and others totaling around 1,000 people, prepared to depart by steamboat for Baltimore. Many southern delegates congregated in Washington on their way to Baltimore and the rumor there was that President Fillmore, if not nominated on the first ballot, would withdraw and throw his support to Webster.[49]

The Whigs of Maryland and Baltimore eagerly awaited their counterparts from around the country and planned a great reception for them. On June 15, a crowd of around 2,000 Baltimore Whigs assembled at Monument Square at 9:00 P.M. and marched to the President Street Station to greet, meet, and welcome about 1,000 Whigs arriving by train from Massachusetts. When the train was delayed, the throng moved on to Bowley's Wharf (located at the Inner Harbor near South Street) to greet the steamboat that carried the Whigs arriving from

Philadelphia. Accompanied by a band and with banners flying, the lively crowd marched back to Monument Square, by which time the Whigs from Massachusetts had arrived, with their own brass band, and joined the merriment. The Fillmore campaign made its headquarters in the principal saloon of Carroll Hall, located just south of Monument Square, while the Webster supporters made theirs in a smaller meeting room upstairs in the same building.[50] Carroll Hall was where the Buchanan supporters had set up their hospitality suite for Democratic delegates during that party's convention only two weeks earlier. As usual, thousands of people came to Baltimore for the convention and the action was not only in the convention hall but also in the streets. One New Hampshire attendee at the convention remembered, years later, the scene:

> The weather was intensely hot during all the days of the convention, and the nights were so hot that the streets were thronged with people who could not sleep. There were some 20,000 visitors to the convention from outside of Baltimore. It was necessary to quiet the restless crowd that gathered about Barnum's Hotel and in Monument-square, on which the hotel fronted. The crowds here gathered varied at different times from 1,000 to 5,000, and here they would remain through nearly the whole night, night after night. To keep them quiet a stand was made before one of the front windows of the hotel, from which speakers would address them. The speakers would vary from dull to lively, from dry to eloquent and entertaining, and unless they were of the latter kind the crowd would become impatient and force them to stop.[51]

At the Hall of Maryland Institute, the convention planners worked to correct some of the problems that had plagued the Democrats at their recently ended convention in the same building. A road covering called tarbark was spread over the streets surrounding the hall to help keep the outside noise from filtering in. The layout of the hall was changed, with the platform moved to the center of the huge room, and it was carpeted. Meticulous decorations had been prepared. On the platform, behind the chair of the president of the convention, a life-size portrait of George Washington was hung. On the opposite wall, a similar-size portrait of the great Whig Henry Clay was placed. Two large banners greeted visitors to the hall, one proclaiming "The Union of the Whigs for the Sake of the Union" and the other "Union and Liberty, Now and Forever, One and Inseparable" the latter being a famous Daniel Webster quotation from the Hayne/Webster debates over nullification in the early 1830s. The gallery behind the president's chair was reserved for members of Congress, state legislators, and invited guests, while the gallery on the opposite side was reserved for ladies. Aware of the need to cultivate the members of the fourth estate, the Whigs made "admirable and ample accommodations" for the press corps attending the convention.[52]

On June 17, 1852, what would turn out to be the last full national convention of the Whig Party of the United States was called to order. It was a hot summer day in Baltimore and, almost immediately, tempers flared from the camps of the competing candidates. Whether by intent or inadvertence, the convention commenced a quarter of an hour before its published starting time of noon, prompting a protest from some delegates. Delegations from all thirty-one states and the District of Columbia were present. George Evans of Maine was named the temporary president of the convention, which then went about the business of organizing various committees. The tradition of the political conventions of the era for committees to consist of one member from every state was followed. For the Scott campaign, which controlled the majority of the large state delegations (New York, Ohio, and Pennsylvania), this meant a dilution of their strength in all committees, since these large states would receive only one committee vote, the same vote as the state with the fewest delegates, Florida, which had only three representatives. Thus, with one member from each state, a Committee on Organization was appointed to name the permanent convention officers, as well as a Committee on Credentials to resolve disputed delegate seats. The formal appointment of a Committee on the Platform was put on hold until the other committees finished their work. The Committee on Organization was the first to report back to the full convention, and nominated John G. Chapman of Maryland as the permanent president of the convention, as well as numerous vice presidents from multiple states. Objections were made, and were overruled, seeking to delay the election of permanent officers and any other business until after the Committee on Credentials reported its recommendations as to who was and was not a proper delegate. The convention then voted to be governed by the procedural rules of the House of Representatives and to allot to each state the number of votes in nominating the presidential and vice presidential candidate equal to that state's total votes in the Electoral College. Both of these were common rules of the conventions held by both major parties in the era. No doubt sensing the divisions in the hall, newly elected convention president Chapman addressed his colleagues assembled in his home state of Maryland and urged unity: "We meet here as Whigs, we meet here as brothers ... I know of no South, or North, East or West, I know but one country, its interests and happiness, as identified with the great Whig Party ... we may differ as to men, but we do not differ as to principles."[53]

One act of unity on the convention's first day was a presentation by the delegates from Philadelphia to the delegates from Kentucky of a large, framed medallion of the great Whig Henry Clay. As the convention was meeting, it was known by all that Clay was on his deathbed in Washington. A few months earlier, in March, Clay had endorsed Fillmore for the nomination, no doubt antagonistic to the nomination of another military leader, Scott, by his party, having twice been bested in the nomination race by two other generals, Harrison and Taylor, whom he felt were politically inept and intellectually inferior. By the time the convention opened in June, Clay was noted to be "more feeble than ever in body ... [and] gives his thoughts no longer to the affairs of the world that he is soon to depart from."[54] The Great Compromiser would die two weeks later, on June 29, 1852. The man who was once famously reported to have said "I had rather be right than be president" died without ever achieving the office he sought for most of his adult life and lost, either in the general election or in the nomination process, in almost every campaign from 1824 to 1848.

On the evening prior to the convention's opening session, the delegations from the southern states met at Carroll Hall and approved what was referred to as the "Southern Platform" for presentation to, and adoption by, the convention.[55] Item number eight of the proposed platform contained the finality provision that was the primary source of the division between northern and southern Whigs. It provided: "That the series of resolutions known as the Compromise ... are recommended and acquiesced in by the Whig Party of the United States, as a settlement in principle and substance ... a final settlement of the dangerous and exciting subjects which they embrace."[56] When this "Southern Platform" was read to the convention on the afternoon of the opening session, its full embrace of the finality of the Compromise angered many northern delegates.

On the second day of the convention, June 18, 1852, there was little substantive work done. Speeches were the agenda for the day. The emotions of those present were evident as delegates and the gallery provided loud applause and vocal approval to various speakers who took to the floor. These demonstrations prompted President Chapman to chide the delegates, saying that "demonstrations of applause [are] unbecoming the dignity of American citizens."[57] The convention then decided to go ahead and name a Committee on the Platform, with one member from each state.

On the third day, June 19, 1852, the Committee on Credentials reported its recommendations, which primarily concerned several disputed delegate seats in New York. Since the committee, consisting of one member from each state, diluted the support of Scott, as might be expected, it recommended that the disputed seats go to Fillmore men. The convention approved the recommendation. The Committee on the Platform also reported on June 19 and recommended adoption of a platform that had only minor changes from the "Southern Platform" that had been presented to the convention previously, including its finality provision as to the Compromise of 1850. The report of this committee was approved by a vote of 227 for and 66 against, with the New York and Ohio delegates comprising a large proportion of the negative votes.[58] Thus, the Scott campaign managers, thought to have the largest block of delegates, were unable to control the reports of the committees and were now saddled with a pro-compromise platform that they did not want, and with the decision to award the disputed New York delegate seats to their primary opponent. There were reports that the Scott team had advised pro–Scott delegates that they were free to vote for the platform, as a gesture of conciliation to the South.[59] Still, it remained to be seen whether this generosity would be reciprocated and whether the pre-convention frontrunner would be derailed.

The convention then proceeded, on a Friday evening, to its main business of the nomination of a presidential candidate. The race was tight. On the first ballot, there were 133 votes for Fillmore, 131 votes for Scott, and 29 votes for Webster. The president won every southern vote except one, and about fifteen scattered northern votes. Scott took most of the North, except for New England, which went to Webster.[60] Through six ballots that evening, the votes fluctuated little, and the convention adjourned for the day.[61] Despite Webster's paltry showing, his men in Baltimore refused to withdraw his name, apparently on firm instructions from Webster himself. A Fillmore supporter wrote to the president shortly after the convention that the Websterites in Baltimore "seemed to me to act like a parcel of school boys, waiting for the sky to fall, that they might catch larks."[62]

In a marathon session on Saturday, June 20, the convention plodded through an additional forty ballots. Again, few votes changed, but the slightest changes in the balloting resulted in applause or disapproval from the delegates and the large crowd in the gallery. On a hot Baltimore summer day, "iced water and fans were considered indispensable requisites for the occasion."[63] The monotony of the voting led the chairmen of some delegations, who reported their state's votes to the full convention, to make the most their moment in the spotlight. On one ballot, Maine voted for "Old Chippewa, General Scott," referring to one of Scott's ancient battle victories in the War of 1812. On another, Maine referred to him as "the hero of Mexico," referring to Scott's more recent military exploits. North Carolina casts its votes for "the great defender of the Constitution" and "the model president," Millard Fillmore. Any observer of modern political conventions, with their flowering roll call descriptions of states and candidates, can readily see how far this art has progressed over the years. As the roll calls went on, ladies in the gallery above the convention floor tossed bouquets of flowers down to delegates supporting their favorite candidate.[64] By early evening on Saturday, the stalemate continued. A resolution was proposed to declare a winner by a plurality vote, instead of a majority, if no candidate had attained a majority by the fiftieth ballot. This required a suspension of the convention's rules and, as such, needed a two-thirds vote, and was soundly defeated with only three votes in its favor.[65]

In the midst of the drudgery of the balloting, controversy was added on Saturday afternoon when word of a *New York Times* article published that morning spread through the convention like wildfire. One of the pro–Scott delegates from New York was Henry J. Raymond, who happened to be the editor of the *New York Times*.[66] Raymond was a close ally of

New York senator William Seward, who was hated in the South for his strong anti-slavery views, and who was one of Scott's primary backers and promoters. Raymond had telegraphed his newspaper from Baltimore with a story reporting that a deal had been struck and that northerners on the platform committee had agreed to support the pro–Compromise platform because "Kentucky, Tennessee, Virginia and one or two others will give Scott the nomination.... The Northern Whigs gave way on the Platform, with this understanding."[67] Outraged members of the platform committee, from the North and the South, took to the floor and denied any such bargain and defended their honor. Following this controversy, the balloting continued. During the fortieth ballot, convention president Chapman "became so much fatigued from his labors" that he handed over his gavel to one of his vice presidents. At 7:00 P.M., the voting continued and the gaslights in the packed hall were lit. After forty-six ballots, Scott had 134 votes (up 3 from the first ballot), Fillmore had 127 votes (down 6 from the first ballot), and Webster had 31 votes (up 2 from the first ballot). (A Virginia delegate left Baltimore on Saturday, which accounts for the missing vote.[68]) At that point, with the stalemate continuing on Saturday evening, the convention adjourned until Monday.

Prior to the convention, Fillmore had written a letter withdrawing from the race and gave it to one of his close friends from New York and one of his floor leaders in Baltimore, George R. Babcock, along with a cover letter to Babcock. In the cover letter, he instructed Babcock, whenever he deemed it proper, to present the letter to the convention's presiding officer. He directed, "In determining the proper time ... you will consider only the cause in which we are engaged.... You will be careful to guard against any premature act or disclosure which might embarrass my friends ... while ... you will not suffer my name to be dragged into a contest for a nomination which I have never sought, [and] do not now seek."[69] Babcock chose to keep the letter in his pocket, apparently after surveys of many Fillmore delegates revealed that not enough of them would be willing to shift to Webster to give Webster the nomination and, thus, presenting the letter would only guarantee a Scott victory.

The day off on Sunday gave each candidate's managers an extra day for attempted deals, the twisting of arms, and more politicking. Obviously, a deal between the Fillmore and Webster forces, who were philosophically aligned, would have been the logical move and would have provided enough votes to secure the nomination. Intriguing offers were put on the table. The Fillmore men proposed that, if Webster could increase his total to forty votes from the North, then Fillmore would defer and his delegates would go to Webster. If, however, Webster could not break the threshold of forty northern votes in Monday morning's balloting, he would then be the one to release his delegates to Fillmore. Webster's men rejected the proposal. Key Fillmore managers took the train to Washington over the weekend to plead with Webster personally, to no avail.[70] One Fillmore delegate who met with Webster late on Saturday urged him to withdraw and endorse Fillmore, only to be sternly rebuffed. He warned Webster that it was a "fearful responsibility you are about to assume by defeating the true Whig party by delaying action."[71] A second, more cunning deal was then proposed by the Fillmore men. If four Webster delegates would shift to Fillmore on each ballot, until Fillmore reached 145 votes (4 short of the nomination), panicked Scott delegates would likely switch to Webster, in order to stop the Webster slide and prevent Fillmore's nomination. It was proposed that, if Webster could get seventy-five northern votes through this process, then Fillmore's team would deliver another seventy-five of their votes to Webster and the nomination would be his. If Webster could not get the seventy-five northern votes on his own through this process, then he would drop out and his delegates would go to Fillmore. The Webster team also rejected this proposal.[72]

A chance visit of an Ohio delegate with the president on Sunday night may have determined the outcome of the race for the nomination. S. W. Ely was the lone Fillmore supporter in the large Ohio delegation, which was otherwise composed of Scott supporters. After the Saturday session, Ely took the train to Washington "with the purpose of getting out of the seething maelstrom at Baltimore" and visited an old friend, John L. Taylor, who was a congressman from Ohio. The two met and discussed the standoff in Baltimore and the real possibility of no nomination at all coming from the convention: "Threats had been made in various quarters of an adjournment 'in a row,' thus aborting the attempt to make a nomination and thus 'breaking up the party.'" On Sunday evening, as Ely and Taylor were walking in front of the White House, debating whether to call upon the president or not, the doors suddenly opened and they were summoned inside. There, they were introduced to President Fillmore and his secretary of the treasury, Thomas Corwin, who were having tea. The president, who had never met Ely before, commented that "my friends are very persistent" in Baltimore and noted that he had received votes from one delegate from Ohio (Ely's vote) and one from Pennsylvania. Ely was unsure whether Fillmore was aware that he was speaking to his lone Ohio supporter or not. Fillmore stated that it was the principles of the party that concerned him most and he lamented the possibility of an adjournment of the convention in disarray and without any nomination. The president told his guests, "If any friend of mine is under the impression that it would give me more pleasure to see them do so than to fix the choice upon Mr. Webster or Gen. Scott, he is very mistaken." As he took the early Monday morning train back to Baltimore, Ely mulled over the president's comments.[73]

While all the weekend deals between the Fillmore and Webster men in Baltimore were being proposed and rejected, President Fillmore and his chief cabinet officer, Secretary of State Webster, who were generally of a like mind on political issues and who were clearly opposed to the nomination of Scott, sat in Washington a few blocks from one another and made no attempt on their own to contact each other or to meet and break the deadlock. The two strong-willed men would eventually each defer to the other, but not until Monday.[74] On Monday morning, as Webster's son, Fletcher, was leaving to board the train to Baltimore to return to the convention, his father gave him a letter finally agreeing to have his name withdrawn. The secretary of state then had a note sent over to Fillmore at the White House the same morning, advising that "I have sent a communication to Baltimore, this morning to have an end put to the pending controversy. I think it most probable that you will be nominated by 1 o'clock." In response, the president sent a note over to his secretary of state saying, no, it was he who was withdrawing: "I had intimated to my friends, who left last evening and this morning, a strong desire to have my name withdrawn, which I assume will be done unless the knowledge of your communication, should prevent it."[75] But it was too late and their delay, as events in Baltimore would unfold that morning, only ensured that both would end up losers and that Winfield Scott would win the nomination.

When the convention resumed on Monday morning, there was "intense excitement" inside the Maryland Institute. All believed the day of decision was at hand. Before the nominating process resumed, however, a Georgia delegate rose to address unfinished business of a personal nature from Saturday. He wanted Henry J. Raymond, who had been named as a replacement delegate from New York, expelled from the convention over the article that Raymond, as editor of the *New York Times*, had written in his newspaper on Saturday alleging that there was a deal among three southern delegations (Georgia, Tennessee, and Virginia) to trade their votes for the nomination to Scott in exchange for the support of some northern delegates for the proposed "Southern Platform" endorsing the finality of the Compromise of

1850. According to the Georgian, the honor of the South had been challenged: "Has the day come when the representatives of a free people, assembled in Convention, are to be charged with corrupt bargaining and intrigue, when if any of one them were guilty of such conduct he ought to be expelled?" Unless Raymond produced the names of the southern delegates who engaged in this treachery, it was argued, he should be expelled from the convention. Raymond, not backing down from the challenge, responded that the article did not specifically accuse anyone of wrongdoing. It just reported that it was "believed" by some northern Whigs that some southern delegations would support Scott on later ballots and, based on this "understanding," the northern Whigs decided to support the proposed platform. In other words, in Raymond's view, he only reported that the northern Whigs were acting on a belief or a suspicion, not a brokered deal. A defiant Raymond declared, "If this be treason or slander, make the most of it." The convention, wanting to move on to the more important matter of nominating a presidential candidate and likely not wanting to make an enemy of one of its own going into an election campaign, who also happened to be the editor of the *New York Times*, voted to lay on the table the Georgia delegate's expulsion resolution, which put an end to the controversy.[76] Whether or not there was a deal in this instance, if every agreement reached at a political convention to trade votes resulted in the expulsion of all of the involved delegates, there would be plenty of empty seats on the floor of many a convention.

The voting process then resumed with the forty-seventh ballot. Scott inched closer on each ballot to the required 149 votes for the nomination: 135, then 137, then 139, then 142, 142 again, and then 148. Bouquets were thrown from the gallery to various delegations as their votes were announced. Ely, the lone Ohio delegate for Fillmore, who had met with the president in the White House on Sunday night, resolved to change his vote, given the president's comments that he would rather see one of his opponents nominated than to have the convention break up with no nominee. As Ely announced his change of vote from Fillmore to Scott and attempted to explain his reasoning to the convention, he was not well received. He recalled the scene years later: "I began my remarks, but was soon choked off by hisses and groans from my compatriots of the week preceding. The fair Baltimoreans, who had showered me with bouquets, now seemed almost frantic with passion, and if one might imagine such hissing beauties were capable of communicating a virile principle, they would have instantly done it. But, by stubbornly standing until the clamor subsided ... I got through satisfactorily, and inaugurated the stampede for Scott."[77] Finally, on the fifty-third ballot, Scott went over the top by ten votes and won the nomination with 159 votes, compared to 112 for Fillmore and 21 for Webster. By the time of the last ballot, the Webster and Fillmore men who had been dispatched from Washington that morning had undoubtedly arrived at the convention in Baltimore, but none was willing to withdraw his candidate's name, nor to defer to the other, despite the stated wishes of their principals. At the end of the last ballot, with Scott victorious, the convention erupted: "The most terrific shouts of applause followed, as also cheering, waving of hats; the ladies waved their handkerchiefs and parasols, the utmost excitement pervading all parts of the room." The sounds of cannon being fired outside the hall were heard. After the noise quieted down, a delegate from New Jersey, where Winfield Scott then resided, took the floor and proclaimed that all of Scott's "associations and feelings were Virginian," as

Opposite: Winfield Scott was the second military hero from the Mexican War to be nominated by the Whigs, who had opposed the war. After winning his party's nomination at a convention held in Baltimore in 1852, Scott's decisive defeat in the election hastened the demise of the party. His vice presidential candidate was William Graham of North Carolina (Library of Congress).

GRAND, NATIONAL, WHIG BANNER.

the Old Dominion was where the general was born. The South had nothing to fear, the New Jerseyan declared, from the nomination of Scott: "The South had been deluded in the belief that her rights were in danger. There were not ten men in Jersey, out of a lunatic asylum, who were in favor of interfering with the rights of the South."[78]

There then occurred another first in American political convention history — a telegraphed acceptance of a presidential nomination. A Tennessee delegate rose and announced that he had a message to read. It was dated from Washington that morning and was from Scott: "Having the honor of being the nominee for president by the Whig National Convention, I shall accept the same, with the platform of principles which the convention has laid down." Delegate Babcock of New York, a Fillmore floor manager and the man who had the president's withdrawal letter in his pocket during the entire convention, rose and stated of the pro–Compromise platform, "The adoption of the platform will bring more joy to Mr. Fillmore's heart than a nomination itself." After more speeches endorsing the nomination of Scott, on a somber note, a delegate from Kentucky rose to announce that this would be the last Whig convention to occur during the lifetime of the party's founder, Henry Clay, who who was breathing his last breaths in nearby Washington. A resolution honoring Clay was passed. It read, in part: "To the venerable patriot in his last moments we tender the language of our inexpressible sympathy and regard, with the assurance that when he may be no more on earth, in our hearts and in the hearts of our children, he will never die."[79] If he had full possession of his faculties, Clay, who died two weeks later, would likely have been irate that his beloved Whig Party had, for the third time in the last four elections, nominated another military hero as its presidential nominee. The convention then adjourned until 5:30 P.M., the only key remaining issue being the filling of the second spot on the Whig ticket.

When the gathering resumed for its evening session, it was announced through a telegraphic message received from Wilmington that "Delaware is now firing one hundred guns for Scott!" The nomination of Scott was made unanimous, resulting in more shouts, applause, and more bouquets of flowers being thrown from the gallery to the floor of the convention. Resolutions designed to soothe the losers were adopted. Fillmore's stewardship in the presidency was praised and a resolution was passed stating that "the Whigs of the United States will ever look on his administration as one of the most successful and patriotic in our history." Webster was honored for being second only "to the illustrious Clay" in the hearts of Whigs and as one who in the future "will be named with praise on every sea and every land in which the banner of the Union may be unfurled." With respect to the vice presidency, two ballots were needed before William A. Graham of North Carolina was nominated to be Scott's running mate.[80] Graham had served as United States senator and governor of the Tar Heel State and as secretary of the navy under President Fillmore. His nomination was seen as a way to placate the disappointed supporters of Fillmore at the convention and also as a way to strengthen the Whig ticket in the South, where Scott was not popular.[81]

How does one explain to an elder statesman that his lifelong dream of the presidency was not to be, and that he not only lost the nomination but also never received more than thirty-two out of almost three hundred votes cast on any ballot at his party's convention? This unenviable task fell to Daniel Webster's Bay State friend and colleague Rufus Choate, who went directly to Webster's house in Washington from the convention in Baltimore. On the day before the convention, Choate, who knew his trip to Baltimore was for a lost cause, had visited Webster "to tell him the sad truth of the matter, but found him so strong in the belief that he would be nominated that it seemed cruel to undeceive him, and he made no attempt to do so." After the convention, Webster received the news with bitterness. Later, "Choate spoke of the interview as one of the most affecting he had ever had, saying that the appearance of the family and everything about the house seemed to remind him of the scenes he had witnessed in families which had lost a beloved member."[82] Webster would never endorse Scott, and died in October 24, 1852, two weeks before the election, many believed due to his disappointment over losing the Whig nomination and his last chance for the presidency.

In the last moments of the convention, when a delegate proposed that the next Whig convention in 1856 be held in Louisville, Kentucky, another delegate rose in opposition and proclaimed that Baltimore was the only place to hold a convention: "In no other part of the Union ... can you find such a hall as this. I venture to remark that there can be no National Convention assembled any where in the Union where such arrangements can be made as have been in this city — so much pains taken, and such satisfaction given.... It is ungrateful on the part of any man to move to change the place of meeting." All resolutions fixing the location of the next convention were defeated, it being decided that the location would be determined at the appropriate time by the party's national committee. Baltimore was praised for "the hospitality and kindness extended" and one portion of the city's population was singled out for special recognition: "During the long time we have been in session we have been honored with the bright eyes and the sunny smiles of the ladies of Maryland, which, to us, have been like hope in a stormy sky. I therefore move, as a compliment, that we give three cheers for their attendance." The cheers were delivered "with stentorian lungs." At 8:00 P.M., the convention adjourned *sine die*.[83]

The delegates did not have much time to relax for, at half past the same hour, a grand Whig ratification meeting began in Monument Square. Speakers located on the east side of the court house, facing Monument Square, addressed a crowd estimated to be ten thousand strong. Given the uncertainly until midday as to the identity of the nominees, the white silken banner above the speakers generically proclaimed that "We Ratify the Nominations." Southern speakers dominated the rally, and they praised the platform, more so than the nominee. Referring to Scott's telegraphed acceptance received that day, one speaker "thanked God for the platform and that Gen. Scott had jumped upon it with lightning speed." The rally continued until midnight.[84] Northern Whigs had their preferred candidate, but southern Whigs had their platform. Little did anyone at the time know that the gathering that just ended would be the last full national convention of the Whig Party.

The Campaign and Election

With the platform of both parties supporting the Compromise of 1850, the campaign of 1852 was fought more on personal attacks on the candidates than on the issues. Pierce was attacked by the Whigs as a coward and a drunk. The Democrats portrayed Scott as vain and he was ridiculed. Two statements he had made in the past were used against him for their comical implications. During the Mexican War, upset with control of military decisions by Democratic politicians in Washington, Scott had written that he was more concerned about "a fire upon my rear" than the enemy in front of him. As in modern times, juvenile bathroom humor existed in the nineteenth century, and the comment was taken out of context and used to embarrass the portly Scott, who weighed more than 350 pounds and who had an "ample posterior." Also during the Mexican War, Scott had missed a visit in the field from a Washington official and explained that he had been eating "a hasty plate of soup" at the time. The fact that soup is impossible to eat from a plate was seen as humorous and Democrats started showing up at Scott rallies around the country, handing out soup bowls, to drive home the ridicule.[85] Scott began to write letters to various supporters and newspapers in June. Democrats were elated at the potential for another embarrassing statement from Scott and proclaimed they would "furnish [him] liberally with stationery."[86]

In mid–September, in a break with precedent and much to the dismay of his Whig handlers, Scott, who was still the commanding general of the United States Army, turned a trip to inspect a military hospital in Blue Lick, Kentucky, into a campaign swing, making several speeches along the way, in Pittsburgh, Cleveland, Columbus, and other cities. He probably should have stayed at home, as the trip and his speeches were not well received. The five-week trip highlighted his weaknesses as a person and as a candidate. He did not address the issues, but spoke of past military exploits. He was criticized for not resigning his military position once nominated, and for then using a military trip to Kentucky as a cover for a campaign swing.[87] In an awkward effort to reach out to immigrant voters, he responded to one Irishman in a crowd that "I love to hear the Irish brogue. I have heard it before on many battlefields, and I wish to hear it many times more!"[88] He repeated in most of his speeches how much he loved and respected the foreign-born, which was criticized by the Democrats as pandering and beneath a presidential candidate, and worried the Whigs that such blatant courtship of Catholic immigrants would alienate many potential Protestant Whig voters.[89]

For his part, Pierce followed the standard script of presidential candidates of the era — he stayed at home and did very little. His college friend, the famous writer Nathaniel Hawthorne, wrote a flattering campaign biography of Pierce that was widely circulated.[90] Meanwhile, he was portrayed by the Whigs as a drunkard, a coward, and anti–Catholic. Pierce had a drinking problem in earlier years, but there was no evidence that it continued. The charges of cowardice stemmed from an incident in the Mexican War when he fainted and had to be carried from the battlefield. Linking both allegations, Whigs joked that the Democratic nominee was the "Hero of Many a Well Fought Bottle."[91] Pierce wrote letters during the campaign defending his record in the war, and wartime colleagues noted that he had sustained a severe knee injury the day before the fainting incident and was in great pain, likely causing the episode. The anti–Catholic charges arose from the fact that the New Hampshire Constitution still contained in 1852 a provision barring Catholics from serving in the state legislature or as governor. Pierce's New Hampshire friends responded that he opposed the provision, but that he was but one man and that changing the state constitution required the vote of two-thirds of the voters in the state.[92]

When the votes were counted, it was an electoral landslide for the Democrats. Pierce won twenty-seven states, compared to only four (Kentucky, Massachusetts, Tennessee, and Vermont) for Scott. The tally was 254 electoral votes for Pierce, with only 42 for Scott. Not since James Monroe ran unopposed in 1820 had there been such a lopsided electoral result in a presidential election.[93] The popular vote was closer, but was still a clear Democratic victory. Pierce had 1,601,274 votes, compared to 1,386,580 for Scott. There was also a candidate of the Free-Soil Party in the race, John P. Hale, who did not influence the outcome and received 156,667 votes, which was only half of Van Buren's total when he ran on the Free-Soil ticket in 1848.[94] For the second time in three elections, a "dark horse" Democratic candidate nominated at a convention in Baltimore had won the presidency. The Whigs were soundly beaten, in both the North and the South, and the question began to be asked — was the 1852 election their death knell, or could they recover?

CHAPTER 9

1856: New and Old: Parties in Transition

Come all ye men of every state, our creed is broad and fair;
Buchanan is our candidate, to take the White House chair.

We'll turn our backs on Frémont, for his principles endorse;
A woolly-headed platform, upon a woolly horse.

But let our hearts for Union be, the North and South be one!
They've worked together manfully, together, they'll work on.[1]

Democratic campaign song, 1856

The Compromise of 1850 had placed a bandage over the slavery issue. When both the Democratic and Whig platforms in 1852 endorsed the "finality" of the compromise, and with the election of Pierce, the wound seemed safely cauterized for the foreseeable future. It was not to be. All this changed in 1854 with the passage of the Kansas-Nebraska Act — the bandage was ripped off, the underlying wound became more severe, and the patient, the United States of America, was set on a path to dismemberment.

Senator Stephen A. Douglas of Illinois introduced his act concerning the Nebraska Territory in the Senate in early January 1854. This land was part of the Louisiana Purchase and, under the Missouri Compromise of 1820, slavery was barred from it, since it was north of the 36 degree, 30 minute north latitude dividing line established by that law between free and slave land. Douglas' motives were uncertain: "Whether he was motivated by personal ambition, Missouri politics, presidential aspirations, railroad rivalries, or just playing the part of an innocent or naïve fool, no one knew."[2] Slave owners in Missouri wanted to expand westward, and Douglas was being pressured by his Democratic colleague in the Senate from Missouri, David R. Atchison, to open up the territory to slave owners. Douglas had business interests in railroads, and in real estate, that would benefit from more rapid westward expansion. Being from Illinois, Douglas would stand to benefit politically from more western states being created. He also needed to mend fences with the South. Douglas had been a key proponent of the Compromise of 1850, with its Fugitive Slave Act, and southerners felt northerners were nullifying the law by not enforcing it and permitting local procedures at the state and local level to evade it.[3] One historian makes a convincing argument that Douglas' primary motivation for introducing a statehood bill for the Nebraska Territory was to secure a northern route for a transcontinental railroad, a project of which he was the leading promoter. Since the railroad would be funded by the sale of government lands adjacent to its route, the territory through which it would pass had to be organized as a prerequisite to construction. Southern senators favored a southerly route for the railroad. Douglas, seeking southern votes for his proposed northern railroad route, sought to gain them by agreeing to the option of slavery in any new territories or states formed out of the land.[4] Most likely, multiple factors played a role in the mind of Stephen Douglas. What is more important for history is not the motivation of the actors, but the law that resulted and its impact on the country.

As it emerged from Congress, the Kansas-Nebraska Act created two new territories, Kansas and Nebraska, and provided that slavery in those territories would be determined by a vote of the citizens residing there. This was the "popular sovereignty" doctrine that had been a part of the Compromise of 1850 as applied to the New Mexico and Utah territories. But those territories were not part of the Louisiana Purchase and were not subject to the slavery prohibition contained in the Missouri Compromise. The Douglas bill, as originally written, did not explicitly overrule the Missouri Compromise. Thus, under Douglas' initial proposal, slavery would be prohibited in these territories under the Missouri Compromise, until they were organized and until territorial legislatures made a pro or con decision on slavery. Southerners, however, successfully amended the bill to explicitly repeal the Missouri Compromise as it applied to the Kansas and Nebraska territories, and it was in this form that the bill passed Congress in March 1854 and was signed into law by President Pierce. The irony of all this was that while the Kansas-Nebraska Act passed Congress and became law, Douglas' transcontinental railroad bill, which likely inspired it, failed in the Congress. It would not be until the next decade that a railroad to the Pacific would be authorized, and "no track would be laid until the sons of the northern and southern Democrats who had stood together to pass the [Kansas-Nebraska] bill were killing one another on the battlefields of Virginia."[5]

As one commentator has noted, the passage of the Kansas-Nebraska Act "opened a Pandora's box of evils" for the nation.[6] Extremists in both North and South were emboldened. Pro-slavery and anti-slavery settlers rushed into Kansas, causing much bloodshed and leading to the establishment of competing territorial governments. The legislation hastened a realignment of the nation's existing political parties. The country's first totally sectional party, the Republican Party, emerged shortly after the act's 1854 passage and had as its founding tenet no expansion of slavery into any territory, period. The Whig Party, which always had a tenuous alliance between its northern and southern factions, and which had been greatly weakened by its losses in 1852 election, was essentially destroyed. The Democratic Party was badly split, but survived.

Into this cauldron, a new political movement was thrown into the mix. Nativism and resentment of the latest wave of immigrants had always been present in the United States. In the late 1840s and early 1850s, more than two million European immigrants came to America. In many northeastern cities, a large percentage of the population was foreign born. Citizens were concerned over increases in crime that resulted from this influx. Immigrants, they believed, took jobs from native-born Americans. Moreover, religion played a significant role, as most immigrants were Catholics and were resented in heavily Protestant America. It was feared that this immigrant tide would take over the country. The leader of U.S. Catholics, Archbishop John Hughes of New York, in 1850 gave voice to these fears by proclaiming that Protestantism was on the decline and that world domination was the goal of the Catholic Church:

> The object we hope to accomplish in time is to convert all Pagan nations, and all Protestant nations.... There is no secrecy in all this.... Everybody should know it. Everybody should know that we have for our mission to convert the world — including the inhabitants of the United States, — the people of the cities, and the people of the country, the officers of the navy, and the marines, commanders of the army. The Legislatures, the Senate, the Cabinet, the President, and all![7]

As a result of this tide of immigration, secret anti-immigrant and anti–Catholic societies, the most predominant of which was called the Order of the Star Spangled Banner, arose and began to have political influence. This order's members formed a political movement and pledged to vote only for native-born American citizens for all political offices, and to oppose all foreigners and Roman Catholics for such offices. Once initiated, new members were then let in on the rituals of the order — secret passwords, signs, and grips, as well as signals of recognition and distress.[8] When asked if they belonged to the order, members responded, "I know nothing about it." Hence, they came to be referred to as the Know-Nothing Party, although their official name was the American Party. This third-party political movement initially became a force in state and congressional elections in 1854. The Know-Nothings were popular in states that had areas with large immigrant populations. In Baltimore, where it was estimated that one quarter of the city's residents were foreign born, most having come from Germany and Ireland, the Know-Nothings won control of the city government in the mid–1850s, no doubt a reaction to the influx of the large number of immigrants in the city.[9]

By 1856, the Know-Nothing movement was of sufficient strength nationwide that it was destined to play a role in the election of the next president of the United States. Ironically, this movement was the antithesis of the first major third-party political movement in the country a generation earlier, the Anti-Mason Party. One was founded on and promoted an organization of secrecy and rituals, while the other denounced them. Somewhat surprisingly, there were alliances between the Know-Nothings and the emerging Republicans, who needed votes from each other to win elections.[10] As the battle for the White House in 1856 began to heat up, this nativist movement, along with support for or opposition to the Kansas-Nebraska Act, would be the key issues before the country.

American/Know-Nothing Convention

The American Party, or the Know-Nothing Party, kicked off the 1856 campaign season with its presidential nominating convention in Philadelphia on George Washington's birthday, February 22, 1856. By then, the party was no longer merely a secret society but a formal political movement and it wanted the force and publicity that a national nominating convention would provide. A total of 227 delegates from the twenty-seven states attended. It was not a successful meeting for the new party, for its members quickly learned that the sectional differences over slavery that divided the major parties also outweighed their shared bonds of nativism and secret rituals. When the northern delegates at the Philadelphia convention proposed a platform plank prohibiting slavery north of the Missouri Compromise line (thereby reinstating that law and repealing the Kansas-Nebraska Act), and which was rejected by the convention, approximately fifty delegates from eight northern states delegates bolted. The remaining delegates of the American Party convention, mostly southern, then nominated Whig former president Millard Fillmore of New York for president and Andrew Jackson Donelson of Tennessee (former Democrat and nephew of Old Hickory himself) for vice president.[11] They adopted a platform proclaiming that "Americans must rule America," favored the election of only native-born citizens for public office, and advocated a twenty-one-year naturalization period for American citizenship. The platform was noncommittal on the slavery issue, and did not repudiate the Kansas-Nebraska Act.[12]

The northerners who had bolted from the American Party convention in February met in New York City beginning on June 12, more than three months later, for their own convention. Calling themselves the "North Americans," the pre-convention favorite for their presidential nomination was Judge McLean of Ohio, a perennial also-ran of various parties in past elections. Republicans feared that a McLean nomination by the North Americans would splinter the antislavery vote and they came up with a cunning, if unethical, plan. They wanted the Republicans and the North Americans to nominate the same candidate, but they did not want their favored candidate, General John C. Frémont, nominated first by the North Americans. They believed that if that occurred, the stigma of nativism would attach to him and alienate potential Republican voters. The calendar presented a dilemma, as the North American convention was scheduled the week before the Republican convention and the North American nominee would have to be named first.[13] Republican leaders, including New Yorkers Greeley and Weed, were present at the convention of the North Americans and, purportedly with the aid of around $30,000 paid to various North American Party leaders and delegates, a deal was struck.[14] A stalking horse plan was decided upon and it was played out to perfection. McLean was dumped as a candidate and, on June 16, Nathaniel P. Banks of Massachusetts, a Republican and the Speaker of the House of Representatives, was nominated as the presidential candidate of the North Americans. Under the secret plan, Banks delayed in accepting the nomination and the convention took a recess for a few days. On June 18, the Republican Party convention met in Philadelphia and nominated Frémont as its standard-bearer. At that point, Banks declined his nomination by the North Americans and urged support for Frémont. The North Americans reconvened on June 19. Over the protests of many of the rank-and-file delegates, who knew nothing of the deal (in this, they truly were Know-Nothings) they also made Frémont their nominee.[15] Of this scheme, one reporter wrote: "May his Satanic Majesty have a place especially hot and sulfurous wherein to roast such humbuggery."[16] Those sly Republicans had just taken over the northern portion of the nativist movement and had succeeded in doing it in such a way as to not alienate their antislavery base.

Democratic Convention

Before the shenanigans of the American Party conventions were fully played out, the Democrats met, beginning on June 2, 1856, for their seventh presidential nominating convention. For the first time in the history of the party, the Democratic convention was not held in Baltimore. This time around, Cincinnati was the host city and the site was Smith & Nixon's Hall, a performance hall and auditorium built by a piano manufacturing company of the same name, which had an adjacent factory.[17] The early June temperature was hot in Cincinnati and one local company sold Ceylon hats to the delegates "to help them keep cool heads in these exciting times."[18] The three leading contenders were the incumbent president, Franklin Pierce, Senator Stephen Douglas of Illinois, and James Buchanan of Pennsylvania. Lewis Cass was again seeking the nomination, but had little support. Pierce and Douglas were closely identified with the divisive Kansas-Nebraska Act, while Buchanan had the good fortune of having been out of the country serving as the United States minister to Great Britain under President Pierce and had avoided taking a position on either side of the issue during the controversy.[19] The Buchanan men walked around the city sporting blue ribbons on their lapels with silver badges shaped to form the Pennsylvania coat of arms.[20] Most observers thought that Buchanan was the favorite going into the convention, but, one observer wrote, the rumors of "plots and counterplots are so numerous, however, that nothing is certain."[21]

Befitting its western location, the opening moments of the convention resembled a barroom brawl. As a speaker was beginning to address the delegates and read the resolution of the party calling for the convention, a loud commotion was heard near the doors at the main entrance to the hall. The doorkeepers, whose job it was to admit only those with tickets to the floor, had been forcibly shoved aside, and in strode approximately twenty Missourians known as the Benton delegation. There were two competing delegations from Missouri in Cincinnati and the other one had presented "prima facie evidence of their regular election" to a subcommittee of the Committee on Arrangements prior to the convention and had been determined to be the legitimate representatives from the Show Me State. Not liking that decision, the Benton group's leader, "a tall impressive looking man, stalked majestically down the aisle, with a military tread, his head erect, and his cane elevated in his hand like a Baronial mace, exclaiming, 'We are the true Democracy of Missouri, and are entitled to seats in this Convention, by God!'" He was followed by his delegation, and seats they took, plopping themselves down on empty chairs and refusing to budge, to the dismay of everyone in the hall. A reporter observed that it "seemed as though a serious riot was about to take place." After a few minutes of "prudent, private counsel" between convention officials and the leader of the renegade Missourians, the situation was defused. It was agreed that the issue of the competing Missouri delegations would be referred to the convention's Committee on Credentials. Once the committee was formed, the gate-crashers got up and marched out of the hall, confident that they had accomplished their mission.[22]

The excitement over, the convention got down to its opening business. In addition to Missouri, it was announced that there were also two competing delegations from New York, reminiscent of the dispute at the 1848 convention between the feuding Barnburner and Hunker delegations from the Empire State. The two 1856 factions had formed from the Hunkers, with many of the anti-slavery Barnburners having bolted the party entirely for the Free-Soil Party in 1848. One faction, the Softs, welcomed the remnants of the Barnburners back into the party, while the other, the Hards, took a hard line on readmitting any of the defectors to the ranks of the Democratic Party. After an opening prayer, the standard committees on credentials, permanent organization, and the platform were formed, consisting of one member from each of the thirty-one states at the convention, with New York excluded from representation.[23]

When the convention resumed for its second day, Tuesday, June 3, the Committee on Permanent Organization reported its recommendation of John E. Ward of Georgia as permanent president of the convention, which was approved by the delegates, along with vice presidents and secretaries from each state except New York.[24] Ward was a Buchanan supporter and his selection by the committee seemed to indicate that the Buchanan forces controlled the majority of the state delegations and, thereby, would control the committees. In his opening address, Ward warned that "our land is convulsed with factions" and criticized the extremists on both sides of the slavery issue that dominated the political debate of the times. One faction, the Republican Party, he described as

> a party which, in the pride of power, assumes to dictate to the consciences of men, and which would allow no man to be fit to serve his country who bowed not with them at the same altar.
>
> The other faction — more dangerous only because it is more numerous — has liberty emblazoned on its banners and deadly treason festering in its heart. It is engaged in an unholy crusade against the Constitution ... in the fond help that they may involve in one common ruin all of the glorious recollections of the past, and all our proud anticipations for the future.[25]

The Committee on Credentials then submitted a partial report, finding that the originally seated Missouri delegation was, in fact, the legitimate delegation from that state and should keep its seats.[26] Thus, the gate-crashers from the previous day were excluded, much to the elation of the delegates who had witnessed their actions with contempt. The committee announced that it still needed more time to resolve the issue of the competing New York delegations. With the platform still not ready, there was little else to do and the convention spent the rest of the day arguing about who should be admitted to the galleries, and whether non-delegates should be permitted on the floor. One Pennsylvania delegate proposed reserving the front rows of the gallery for ladies, which aroused the ire of an Indiana delegate, who fumed that, while he "would yield to no man in gallantry," women had no business at a convention and that he would "rather see the vilest Know Nothing or Black Republican in the world there than have the gallery filled with petticoats."[27]

A proposal to let members of the nonvoting delegation from the District of Columbia on the floor and to participate in debates was objected to by one Illinois delegate, who stated that "the object of taking the Convention from Baltimore was to get clear of congressional influence."[28] All of these motions were tabled, as was a similar motion to permit access to the convention floor by members of Congress who were in Cincinnati and who were not delegates.[29]

On its third day, June 4, the convention heard the report from its Committee on Resolutions on the proposed platform for the party. On the slavery issue, the committee strongly endorsed the popular sovereignty policy of the 1864 Kansas-Nebraska Act. The committee recommended that:

> the American Democracy recognize and adopt the principles contained in the organic laws establishing the Territories of Kansas and Nebraska, as embodying the only sound and safe solution of the "slavery question" upon which the great national idea of the people of this whole country can repose in its determined conservation of the Union — NON INTERFERENCE BY CONGRESS WITH SLAVERY IN STATE AND TERRITORITY, OR IN THE DISTRICT OF COLUMBIA.
>
> That by the uniform application of this Democratic principle to the organization of Territories and the admission of new States, with or without domestic Slavery, as they may elect, the equal rights of all the States will be preserved intact.[30]

The platform was unanimously approved, with the exception of some planks dealing with some foreign policy issues, which were voted upon separately later in the day. No votes were cast on the platform from New York, its delegate situation still being unresolved.[31]

Unlike the 1848 Democratic convention, the issue of the competing New York delegations was peacefully resolved when both factions agreed to accept the Solomonic ruling of the convention as to their seating. The majority report from the Committee on Credentials recommended that the New York delegation headed by former governor Horatio Seymour (the "Softs") be given forty-four delegate seats, and that the delegation headed by Samuel Beardsley (the "Hards") be given twenty-six delegate seats, with each delegate entitled to cast one-half vote, as New York had a total of thirty-five votes under the rules adopted by the convention. It also proposed that the unit rule would not apply to New York. The minority report of the Committee on Credentials recommended that each of the two factions be given thirty-five delegate seats, with each being entitled to cast seventeen of New York's delegate votes, with the remaining vote being given on alternate ballots to each faction, and with the Softs being given the first extra vote. The minority report was approved by the convention by a vote of 137 yeas to 123 nays and, surprisingly, both of the feuding camps from the Empire State agreed to this solution.[32]

The convention then proceeded to nominations for the presidency. Once again, the time-honored two-thirds rule used by the Democrats in prior conventions was adopted. Four names were placed in nomination: James Buchanan, the sitting minister to Great Britain; Franklin Pierce, the incumbent president; Lewis Cass, the party's nominee in 1848; and Stephen Douglas, the up-and-coming senator from Illinois. During the convention the Pierce and Douglas forces had colluded and hoped to draw enough votes to deny a two-thirds vote for Buchanan, and to turn the convention to one of them, or to a "dark horse" candidate. They agreed on a plan for Pierce to run strongest first and, if he progressed with each ballot and it appeared as though he could overtake Buchanan, then the Douglas delegates would support him. If, however, Pierce did not gain votes with each ballot, then his supporters would switch their votes to Douglas. On the first ballot, Buchanan led with 135 votes, to 122 for Pierce, 33 for Douglas, and 5 for Cass.[33] After fourteen ballots, Buchanan was gaining and Pierce was faltering, with 152 for Old Buck and 63 for the president.[34] Pursuant to the plan, the New Hampshire delegation withdrew Pierce's name and they endorsed Douglas. Over the next two ballots, Douglas picked up some steam, but never caught Buchanan. The closest he got was 122 votes, compared to 168 for Buchanan.[35] With a total of 296 delegate votes, a tally of 198 was needed under the two-thirds rule for the nomination. On the seventeenth ballot, the Douglas forces, who probably could have held firm and prevented a two-thirds vote for Buchanan, capitulated. A withdrawal letter from Douglas, written from Washington on June 4 and received in Cincinnati by telegraph, was read by W. A. Richardson, Douglas' floor manager. In a "solemn and impressive manner," Richardson read Douglas' words to the delegates:

> From the telegraphic reports in the newspapers, I fear that an embittered state of feeling is being engendered in the Convention, which may endanger the harmony and success of our party. I wish you and all my friends to bear in mind that I have a thousand fold more anxiety for the triumph of our principles than I do for my own personal elevation.
>
> If withdrawal of my name will contribute to the harmony of our party or the success of our cause, I hope you will not hesitate to take the step ... if Mr. Pierce or Mr. Buchanan, or any other statesman who is faithful to the great issues involved in the contest, should receive a majority of the Convention, I earnestly hope that all of my friends will unite in insuring him two thirds, and then in making his nomination unanimous.
>
> S. A. Douglas[36]

On the next ballot, Buchanan won the nomination by a unanimous vote.[37] The Douglas men hoped that their candidate's honorable act would create goodwill and put him in a favored position for the nomination in 1860. A young Kentuckian, John C. Breckinridge, only thirty-five years old (the minimum age permitted under the Constitution for the presidency and vice presidency), received the nomination for vice president on the second ballot over several other candidates, including John A. Quitman of Alabama, who was the preferred choice of many southern delegates. Breckinridge was a delegate to the convention and rose when he was nominated and asked to have his name withdrawn, a request that was ignored.[38]

Buchanan was offered by the Democrats to the country as an experienced and steady hand at the helm of the ship of state. There would be no surprises with Old Buck in the White House: "The Democrats had settled on candidates and policies which represented their wish merely to hold the old structure together. No new faces or policies would be offered to the public; the course of the past decade would remain unaltered and the voters, nervous and fearful of the future, would be offered security, experience, and a continuation of the status

JAMES BUCHANAN,
DEMOCRATIC CANDIDATE FOR PRESIDENT OF THE UNITED STATES.

Like his predecessor Franklin Pierce, James Buchanan of Pennsylvania was a northerner with southern leanings, which enabled him to secure enough cross-sectional votes to win the Democratic nomination at a convention held in Cincinnati in 1856, and to also win the election *(Library of Congress)*.

quo."[39] The next presidential nominating convention to meet during the 1856 campaign would offer a much different vision to the country.

Republican Convention

Two weeks after the Democrats met in Cincinnati, the first presidential nominating convention of the Republican Party met in Philadelphia on June 17, 1856, at the Musical Fund Hall, a structure that had originally been built as a Presbyterian church. It was located at the corner of Locust and what was then called Darien Street. The Philadelphia Musical Fund Society purchased the church in 1823 and remodeled it into a concert hall.[40] By 1856, many of the leading anti-slavery northern Whigs, such as William Seward, Horace Greeley, Thurlow Weed, and others, had formally joined this new party. It was clearly a sectional meeting—there were delegates from all of the free states, but only three border slave states (Delaware, Maryland, and Kentucky) and one southern state (Virginia) sent representatives to Philadelphia. At the convention, a rule was adopted that the nomination would be determined by a majority vote. As a new party, the Republicans established at least one new convention procedure. Each state was allotted three delegate votes for each of its votes in the Electoral College, whereas prior conventions had allotted only one or two. Thus, while only slightly more than half of the states were represented, there were more than 560 voting delegates.[41] With so many delegates, it soon became clear that "the room engaged was entirely too small to contain the half of those who were entitled to spaces." Despite this, more people were admitted to floor. When it was announced that a committee of six from a disaffected group of New York Democrats (called the "Council of One Hundred," once part of the old anti-slavery Barnburners) were present in the hall, they were greeted with enthusiasm. It was moved that they be given seats on the floor, and the New Hampshire delegation even offered to let the honorary guests sit on their laps.[42] The delegates were enthusiastic and uncompromising in their causes — the admission of Kansas as a free state and the prohibition of slavery from all of the territories. Most of the delegates were righteous, serious-minded men who were determined to stop the spread of slavery. As one observer asserted, the gathering seemed more like a "Methodist conference than a political convention."[43]

The delegates heard a fiery opening speech from the convention's temporary president, Judge Robert Emmet of New York:

> We are here for noble and high and holy purposes. They may laugh at us. They may call us Black Republicans and Negro-Worshippers.... They may say that we mean to concentrate and gather under our wings all the odds and ends of the parties — all the isms of the day. Be it so. Let them come to us with all their isms. We will merge them all in that great ism, patriotism....
>
> We come not to treat slavery as a moral question. Slavery is, so far as our functions are concerned with it, a political evil.... Whether it be moral or immoral, it exists here among us, and we must manage it as well as we can. We must repress it. We must prevent it from being, as its nature always urges it to be, aggressive.... We must keep it back....
>
> Let us, then, fellow citizens, proceed to the good work and I trust that the result will be that we will strangle this hydra of the Union which is now menacing our liberty and our peace; that we will extirpate this canker that is eating our very vitals, and extinguish the smouldering fire of treason and disunion that is under our feet at this very moment, and which may burst forth in an instant and swallow up all the fair liberties which have been our boast and pride since the establishment of this Republic.... We have a high duty to perform, and I am sure at the close of this convention the people will say with one acclaim, "Well done, good and faithful servants."[44]

The platform adopted in Philadelphia ratified the party's stance of no extension of slavery into the territories: "We deny the authority of Congress, of a Territorial Legislature, or any individual, or association of individuals, to give legal existence to slavery in any Territory of the United States, while the present Constitution shall be maintained." The platform also denounced the violence in Kansas and called for the admission of Kansas as a free state, denounced polygamy, and endorsed the construction of a transcontinental railroad.[45]

Taking a cue from the old Whig strategy of nominating a popular military figure, key Republican leaders had decided well before the convention that General John C. Frémont would be their strongest candidate. Others seeking the nomination were Ohio governor Salmon P. Chase and another Ohioan, Justice John McLean of the U.S. Supreme Court who, at age seventy-one, was making yet another attempt at the presidency.[46] New York's William Seward also flirted with making a serious run, but held back and his name was withdrawn early in the proceedings. Frémont was the frontrunner going into the convention. A resident of California in 1856, Frémont had gained military fame, not in battle, but as an explorer of the American West. Early in his career, he had explored the Dakotas as a young officer, and had led exploratory expeditions in the 1840s to the Rocky Mountains, to Oregon, and to California.

MUSICAL FUND HALL, PHILADELPHIA, PENNSYLVANIA.

The Musical Fund Hall in Philadelphia was the site of the first Republican Party convention held in 1856. Still standing, the building has been substantially altered and now serves as condominiums *(Library of Congress)*.

Nicknamed "The Pathfinder" in recognition of his western treks, Frémont had published reports from his expeditions and these had made him popular with the public and a household name.[47] Frémont's political skills were slight and, as he was the candidate of a first-time political party, Republican leaders did not really expect him to find a path to the White House in 1856. The goal was to run a respectable race and lay a foundation for future elections. Frémont supported the Republicans on the slavery issue, but he would not be a lightning rod for the opposition, as some other possible Republican nominees would have been. Passionate in nature and rash in judgment, Frémont was only forty-three years old in 1856.[48]

At the convention, before the balloting began, a letter was read from Chase withdrawing his name. Interestingly, just prior to the Chase letter being read, a supporter of McLean had withdrawn his candidate's name, only to announce later in the day that he "withdrew the withdrawal this morning made by him" and that McLean was back in the race. Apparently,

JNO C. FREMONT. WM L. DAYTON.
THE CHAMPIONS OF FREEDOM.

General John C. Frémont earned fame not on the battlefield but as an explorer of the American West. Nicknamed "The Pathfinder," he was the first nominee of the Republican Party for the presidency at the 1856 convention held in Philadelphia. William Dayton of New Jersey was Frémont's running mate *(Library of Congress).*

with Chase out of the contest, McLean supporters thought that their man stood a chance in a head-to-head contest with Frémont. They were wrong. Frémont prevailed handily on the first ballot with 359 votes, compared to 190 for McLean, and became the first nominee for president of the United States by the Republican Party.[49] The usual motion was then made and approved to make the nomination unanimous, at which time a large canvas banner proclaiming "For President, John C. Frémont," was stretched across the length of the hall. The enthusiasm of the delegates increased when, "as if by magic, there was thrown among the delegates a vast number of small American flags, having inscribed on them the name of Frémont. These were caught up and waived over the multitude, and then broke out again that strong, enthusiastic cheering that had greeted the first declaration of the vote.... The hearts of the strong men who had come up to choose their standard-bearer were in their cheers, and they could not be suppressed."[50]

Former senator William L. Dayton of New Jersey received the Republican nomination for vice president on the first ballot, beating handily the second-place finisher, a former one-term Whig congressman from Illinois, Abraham Lincoln.[51] With its ticket in place, the

Republican Party entered its first presidential campaign with the slogan of "Free Speech, Free Soil and Frémont!"

Old Line Whig Convention

Hunters tell stories of deer that, after having been shot, continue to run for a while, oblivious to the fact that they have been mortally wounded and death is imminent. So it was that the almost forgotten and nearly dead Whig Party, which brought up the rear in the 1856 presidential nominating conventions. Milliard Fillmore was more clever than he is given credit for in history books. Former Whigs loyal to him had taken over the leadership of the American or Know-Nothing Party in 1854 and turned it into a broader-based political movement focused on more than just nativism.[52] After the Kansas-Nebraska Act had totally disrupted sectional harmony, Fillmore and his friends hoped to use the American Party as a vessel for the emergence of a pro–Union party that would attempt to heal the breach between North and South and save the country. To keep his name in the headlines, Fillmore traveled. In spring 1854, he made two extended trips, one to the South, and one to the West, where he was feted with public receptions in many cities. Fillmore paid homage to the late Whig leader, Henry Clay, by visiting his grave in Lexington, Kentucky. As an ex-president, he was well received wherever he went and remained above the political fray.[53] When the Know-Nothings showed success in the fall 1854 elections, Fillmore decided to cast his lot with the movement and to try to change it to a pro–Union movement. As one of Fillmore's biographers has commented, "If the idea of using the disguise of an anti-foreign movement to promote national unity troubled his conscience, he left no record of apprehension."[54] In early 1855, he became a member of the Order of the Star Spangled Banner, receiving the order's secret rites in his home. Fillmore then set off on an extended tour of Europe, again appearing to be above politics, and left it to his associates to do their work and secure his nomination for another term in the White House on the American Party ticket.[55] In England, he was admired wherever he went. Queen Victoria purportedly referred to him as the most handsome man she had ever seen. In France, he came to the aid of a political rival from New York, Horace Greeley, who had been imprisoned by French authorities over a debt. Fillmore posted his bail and Greeley was freed. In Rome, he hesitantly agreed to an audience with the pope (somewhat awkward for the man who was trying to take control of the anti–Catholic movement in America) and was relieved when the Holy Father received him sitting down and did not offer his hand, sparing the American from having to kneel or to kiss the papal hand and ring.[56] By the time Fillmore returned home in June 1856, he had been nominated for the presidency by the southern portion of the American Party at their convention in February and was about to also be nominated by the remnants of his old party, the Whigs.

The last convention of the Whig Party assembled at the Hall of the Maryland Institute in Baltimore on September 17, 1856, less than two months before election day. The hotels of Baltimore were filled and there were the usual warnings in the newspapers to be aware of pickpockets "as the city is infested with a party of cunning pickpockets from the Northern cities."[57] Apparently, Baltimore newspapers did not believe pickpockets were a native species.

The hastily convened gathering was only a shadow of the grand Whig conventions of the past. Approximately 150 delegates from twenty-two states attended. Nine states — New Hampshire, Rhode Island, Maine, Vermont, California, Wisconsin, Texas, Mississippi and South Carolina — sent no delegates. A platform was erected in the center of the hall. A rostrum was built on the west side of the platform with elevated seats for the presiding officers. American flags and red, white, and blue bunting decorated the long and narrow room.[58]

When the opening gavel came down at noon, New York's Washington Hunt was named the temporary president of the convention. In his opening remarks, Hunt noted that the convention was meeting on the sixtieth anniversary of George Washington's farewell address to the nation, in which the father of the country had warned against the formation of sectional parties. Commenting on Baltimore's monument to the nation's first president, Hunt noted, "Yesterday morning as [I] viewed the statue of Washington, on the noblest monument ever erected to his memory, [I] thought [I] saw a shade of sadness and a frown pass over his brow, at the sectional strife" that was dominating the politics of the day. Pleading for his party's continued relevance, Hunt proclaimed: "It has been preached that the Whig party is dead, but it is not so.... Let us contend for the principles of Clay and Webster."[59] The convention then appointed a Committee on Permanent Organization, which deliberated and returned a short while later and proposed Edward Bates of Missouri as the convention's president, along with one vice president from each state represented and eight secretaries. After approval of the officers, a Committee on Resolutions was appointed and an afternoon recess was taken.[60]

When the convention resumed for a short late afternoon session, a series of speakers proclaimed the Whigs and Millard Fillmore as the only hope for the nation to avoid civil war. Francis Granger of New York spoke "as a Whig and nothing but a Whig." He stated that only Fillmore could save the Union and that no platform was needed: "All platforms had done of late years was to furnish the planks on which to lay the bodies of dead candidates." Alexander Rives of Virginia condemned the repeal of the Missouri Compromise as the cause of the country's present ills. The convention adjourned for the day shortly after 7:00 P.M.[61]

The politicking was not over for the day. The delegates met at Monument Square for an evening rally. The outdoor decorations were elaborate. A six-columned "Temple of Liberty" had been erected at the east end of the courthouse facing Calvert Street. Topped by American flags, the speakers' stand had above it a painted eagle, holding a ribbon with the names of "Fillmore & Donelson." Statues representing Liberty and Justice were on each side and a large portrait of Fillmore completed the décor. All were brightly lit by gas lights. A glee club sang a newly composed campaign song and the speeches then began. As with many campaign rallies of the era, the event had a formal organization, and a presiding president and various vice presidents for the evening were named. The candidates of the other parties, Frémont, the explorer, and Buchanan, the old political warhorse, were derided: "One candidate for president had shown himself bold and daring and had supped on mule soup and dined on grasshopper pus ... [while the other had] sacrificed his own personal respect on the platform of a party." Only Fillmore, they proclaimed, could save the Union. Midway through the evening, a second group of speakers addressed the crowd from the balcony of the Gilmor House, adjacent to the courthouse on Monument Square. At the end of the festivities, resolutions endorsing the nominations of the convention for president and vice president (which would not officially occur until the next day) were approved and the conclave broke up just before midnight, amid loud cheers.[62]

When the convention resumed for its morning session on September 18, 1856, the platform in the hall had been enlarged to more comfortably accommodate the delegates. More ladies were present in the gallery. Interestingly, instead of a roll call vote of the states, the Committee on Resolutions, which was formed to prepare the party's platform, reported that it was unanimously recommending the nomination of Millard Fillmore for president and Andrew J. Donelson for vice president. This proposal of making the nominations a plank in

MILLARD FILLMORE,

AMERICAN CANDIDATE FOR PRESIDENT OF THE UNITED STATES.

Former president Millard Fillmore returned to the political arena in 1856 as the candidate of the southern wing of the American, or Know-Nothing, Party, seeking to turn that nativist party into a unionist movement. Although Fillmore also won the nomination of the dying Whig Party, he carried only one state in the 1856 election *(Library of Congress)*.

the platform was a somewhat unusual procedural maneuver. Some levity followed over the use of Donelson's middle initial being stated, rather than his full middle name of Jackson, which was how he was generally known. The irony of a Whig convention nominating the nephew of Old Hickory, who was the party's nemesis and its original reason for being, was not lost on many of those present. A motion by a North Carolina delegate to strike the nomination of Donelson and to have only a presidential nomination, was withdrawn, in the interest of the party unity. The nominations were finalized, following which the delegates gave three cheers for Fillmore, three cheers for North Carolina, and three cheers for the Whig convention. Nominating Donelson was apparently all the Whigs could stomach, as no cheers were offered for him.[63] The Whig Party, born in opposition to Andrew Jackson, would end its days having nominated his nephew for vice president. Both Henry Clay and Andrew Jackson likely turned over in their graves at the news.

The platform was brief. It pronounced that the Whig Party had "no new principles to announce — no new platform to establish — but are content broadly to rest where their forefathers have rested — upon the Constitution of the United States ... wishing no safer guide, no higher law." It declared "as a fundamental article of their political faith, the absolute necessity of avoiding geographical parties." The Whigs warned that the election of either Buchanan or Frémont "must add fuel to the flame which now threatens to wrap our dearest institutions — one common ruin."[64]

Looking back, the closing speeches of the convention, admittedly with the knowledge of history that the Whigs would never convene again, seem out of touch with reality and sound like the proverbial whistling through the graveyard. Delegate Pearce of Maryland shouted, "My god ain't this a good time. I feel like I just saw again that same old Coon," referring to the popular symbol of the Whig Party in its heyday. Fillmore was praised as "a known and tried man" who occupies "a middle ground." Buchanan is "out of the question" as president and Frémont "is only distinguished for his equestrian performances." Delegate Morehead of North Carolina proclaimed: "The great Democratic party have their train on the highway of the country rushing to destruction, with the bridge before them and the draw up; and seeing the danger, they are exclaiming to the Whigs: 'Brake — Brake' and save us!" Delegates from several states announced that their states would definitely go for Fillmore in the election, except for one honest Ohio delegate, who announced that there was "very little hope" of Fillmore winning the Buckeye State, but that they hoped to give him "a very respectable vote." Convention president Bates ended the proceedings by stating that the Kansas-Nebraska Act had been unleashed in the country by Senator Douglas of Illinois as a way to get his friend, Senator Atchison of Missouri, reelected and "as an electioneering scheme for the presidency." Now, only Fillmore could save the country and the convention had chosen him "because he was a Whig, and nothing but a Whig."[65] The fact that Fillmore (as well as Donelson) were also the candidates of the southern portion of the American, or Know-Nothing, Party, having been nominated by that party in convention seven months earlier, barely passed the lips of the Whigs in Baltimore, lending further credence to the fact that their time had passed and that they were ignoring realities.

The Campaign and Election

With three candidates in the race, there were really two elections in the campaign of 1856. Buchanan was the only national candidate. He competed against Fillmore in the South (where the Republicans were not even on the ballot in most states) and against Frémont in the North. It was felt that Buchanan would carry most of the South, although some thought that Fillmore could pick off a few states and prevent an Electoral College majority by either Buchanan or Frémont, and thereby throw the election into the House of Representatives. The battleground states were in the North and that is where the attention was focused. As usual, the candidates themselves took no active role in the contest. The Democrats portrayed the Republicans as disunionists and argued that a vote for them would lead to dire consequences for the country. The hope was that moderate northerners would turn to Buchanan as the tried and steady hand at the helm and as the only candidate who could save the Union. Frémont was savaged by the Democrats on numerous fronts. He was ridiculed as "a man whose only merit, so far as history records it, is in the fact that he was born in South Carolina, crossed the Rocky Mountains, subsisted on frogs, lizards, snakes, and grasshoppers, and captured a woolly horse." He was attacked as a drunkard and as a secret Catholic, as he had been married by a Catholic priest when he and his bride eloped and no other official could be found to perform the ceremony. Republicans attacked Buchanan as an old fogy whose time had passed. He was a lifelong bachelor, and there were whispers about his sexuality. The new Republican

Party ran an energetic campaign, with speakers fanning out across the North and West and rallies, torchlight parades, glee clubs, among other festivities.[66]

When the votes were counted, Buchanan emerged the victor, beating Frémont by over 400,000 votes and Fillmore by almost a million. The actual vote totals were 1,832,955 (45 percent) for Buchanan, 1,399,932 (33 percent) for Frémont, and 871,731 (22 percent) for Fillmore. In the Electoral College tally, Old Buck racked up 174 votes, to 114 for the Pathfinder, and 8 for the former president. Fillmore carried only Maryland, but he lost Kentucky, Tennessee, and Louisiana by narrow margins, and a shift of only 15,000 votes scattered over those three states would have deprived Buchanan of an electoral majority and the election would have been decided by the House of Representatives. It was a violent election day in places. The Know-Nothings controlled the city government of Baltimore and used force to keep opponents from the polls. Ten people died and 150 were wounded in Baltimore as a result of violence and riots on the day that the nation went about electing its next leader.[67] Nationally, the stories of the election of 1856 were of the increasing alignment of the parties along sectional lines, and of the strength that the Republicans showed in their first presidential election. While the South was solidly Democratic, despite the fact that no Republican votes at all were cast in twelve southern states, Frémont had won eleven of the sixteen northern states and had come within thirty-one electoral votes of winning the presidency.[68] It was a solid base for the new party to build upon. It remained to be seen, if a Republican ever won the White House, whether fears of disunion were real or imagined.

CHAPTER **10**

1860: Two-Act Tragedy

We'll go for the son of Kentucky, the hero of Hoosierdom through,
The pride of the "Suckers" so lucky, for Lincoln and Liberty, too!

They'll find by felling and mauling, our railsplitting statesman can do;
For the people everywhere are calling, for Lincoln and Liberty, too!

Hurray for the choice of the nation, our hero so brave and so true,
We'll go for the great reformation, for Lincoln and Liberty, too![1]

Republican campaign song, 1860

As the election year of 1860 began, the nation's political parties decided on new cities to host their conventions. The Whig Party had disbanded. The Democratic Party had selected Charleston, South Carolina, for its convention, while the emergent Republican Party would be holding its convention in Chicago, Illinois. With a new party alignment and a new political era about to begin, conventions in Baltimore appeared to be a thing of the past. As fate would have it, however, in a turbulent campaign with many unforeseen twists and turns, by mid–year Baltimore would end up as the site of three presidential nominating conventions. With the nation lurching toward disunion and civil war, its eyes would once again be focused on Baltimore.

Constitutional Union Party Convention

Although the Whig Party was no more, many Whigs were not yet willing to join the Republicans, and certainly not the Democrats. In a last-ditch effort to avoid a total breakdown between North and South, Senator John J. Crittenden of Kentucky called a meeting of fifty like-minded current and former members of Congress in Washington in December 1859. Mostly former Whigs, the attendees reached out to the members of another virtually defunct party, the American (Know-Nothing) Party, and agreed to form a new coalition with the goal of saving the Union. Like the proponents of the Compromise of 1850 a decade earlier, they wanted to take the slavery issue off of the political agenda. This meeting in the Federal City in late 1859 resulted in the creation of a new political party, the Constitutional Union Party, and its founders published an address to the American people on February 22, 1860, George Washington's birthday:

The people everywhere are disturbed with fear of some disastrous crisis. Many are alarmed for the safety of the Union ... there has been manifested a design in the movements of influential political leaders to force the country into an organization of parties founded on the question of slavery.... The two great parties in the country — the Democratic and Republican — have been the chief actors in this fatal contest, if not its authors.... After having so long agitated the country by their reciprocal assaults, these parties are now preparing for a sectional struggle, far exceeding in violence any that has yet occurred, the results of which may be disastrous for the country.

Solemnly impressed with these facts, a number of gentlemen from different parts of the country, among whom were members of the present Congress and of Congresses of former date, recently assembled in the City of Washington to deliberate on measures for averting dangers to which they may lead. It was the unanimous opinion of the meeting that immediate steps should be taken to organize a "Constitutional Union Party," pledged to support "The Union, the Constitution, and the enforcement of the laws."

[N]either of the two parties who are now seeking to obtain control of the Government can be safely entrusted with the management of public affairs. The only way to rescue the country from their hands is to organize a party ... [t]o remove the subject of Slavery from the arena of party politics, and leave it to the independent control of the States in which it exists, and to the unbiased action of the judiciary.

To this end, we propose that a convention be immediately held in each state ... [t]hat each of these conventions shall make a nomination of two candidates for the Presidency ... one of which candidates, at least, shall be a citizen of some other State than that in which he is nominated ... that these two candidates from each state shall be submitted to the consideration of a general convention, to be assembled at Philadelphia ... which general convention shall be empowered to select from the whole number of nominations transmitted to it a candidate for President and Vice-President, as the candidates of the Constitutional Union Party.[2]

This manifesto to the American people was signed by twenty-nine members of the new party's National Executive Committee, including its chairman, John J. Crittenden of Kentucky, William C. Rives of Virginia (the former Democrat who lost that party's vice presidential nomination to Richard M. Johnson at the 1836 Democratic convention), William Graham of North Carolina (Whig candidate for vice president in 1852), John Pendleton Kennedy of Maryland (former Whig congressman), and William "Parson" Brownlow of Tennessee (a noted Whig newspaper editor).

Within a few weeks of the call for the Constitutional Union Party convention to be held in Philadelphia, the location of the gathering was changed to Baltimore and it was scheduled to begin on May 9, 1860. As it turned out, it would be the first convention to nominate a candidate in the 1860 campaign, with the Democrats having met and disbanded in disarray at Charleston in April, and with the Republicans not scheduled to meet until May 16 in Chicago. The site of the convention was the former First Presbyterian Church building on the northwest corner of Fayette Street and North Street (now Guilford Avenue). This church had been the location of the 1835 Democratic convention that nominated Martin Van Buren for the presidency.

Many church members at that time had been appalled that their sanctuary (to which the Democrats had moved mid–convention when looking for a larger space) had been used for a political event and passed a resolution stating that the church would never again be used for secular purposes without full approval from the congregation and church officials. This prohibition was no longer in effect in 1860, however, since the church building and the land on which it sat had been sold by the Presbyterians to the United States government in 1859. The structure was scheduled for demolition and a new federal courthouse was planned for the site. The last church services were held in the building in September 1859, following which the First Presbyterian Church of Baltimore moved to its new sanctuary, located at Madison Street and Park Avenue in Baltimore.[3] In spring 1860, the old church building sat empty. It is perhaps fitting that the Constitutional Union Party, which consisted largely of old men from the dead Whig Party whom many viewed as having been passed over by time and events, chose for their convention a church building that had outlived its usefulness. The building was about to be destroyed, as was the union of the states that the Constitutional Unionists were trying to preserve. The brief history of this party shows a hoping-against-hope mentality that a "can't we all just get along" approach would save the country. It was well-meaning but, as events would soon indicate, would prove to be naïve.

In the days prior to the convention, as usual, Baltimore's major hotels began to fill up with delegates. Barnum's City Hotel recorded over four hundred arrivals, with delegations from Pennsylvania, Ohio, New Jersey, Missouri, Mississippi, Kentucky, Delaware, North Carolina and Georgia lodging there. Most of the delegations also reserved parlor rooms in Barnum's for their meetings. The Virginians were at another hotel on Calvert Street, while the New Yorkers were a few blocks to the west at Eutaw House. Some smaller delegations stayed in private boardinghouses.[4] Nine states (New Hampshire, Iowa, Michigan, California, Oregon, Iowa, Florida, Louisiana, and South Carolina) failed to send any representatives. The old church building was adorned with red, white, and blue decorations, and a full-length portrait of George Washington was hung behind the president's chair at the front of the sanctuary, with flags adjacent to the portrait and an American eagle above it. There was seating for about 700 people on the floor, with space for about 300 more for the gallery in the church's balcony. As usual at conventions of the era, the "best gallery is appropriated to the ladies," in this case, the west gallery.[5]

Seventy-two-year-old John J. Crittenden, the party's founder, had adamantly refused to be a candidate for the presidential nomination. The pre-convention favorites were John Bell and Sam Houston. Bell, of Tennessee, had a long career as a member of Congress, serving in both the House and the Senate. He was sixty-four years old, a lawyer and a slave owner. Bell had started his congressional career in the late 1820s as an Andrew Jackson Democrat, breaking with Old Hickory by the end of his second term and becoming the primary in-state Democratic opponent of the Jackson political machine in Tennessee. He then gravitated to the Whigs and entered the Senate as a member of that party in 1847, serving until 1859. A serious man, Bell was more interested in policy than in people and had made many enemies over his long political career.[6] Sam Houston, a former Democrat, the hero of the 1836 Battle of San Jacinto in Texas' war for independence from Mexico, and the former president of the Republic of Texas before it joined the United States in 1845, was a far more popular and national figure than Bell. Houston, however, was not known for his intellectual prowess. Reporter Murat Halstead of the *Cincinnati Commercial* newspaper attended all of the 1860 political conventions and later compiled his writings from the conventions in an excellent book of his observations and commentaries on the proceedings. Of Houston, Halstead wrote that he was "a rather good old soul, as we all know, but the most shallow of the shallow politicians who have been engaged for some years in attending to the affairs of our beloved country."[7] Other candidates were William C. Rives of Virginia, Justice John McLean of Ohio (a perennially possible nominee of multiple parties going back to the 1830s), and William Graham of North Carolina, who had been Winfield Scott's Whig running mate in 1852.[8]

At noon on May 9, Crittenden took the stage, to the cheers of a full house in the historic

This view from the pulpit of Baltimore's First Presbyterian Church shows the balconies from which onlookers cheered the delegates to the one and only convention of the Constitutional Union Party in 1860 *(Enoch Pratt Free Library).*

Two Steeple Church. The first, and last, presidential nominating convention of the Constitutional Union Party was underway. Twenty-two states were represented, with approximately 250 delegates. Like the mood of the country, the weather was gloomy, and it was raining. After an opening prayer pleading for national unity ("Rebuke every spirit that would attempt to alleviate any portion of our country from the rest ... may a flame of pure and devoted patriotism be shed forth upon the whole indivisible..."),[9] Crittenden proposed as temporary president former New York governor Washington Hunt, whose nomination was approved by acclamation. Hunt then delivered what amounted to the convention's keynote speech, striking themes eerily reminiscent of the opening address he himself had made just four years earlier when he had also served as temporary chairman of the last Whig Party convention, which had been held just a few blocks away at the Maryland Institute. This time, Hunt proclaimed:

> We have come on a mission of peace to strengthen the chains of union and to revive the spirit of national affection in the land, and to proclaim that we are and ever intend to be one, bound together by common ties.... We are brought together by no partisan influences, for in times like these the interest of party and the schemes of personal ambitions become utterly insignificant and worthless.... Let us know no party but our country, and no platform but Union.... The once proud and invincible Democracy, which has wielded the powers of Government for many years, has been rent in twain by the fell spirit of sectional discord, and has [run] aground upon the shoals and breakers of Popular Sovereignty and Territorial Government. I fear it is beyond the power of any surgical or medical skill.... We

have another party, which proposes mainly to deal with this same subject ... and the question is presented to us as a great pertinent issue of the day: whether Slavery should be extended where the winter temperature is many degrees below zero, and in which, I will venture to say, no slave-owner could be induced to emigrate and settle. And while we are called upon to discuss this miserable abstraction to enter into the Presidential election upon it, nothing is stated, nothing is proposed in regard to the great functions and duties of the General Government, which concerns the people of the United States at large.[10]

Hunt's address was well received; too well received, according to reporter Halstead, who observed, "The convention insisted on applauding nearly every sentence, and several times refused to let him finish a sentence. It was worse than the applause given by an Irish audience at an Archbishop's lecture. The Americans must never laugh at the Irish for their irrepressible disposition to applaud."[11] The convention then appointed two committees, one a Committee on Permanent Organization and the other a Committee on Credentials, and then took a recess.

When the convention in the packed church resumed for its second session of the day on a rainy spring afternoon in Baltimore, drenched spectators on the outside looked in on the proceedings through the building's large windows. The Committee on Permanent Organization gave its report and recommended that temporary president Washington Hunt also serve as permanent convention president. It also nominated nineteen vice presidents, one from each state then represented. Before the convention's end, three additional state delegations arrived, one of which had been delayed by an accident on the Baltimore & Ohio Railroad. Eleven secretaries were also named. The committee's report was read by Andrew Jackson Donelson, the former president's nephew and the vice presidential candidate of the American Party and the Whigs in 1856. All nominations were approved by acclamation. Hunt then addressed the convention again briefly, again urging moderation and harmony.[12]

A debate then ensued over whether to proceed first to the nominating process, or to establish a platform for the party. Interestingly, the delegation from Texas (home of Sam Houston, a major contender for the nomination) had not yet arrived. Attempting to inject some levity into the proceedings, delegate Coombs of Kentucky proposed that three platforms, one for each party, should be adopted. For the divided Democrats, who could not agree whether to have slavery in the territories or not, he proposed a two-plank platform — one excluding slavery in the territories and the other forcing slavery in the territories, both planks to be adopted unanimously and without debate. Second, for the Republicans, Coombs proposed a modified version of the blue laws of Connecticut, which had prohibited the kissing of wives on Sundays and demanded the burning of all witches at the stake. He suggested a platform for the Republicans permitting the kissing of young wives on the Sabbath and the burning of only old witches. For the Constitutional Union Party, he suggested that only a one-sentence platform was needed: "The Constitution as it is, and the Union under it now and forever." As Coombs was speaking, the delayed Texas delegation, led by its chairman, A. B. Norton, arrived in the hall to a round of three cheers for the Lone Star State. Norton sported a beard down to his waist. The jocular Coombs, now on a roll, joked to the convention that Norton had vowed fifteen years earlier not to shave until Henry Clay was elected president.[13] Clay had died in 1852.

The levity over, the convention then resumed serious discussion of a platform. A Committee on Resolutions was appointed, with one member from each state, and the committee was directed to work overnight and report its work at 10:00 A.M. the following morning. With that, the convention adjourned for dinner and for the evening. After dinner, the Committee on Resolutions met at 8:00 P.M. at Eutaw House and made quick work of its business. Perhaps the 10:00 A.M. deadline the following morning for its final product helped to shorten and stifle debate. Declaring that political platforms "had the effect to mislead and deceive the people, and at the same time to widen the political divisions of the Country," the committee adopted a no-frills "mom and apple pie" platform: "Resolved, that it is the part of patriotism and of duty to recognize no political principles, other than the Constitution of the Country, the union of the states and the enforcement of the laws." Who could disagree with that? Their work done, the committee then enjoyed the offerings of an evening in Baltimore.[14]

When the convention resumed on the morning on May 10, two additional state delegations, from Minnesota and Florida, had arrived. The report of the Committee on Resolutions was read. The first portion, concerning the brief platform, was approved with little discussion. The second portion, concerning the method of voting during the nomination process, generated much debate. The committee had proposed letting each state determine how its votes would be cast, thus allowing a majority of a state's delegates to impose the "unit rule" used by the Democrats at their conventions and casting all of that state's votes for the candidate favored by the majority of that state's delegates. It also proposed the traditional rule of each state being allotted its number of votes in the Electoral College. After much discussion, a proposed modification made by a Virginia delegate was adopted: the chairman of each delegation would announce the vote of each delegate in his state, as instructed by each delegate. If there were no delegates present from any congressional districts in the state, then the majority of the delegates would decide how to cast the votes of those districts, and where two delegates were present from a district but could not agree, then half-votes would be cast on behalf of that district. This modified "unit rule" formula was approved by the convention.[15]

The rules decided, the voting for the presidential nomination began shortly before noon. The roll call of the states was done alphabetically, as opposed to the traditional method of starting in the northeast with Maine. As the roll call began, the Maryland delegation asked to be excused for fifteen minutes, apparently not able, as one commentator comically noted, to fully get the complicated voting rules "through its head without a surgical operation."[16] The voting turned out to be somewhat of a surprise. Many had thought Sam Houston, the old Texas Democrat, would win the nomination on the first ballot. But, as it turned out, a convention comprised mainly of former Whigs was hesitant to support a former Democrat, no matter his war hero status. Houston had also alienated the former members of the American Party, some of whom were delegates at the convention, by stating during Texas elections in 1859 that he did not favor their key issue, nativism. Kentucky supported its native son, Crittenden, as did a few other delegations, despite his stated opposition to being a candidate. On the first ballot, 254 votes were cast, with a majority of 128 required for the nomination. With 68 votes Bell was in the lead, compared to 57 for Houston, 28 for Crittenden, 25 for Edward Everett of Massachusetts, 21 for John McLean of Ohio, 13 for William Rives of Virginia, and the remaining votes scattered among three others. As the states were called on the second ballot, Bell began to pick up votes from the fading lesser candidates. As the roll call progressed, last-minute appeals were made by delegates favoring the top candidates. As Halstead commented: "A New York delegate had something to say of Washington, the American Eagle, the Washington Monument, the Battle Monument, and striking upon expediency, availability, etc., wound up with a screech for Sam Houston.... Pendleton of Ohio declared that Ohio wanted a Southern Whig ... [which] was understood to be a stroke for Bell. Houston's long-haired friend from Texas, made a wild speech for him. He (long hair) was an old friend of Henry Clay — loved, admired, and revered him, and followed him through his days of adversity. But Sam Houston was the man."[17] By the time the alphabetical roll call reached the last state, Virginia, Bell was only three votes shy of victory. All of Virginia's votes had been given to two favorite son candidates on the first ballot. After a dramatic pause for consultation, the chairman of the Old Dominion's delegation cast thirteen of the state's fifteen votes for Bell, putting him over the top. The convention erupted in cheers. As various states began to switch their votes to Bell, another one of those Baltimore convention moments of panic occurred. A loud noise in the east gallery was heard, leading many to think the old church was collapsing, and resulting in some people jumping out of the windows and others rushing for the doors. Once again, a broken bench was determined to be the culprit and order was quickly restored.[18]

After Bell's nomination was declared unanimous, the delegates heard an echo from the American Revolution. Delegate Major G. A. Henry of Tennessee, an elderly gentleman, began a speech praising the Union and thanking the convention for the nomination of Bell, his home state colleague. When it was shouted out by a delegate that the speaker was the grandson of Patrick Henry, the great orator of the American Revolution, the convention gave him three cheers and hung on his every word:

> We are Union people; shall we throw this Union away? How can we avoid the responsibility of standing up to defend it? With what face could we meet the wondering nations, if ... we throw away the richest heritage God ever gave to man.... If such must be our country's early doom; if all her pride, her power, her cherished hopes, our stripes, our stars, our heritage of glory, and the bright names we have taught our children to revere — if all must end in this, never let free man meet free man again...
>
> Tear down your flag; burn your Capitol; dismiss your navy; disperse your army; let our commerce rot; overturn all your monuments, here in Baltimore and everywhere else; give to the flames the once loved record of our father's deeds; scatter the sacred dust of Washington ... teach your boys to forget his name, and never let the pilgrim's foot tread the consecrated graves of Mount Vernon. Can we surrender all these bright and glorious hopes? If we can, then we of the Union party are the most recreant of all mankind, and the curses of all time will cling upon us like the shirt of Nessus.[19]

It was not "Give me liberty, or give me death!," but it was close. The grandson of Patrick Henry had revived the family name for great oratory. Even the often cynical reporter, Halstead, was moved and called it the speech of the convention. "The old man was in good earnest, and his effort was immensely acceptable. In truth, I have seldom heard a speech better calculated to arouse popular feeling."[20] In a convention known to give excessive applause and cheers, Henry received twenty-five cheers at the conclusion of his moving remarks, a record number.[21] After a brief patriotic speech by a Mississippi delegate, the convention then recessed until 5:00 P.M.

When the convention resumed, the only remaining business was the selection of a vice presidential nominee. With the nomination of Bell from Tennessee for the top spot, all agreed that a northerner was needed to balance the ticket. Former senator Edward Everett of Massachusetts was the consensus choice. Everett was one of the most distinguished orators of the day. Three years hence, at the dedication of the Gettysburg cemetery in November 1863, he would be the featured speaker and would give a two-hour address, compared to Abraham Lincoln's two minutes of remarks. Everett, 67 years old in 1860, was a Harvard graduate, and a former professor and president of that institution. He had served in the House of Representatives, as governor of Massachusetts, in the Senate, and briefly as minister to England and as secretary of state during the Whig administrations of Harrison and Fillmore. He was a well-known writer, scholar, and orator, and was a leader in the effort to purchase George

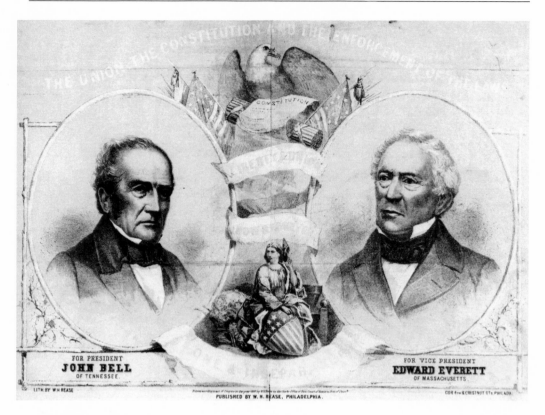

THE UNION THE CONSTITUTION AND THE ENFORCEMENT OF THE LAWS

FOR PRESIDENT
JOHN BELL
OF TENNESSEE.

FOR VICE PRESIDENT
EDWARD EVERETT
OF MASSACHUSETTS.

PUBLISHED BY W. H. REASE, PHILADELPHIA.

John Bell (left) of Tennessee was the 1860 nominee of the Constitutional Union Party, along with running mate Edward Everett of Massachusetts. They ran on a platform to remove the slavery issue from political debate *(Library of Congress)*.

Washington's Mount Vernon home and to maintain it as a historical site.[22] Although there was no opposition to Everett's nomination, at a convention prone to lengthy applause and cheers, there were numerous speeches nominating and praising him, which took up three hours before his nomination was approved by acclamation. A distinguished-looking and handsome man, Everett was known to be a favorite of the ladies of the country and, for this reason, many of the speeches urged the women of the country to persuade their husbands and sweethearts to support the Bell/Everett ticket.[23] After approving nominations for the party's National Central Executive Union Commission, the convention adjourned in high spirits and with hope for the coming campaign. Perhaps, just perhaps, they thought, the Union could be saved.

With the official business of the convention over, the traditional evening rally was held just a couple of hours later. Once again, Baltimore's Monument Square, located only a few steps away from the old First Presbyterian Church, was the setting. An elaborate one-hundred-foot-long stage had been erected, with two thirty-six-foot towers at the north and south ends. On one tower, there was a life-size portrait on Washington; on the other, a life-size portrait of Clay. The name of John Bell was on one tower; that of Edward Everett on the other. A large archway, equal in height at its top to the towers, was inscribed with the words "The Union, the Constitution, and the Enforcement of the Laws." It was perhaps the only time in American history when a political party's entire platform could be written on a stage decoration. Gas lights lit the stage, bands played, and speeches were made. Rockets were fired from the yard of the courthouse. An estimated 8,000 to 10,000 people jammed the square for the festivities. Halstead described the scene as giving "an exceedingly brilliant appearance. I imagine nothing more complete in design, or elaborate on execution, was ever in the United States constructed to serve a similar purpose."[24]

The enthusiasm of the delegates to the Constitutional Union Party convention could not mask the widening divisions facing the country. The central political issue of the era, slavery, was hardly mentioned. The party's approach was to let each state decide the issue of slavery within its borders and to let the Supreme Court decide the matter in the territories, with the Congress and the president having no roles. Nationally, the convention was viewed as a meeting of old men whom time had passed by. It was noted that few of the delegates were under the age of sixty and that the gathering presented a "shopworn, graying image" to the country.[25] A joke in the *New York Tribune* shortly after the convention had a person inquiring of a delegate returning from Baltimore:

QUESTIONER: Why didn't you nominate Choate?
DELEGATE: Choate — Why, he is dead!
QUESTIONER: Oh, I know it, but he has not been dead a very long time.[26]

Rufus Choate, a former Whig senator from Massachusetts, had died in July 1859. The *Tribune's* editor, Horace Greeley, commented of the party's platform: "It belongs to the year 1830, and not to the time in which we live."[27]

From a twenty-first-century perspective, it is easy to criticize the Constitutional Unionists, as Greeley and others did at the time, as old men out of touch with the times. It should be remembered, however, that no candidate in the election of 1860 advocated the abolition of slavery in the existing southern states. The issue was slavery in the territories. California and Oregon were already admitted to the Union as free states. Existing laws already established that popular sovereignty would determine the issue of slavery in the Mexican Cession lands and in the Kansas-Nebraska territories, at least once they became states. As a practical matter, the Constitutional Unionists felt that there was not much left to be decided and, of the remaining land, most of it was not suitable for the institution of slavery. In their view, was it worth destroying the Union over the right to take a slave to Montana, a right that no southern slave-owner would likely ever exercise? Major Henry's speech to the convention eloquently expressed, from the perspective of the Constitutional Unionists, all that was being put at risk by extremists on both sides of the territorial slavery issue. To the Constitutional Unionists, love of country overcame all.

Democratic Convention

The Front Street Theater was one of the leading performing arts theaters in Baltimore in the mid-nineteenth century. Located on the northwest corner of Front and Low Streets, just west of the present United States Post Office on Fayette Street in downtown Baltimore, the theater opened its doors in September 1829. The building faced Front Street and ran approximately one hundred fifty feet along Low Street. Four stories high, with a main seating floor and three balconies, the theater could seat approximately 2,500 people. The rear of the property bordered on the Jones Falls, a river (now underground) that runs through the middle of the city. After a fire destroyed the original theater in 1838, the structure was rebuilt and reopened in less than a year.[28]

In the performing arts, the Front Street Theater is best remembered as the site of four Baltimore performances during the 1850 American tour of the famous opera singer, Jenny Lind, known as the Swedish Nightingale. Lind's tour created a national sensation and she sold out theaters throughout the country. With a face value of three dollars each, tickets for her Baltimore shows were scalped for much higher prices. A Baltimore businessman paid one hundred dollars for the first choice of seats for the opening concert.[29] Lind was accompanied by a forty-two-piece orchestra. The *Baltimore Sun* reported that the audience for Lind's concerts was "much surprised by her personal appearance, so far excelling in good looks the engraved representations that have foreshadowed her coming, as they were in the superiority of her powers as a vocalist over all others that have ever appeared in this city.... Her execution was faultless and wonderful. In truth her voice was like the warbling of a bird, so soft, so sweet, so delicately clear."[30]

A decade later, the Front Street Theater would play host to performers of a much different sort than the Swedish Nightingale. Political actors would take the stage for the second act of a two-act tragedy that was this Democratic Party's presidential nominating convention of 1860. With a run of nine weeks, this play would have more than its share of villains, no heroes, and would leave the United States on an almost certain path toward disunion and civil war.

The opening act of the Democratic convention began in Charleston, South Carolina, on April 23, 1860. After its 1856 convention in Cincinnati, the party decided, in an effort to promote sectional harmony and unity, to move its quadrennial convention to the South in 1860. In Cincinnati, the party had adopted as its platform the principle of "popular sovereignty" advocated by Senator Stephen Douglas of Illinois and others, which held that, when a territory became a state, its people, through their elected representatives, could "form a constitution, with or without domestic slavery, and be admitted to the Union upon terms of perfect equality with the other states." It also adopted "the principles contained in the organic laws establishing the Territories of Kansas and Nebraska as embodying the only sound and safe solution of the Slavery question ... and non-interference of Congress with Slavery in the Territories or in the District of Columbia."[31] There was an unanswered question in the 1856 platform — if Congress could not do so, could the people of a territory restrict slavery during the territorial period, or could such restrictions be imposed by the people only upon statehood? It was over this relatively narrow issue that the Democratic Party would divide in 1860 and which would lead to secession and civil war. In his famous 1858 debates in Illinois with Abraham Lincoln during his reelection campaign for the United States Senate, Douglas had gone on the record as stating that the people of a territory could limit slavery by local legislation during the territorial period. Southerners derisively referred to this as "squatter sovereignty" and held the view that their "property"— slaves — had to be protected by the federal government in the territories, since the territories were owned in common by the people of the entire United States and since the Constitution recognized their "domestic institution."[32] Thus, Douglas, who many believed had included "popular sovereignty" in the Kansas-Nebraska statehood bill of 1854 (which overruled the Missouri Compromise prohibition of slavery north of the 36 degree, 30 minute north latitude) as a way to curry favor with southerners and promote his proposed transcontinental railroad and presidential aspirations, was, by 1860, being branded a villain in the South for favoring the same doctrine during the territorial phase.

Going into the Charleston convention, Douglas was the leading candidate for the Democratic nomination. He was thought to have a majority of the delegates, but under the precedent-honored two-thirds rule adopted by past Democratic conventions, his nomination was by no means certain. There was no anti–Douglas candidate upon which the opposition, split into three groups, had united. One group consisted of the supporters of the unpopular incumbent Democratic president, James Buchanan, who was not seeking reelection. The bad blood between Buchanan and Douglas stemmed from Douglas' refusal to support the pro-slavery

Lecompton constitution for the statehood of Kansas, which Douglas claimed was drafted by an unrepresentative convention.[33] The main opposition to Douglas, however, came from those who advocated the extreme southern position. Known as "fire-eaters," they were led by William L. Yancey of Alabama. Their view was that the Constitution mandated slavery in the territories and that there could be no interference by Congress or territorial legislatures prior to statehood. They had been emboldened by the 1857 decision of the Supreme Court in *Dred Scott v. Sandford*, which held that enslaved people were property, not citizens, that the Missouri Compromise was unconstitutional, and that Congress had no power to prohibit slavery in the territories. The third group opposing Douglas going into the convention consisted of moderate southerners and several delegates from border states. They were wary of both Douglas and the "fire–eaters" and were thought to hold the balance of power in a divided convention.[34]

The eighth presidential nominating convention of the Democratic Party opened at Institute Hall on April 23, 1860, in the one-hundred-degree heat of a Charleston spring. Heat, in temperature and tempers, would characterize the proceeding. There were 303 delegates representing thirty-two states.[35] Built in 1854, Institute Hall, located in the one hundred block of Meeting Street, seated 3,000 people and was the home of the South Carolina Institute, an organization created to promote "art, ingenuity, mechanical skill and industry" in the Palmetto State.[36] It was widely known before the convention that the Democratic parties of the states of the Deep South had instructed their delegates to walk out of the convention if it did not adopt a platform favoring full federal protection of slavery in the territories. Douglas' fate was sealed when the convention, with the surprising support of his own delegates, approved the adoption of a party platform before the nomination of a presidential candidate. Apparently, their thinking was that the departure of a few extreme southerners upon the adoption of a moderate platform would make it easier for Douglas to receive the two-thirds vote required for nomination.[37] It was the first of several missteps by the Douglas team.

A platform committee was named, with the traditional single member from each of the thirty-two states represented at the convention. After days of committee meetings, the platform committee finally submitted its divided report on the fifth day of the convention, Friday, April 27. The majority report, supported by committee members from fifteen southern states, and by California and Oregon, required federal protection of slavery in the territories. A minority report, supported by members from fourteen northern states, called for reaffirmation of the party's 1856 Cincinnati platform, with the addition of acceptance of any decisions by the Supreme Court on slavery in the territories. A third platform committee proposal, supported by only one vote, that of the Massachusetts committee member, Benjamin F. Butler, favored simply reaffirming the Cincinnati platform. For two days, Friday and Saturday, the convention heatedly debated these platform proposals, with no resolution. The convention did not meet on Sunday, and the showdown would come on Monday, April 30.[38]

And a showdown it was. The Douglas forces mustered support to approve the minority report of the platform committee, by a vote of 165 yeas to 138 nays. Once this vote was taken, the Alabama delegation, acting on instructions from its state convention, announced its withdrawal from the convention. The Alabamans were led by William Lowndes Yancey, the same man who had walked out of the 1848 Democratic convention in Baltimore over that convention's refusal to adopt virtually the same proposal of non interference with slavery in the territories that had now also been rejected in Charleston. Unlike in 1848, however, this time Yancey had more than one other delegate accompany him out onto the street. In quick order, the same announcement followed from similarly instructed deep South delegations — Arkansas, Florida, Louisiana, Mississippi, Texas, and South Carolina all joined the Alabamans in heading

This is an interior scene of Institute Hall in Charleston during the 1860 Democratic convention. The party's plan of uniting its factions by moving its convention in the South backfired when the many southern delegates walked out. Since the remaining delegates were unable to nominate a candidate, the party had to reconvene its convention in Baltimore several weeks later *(Library of Congress)*.

for the exits. In all, the majority of each of these delegations, more than fifty delegates, got up and walked out of the convention, to the cheers of the pro-southern Charleston gallery observing the proceedings. The delegations from Georgia, Virginia, and Delaware then asked for an adjournment for the day so that they could go into consultation, which was granted.[39]

The next day, May 1, the news only got worse for the Douglasites. The majority of the Georgia delegation withdrew, as did a delegate from Delaware and two additional delegates from Louisiana. Virginia, considered the bellwether of the upper South, decided to remain. However, when convention president Caleb Cushing ruled, and the remaining delegates sustained his ruling, that two-thirds of the original 303 delegates were still required for nomination, all hope was lost for the Douglas floor managers. They would need votes from four of every five remaining delegates, 202 votes, to win the prize, a near impossibility.[40] The convention then proceeded with the hopeless task of trying to nominate a candidate. On the first ballot, Douglas received 145½ votes, to 107½ scattered among several other candidates. After three more long days and fifty-seven ballots, there was little movement from the tally of the first ballot and, recognizing the futility of continuing further, the convention decided to adjourn and to reconvene in Baltimore on June 18.[41] The bolted southern delegates, who had assembled at another hall in Charleston and who had been expecting a conciliatory call from their brethren to rejoin them and agree on a compromise candidate, were stunned. Their bluff had been called. Thus ended act one.

There was a six-week intermission before the convention resumed in Baltimore in mid–June. The streets of Baltimore bustled with activity over the weekend before the opening on June 18 of the second act of the Democratic Party's presidential nominating convention. The Saturday afternoon train of the Northern Central Railroad deposited the Illinois and Ohio delegates at Calvert Station. Each delegation was accompanied by its own uniformed band, the Great Western Brass Band of Chicago and Mentor's Band from Cincinnati. With the bands playing, the two delegations marched in unison the few blocks from the train station to their lodgings at the Gilmor House on Monument Square. All of the major hotels in the city were filled. Barnum's City Hotel registered more than one thousand guests from virtually every state in the Union. Eutaw House was the host of more than five hundred, including delegations from New York, Connecticut, Vermont, Indiana, and Louisiana. Maltby House was the temporary home of delegates from Delaware, Michigan, Pennsylvania, Virginia, and others.[42] In all, more than ten thousand people had streamed into Baltimore to see the final scenes of the drama that had begun in Charleston.

Baltimore's Front Street Theater was appropriately modified and decorated for its moment in the nation's spotlight. The main level of the theater and the stage were reserved for delegates and the press. The president's chair was on a platform at the west end of the stage, the area of the building closest to the Jones falls. At the rear of the stage there was "a rich and beautiful

The Front Street Theatre in Baltimore was the site of the reconvened Democratic convention in 1860, which nominated Stephen Douglas of Illinois for the presidency. It was also the site of the 1864 Republican convention that nominated Abraham Lincoln for a second term *(Enoch Pratt Free Library).*

scenery to relieve the heaviness of the unplastered walls." The stage itself was "handsomely decorated with festooned wood and the national standard." There were desks for one hundred reporters on the stage and, for the first time in American political convention history, telegraph lines were installed inside the convention hall, running to the Sun Iron Building at Baltimore and South Streets a few blocks away, and from there to the entire country. A large American flag was hung across the street in front of the theater, inscribed with the motto (or perhaps the hope and prayer) "We Will Support the Nominee." The dress circle was reserved for ladies, who were not required to have tickets. Seating in the public galleries in the upper two balconies required tickets, which had been distributed free of charge by convention president Caleb Cushing at Barnum's Hotel over the weekend before the convention. These gallery tickets were, in turn, being scalped for between two and five dollars each. Baltimore police were out in force, with special detachments deployed at the Front Street Theater and at the major hotels, as the convention also attracted the usual thieves and pickpockets who were "expecting a rich harvest."[43]

The convention did not get off to a smooth start, due to confusion over the time of the opening gavel. The established time was 10:00 A.M., but some thought it was noon. Convention president Caleb Cushing of Massachusetts, continuing in his role from Charleston, called the proceedings to order shortly after 11:00 A.M. with a roll call of the states. Twenty-four states were called and twenty-two answered that they were present, with Kentucky and Connecticut absent. The eight southern states whose delegations had walked out in Charleston (Alabama, Arkansas, Florida, Georgia, Louisiana, Mississippi, South Carolina, and Texas) were not called, and no delegate tickets for admission to the floor had been given out for those states. There was an opening controversy over the distribution of delegate tickets to the admitted states. A Delaware delegate complained some members of his delegation had not been given tickets and had been refused admission by the sergeant-at-arms. Cushing responded that the tickets were supposed to have been distributed to all delegation chairmen and, if a chairman did not get his allocation, he should speak up. Others in the hall were unable to hear this verbal exchange, which led to one of the few moments of levity at the convention. A New York delegate advised the disgruntled Delaware delegate that "he is now speaking from the stage of a theater, and it is important that he should face those in the rear, and address them, and not the chair," if he desired to be heard. When the flustered Delaware man responded that "I am not a theater man ... [having] never attended a theater ten times in my life," the culturally seasoned New Yorker retorted that, "Well, you are making your debut then, and we want to hear what you say."[44] Following this exchange, another roll call was done and, by this time, the missing Kentucky and Connecticut delegations had arrived. A Lutheran minister from Baltimore then delivered the opening prayer: "And we pray Thee, O God, that the compact Thou hast blessed may be perpetuated in all its integrity and beauty by the cement of Thy favor."[45] If ever a political convention needed assistance from the Almighty, it was this one.

President Cushing then delivered his opening address, which primarily reviewed the actions taken at Charleston. The convention had voted to adopt the minority report of the platform committee. A motion to reconsider the platform was still pending when the convention adjourned. With respect to the nomination of a presidential candidate, Cushing reviewed that the two-thirds rule had been adopted in Charleston but, after numerous ballots, no candidate had met this threshold. He then added a third issue that now faced the Baltimore convention — the seating of delegates. Before adjourning in Charleston, the convention had adopted a resolution directing the Democratic parties in those states where delegates had walked out of the convention "to make provision for supplying all vacancies on their respective delegations to this Convention, when it shall re-assemble."[46] Several states had done this and had selected new delegates, who had come to Baltimore. The problem was that most of the seceding delegates at Charleston had also shown up in Baltimore and wanted their seats back. While the fireworks in Charleston had been over the platform, in Baltimore they would be over whether and to what extent the seceding delegates would be permitted to rejoin the proceedings. In an eerie foreshadowing of questions that the country would face a few years hence during the Reconstruction era at the conclusion of the Civil War, questions were asked as to what was the meaning of secession, was it legal, could it be revoked and, if so, what would be the terms for readmission?

The convention first debated what amounted to a loyalty oath. A resolution was proposed that all vacant seats at Charleston be referred to a credentials committee "with the distinct understanding, however, that every person occupying a seat in this convention is bound in honor and good faith to abide by the action of this convention, and support its nominee."[47] The same arguments for and against this proposal were raised as were debated at the 1848 Democratic convention in Baltimore when a loyalty oath was proposed before seating the feuding Barnburner and Hunker delegations from New York. Some argued that any requirement imposed on the southern delegates to support the nominee was a requirement that was not being asked of the rest of the delegates. After debate on this resolution, it was rejected with 107½ votes in favor and 140½ against. New York, the largest delegation at the convention, cast its thirty-five votes against the resolution.[48] With a thirty-three vote difference between the yeas and nays, it became apparent at the outset of the convention that the Empire State held the balance of power. Shortly after 2:00 P.M., the convention voted to adjourn its morning session.[49]

When the convention resumed for its evening session at 5:00 P.M., the debate over the fate of the seceded southern delegates continued. A Pennsylvania delegate, Gilmore, proposed that the president of the convention be authorized to issue tickets of admission to the delegations from Arkansas, Florida, Texas, and Mississippi (where there were no competing delegations for those seats) and to have a Committee on Credentials appointed to determine whom to seat from the competing delegations from Alabama, Delaware, Georgia, and Louisiana.[50] An Iowa delegate then proposed that the Gilmore resolution be amended and that the following language be added:

> Resolved, that the citizens of the several states of the Union have an equal right to settle and remain in the Territories of the United States, and to hold therein, unmolested by any legislation whatsoever, their slave and other property; and that this Convention recognizes the opinion of the Supreme Court of the United States in the Dred Scott case as a true exposition of the Constitution ... and that the members of the convention pledge themselves, and require all others who may be authorized as delegates, to make the same pledge, to support the Democratic candidates, fairly and in good faith, nominated by the Convention according to the usages of the National Democratic Party.[51]

This resolution was totally contrary to the Douglas position of permitting restrictions on slavery in the territories during the territorial phase and would amount to an adoption of the majority platform committee report that had been rejected at Charleston. An angry Pennsylvania delegate, Congressman William Montgomery, rose in opposition and gave what reporter Halstead called "the speech of the day." Montgomery, a Douglas supporter, said that, as delegates, all were honor bound to support the nominee of the convention. With respect to the southerners who walked out at Charleston, he said, "They declared it. It was not our act, but theirs. They put themselves from us, not we from them.... We adjourned for what? For the purpose of enabling those states in the South, whose delegates had seceded, to fill up the places of those who had left us." Under these circumstances, Montgomery implored, it was not too much to ask the bolters to give an oath to support the nominee as a condition for readmission.[52] According to Halstead, the speech was "more than red hot" and "by the time he had concluded, the political atmosphere was at the temperature it reached in Charleston just before the explosion."[53] Interestingly, the official proceedings of the convention, which were approved and published after the convention by the Douglas team, do not record any of Montgomery's remarks and simply state that he "addressed the Convention in opposition to the last amendment offered."[54] Apparently, it was felt that publication of the inflammatory language would not serve any useful purpose to Douglas in the campaign. Although the convention then adjourned for the day with no votes being taken on the pending resolution, the political activity for the day was far from over.

On the evening of June 18, Baltimore's Monument Square was again the venue for nighttime political rallies, as it had been during the numerous prior presidential nominating conventions in the city. During this convention, however, even the evening rallies would be contentious. If the move five hundred miles north from Charleston to Baltimore was intended by party leaders to ensure a friendly local population that supported Douglas, the plan did not work. The home of Marylander Reverdy Johnson, which was on Monument Square, was the headquarters of the Douglas brain trust, while the leading southerners lodged at adjacent

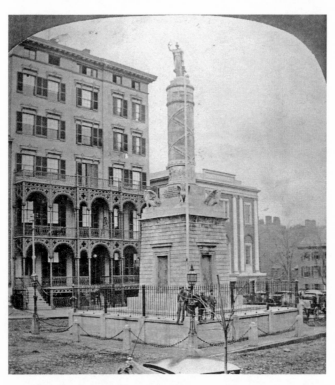

This photograph shows the west side of Baltimore's Monument Square as it looked at the time of the 1860 Democratic convention. Behind the Battle Monument to the left is the Gilmor House, the hotel from which southern speakers in 1860 addressed crowds in the square during evening rallies. To the right is the Baltimore Courthouse, where many speakers also addressed evening rallies during several of the conventions held in the city *(Enoch Pratt Free Library)*.

Gilmor House. To the pleasure of a large crowd gathered in the square, around 8:00 P.M., three bands began, alternately, to play music — a Pittsburgh band played from the balcony of Barnum's, Chicago's Great Western band performed from the balcony of the Gilmor House, and Cincinnati's Mentor's Band entertained from Guy's Monument House, which was located across the square. The early evening belonged to the Douglas backers. Shortly after 9:00 P.M., pro–Douglas speeches started from the steps of the Johnson house. Around 10:00 P.M., however, calls rang out from the opposing viewpoint, with shouts of "Yancey, Yancey, Yancey!" coming from the crowd. The Alabaman, Yancey, who had led the walkout in Charleston, soon appeared on the balcony of Gilmor House and made a fiery speech supporting the southern position, followed by other speakers. Meanwhile, the pro–Douglas speeches continued from the Johnson house. The scene was reminiscent of the one sixteen years earlier, in 1844, when the Democratic convention and the Tyler convention met at the same time in Baltimore and held competing evening rallies on Monument Square. As Halstead reported, there were "two mass meetings of the Democracy, side by side, both in full blast for about three hours." The southerners carried the evening, lasting until 1:00 A.M. and hearing a second "silver-toned" speech from their hero, Yancey. Through it all, Baltimore's "citizens swarmed forth enjoying the pleasant air, the excellent music discoursed by half a dozen bands, and the excitement of the politicians who were in fervent heat and violent commotion."[55]

On the morning of the second day of the convention, Tuesday, June 19, 1860, tempers seemed to have cooled somewhat. Most of the inflammatory resolutions from the previous day were withdrawn and the convention passed a resolution in its morning session simply referring all disputed delegate seats to the Committee on Credentials.[56] Four members of the Charleston credentials committee, from Oregon, Delaware, Kentucky, and California, announced that they no longer wished to serve and replacements were named. There being no business to conduct until the issue of the seating of delegates was resolved, the convention adjourned until 5:00 P.M.[57] When the convention resumed for the evening session, the Committee on Credentials announced it had not yet completed its report. The issue of tickets for the seating of undisputed delegates was again brought up by a delegate, Fisher, of Virginia, who accused president Cushing of keeping out dozens of legitimate delegates: "I know, sir, there are fifty representatives from different portions of the country on your outside now that cannot get admittance because you have a police there that have the physical power to keep them out of this body."[58] An angry Cushing responded that he had set up a system whereby delegate tickets were delivered by the convention's sergeant-at-arms to the chairman of each state delegation and it was not his fault if some of the state chairmen failed to properly deliver them to the appropriate persons. He stated that the gatekeepers were needed to keep non-ticketed persons from having access to the floor of the convention and, if the convention wanted to assign the responsibility for tickets to someone other than himself, he would be glad to be relieved of it.[59] A Pennsylvania delegate, Randall, explained the nature of the problem. Apparently, due to the counterfeiting of tickets, "a change in the tickets were made and announced. Members of the convention were requested to change their blue tickets for red ones. They did not change them, and the consequence was, when they came with the blue tickets, they were refused admission, but as soon as the door-keepers understood it they were admitted without difficulty."[60] The ticket controversy explained, and unable to transact any business with the credentials dispute still pending, the convention adjourned for the day. According to Halstead, a heavy downpour at the time of adjournment kept many delegates in the theater, during which time several persons amused the crowd while waiting for the rain to clear.[61]

The third day, Wednesday, June 20, 1860, was equally uneventful inside the Front Street Theater. The Committee on Credentials still was not ready to report. The morning and evening sessions lasted only a few minutes, in order to that the delegates could be advised as to the progress, or lack thereof, of the committee. Cushing did read to the convention a hostile letter he had received from the chairman and four members of the Florida delegation. It had been reported in a newspaper that the Floridians had presented their credentials to Cushing and wished to be admitted to the convention. Lest there be no misunderstanding, the delegation requested that Florida "be omitted from the list of those States represented, or seeking to be represented, in the Convention over which you preside, until they shall themselves notify you of their desire to participate in your proceedings."[62] The angry Floridians, who were in Baltimore, apparently wanted to watch from a distance and see how the convention treated the delegates from Florida and other southern states who had bolted from the proceedings at Charleston before committing themselves to any participation in Baltimore.

While there was lack of activity on the floor, there was plenty of action going on elsewhere in Baltimore. Tempers were rising to the level of violence. At a meeting of the Committee on Credentials, a fight broke out between representatives of two rival Arkansas delegations, William Hooper and Thomas C. Hindman, the latter being a congressman. Hooper denounced all conventions as composed of "demagogues, tricksters, and political pettifoggers" and shook his hand in Hindman's face, whereupon the latter "slapped him violently on the face" and started to draw his pistol before other members of the committee intervened.[63] A similar dispute arose between two Virginia delegates, Yost and Brannan. Angry words and a slap to the face occurred, leading to a challenge for a duel, but the controversy was settled without bloodshed. A more serious dispute occurred between two Delaware men, Whitely and Townsend, both of whom were vying for the same delegate seat. Whitely, a congressman, had originally held the seat, but walked out at Charleston, and Townsend had been named as his replacement. The two fought on Tuesday evening and "language of an exciting personal character" passed between them. One report had Whitely sustaining a black eye. Vowing revenge, Whitely went to the hotel where Townsend was staying, the Maltby House, at 5:00 A.M. the next morning and lay in wait for his opponent. As Townsend walked by at 5:15 A.M. on his way to the washroom, Whitely "struck him a violent blow on the side of the head" and the two "kept striking rapidly at each other." When both went to the floor, Townsend ended on top and held the advantage in the encounter until the hotel's landlord separated the two and called the police. Upon getting up, Whitely thrust his hand into his pocket, as if reaching for a gun. The alert Townsend spotted a pistol on the floor and "instantly secured it," placing it in his own pocket, saying, "I will take care of this for the present."[64] Baltimore's finest arrived and took Whitely away to the station house. The following day, after a dispute on the convention floor between two Pennsylvania delegates, Randall and Montgomery, the son of Randall spotted Montgomery walking near the convention hall during a recess. On behalf of his father, the younger Randall "dealt him several blows to the face, causing the blood to flow profusely." Montgomery recovered and knocked his assailant to the ground, at which time both were separated by onlookers.[65] Delegates beating each other up right and left did not bode well for a peaceful resolution of the issues facing the convention.

On the morning of the convention's fourth day, Thursday, June 21, the Great Western Brass Band was in an upper gallery of the Front Street Theater and entertained the arriving crowd and delegates prior to the call to order at midmorning. After an opening prayer invoking "the spirit of Justice and compromise," President Cushing called for the long awaited report from the Committee on Credentials. Just as the chairman of the committee was about to rise, in another bad omen, a loud crash was heard in the theater. No Baltimore political convention, it seems, would be complete without some structural failure of the building and a resulting panic. Delegates to the sides and rear of the main floor looked to the center area in front of the stage, where the sound came from, and, to their dismay, saw the New York and Pennsylvania delegations "sinking out of sight." A "scene of the wildest excitement ensued" as the delegates, thinking that the building was collapsing, rushed for the exits. In the commotion, the *Baltimore Sun* reported that "several small sized delegates were knocked down and trodden under foot by their terrified compatriots." In addition, "Two or three excited individuals made a bolt for the windows which open upon the right and left of the stage, achieved a speedy though not very graceful exit through those orifices, and took to their heels. For aught we can tell, they may be running yet."[66] Reporter Halstead noted that many ran in his direction and toward the president's chair on the stage: "Delegates rushed in masses to the windows, and climbed, nimbly as monkeys, over the chairs of the reporters seeking, according to appearances, to place themselves under the protection of the president."[67]

From above, those in the galleries could see the cause of the problem, which was not as severe as it seemed to those at its epicenter. Due to the mass of people in the theater, a beam supporting the temporary flooring covering the orchestra pit had given way, causing the floor in about a fifty-foot radius to sink about three feet, forcing all in the area "into one wedged mass, from which they extricated themselves as rapidly as possible, and fled in all directions to distant parts of the house."[68] The main floor was cleared, the cause of the problem was discovered, and the convention recessed for an hour while carpenters repaired the broken beam. During the intermission, the inevitable jokes about the failure of the party's platform spread around the theater, while a brass band from Philadelphia entertained the galleries.[69]

The floor repaired, the convention moved to the business of determining who would be entitled to take seats on it. Delegate Krum of Missouri, chairman of the Committee on Credentials, rose to announce that the committee was divided and would be presenting three different reports to the convention for consideration. The majority report, which Krum supported and presented, noted that there were delegations from five states (Alabama, Florida, Louisiana, Mississippi, and Texas), that were wholly vacant after the secession at Charleston and that three state delegations (Arkansas, Delaware, and Georgia) were partially vacant. There were also some disputed individual seats in Massachusetts and Missouri.[70] No delegates from South Carolina were present in Baltimore and seeking readmission. The majority report also concluded that no delegates from Florida should be seated, as no one from that state had appeared before the committee with credentials. Three states (Delaware, Mississippi, and Texas) did not have disputed delegations and the majority report recommended readmission of the seceded Charleston delegates from those states that wanted to return to the convention. Those were the easy decisions. With respect to the remaining four states at issue, the majority report recommended that all competing delegates from Arkansas and Georgia be seated, but that they each be given partial votes to be cast toward their state's Electoral College allotment of votes at the convention. Concerning Alabama and Louisiana, the majority report recommended the total exclusion of the seceded Charleston delegates from those two states and the seating of the replacement delegates that had been appointed after the Charleston convention. Committee chairman Krum presented the majority report as a carefully crafted compromise, given the "new, complex and unusual questions, that have arisen since the session at Charleston.... The Committee ... desired to do justice and to discharge those duties with fidelity, and in their behalf I deserve to say that they have labored with an industry that I have never seen surpassed and rarely equaled."[71]

The minority members of the Committee on Credentials were not impressed. Their spokesman, delegate Stevens of Oregon, addressed the convention and presented their alternative report. This report was signed by committee members from nine states (California, Delaware, Kentucky, New Jersey, North Carolina, Oregon, Pennsylvania, Tennessee, and Virginia).[72] Stating, "We differ radically from the majority of the committee, both in much of the action we recommend to the Convention and the principles which should control each action,"[73] the minority report called for the seating of *all* of the delegates who had bolted at Charleston and for *all* of the replacement delegates to be excluded. According to the minority report, the seceding delegates were "duly accredited to Charleston. They withdrew and never resigned. They returned to their respective constituencies ... [and new state conventions met, which] approved their course, continued their powers, and accredited them to Baltimore."

Stevens criticized the proceedings at which the replacement delegates were named by several of the states as not being the true conventions of the Democratic Party of those states and as having been held without any official sanction.[74] A second minority report by a single delegate, Gittings of Maryland, agreed with the majority in all respects except as to the Alabama delegation, since he believed that the seceding delegates from that state had been recertified at a properly accredited state convention held in Alabama after the departure at Charleston.[75] The gauntlets now thrown, the New York delegation, whose thirty-five votes would likely determine the outcome of the seating contest, requested a recess to ponder its options. This was granted and the convention adjourned until 4:30 P.M.[76] According to reporter Halstead, the New York delegation had caucused and had only narrowly favored the majority report of the Committee of Credentials. The impression of many was that the New Yorkers "were at the last minute proposing to slaughter Douglas."[77] Rumors were circulating that the southerners, if New York voted in favor of the minority report to seat all of the seceded Charleston delegates, would agree to any presidential candidate chosen by the Empire State — anybody but Stephen Douglas.

When the convention resumed for its evening session, the large number of seats reserved in the front and center of the main floor for the Empire State remained vacant. A half hour went by and, still, no New Yorkers. Shortly after 5:00 P.M., a member of the New York delegation appeared, apologized for the delay, and advised that his colleagues were still "in consultation and will be unable for some length of time to record their votes" on the credentials reports. A roll call was taken and, by vote of 161 yeas and 48 nays, the convention acceded to the wishes of the New Yorkers and agreed to adjourn until the following day.[78]

That evening, there again were competing Douglas and anti–Douglas rallies in Monument Square, which only hardened the ill will between the two sides.[79] The Douglas speakers proclaimed the virtues of their man from the Reverdy Johnson house, while, only a few feet away, "hundreds of noisy fellows yelled 'Yancey! Yancey!'" from the top of their lungs until the silver-tongued Alabaman appeared from a balcony of the Gilmor House and again espoused the merits of the southern cause. Adding to the mix, a large group of Baltimore gang members appeared in the crowd, shouting "Three cheers for Bell and Everett!," the candidates of the Constitutional Union Party who had been nominated in Baltimore one month earlier. As Halstead observed the scene, he noted that "the cauldron boiled and bubbled more and more."[80]

On Friday, June 22, 1860, the American Civil War began. Shots would not be fired until the following April at Fort Sumter, but the die was cast on this early summer day at the Front Street Theater in Baltimore. On this day, the great Democratic Party of the United States irreconcilably split, foreshadowing the split of the nation within a matter of months. After more discussion of the pending reports, a motion to substitute the minority report of the Committee on Credentials for the majority report was rejected by a vote of 100 yeas to 150 nays, with New York's thirty-five votes being cast against the minority report and deciding the contest.[81] At this point, votes were taken on each of the recommendations of the majority report. One by one, these were approved. When the Alabama recommendation was reached, the vote was 148 yeas to 100 nays in favor of seating the replacement Alabama delegates and excluding the Yancey-led Charleston delegation.[82] The southern fire-eaters were smoking. Next up was Georgia. The majority report had proposed seating both the Charleston and replacement delegations, with partial votes given to each. New York, which had been trying to broker a deal between the two factions, voted against the majority report's proposal as to Georgia, causing it to fail by a vote of 106 yeas to 145 nays.[83] New York then proposed seating the seceded Georgia delegates, which was passed.[84] Next, a motion to table a motion to reconsider the earlier rejection of the entire minority report was brought to a vote and, again, the

New Yorkers voted with the majority, leading to a tally of 113 yeas and 138 nays.[85] The minority report was on life support, but it still lived. What were those Yankees up to? That was the question perplexing everyone as the convention voted at 2:40 P.M. to adjourn and to not reconvene until 7:00 P.M.[86]

During the afternoon recess, Halstead reported that "the New York delegation was denounced on every side as composed of tricksters and bargainers." Rumors swirled around the convention hall and the major hotels that Douglas had sent word to withdraw his name in the interest of party unity, but those rumors were flatly denied by the key Douglas men.[87] During the recess, the New Yorkers offered the southerners a deal — New York would vote to admit all of the seceding Charleston delegates with the exception of Yancey and his delegation from Alabama. The southerners rejected this compromise and both parties walked away from the negotiations.[88] Thus, the fate of the convention came down to a disagreement over the admission of one state's delegation — Alabama.

When the convention reconvened a few minutes after 7:00 P.M., it did not take long for the fireworks to begin. All negotiations having broken down, the convention quickly voted, and rejected the motion to reconsider the minority report by a count of 113 yeas to 139 nays, with New York's thirty-five votes again making the difference in the outcome.[89] Delegate Russell of Virginia then sought and obtained the attention of President Cushing for an announcement. According to reporter Halstead, Russell, standing in his chair, was "very pale, nervous and solemn."[90] He announced to the hushed theater that, with the seating of delegates now "final, complete and irrevocable," it is "my duty now, by direction of a large majority of the delegation from Virginia, respectfully to inform this body that it is inconsistent with their convictions of duty to participate in its deliberations ... the reasons which impel us to take this important step will be rendered to those to whom only we are responsible, the Democracy of the Old Dominion. To you, sir, and to the body over which you preside, I have only to say in addition, that we bid you a respectful adieu."[91] With that, most of the Virginians got up and walked out of the Front Street Theater. The Old Dominion, the bellwether of the upper South, was leading the walkout. Next, eight of the ten North Carolina delegates announced their withdrawal. Tennessee's delegation then announced, by a vote of twenty to four, their withdrawal.

The delegates from Kentucky announced that they would be withdrawing for consultation in order to decide their final action.[92] And so on it went. Reverdy Johnson of Maryland, a key Douglas supporter, rose to announce that a portion of the Maryland delegation would also be leaving the convention.[93]

An angry delegate Smith of California then took to the floor and berated the Douglas men controlling the convention. Once again, the Douglas-issued official proceedings of the convention do not contain Smith's words, stating only that they were "of an uncivil and personal character."[94] Reporter Halstead, however, recorded Smith's outburst, and the reaction to it, for history:

> California is here with a lacerated heart, bleeding and weeping over the downfall and destruction of the Democratic Party. [Applause & laughter]. Yes, sir, the destruction of the Democratic party, consummated by assassins now grinning upon this floor [loud cries of "Order," "order," "put him out,]" and great confusion...
>
> This convention has properly been held in a theater, and upon that stage, a play has been enacted this evening that will prove a tragedy of which the Democratic party will be the victim. [Mingled hisses and applause.] I then do state that these have been wrongs perpetuated upon the Democracy of that deep and damning character that it does not permit California longer to participate in the proceedings of this irregular convention.[95]

Smith was not done. He went on to charge the Douglas men of perpetuating a "trick" on the convention at Charleston, which, he charged, enabled the minority to control the majority. When his fifteen minutes of speaking time had expired, Smith would not give up the floor. According to Halstead, "He was as hard to choke off as a bull-dog, but all the Douglas men in the house, aided by the president, succeeded in getting him down."[96]

The bad news from the West continued for the Douglasites. As soon as they got the Californian Smith muzzled, delegate Stevens of Oregon, who was a member of the Committee of Credentials and who had presented the now rejected minority report to the convention, rose and announced that he had a "most melancholy duty to perform." The Oregon delegation would also be withdrawing, because "[b]y your action today, gentlemen as much entitled to seats as ourselves, in our opinion, are excluded from the floor."[97]

A Georgia delegate, Gaulden, then took the floor, proclaimed that he was staying at the convention, that he was for the Democratic Party, and that he was unapologetically for slavery:

> I am a pro-slavery man in every sense of the word, aye, an African slave-trademan.... This institution of slavery, as I have said elsewhere, has done more to advance the prosperity and intelligence of the white race, and of the human race, than all else together. I believe it to be founded upon the laws of nature and upon the law of God ... I glory in being a slave-breeder myself ... I think I shall live to see the day when the doctrines which I advocate tonight will be the doctrine of Massachusetts of the North.

According to Halstead, "Mr. Gaulden's speech was generally laughed at, but he was in sober and resolve earnest.... Nothing delights him more than to tell of ... his plantation."[98] Once again, the Douglas-issued official proceedings of the convention do not contain Gaulden's extreme pro-slavery and controversial words, which the Douglas campaign surely did not want known by the northern public, as they would have been read with disgust by many and result in their opposition to any candidate nominated at a convention where such words were spoken. If not for Halstead, all we would know was that Gaulden "addressed the Convention in an eloquent manner, advocating the maintenance of the integrity of the National Democratic party."[99] At 10:30 P.M., after an eventful evening, the convention adjourned for the day.

When the convention reassembled on the morning of Saturday, June 23, 1860, the Front Street Theater gave the appearance of hosting a sparsely attended weekend matinee performance. There were plenty of empty seats on the main floor and in the balconies, for there was a new competing show in Baltimore opening that day. If the Douglas forces controlling the convention thought things could not get worse after the disastrous events on Friday, they were wrong. The Kentuckians announced that, as a result of their overnight consultations, ten of their fifteen delegates were withdrawing and the remaining five were suspending their participation in the convention with "full liberty to act as future circumstances may dictate."[100]

Then came the bombshell of the day. After a motion was made to proceed to a roll call on the nomination of a presidential candidate, the convention's president, Caleb Cushing, from Massachusetts, of all places, announced he was stepping down. He stated that he had remained in his post after the withdrawal of delegates at Charleston,

> But circumstances have since transpired which compel me to pause. The delegations of a majority of the States of this Union have, either in whole or in part, in one form or another, ceased to participate in the deliberations of this body ... I deem it is my duty to resign my place as presiding officer of this Convention in order to take my seat on the floor as a member of the delegation of Massachusetts ... and to abide by whatever may be its determination in regard to its further action in the Convention.[101]

When Cushing announced he was stepping down as president, cheers and applause rang out in the theater, for two entirely different reasons. According to reporter Halstead, delegates from many northwestern states "cheered him violently as he retired from the chair," in elation over getting rid of him, while the applause from the galleries was supportive of Cushing's stance in sympathy with the cause of the departed delegates.[102] One of the convention's vice presidents, David Tod of Ohio, quickly replaced Cushing in the president's chair. The affront to one of their own by the delegates did not sit well with the Massachusetts delegation. As the roll call of the states for the nomination of a presidential candidate began, delegate Benjamin F. Butler of the Bay State repeatedly tried to be recognized, but was overruled by the new presiding officer. When Massachusetts was reached in the roll call, Butler finally had the floor and announced that a majority of his state's delegates "do not propose further to participate in the doings of the convention," and presented a note to the chair, dated the previous day, giving the stated reason as the exclusion of a Massachusetts delegate, Hallett, who had been unable to attend the convention in Charleston and whose seat was taken there by a substitute, Chafee, who was deemed by the Baltimore convention to now be the proper holder of the seat. The note was signed by fifteen Massachusetts delegates, including Cushing.[103] Since the note was dated the previous day, Cushing obviously knew he would be withdrawing from the convention when he stepped down as the presiding officer that morning. Butler left with a parting shot, stating that he "would not sit in a convention where the African slave trade was upheld," referring to the speech given the previous day by the Georgia delegate, Gaulden.[104] Butler, who had brought a personal bodyguard with him to the convention, "a Boston prize fighter who stood near with a bulldog expression," then led the walkout of the fifteen Bay Staters from the theater.[105]

The convention was now in a real quandary. When it began, there were 303 delegate seats. Under the Democratic Party's two-thirds rule, which had been reaffirmed just weeks earlier at Charleston, 202 votes were needed for the nomination. Moreover, under the ruling of then President Cushing after the walkout at Charleston, a ruling which had been affirmed by the convention, the two-thirds rule applied to the total number of delegates at the beginning of the convention, not to the number remaining after the walkout. Now, in Baltimore, there was an even larger walkout than at Charleston and more than one-third of the delegates in Baltimore had now withdrawn. How does a convention that has a two-thirds rule nominate a candidate with less than two-thirds of the delegates present? The answer was to change the rule, but to do it in a way in which it appeared that no change had been made.

The first ballot was then taken. During the roll call of the states, it was the remarks of the few remaining southern delegates that stood out. The sole remaining North Carolina delegate cast his single vote for Douglas and spoke eloquently of his love for the Democratic Party:

> I stand alone for North Carolina.... I have a birthright amidst the national Democracy which I never intend to forfeit.... Although my friends have gone — friends with whom I have heretofore rallied in many a fiercely fought contest. I bid them good bye with sorrow, saying naught against their motives. They have gone from us, and, as I think, with strange gods, but I intend to worship where I have done heretofore.... Soon a great battle is to be fought, which, in a probability, will decide the destinies of my country....
>
> I expect to stand on the deck of the old Democratic ship, launched eighty-four years ago, freighted with the hopes and interests and destinies of the country, as I have stood upon her when "she walked the waters like a thing of life," and seemed to dare the elements to strife. Now, in the midst of storms and tempests, I expect to stand by her, and I hope and believe she will outride the storm, and lead us to the haven of a glorious destiny.... But if she must go

> down amid the dark waters of division and sectionalism, I expect to cling to the last spar that
> floats upon the troubled waters, and go down with the hopes and interests of the country.[106]

One of the Alabama replacement delegates proclaimed: "Shall it be said that in 1860, here in Baltimore, the grave of this Union was dug? The Star Spangled Banner still waves over us — shall it continue to wave?... The struggle for disunion is putting forth its last efforts. But the people will rally around us." He cast Alabama's nine votes for Douglas. A Louisiana replacement delegate cast his state's votes for Douglas, stating, "Louisiana is unwilling to risk her future and the future of this Union upon impracticable issues and purely theoretical abstractions."[107]

When the votes on the first ballot were tallied, a total of 190 votes had been cast, of which Douglas received 173, with 17 scattered votes for other candidates.[108] Delegate Church of New York then proposed that Douglas be declared the nominee, "having now received two-thirds of all the votes given in the Convention.[109] Much discussion ensued. The thrust of the argument of the supporters of the resolution was that the two-thirds rule as laid down in Charleston was simply an interpretation of the rule by the convention's then-president (the now departed Cushing), that the convention had sustained his ruling, and "all that is now necessary is to rescind the vote sustaining the decision of the Chair."[110] As one of the few remaining Virginia delegates noted, "We are called upon now to do what we ought to have been done at Charleston, otherwise we must stay here and ballot and ballot, and ballot without ever nominating. If we had adopted the resolution at Charleston, as we ought to have done, we would have concluded long since."[111] A second ballot was decided upon, which resulted in 194 total votes cast, with 181 of those going to Douglas.[112] This was an increase of eight votes over his first ballot tally, but still short of the two-thirds requirement of 202 votes, as determined in Charleston, and an impossible number to reach with less than 202 delegates remaining at the convention. A Virginia delegate, Hoge, then re-offered the earlier resolution of delegate Church of New York, declaring Douglas the nominee "having now received two-thirds of all the votes given in this Convention ... in accordance with the rules governing this body, and in accordance with the uniform customs and rules of former Democratic National Conventions."[113] Not really, but close enough. The resolution was unanimously approved on a voice vote and, two months after the 1860 nominating convention of the Democratic Party opened in Charleston on April 23, the party finally had a nominee for the presidency. Amid applause, the waving of hats, and a band in the upper gallery playing "Hail to the Chief," three cheers were given for Stephen A. Douglas of Illinois each time his name was called.[114] In the round of speeches following the nomination, a Pennsylvania delegate, Dawson, praised the heritage of the convention's host city and state:

> If here in this beautiful city which looks out upon the Chesapeak [sic], we could have
> needed any incitement to a broad patriotism in our deliberations, it should have been
> found in the associations in the midst of which we are assembled, for it was at Annapolis at
> the close of the Revolution that Washington resigned his commission. It is also within sight
> of the spot at which we are convened that imposing monuments rise to the greatness of his
> memory and to the patriotism of the sons of Maryland.[115]

The convention then adjourned until 7:00 P.M.

The remaining item on the agenda for the evening session was the selection of a vice presidential nominee. Even in this choice, this snake-bitten convention would suffer a final humiliation. In a gesture of appreciation to the southern delegates who remained at the convention, it was agreed that they could select a candidate for the second spot on the ticket with Douglas. The southerners caucused during the recess and announced at the opening of the evening session that their choice was Governor Benjamin Fitzpatrick of Alabama, who was lauded as "a self-made man — a man in the prime of life — a man of vigorous intellect — a man of great administrative talent — a popular Governor of his own State — a national man — a life-long Democrat." On a roll call vote, 199 votes were cast (interestingly, five more than had voted in the second presidential ballot), with all but one vote going to Fitzpatrick.[116] It was no coincidence that a son of Alabama had been put in the vice presidential slot; that was the state whose delegation had led the secession at Charleston and which was the focus of the credentials battle in Baltimore.

Within forty-eight hours after the convention adjourned, however, Fitzpatrick responded with a firm "No, thanks." The Alabama governor, who was in Washington, met on June 25 with the committee appointed to formally advise him of his nomination and responded the same day by declining it. Noting that the Republicans and the Constitutional Union Party had held united conventions, Fitzpatrick lamented the "melancholy spectacle" of his divided party and noted that "designation as a candidate for the high position would have been more gratifying to me if it had proceeded from a united Democracy — united both as to principles and to man."[117] The same day, June 25, the National Democratic Committee met at a hotel in Washington and named Herschel V. Johnson, a former senator and former governor of Georgia, as the replacement vice presidential nominee. Johnson quickly accepted.[118]

In one of its last acts before leaving the Front Street Theater and adjourning, the convention tweaked its platform in an attempt to make it more palatable to southern voters. At the request of a Louisiana delegate, Wickliffe, the convention overwhelmingly approved a platform amendment stating that "during the existence of the Territorial Governments the measure of restriction, whatever it may be, imposed by the Federal Constitution on the power of the Territorial Legislature over the subject of the domestic relations, as the same has been or shall hereafter be finally determined by the Supreme Court of the United States, should be respected by all."[119] In other words, if the Constitution does limit the ability of territorial legislatures to restrict or prohibit slavery prior to statehood, then the Supreme Court has the final say. It was the final split hair over strong opinions concerning a narrow issue that would plunge the nation into civil war.

The nomination of Stephen A. Douglas at the Front Street Theater was not the only presidential nomination made in Baltimore on June 23, 1860. The delegates who had withdrawn from the convention, numbering slightly more than one hundred, walked a few blocks southeast of the theater and opened their own convention at the Hall of the Maryland Institute on the same Saturday. This grand hall, which had been the site of three prior presidential nominating conventions in Baltimore, now hosted a fourth such gathering. The hastily called convention was the hottest ticket in Baltimore that day and the gallery, which opened at 11:00 A.M., quickly filled. In the competition for public attention, this newly opened drama outdrew the closing act of the week-old show that had been playing at the Front Street Theater.

When the opening gavel fell at 12:30 P.M., this meeting of like-minded individuals was in a festive mood. The *Baltimore Sun* noted that "[a]ll restraint of feeling had disappeared, and a spirit of the most cordial unanimity and harmony characterized every man and every feature."[120] A large American flag hung at the south end of the hall. Reporter Halstead, who had hurried over from the other convention, observed that Garrett of Virginia "seemed as pleased as a school-boy with new boots." Of the man who had started it all with his delegation's secession at Charleston, Yancey of Alabama, Halstead commented, "Yancey, who always wears a surface smile, twisted about in his seat with the unrest of intolerable felicity, laid his head first upon one shoulder and then upon the other, and glowed with satisfaction."[121] Delegate

Russell of Virginia was named the temporary president and declared this proceeding to be the National Democratic Convention, not the gathering from which they had just departed. With the gallery full, members of the public were also permitted to fill vacant seats on the main floor. The convention quickly appointed a Committee on Permanent Organization of five members, a Committee on Credentials, and then adjourned for the afternoon.[122]

When the gathering resumed for its evening session shortly after 5:00 P.M., the Committee on Permanent Organization, having concluded its deliberations, announced its recommendation for president of the convention. A familiar name, Caleb Cushing of Massachusetts, was nominated, which resulted in wild applause from the delegates and the gallery. Yes, that Caleb Cushing, the man who had resigned as president of the Front Street Theater convention because it was no longer representative of a majority of the states of the Union, was now nominated, and accepted, the presidency of an even smaller and less representative gathering of Democrats. His fellow Bay Stater, Benjamin F. Butler (who, within a year, would be a Union army general and lead a military occupation of Baltimore) was proudly at Cushing's side as a member of the Massachusetts delegation. Butler's presence at, and full participation in, this rump convention comprising primarily pro-slavery Southerners is one of, if not the most, supreme ironies of the campaign of 1860.

Cushing then took his seat at the president's chair with a "burst of applause, which fairly shook the solid walls of the Institute and made glass tingle in the casements."[123] The convention then went about its business at hyper-speed. The Committee on Credentials reported that there were slightly more than one hundred delegates present from twenty states. For a platform, the convention adopted the majority platform committee report from the Charleston convention "without the crossing of a 't' or dotting of an 'i.'" The most significant of the planks was the statement that the government of a territory "is provisional and temporary, and, during its existence, all citizens of the United States have an equal right to settle with their property in the territory without their rights either of person or property being destroyed or impaired by congressional or territorial legislation."[124]

Wasting no time, the convention then moved to the nomination of a presidential candidate. Four names were placed in nomination: John C. Breckinridge of Kentucky, the sitting vice president of the United States; Daniel S. Dickinson of New York; Joseph Lane of Oregon; and R. M. T. Hunter of Virginia. The names of Lane and Hunter were quickly withdrawn and the first ballot proceeded with only the names of Breckinridge and Dickinson, the former receiving fifty-one votes and the latter twenty votes. Under the rules adopted, where only one delegate was present from a congressional district, that delegate was entitled to cast only one-half of a vote, which accounts for the low total number of votes cast by the approximately one hundred delegates. It was then proposed that Breckinridge be nominated by acclamation, which was approved. Moving to the vice presidency, only one name was placed in nomination, Joseph Lane of Oregon, and he was quickly nominated.[125]

The convention concluded its one-day session with a late evening speech from its symbolic leader, the fire-eater of fire-eaters, William Lowndes Yancey of Alabama. Although the *Baltimore Sun* reported that Yancey "made an eloquent, patriotic and lengthy speech, which throughout was widely cheered,"[126] Halstead had a different take on the oration. After praising Yancey for his speaking skills, the Cincinnati reporter felt that he went on for far too long and, as a result, lost his audience:

> There is not the slightest symptom of the fanatic about him.... But you don't know him until you have heard him speak. His voice is clear as a bugle-note, and at the same time

singularly blended with its music is a sharp high metallic ring, like that of a triangle of steel. This peculiar voice, always clear and sharp, pierces to a great distance, and would instantly command attention in any assembly.

And with all of Mr. Yancey's power it is due to the truth to say that he was guilty of that terrible offense on such an occasion — too much speaking — and contrived to use up very handsomely the brilliant reputation with which he came to Baltimore, as an orator of the first order.... His speech was a disenchanter. He was not calculated to assist his party at all, but rather to place embarrassments in its way. He denied being a disunionist, but his talk respecting the Union did not indicate any warmth or affection for our common nationality.... He had the bad taste, too, to enter largely into Alabama politics, and gave details of matters purely local in their nature. The people left the hall by the hundreds; yet he spoke on, as if unconscious that instead of captivating the multitudes he was boring them. Cushing became uneasy, nervous, and fidgety ... when he concluded it was evident that there would not be any more speech making. If the eloquence of Yancey had become a weariness, who would dare propose to stand up before the jaded crowd, sick, as all were, of the very sound of the human voice.[127]

With that, June 23, 1860, one of the most eventful days in Baltimore history, came to an end. Since sunrise, two separate conventions had nominated two separate candidates, Douglas and Breckinridge, both Democrats, for the presidency. At the beginning of the year, Baltimore had been slated to be a mere observer of the 1860 campaign. By the end of June, however, the city had hosted three presidential nominating conventions and three of the candidates in the race for the White House had been nominated in the Monumental City.

Republican Convention

There was, of course, a fourth candidate nominated by his party in the election of 1860: Abraham Lincoln, a man who would win the election and go on to become, in the view of many, the greatest president in American history. In between the Democratic debacles in Charleston and Baltimore, the Republican Party held its second presidential nominating convention in Chicago, beginning on May 16, 1860. Other than the Democratic convention in Cincinnati in 1856, no other major party convention had ever been held outside of the East Coast. By 1860, Chicago had a population of just over 110,000, ranking it near the bottom of the ten largest cities in the United States. Advancements in rail transportation made travel to Chicago relatively quick and easy. A group of New York delegates left Buffalo left by train at 6:00 A.M. and were in the Windy City shortly after 9:00 P.M., a trip lasting just over fifteen hours. They rode on rails that "were as firm as the rock of Gibraltar" and, en route, "along the road at every depot and at every station crowds of people were seen, waving their handkerchiefs, shouting for this or that favorite" candidate. On the eve of the convention, it was reported in Chicago that "the city swarms like a bee-hive. Hotels are full ... and on every side is in progress the work of president-making."[128] The convention's delegates, reporters, and onlookers gathered at the city's most exclusive hotels, the Richmond House (located at South Water Street and Michigan Avenue), the Tremont House (southeast corner of Dearborn and West Lake Streets), and the Sherman House (northwest corner of North Clark and West Randolph Streets).[129]

The convention was held at a just-completed arena called the Wigwam, located on the southeast corner of Lake and Market Streets, near the Chicago River. Built entirely of wood

The Wigwam in Chicago was a wooden structure built for hosting the 1860 Republican convention. The building got its name because the chiefs of the Republican Party would be meeting there to select a presidential nominee.

in just over one month, the Wigwam, which held more than 10,000 people, was built specifically for the purpose of hosting the Republican convention and was given its name because the "chiefs" of the party would be meeting there.[130] Only about one-third of space in the building was allotted for delegates, the rest being for onlookers. "The roof was arched and well supported by posts and braces, as were the galleries, and around all these were twined evergreens and flowers. The whole space over the platform was festooned with evergreens and drapery showing the National colors, the red, white, and blue." The arrangements committee also "brought in busts of American notables, ordered great allegorical paintings of Justice, Liberty, and the like, to suspend on the walls, borrowed a whole series of Healy portraits of American statesmen [and] made the Wigwam ... gay and festive."[131] A chair on the platform, which "attracted a great deal of attention," was specially made for the convention, consisting of wood from each of the nation's thirty-four states. The gavel used by the chairman of the proceedings was fashioned from a wooden fragment from the U.S.S. *Lawrence*, the flagship of Commodore Oliver Perry during the War of 1812.[132]

The pre-convention favorite for the 1860 Republican nomination was New York's William H. Seward, who was very popular in the North for his strong anti-slavery stance, but who was viewed as perhaps too strident on the issue to attract votes in the border and western states. In addition to Lincoln, the other major candidates were Edward Bates of Missouri, Salmon P. Chase of Ohio, and Simon Cameron of Pennsylvania. The Bates effort was being led at the convention by New York's Horace Greeley, the editor of the *New York Tribune*, a former ally of Seward and of Seward's political mentor, Thurlow Weed. Greeley, who had been denied a seat as part of the New York delegation, had privately been holding a grudge against Seward and Weed since 1854 over their failure to support his desire to run for statewide office in New York.[133] In Chicago, he managed to get a seat as a delegate to the convention from Oregon, of all places, when a delegate from that new state was unable to attend and named Greeley as his proxy. When Greeley's name was announced from the podium as Oregon's representative on the platform committee, "[i]t was received with universal applause and cries of 'When did you move?' from those near him."[134] Greeley would use his official position at the convention to extract revenge against Seward. As he made the rounds through several hotels in the city to lobby against Seward, one Seward supporter managed to pin a Seward for president sign on the back of Greeley's coat, which Greeley unknowingly wore for a short time, and which was "considered quite a good joke" by all but Greeley.[135] The Lincoln strategy in Chicago was simple — offend no one and become the second choice for the nomination among the supporters of all of his opponents. As events would turn out, it was a strategy that the Lincoln team played out to perfection, with some help from Greeley.

Reporter Halstead was also at the Republican convention and made observations of the scene in the lobby of one of the large Chicago hotels where delegates were staying, comments that are likely still applicable to political conventions of the modern era:

> The amount of idle talking that is done, is amazing. Men gather in little groups, and with their arms about each other, and chatter and whisper as if the fate of the country depended upon their immediate delivery of the mighty political secrets with which their imaginations are big. There are a thousand rumors afloat, and things of incalculable moment are communicated to you confidentially, at intervals of five minutes. There are now at least a thousand men packed together..., crushing each other's ribs, tramping each other's toes, and titillating each other with the gossip of the day; and the probability is, not one is possessed with a single political fact not known to the whole, which is of the slightest consequence to any human being.[136]

When the doors of the Wigwam opened on Wednesday, May 16, there were two areas for the public. Behind the platform on the main floor where the delegates were seated, and behind an adjacent area for alternates and special guests, there was a large open area, without seats, that could accommodate about 4,500 people. Reserved for men, this area had large landings that rose gradually from the platform to the front of the building and allowed a standing-room-only view of the proceedings.[137] Within five minutes of the doors being opened on each day of the convention, this area was packed. A more preferred area to watch the proceedings was from the gallery above the main floor, which had benches for sitting, and which provided an overhead view of the delegates from three sides of the building. The gallery, which could hold more than 2,000 people, was reserved for only those gentlemen who were accompanied by ladies. Eager to get inside and to be able to sit down, men grabbed schoolgirls and women off the sidewalks and paid them a quarter or a half dollar to accompany them through the doors. One woman picked up a few dollars by escorting one man through, then doubling back and repeating the process several times with different suitors, until she was "afraid of arrest if she carried the enterprise any further." One young Republican paid an Indian woman who was selling moccasins on the street to accompany him in, only to be turned back by a policeman at the door on the basis that "the squaw was not a lady," his protests against the decision falling on deaf ears.[138]

The convention was called to order by Edwin Morgan of New York, the chairman of the Republican National Committee. David Wilmot of Pennsylvania was named the temporary president of the proceedings. It was Wilmot who had, as an obscure Democratic congressman in 1846, introduced in the House of Representatives the famous "proviso" bearing his name that attempted to exclude slavery from any territory gained from Mexico in the Mexican War. He was introduced as "the man who dares to do the right, regardless of the consequences."[139] After a short speech from Wilmot and an opening prayer, the convention went about the business of appointing the standard committees on permanent organization, credentials, rules, and the platform. Much of the first day was spent arguing over an offer by the Chicago Board of Trade inviting the delegates to a boat ride, "a short excursion on Lake Michigan," which would be departing at 5:00 P.M. that afternoon. After initially voting to accept the offer, several delegates objected that the timing would keep the convention from going about its work and would likely cause the delegates to incur additional expenses by extending the convention for an extra day. An Ohio delegate protested, "I want it understood that I came here to work and am not going on the lake, nor is any delegate who came to work." After much debate, the convention decided that business came before pleasure and tourism, adopted a motion to reconsider, and reversed its initial decision to adjourn early for the afternoon cruise. It appointed a five-member committee to meet with the Chicago Board of Trade "so that at our adjournment we will meet them and cordially accept the invitation and take this excursion."[140]

As the convention opened for its second day on Thursday, May 17, a letter was read from the podium making a plea from the throng outside the Wigwam: "Sir — Can you not arrange to send out some effective speakers, to entertain 20,000 Republicans and their wives, outside the building?"[141] The crowd outside received news of the proceedings through a relay system. A man was stationed at one of the open skylights on the roof, who repeated what he could hear to another man standing several feet away on the roof, who relayed it to the next man, and so on, until it could be shouted to the masses outside.[142] The convention's second day was spent receiving and debating the reports of the various committees appointed the previous day.

The Committee on Order of Business and Rules recommended that there be two delegate seats allotted for each state's Electoral College votes (a reduction from the three allotted at the first Republican convention in 1856), that the platform be adopted before the nominations, that the states be called in their geographic order beginning in the northeast with Maine, that the rules of the House of Representatives apply, and that "304 votes, being a majority of the whole number of votes when all of the states of the Union are represented at this convention ... shall be required to nominate the candidates of this Convention for the offices of president and vice president." This latter provision was objected to and was, in effect, similar to the two-thirds rule used at Democratic conventions, since most of the southern states were not represented at the convention in Chicago and there were only 465 delegate seats. A minority report from the rules committee was presented, which favored a simple majority of the voting delegates present be required for nomination, and the convention overwhelmingly approved this substitution and adopted it, along with the remaining provisions of the committee's report. George Ashmun of Massachusetts was named the convention's permanent president.[143]

The report of the Committee on Credentials was received next. A total of twenty-four states, including six slave states, had sent delegations to the convention, plus two territories (Kansas and Nebraska), and the District of Columbia. Many delegates from northern states objected to votes being given to the slave states represented in Chicago, since the Republican Party hardly existed in many of those states and it was felt that the delegates were not representative of an organized statewide party. After much debate, these states were given votes, but at a reduced number. The two territories were allotted six votes each, and the District of

Columbia was given four votes, despite its lack of votes in the Electoral College.[144] This was consistent with the practice followed by the old Whig Party, and was different from the Democratic Party, which limited votes at its conventions to only fully organized states with votes in the Electoral College.

The report from the Committee on Resolutions was unambiguous on the key issue that gave rise to the Republican Party — no extension of slavery into the territories: "That the normal condition of all of the territory of the United States is freedom ... and we deny the authority of Congress, or of a territorial legislature, or of any individuals, to give legal existence to slavery in any territory of the United States." The platform did not call for the abolition of slavery in the states where it existed and recognized that "the right of each state to order and control its own domestic institutions according to its own judgment exclusively, is essential to the balance of power on which the perfection and endurance of our political fabric depends." It denounced any attempts at disunion, from whatever source, called for the immediate admission to the Union of Kansas as a free state, called for a transcontinental railroad, and opposed any attempts to change naturalization laws to make it more difficult for immigrants to become citizens. After some debate over an amendment to add language to the platform quoting and endorsing the first paragraph of the Declaration of Independence (during which one delegate stated that he also believed in the Bible and the Ten Commandments, but did not see the need to include them in the party's platform), the report of the platform committee was approved, with Thomas Jefferson's words that "all men are created equal" and are entitled to "life, liberty, and the pursuit of happiness" included. Upon the conclusion of the roll call vote on the platform, "the delegates and the whole of the vast audience rose to their feet in a transport of enthusiasm, the ladies waving their handkerchiefs, and the gentlemen their hats, while for many minutes the tremendous cheers and shouts of applause continued, and again and again were renewed and requested."[145]

The balloting for the nomination was done on the third day of the convention, which was Friday, May 18. After observing the proceedings on the first two days, the Lincoln floor managers recognized the positive effect that the noise produced by a favorable crowd inside the large hall could have on a candidate's chances and perceived momentum. "Honest Abe's" team then implemented a plan not worthy of their candidate's nickname. The Lincoln convention managers printed thousands of counterfeit tickets for admission to the convention on the third day, forged the signatures of convention officials on the tickets, handed them out to Lincoln supporters, and told them to get to the hall very early the next morning. The recipients of the tickets did so, the fake tickets were not detected, and the pro–Lincoln supporters packed the Wigwam. One local man "reputed to be able to shout across the breadth of Lake Michigan was summoned to take a prominent position, and another equally leather-lunged galoot ... was imported to do the same in another quarter, both with instructions to lead a tempest of cheers whenever Lincoln's name was mentioned."[146] Later that morning, more than a thousand Seward supporters assembled at the Richmond House, where the New York delegation was staying, and "marched away after their band of music — the band in splendid uniform and the Sewardites wearing badges ... the procession was four abreast, filing away in a cloud of dust, and one of their orators mounted upon a door-step, with hat and cane in his hands, was haranguing them as a captain might address his soldiers who were marching into battle."[147] By the time the Seward parade through the streets of Chicago arrived at the Wigwam, a couple of hours after the Lincoln supporters had shown up, they were denied admission despite holding valid tickets. The hall was already filled with the Lincoln supporters holding the counterfeit tickets.[148]

This drawing depicts the scene inside the Wigwam at the 1860 Republican convention in Chicago. More than 10,000 people packed the arena on the day of the nomination vote, some of whom were Lincoln supporters given counterfeit tickets by the Lincoln campaign team, in order to create momentum in the hall for the underdog Lincoln *(Library of Congress)*.

Meanwhile, backroom deals were being cut, purportedly offering cabinet seats in exchange for support of Lincoln. When Lincoln sent word to Chicago to "make no contracts that will bind me," his men in the trenches ignored their boss, one stating bluntly: "Lincoln ain't here, and don't know what we have to meet, so we will go ahead, as if we hadn't heard from him, and he must ratify it."[149] There were rumors that Simon Cameron of Pennsylvania was offered, or it was strongly implied to him that he would be offered, a cabinet seat if he would drop out of the race.

With 465 delegates present, a majority of 233 was needed for the nomination. Seven names were placed in nomination — the frontrunners, Seward, Lincoln, Bates and Chase, and also three lesser contenders, William Dayton of New Jersey, Cameron of Pennsylvania, and the perennial name that seemed to crop up many of the conventions of the era, Justice John McLean from Ohio. Seward's men were confident of victory. On the first ballot, Seward led with 173 votes, Lincoln with 102, Cameron with 50 , Chase with 49, Bates with 48, and the few remaining votes were scattered among other candidates. On the second ballot, Lincoln made his move when 44 of Cameron's votes from Pennsylvania switched to him.[150] With the pickup of additional second ballot votes in New England and in Delaware, Lincoln, with 181 votes, was only 3 votes behind Seward's 184 votes and clearly had the momentum, and a large cheering crowd in the Wigwam, to press it forward.[151] The small Oregon delegation, with five votes, had supported Bates on the first two ballots. However, persuaded by Greeley, the Oregon delegates cast their votes for Lincoln on the third ballot, which, along with the switch of other votes to the Illinoisan on the third ballot, put him well over the top and he won the nomination. Seward's supporters were in a state of shock, "Grown men wept like boys, faces drawn, white and aged as if ten years had passed in that one night of struggle."[152] The rest of the crowd, inside and outside, was jubilant: "The scene at this time beggars all description. Eleven thousand people inside the building, and 20,000 to 30,000 outside, were yelling and shouting at once; the cannon sent forth roar after roar in rapid succession; the delegates tore up the sticks and boards bearing the names of the several states, and waived them aloft over the heads of the vast multitude. Hats and handkerchiefs were waving, and the whole scene was one of the wildest enthusiasm."[153] Hannibal Hamlin of Maine, a former Democrat, was nominated on the second vice presidential ballot at the Chicago convention to be Lincoln's running mate.

It is said that revenge is a dish best served cold. Many of Seward's supporters attributed his unexpected defeat to Greeley: "Behind the scenes, in the unconscious shiftings of the convention, worked the great editor of New York, the man whom Oregon had sent there, the man whom the leaders of the party in his own state tried to shut out of the convention, the man, moreover, who, in the words of Seward's friends, turned the trick to the favorite of Illinois and thus worked out an old grudge that that had smouldered many years in ... [his] bosom."[154] Despite his defeat at the hands of Lincoln, Seward would, after the election, swallow

The beardless Abraham Lincoln of Illinois was nominated as the Republican standard-bearer in 1860, beating the favored William Seward of New York for the nomination. Hannibal Hamlin of Maine was nominated as the vice presidential candidate on the ticket with Lincoln *(Library of Congress)*.

his pride and accept Lincoln's offer to be secretary of state and would ably serve his former foe in that position throughout the Civil War.

The Campaign and Election

After attending all of the political conventions in 1860, reporter Murat Halstead of the *Cincinnati Commercial* was more cynical than ever. He advocated abolishing the presidential nominating convention system, which he referred to as the caucus system or, derisively, as "King Caucus." In Halstead's view, the convention system "in whatever party organization operative, is a system of swindling, by which the people are defrauded out of the effective exercise of the right of suffrage. There is no honesty in caucuses, no sound principle or good policy, except by accident; and the accidents that furnish the exception are rare indeed." He continued his criticism of "King Caucus" by arguing that "his platforms of principles are elaborations of false pretenses — his nominees are his obsequious viceroys — and he is the power behind the chairs of our chief magistrates, and under the tables of our cabinets, far more potent than those who visibly assume authority. If a Republican form of government is to be preserved in our confederacy, the people must make a bonfire of his throne."[155] As is often the case with critics, Halstead did not elaborate on what type of new system he would favor to replace presidential nominating conventions.

Perhaps more ink has been used in writing about the campaign and election of 1860 than for any other presidential election in American history. The intricacies are beyond the scope of this book. There were four major candidates in the contest, each with a different position on the key issue — slavery in the territories. Douglas and the northern Democrats favored popular sovereignty at statehood, and agreed that there could be restrictions on slavery by territorial legislatures prior to statehood. Breckinridge and the southern Democrats viewed any restriction on slavery in the territories as unconstitutional and forbidden. Bell and the Constitutional Unionists wanted to leave the entire issue up to the Supreme Court, while Lincoln and the Republicans opposed any extension of slavery into the territories under any circumstances. There were essentially two separate contests, one between Lincoln and Douglas in the North and the other between Bell and Breckinridge in the South. Lincoln was not even on the ballot in most southern states. Of the four candidates, Douglas was the only one to break with tradition and actively campaign. Douglas believed that the survival of the Union was at stake in the election and that he was the only candidate in the race who could save the country. He traveled the nation as no presidential candidate had ever done. In June, he was in New York and New England; in August he was in Virginia and North Carolina; in September he spoke in Baltimore and then went on to Pennsylvania, Ohio, Indiana, and his home state of Illinois. When the results of October state elections in the key states of Pennsylvania and Indiana showed Republican victories and foreshadowed a likely Republican presidential victory in November, Douglas pressed on, not for his own sake, but for the sake of the Union. He declared that "Mr. Lincoln is our next president.... We must try to save the Union. I will go South." And so he did, speaking late in the campaign at Memphis, Nashville, Chattanooga, Atlanta, Macon, Selma, and Montgomery, all the way urging his audiences to support the Union, no matter the outcome of the election.[156]

Election day in 1860 was on November 6 and, when the votes were counted, a million more people had voted against Lincoln than for him, but he won the presidency. The Railsplitter from Illinois won 1,866,452 votes, while the Little Giant from the same state finished second in popular votes with 1,376,957, followed by Breckinridge with 849,781 and Bell with 588,879. Lincoln had, however, a commanding Electoral College lead with 180 votes, compared to 72 for Breckinridge, 39 for Bell, and only 12 for Douglas.[157] Lincoln won the electoral votes of every northern state except New Jersey, which apportioned its votes between him and Douglas. Breckinridge won eleven of the fifteen slave states, while Bell won only three states (Kentucky, Tennessee, and Virginia), and Douglas won only one state, Missouri, outright.[158] For the first time in American history, a totally sectional party had won the American presidency. The South then made good on its threats. On December 20, 1860, South Carolina became the first state to secede from the Union, followed by six other states of the lower South before Lincoln took the oath of office on March 4, 1861.[159] A month after Lincoln's inauguration, shots would be fired at Fort Sumter, the Civil War would begin, and four more states from the upper South would leave the Union.

CHAPTER 11

1864: Keeping the Same Horse

Old Abe and Mac have just begun, the White House race to run.
But Abra'm's legs were made to go, while Mac was always voted slow.

By all wise men 'twill be confessed, that Lincoln's chances are the best.
For while the Mackites make the noise, the voting's done by Union boys.

So out of the way Mac the digger, out of the way, Mac, the digger,
Don't you wish your chance was bigger?[1]

Republican campaign song, 1864

When the campaign season for the 1864 presidential election began in earnest in the spring of that year, a civil war that many in the North had predicted would last only three months was ending its third year. It had turned out to be a long and bloody war, with no end in sight. As one commentator has noted, "the most remarkable fact about the 1864 election is that it occurred."[2] Secretary of State William H. Seward warned, "The country is entering a new and perilous time, a canvass for the presidency in time of civil war."[3] Subsequent history has shown that democratic nations in the midst of bloody civil wars usually suspend, postpone, or cancel scheduled elections, but not the United States of America in 1864. The successful conclusion of the war and the martyrdom of Abraham Lincoln after his assassination obscures the political reality that existed in 1864. Lincoln was by no means assured of renomination by the Republican Party and, if successful in getting the nomination, his reelection as president for a second term was equally questionable. Lincoln's own secretary of the treasury, Salmon P. Chase of Ohio, openly flirted with seeking the nomination in the first few months of 1864 and had the support of some leading Republican officeholders.[4]

A group of extreme Republicans called the Radicals, who were upset with Lincoln over what they felt was lax prosecution of the war and over his hints of resisting harsh sanctions against the South at the war's end, went so far as to hold their own presidential nominating convention in Cleveland on May 31, 1864. They nominated the 1856 Republican Party standard-bearer, John C. Frémont, for the presidency. The platform adopted in Cleveland called for suppression of the rebellion "without compromise" and amending the Constitution to limiting the president to only one term.[5] In accepting the nomination, Frémont decried the wartime extension of executive power by the Lincoln administration, its "disregard of constitutional rights, by its violation of personal liberty and the liberty of the press," and denounced

Lincoln: "While we are saturating Southern soil with the best blood of the country in the name of liberty, we have really parted with it at home."[6]

Other Republicans proposed delaying the party's nominating convention until September, hoping that the delay would allow the "dump Lincoln" movement more time to gain support.[7] The bad news from the war continued. Just days before the Republican convention was scheduled to begin in early June, the Battle of Cold Harbor was taking place outside of Richmond, which resulted in a Union loss with massive casualties. Lincoln himself was not optimistic about the outcome of the convention. A visitor to the White House a couple of weeks before the convention noted, "I was surprised to find Lincoln apprehensive that he may not be renominated." When assured by his guest that a majority of the delegates going to the convention were pledged to support him, a cautious Old Abe responded, "I don't forget that I was nominated for president in a convention that was two-thirds for the other fellow."[8]

Republican/Union Convention

It was against this backdrop that the Republican Party opened its third presidential nominating convention in Baltimore on Tuesday, June 7, 1864. The location of the convention was a surprising choice for the Republicans because Maryland, in general, and Baltimore, in particular, had not been kind to Abraham Lincoln. Out of 92,502 votes cast by Marylanders in the election of 1860, Lincoln received only 2,294, a paltry 2.5 percent.[9] Baltimore was known throughout the war to be a city teeming with southern sympathizers.

In February 1861, while Lincoln was en route to Washington for his inauguration during a grand twelve-day railroad tour of many northern states, rumors of an assassination plot in Baltimore reached his entourage. Lincoln and his top advisors, convinced by private detective Allan Pinkerton that the plot was real, decided that the scheduled public daytime arrival of Lincoln in Baltimore was too risky, and a change of plans, unannounced to the public, was made. Rather than a public midday arrival from Harrisburg on Saturday, February 23, 1861, via the Northern Central Railroad at Calvert Station, the president-elect of the United States was smuggled, some say while wearing a disguise, through the streets of Baltimore hours earlier, at 3:30 A.M. He had secretly been moved from Harrisburg to Philadelphia and then put on a train operated by the Philadelphia, Wilmington and Baltimore Railroad to Baltimore, arriving at President Street Station hours before dawn.[10] Once there, Lincoln's sleeping car was pulled by horses from the President Street Station, along Pratt Street, to the Baltimore & Ohio Railroad's Camden Station, a distance of about one mile. At Camden Station, the sleeper car with the unidentified passenger was coupled to a B & O locomotive and train heading on a regular run to Washington, forty miles away.[11] It was along these same B & O tracks between Baltimore and Washington that thousands of delegates, politicians, and others, in better days, since the 1830s, had openly and proudly traveled to attend political conventions in Baltimore to nominate candidates for the presidency of the United States. Now, in darker days, a man who received such a nomination, and who had won the presidential election, was forced to pass secretly, under threat of assassination, in the middle of the night along this same route from the Monumental City to the Federal City.

The news from Baltimore and the rest of Maryland did not improve for Lincoln once he was inaugurated on March 4, 1861. After only a few weeks in office, the Lincoln administration was shocked on April 19, 1861, when soldiers from the Sixth Massachusetts Volunteers were attacked by a Baltimore mob while marching along Pratt Street in Baltimore from the

President Street Station to Camden Station, the exact same route through which Lincoln had been smuggled in the dead of night only two months earlier. The Pratt Street riot left four soldiers and approximately one dozen Baltimoreans dead.[12] In reaction, in May 1861, federal troops under the command of General Benjamin F. Butler of Massachusetts, occupied Baltimore. Butler seized control of the city, established his headquarters on Federal Hill overlooking the Inner Harbor, pointed his cannon toward the city, and ordered his soldiers to patrol the streets.[13] This was the same Benjamin F. Butler who, less than a year earlier, as a Massachusetts delegate to the Democratic convention in Baltimore, had bolted the convention at the Front Street Theater and joined the "rump convention" of southerners that had also met in Baltimore. How times had changed. The man who had stood with southerners in Baltimore as a politician in 1860 was now, as a Union general in 1861, leading a military occupation to suppress southern sympathizers in the same city.

By fall 1861, Baltimore and Maryland were still considered by the United States government to be full of Confederate sympathizers. In September, detective Allan Pinkerton, by then civilian chief of General George B. McClellan's secret service force, traveled to Baltimore and arrested more than a dozen prominent citizens of the city, including the mayor. Concerned that the Maryland legislature would pass a resolution of secession, which would leave Washington an isolated Union island surrounded by a Confederate sea, Secretary of War Simon Cameron and McClellan directed General Nathaniel P. Banks to arrest all members of the Maryland legislature who were suspected of being disloyal to the Union.[14] The legislature had been meeting in special session in Frederick, one of Maryland's more pro–Union cities, since late April 1861. Although there were probably not enough votes to pass a resolution of secession, the body had passed, before taking a recess in early August, a resolution directed to President Lincoln protesting the occupation of Maryland by Union troops. As ordered, General Banks sent, on September 16, the following instructions to his commanding officer in Frederick: "It becomes necessary that any meeting of this Legislature, at any place or time, shall be prevented.... You will hold yourself and your command in readiness to arrest members of both Houses ... among whom are to be specially included the presiding officers of the two houses, secretaries, clerks, and all subordinate officials. Let the arrests be certain, and allow no chance of failure."[15] When the legislature met the following day in Frederick for the scheduled resumption of the session, more than twenty legislators and legislative officials were arrested by federal troops, effectively ending the session, as well as any possible vote for secession.[16] Maryland was to remain in the Union, like it or not.

Three years later, the Republicans, despite their past problems with the city, decided to meet in Baltimore for their 1864 convention. Political dirty tricks did not begin in modern times. In an effort to delay or derail the convention, some Radical Republicans, led by Maryland congressman Henry Winter Davis, rented the primary convention hall in Baltimore, the Maryland Institute, for the week of the convention, so that it could not be used for the Republican convention.[17] Lincoln's secretary of the navy, Gideon Welles, recorded in his diary on May 13, 1864, three weeks before the convention:

> Tonight Governor Morgan informs me that the hall for which the convention is to meet has been hired by the malcontents, through the treachery and connivance of H. Winter Davis, in whom he confided. He called me as to advise as to the course to be pursued. Says he can get the theater, can build a temporary structure, or he can alter the call to Philadelphia. Advised to try the theater for the present.[18]

Within a few days, a committee of the City Council of Baltimore responsible for arrangements for the convention had procured the Front Street Theater as the alternative site of the convention, with the City of Baltimore paying all of the costs.[19] The show would go on.

The choice of the Front Street Theater was fitting in two ways. The incumbent president loved attending the theater, especially Shakespearean plays, to take his mind off of the burdens of the war and of his office. Also, it was the same building in which the Democratic Party had met in 1860 and had self-destructed, resulting in Lincoln's election to the presidency. The political show about to open at the Front Street Theater with a matinee performance on June 7, 1864, had a large cast, no fixed script, a lead actor who remained in Washington, multiple candidates vying for the best supporting actor role, and an unknown closing act.

The Republican Party, in an effort to include Democrats who supported the Union's position in the war, joined with the National Union League in holding the convention and it was officially held under the name of the National Union Convention. In a proclamation calling for the convention, issued on February 22, 1864, the Executive Committee of the Republican Party limited the invitation to "each state having representatives in Congress," thereby excluding delegates from states that had seceded from the Union.[20] Despite this, some delegates from those states showed up in Baltimore, which provided much of the controversy at the convention. Anyone walking the streets of the city could readily see that a political convention was in town. The Ohio delegation lodged at Barnum's City Hotel and hung from one of the hotel's balconies a large white flag with a tricolor border proclaiming "Ohio True to the Union." A few blocks away, at the Eutaw House, a large canvas banner proclaimed the name of Abraham Lincoln for a second term.[21] In preparation for the convention's opening session at noon on June 7, a military band from Baltimore's Fort McHenry, located only a couple of miles away, was seated in the theater's gallery and entertained the arriving crowd with patriotic tunes. More than six hundred delegates and alternates were at the convention, along with a huge number of onlookers. Many had to be turned away, as even all standing room was occupied.[22] Arrangements for reserving and decorating the hall were done by the City Council of Baltimore. The stage was enlarged and extended over the parquet with the president's desk at the rear, under a canopy of American flags. The dress circle of the theater was reserved for ladies and their accompanying gentlemen. Pages wore red, white, and blue badges. There were several messengers whose job it was to take messages from the reporters to the three telegraph machines of the American Telegraph Company located in the lobby of the theater, where they would be distributed to the entire country.[23] Several young men were on hand to distribute ice water to the hot and thirsty crowd. The City of Baltimore had also stationed a large police force in and around the theater to preserve order.[24] As often occurs with a large gathering of people, then and now, pickpockets were present. One New York delegate reported that his wallet, with eighty dollars in it, had been relieved from his person while he was attending a pre-convention outdoor event.[25]

The convention was called to order at noon on June 7 by Edwin D. Morgan, the chairman of the National Union Executive Committee and a former governor of New York. Morgan had met with Lincoln in the White House a couple of days before the convention and the president had told him of his desire to have the convention support an amendment to the Constitution outlawing slavery and requested that the issue be brought before the delegates at the outset of the proceedings.[26] Morgan complied. In his opening address, he reviewed the events since the party last sat in convention in Chicago in 1860, and he called for further action at this convention. The party had nominated and elected Lincoln, "but with success came rebellion; and with rebellion of course came war; and war, terrible civil war, has continued with varying success ... this has all been caused by slavery ... [and the party] will fall short of accomplishing its great mission, unless among its other resolves, it shall declare for such an amendment of the Constitution as will positively prohibit African slavery in the United States."[27] After prolonged applause and three cheers for his remarks, Morgan introduced the temporary president of the convention, Robert J. Breckinridge of Kentucky. A nationally known Presbyterian minister, the sixty-four-year-old Breckinridge was a strong supporter of the Union and of Lincoln, but he was not a Republican. His family situation was typical of many in the border states during the Civil War — his nephew, John, had been vice president of the United States under James Buchanan, was the nominee for president of the southern Democrats at their convention in Baltimore in 1860, and then became a Confederate general during the war. Two sons of the elder Breckinridge were serving as officers in the Confederate army at the time of the 1864 convention. Being from a border state that still had slavery, Breckinridge noted that he did not support Morgan's call for a constitutional amendment to prohibit slavery. He stated, "I do not know that I would be willing to go so far as probably he would," and reminded all that the 1860 Republican convention in Chicago had "virtually, did explicitly say, that they would not touch slavery in the States" where it then existed.[28] In an appeal for unity and in support of a broad coalition to finish the job of the war, Breckinridge declared, "As a Union Party, I will follow you to the ends of the earth, and to the gates of death! But as an Abolition party — as a Republican party — as a Whig party — as a Democratic party ... I will not follow you one foot." After these remarks, an opening prayer was given by the Reverend McKendree Reily of the Methodist Episcopal Church of Baltimore, who commented upon the city's southern leanings: "We praise thy name that the Convention holds its session in the city of Baltimore, from whose breezes, but a short time ago, early in the present conflict, the banner of our common country was exiled."[29] The prayer, lasting ten minutes, was described as "a feeling prayer" with the delegates generally standing, and listening with deep attention.[30] After appointing three committees — a Committee on Credentials, a Committee on Permanent Organization of the convention, and a Committee on Platform and Resolutions for the party — the convention then voted at 3:00 P.M. to adjourn until 7:30 P.M. in order for the committees to begin their work. Each committee consisted of one member from each state's delegation, but only from those states whose credentials were not being questioned.[31]

When the convention resumed for its evening session, the Committee on Permanent Organization recommended that William Dennison of Ohio be named permanent president of the convention, which was approved. The committee also named one convention vice president and one secretary from each of the states that were represented at the convention. In his opening address, Dennison called for the "complete suppression of the rebellion" and for slavery to "be made to cease forever in every state and territory of the Union."[32] Another committee was then appointed to address the order of the business of the convention. With the Committee on Credentials still not ready to report, a motion to adjourn for the evening was made. Before the motion could be ruled upon, however, delegate G. W. Patterson of New York moved that the convention hear an address from "Parson" Brownlow of "East Tennessee," who was described as a person "who has experienced some of the trials of Tennessee." As would become obvious later in the convention, this was the first step in an orchestrated plan by party leaders to dump Vice President Hannibal Hamlin of Maine from the second spot on the ticket and replace him with Andrew Johnson of Tennessee, with the purpose of gaining the support of voters in the border states. Tennessee had seceded from the Union and was part of the Confederacy. It did not have representatives in Congress and was not one of the states yet recognized to participate in the convention. It would not do to put a candidate on the ticket from a state not represented at the convention, and Brownlow's speech was intended to correct this problem.

William "Parson" Brownlow, a Methodist minister, was an anti-slavery Whig from Tennessee and, before the war, had been the editor of the *Knoxville Whig* newspaper. When Tennessee seceded, he was arrested by the Confederates early in the war and was jailed for a few several months. He was released under a flag of truce in 1862 and later made a speaking tour of the North in support of Lincoln and the Union cause.[33] Brownlow had been a longtime political foe of Andrew Johnson before the war and now spoke to the convention on behalf of his home state and his former foe. Announcing at the outset of his remarks his poor physical condition and the difficult journey he had taken to get to Baltimore, Brownlow pleaded with the convention:

> I am a very sick man and ought to be in my bed, and not here. I have journeyed on, how-
> ever, through great tribulation to meet you ... I heard when I came to town that you had
> some doubts in your mind about the propriety of admitting the delegation from Ten-
> nessee,—a state in rebellion. I hope you will pause, gentlemen, before you commit so rash
> an act as that, and thereby recognize secession. We don't recognize it in Tennessee. We deny
> that we are out. We deny that we have been out ... I pray you not to exclude us. We have a
> full delegation from Tennessee—a patriotic delegation ... and the idea I suggest to you as
> an inducement not to throw out our delegation is, that we may take it into our hearts,
> before the thing is over, to present a candidate from that State in rebellion for the second
> office.... We have a man down there whom it was my good luck and bad fortune to fight
> untiringly with the last twenty-five years—ANDREW JOHNSON. For the first time three
> years ago, we got together on the same platform, and we are now fighting the devil ... and
> JEFF DAVIS, side by side.[34]

Brownlow's address was well received by the convention, following which the meeting adjourned for the day. The "Andy Johnson for vice president" bandwagon had started to roll. Lincoln's friend and bodyguard, Ward Hill Lamon, who was at the convention, telegraphed the president after Brownlow's speech and summarized the first day's proceedings: "Enthusiastic unanimity beyond even my expectations. Preliminaries not yet settled. Nomination to be made tomorrow."[35]

Lincoln had two young secretaries, John Nicolay and John Hay, who worked with him daily and who lived in the White House. A third man, William Stoddard, also worked as a secretary for Lincoln from time to time, but was not as close to the president as were Nicolay and Hay. Years after Lincoln's death, in 1890, Nicolay and Hay would publish *Abraham Lincoln: A History*, a detailed ten-volume biography based on their work for, and observations of, the president. In June 1864, Lincoln sent Nicolay to Baltimore to be his eyes and ears at the convention. Stoddard also attended, apparently on his own. In the days prior to the convention, many of the delegations from various states spent a day or two in Washington, some of which were received by the president. When the delegation from South Carolina, the state which had started the rebellion, stopped by, Hay told the president, "They are a swindle," and recommended that he not see them. The ever-generous Lincoln agreed to see them, remarking to Hay, "They won't swindle me."[36] Members of the Radical Republicans in Congress also met with the delegates coming through Washington, in a last-ditch effort to derail a Lincoln renomination. Navy secretary Welles also met with several of the delegates and encouraged them to support the president. He felt, however, that the delegates were getting another message elsewhere in their Washington meetings, at the instigation of another member of Lincoln's cabinet.

Welles wrote in his diary, "There is a spirit of discontent among the Members of Congress, stirred up, I think, by the Treasury Department. Chase has his flings and insinuations against the president's policy, or want of policies. Nothing suits him."[37] Welles noted on June 4 that there were "attempts made by members of Congress to influence" the delegates before they boarded the B & O trains to Baltimore.[38]

Upon arriving in Baltimore, the Lincoln men were confident but concerned. Lincoln's attorney general, Edward Bates, who was in Baltimore, observed, "The radicals are here in great force."[39] As one commentator noted, "There was a radical grumpiness, an anti–Lincoln, anti–Blair, anti–Seward, anti-cabinet bias, a feeling that all things they detested about this administration were being crammed down their throats."[40] There were meetings everywhere. The New Yorkers, seemingly always divided amongst themselves, were headquartered at the Eutaw House, along with several other delegations from eastern states. Barnum's City Hotel was the Baltimore home of the large Pennsylvania delegation, as well as those from several western states.[41]

A meeting of the Grand Council of the Union League was held in Baltimore the evening before the Tuesday opening of the convention. Union League organizations were founded throughout the North during the war and were political and patriotic in nature, supporting the war effort with fundraising for the Republican Party, helping to recruit volunteer soldiers, distributing literature in support of the war, and providing relief to soldiers in need. This group was dominated by Radical Republicans hostile to Lincoln, who wanted the war prosecuted more vigorously and the South held accountable at its conclusion. If there was to be an attempt to block the president's renomination at the convention, it would likely come from the Grand Council's meeting. One of Lincoln's secretaries, Stoddard, attended the meeting and was appalled by the denunciations of the president and the administration made by a Radical senator and by a congressman, whose names he did not disclose. They portrayed an administration full "of malfeasance, of tyranny, of corruption, of illegal acts, of abused power, of misused advantages, of favoritism, fraud, timidity, sluggish inertness, local wrong and repression." A startled Stoddard heard this "long and shameful indictment," and wondered "[h]as Lincoln no friends left?" At that point, according to Stoddard, the lanky senator Jim Lane of Kansas spoke up forcibly and, perhaps, saved the Lincoln presidency. Lane had a reputation in Washington as being ill-mannered and a womanizer, and he was an unlikely person to speak with any moral authority in support of the president. Yet, according to Stoddard, with a voice that "would go through a wall," Lane stared down the opposition, was brutal in his criticism of them, and made arguments "pulling apart the indictment against Lincoln." He argued that failing to renominate Lincoln "would sunder the Union, make permanent the Confederacy, re-shackle the slaves, dishonor the dead, and disgrace the living." After Lane's moving speech, the mood in the meeting totally changed and the Grand Council voted to endorse Lincoln's renomination, with only nominal votes in opposition.[42]

The issue of the vice presidency was far less certain. The incumbent vice president, Hannibal Hamlin of Maine, had increasingly aligned himself with the Radical Republicans in Congress. It was rumored before the convention, but never confirmed, that Lincoln wanted to dump Hamlin and replace him with a pro-war Democrat, in order to have a broader base of support for votes in the 1864 election. Any open attempt by the president to replace Hamlin, however, would cost him votes in New England. Andrew Johnson of Tennessee was placed on the ticket. The still unsolved mystery of the 1864 National Union Convention is whether, and to what extent, Abraham Lincoln planned and participated in this outcome.

The "did Abe or didn't he" debate over the 1864 vice presidential nomination erupted with furor in the national press in 1891, a full generation after the convention. The precipitating cause at that time was the death on July 4, 1891, of former vice president Hamlin. His body was hardly cold when Alexander K. McClure, then the editor of the *Philadelphia Times* and an influential Republican politician in Pennsylvania during the war, published an editorial in his paper on July 6, 1891. McClure alleged that, shortly prior to the convention, he was summoned by Lincoln himself to the White House and was told by the president that he wanted Andrew Johnson on the ticket and that McClure was to go to Baltimore and accomplish that result. He stated that Simon Cameron of Pennsylvania and Henry J. Raymond of New York (a delegate, chairman of the 1864 convention's platform committee, and editor of the *New York Times*) were also similarly recruited by Lincoln.[43] By 1891, any attempt to associate the martyred Lincoln with the discredited Johnson was considered blasphemy. Andy Johnson had shown up drunk at his inauguration as vice president on March 4, 1865, and things generally went downhill from there, including his impeachment by the Radical Republicans in the House of Representatives in 1868 and his escape from conviction and removal from office by only one vote at his trial in the Senate.[44]

Lincoln's defenders against McClure's charges in 1891 were led by John Nicolay, one of the president's White House secretaries, who adamantly denied that Lincoln preferred Johnson as the vice presidential nominee, or that he did anything to promote Johnson before or at the convention. McClure and Nicolay traded accusations in the newspapers for a few weeks and each provided evidence that they claimed supported their position, with some support from the recollection of others, but with little contemporaneous documentation from 1864. Viewing all of the evidence, it seems clear that Lincoln wanted to remove Hamlin from the ticket and replace him with a Democrat who supported the war; whether he named or insisted on Andrew Johnson as the primary candidate is less clear.

About three months before the opening of the convention, the historical record is undisputed that Lincoln did offer the vice presidency to another pro-war Democrat, General Benjamin Franklin Butler, from Massachusetts. Butler was a staunch Democrat before the war and had been a delegate to the 1848 and 1860 Democratic conventions. At the 1860 convention in Charleston, he voted for Jefferson Davis to be the Democratic Party's standard-bearer on all fifty-seven ballots before the convention adjourned and met again in Baltimore. As discussed in the previous chapter, it was Butler who had led the walkout of the Massachusetts delegation from the Democratic convention at the Front Street Theater in Baltimore in 1860, and who then participated in the rump convention of southern Democrats that had nominated John C. Breckinridge for the presidency. Like many politicians, Butler became a general during the Civil War. In the spring of 1864, Butler made a decision that resigned him to forever being one of history's footnotes.

Lincoln and his top aides, particularly Secretary of War Stanton, having made a decision to replace Hamlin with a pro-war Democrat, sent Simon Cameron of Pennsylvania in the spring of 1864 to Fort Monroe, Virginia, where Butler was then serving. The purpose of the trip was to offer Butler the vice presidential spot on the ticket with Lincoln. Cameron recounted the meeting in an interview given in 1873:

> Lincoln and Stanton thought highly of Butler, and I will now tell you another fact that is not generally known, and which will show you how near Butler came to being President instead of Andrew Johnson. In the spring of 1864, when it was determined to run Mr. Lincoln for a second term, it was the desire of Lincoln and also that of Stanton who was the one man of the cabinet upon whom Lincoln thoroughly depended, that Butler should run on the ticket with him as candidate for Vice President. I was called upon in consultation and heartily endorsed the scheme. Accordingly Lincoln sent me on a mission to Fortress

> Monroe to see General Butler, and to say to him that it was his [Lincoln's] request that he
> [General Butler] should allow himself to be run as second on the ticket.[45]

Butler, writing in 1891 to McClure, advised that he had heard in the spring of 1864 that
Hamlin was not to remain on the ticket, for reasons unknown, and he corroborated Cameron's
visit and offer:

> Within three weeks afterward a gentleman [Cameron] who stood very high in Lincoln's
> confidence came to me at Fort Monroe * * * *the gentleman informed me that he came from
> Mr. Lincoln; this was said with directness,* because the messenger and myself had been for a
> considerable time in quite warm, friendly relations....
>
> He said: "The President, as you know, intends to be a candidate for re-election, *and as his
> friends indicate that Mr. Hamlin is no longer to be a candidate for Vice President,* and he is from
> New England, the President thinks his place should be filled by someone from that section;
> and ... he believes that being the first prominent Democrat who volunteered for the war, your
> candidature would add strength to the ticket, especially with the war Democrats, and he
> hopes that you will allow your friends to cooperate with his to place you in that position."[46]

Butler flatly declined the offer, advising Cameron that he wanted to finish the military campaign in which he was then involved and did not wish to spend his days as vice president
breaking tie votes in the Senate. According to Butler's account of the conversation years later,
likely apocryphal, he jokingly told Cameron that there was no way he would accept the offer
unless Lincoln gave his bond that would die within three months after his inauguration.[47]
Almost exactly one year later, in April 1865, when Butler heard of the events at Ford's Theater
in Washington, he had to have wondered how the 1864 convention at the Front Street Theater
in Baltimore could have ended, how he could have been nominated in 1864 for vice president
by the Republicans in the very same building that he walked out of in 1860 as a Democrat,
and of what might have been.

In trading accusations over Lincoln's alleged engineering of the Andrew Johnson nomination, both Nicolay and McClure were fortunate that the age of dueling had ended before
1891, or challenges would have been issued and one of them would likely have ended up shot
by the other. Upon learning of McClure's allegations in his Philadelphia editorial of July 7,
1891, Nicolay promptly sent a public telegram to former vice president Hamlin's grieving
widow, consoling her for her loss and stating that McClure was "entirely erroneous" and that
"Lincoln's personal feelings, on the contrary, were for Mr. Hamlin's renomination, as he confi-
dentially expressed to me, but he persistently withheld any opinion calculated to influence
the convention for or against any candidate."[48] McClure wasted no time in firing back, with
gloves off, through another editorial in his paper published on July 9:

> The ignorance exhibited by John G. Nicolay in his public telegram to the widow of
> ex-Vice President Hamlin is equaled only by his arrogance in assuming to speak for
> Abraham Lincoln in matters about which Nicolay was never consulted and of which he
> had no more knowledge than any other routine clerk about the White House.... I was one
> of those called to the inner councils of Abraham Lincoln ... there were not only scores of
> confidential conferences in the White House of which John G. Nicolay never heard, but no
> man ever met or heard of John G. Nicolay in such councils. He was a good, mechanical,
> routine clerk; he was utterly inefficient as secretary to the President: his removal was
> earnestly pressed upon Lincoln on more than one occasion because of his utter want of tact
> and fitness for his trust, and only the proverbial kindness of Lincoln saved him from dis-
> missal. He saw and knew President Lincoln; the man Abraham Lincoln he never saw and
> never knew.[49]

And so on it went. McClure denounced Nicolay's fitness to be a biographer of Lincoln and charged, "It would have been well for both Lincoln's memory and for the country had such a biographer been drowned as a pup."[50] Nicolay responded: "I will not reply to your personal abuse, it proves nothing but your rage and wounded vanity at being exposed in a gross historical misstatement."[51] Nicolay further questioned, if McClure was on a mission from Lincoln to go to Baltimore and to dump Hamlin and nominate Johnson, why McClure, as a Pennsylvania delegate, had voted with the entire Pennsylvania delegation for Hamlin on the first ballot. He belittled McClure as a "pretended agent to manipulate a national convention who had not influence enough in his own delegation to control his own vote."[52]

There is yet another theory, which can be called the "feuding New Yorkers" theory, about how and why Johnson was placed on the ticket by the 1864 convention in Baltimore. After all, what would a nineteenth-century political convention be without controversy and intrigue amongst the politicians from the Empire State? Lincoln's secretary of state, William Seward, was a New Yorker and had been the leading candidate for the Republican nomination against Lincoln in 1860. While loyal to Lincoln, Seward undoubtedly wanted to succeed Lincoln in the presidency and believed the best way to accomplish this was to maintain his top status in the cabinet during Lincoln's second term. With Lincoln's decision to place a pro-war Democrat on the ticket, Seward had to block one pro-war Democrat, Daniel S. Dickinson, from getting the vice presidential nomination. Dickinson was from New York, and Seward and his supporters knew that it would be impossible for Lincoln to have both his vice president and his secretary of state from the Empire State. The anti–Seward faction of the Republican Party in New York openly promoted a "Dickinson in, Seward out" movement, and Dickinson received pre-convention support from parts of New York, in New England, in the West, and in the border states.[53] The Seward faction in New York favored the renomination of the incumbent Vice President Hamlin, which would protect Seward's seat in the cabinet.

As the convention opened, Dickinson and Johnson were seen as the leading challengers to Hamlin for the vice presidential nomination. On Monday night, June 6, several of the state delegations met in individual caucus meetings at their hotels in Baltimore. In the early evening meetings, the Pennsylvania delegation expressed unanimous support for Hamlin, as did New Jersey, Kansas, Wisconsin, Minnesota, Iowa and Missouri. At 10:00 P.M., the New York delegation supported Hamlin with 28 votes, to 16 for Dickinson, 8 for Tremaine, only 4 for Johnson, and the rest scattered among other candidates. Hamlin's vote counter at the convention, Lot M. Morrill, upon hearing these favorable results for his man, assumed that the battle was won and went to bed. He should have stayed up, for late-night meetings totally changed the complexion of the race. In a caucus held after 10:00 P.M., the Massachusetts delegation decided that the party needed to nominate a pro-war Democrat, and switched from Hamlin to Dickinson. The Bay State's delegation sent a message to its Empire State colleagues asking them to nominate Dickinson on the floor at the convention. The Seward faction of the New York delegation, needing to block Dickinson, desperately switched its allegiance from Hamlin to Andrew Johnson. They were willing to support a pro-war Democrat, so long as he was not a New Yorker named Dickinson. In meetings lasting until 1:30 A.M., the New Yorkers remained badly divided, with 32 votes for Johnson, 26 for Dickinson, and 8 for Hamlin.[54] This was followed by a three-hour meeting of the New York delegation on the morning of June 7, with the two factions going at each other, during which the "caucus degenerated into a quarrelsome discussion of whether Seward or Dickinson should have a post in the national government."[55] Another man, Judge Joseph Holt of Kentucky, was suggested by Thurlow Weed, the longtime New York power-broker and leader of the Seward faction. Prior to the convention, Leonard Swett of the Illinois delegation, who was a good friend of Lincoln, also floated a trial balloon for Holt. Lincoln's man at the convention, John Nicolay, wanting to be sure of Swett's loyalty to Lincoln, sent a telegraphic message from Baltimore to Lincoln's other secretary, John Hay, who was at the White House, and asked him to question Lincoln on the possibility of Holt as a running mate. Lincoln, through Hay, wired the following response to Nicolay in Baltimore: "Swett is unquestionably all right. Mr. Holt is a good man, but I had not heard or thought of him for V.P. Wish not to interfere about V.P. Cannot interfere about platform. Convention must judge for itself."[56] This response from the White House was shared by Nicolay with others in Baltimore. The race for the second spot on the ticket was wide open, or at least that is what Lincoln wanted Nicolay to think.

As the convention opened for its second day, June 8, the theater began to fill up well before the 11:00 A.M. opening gavel. After an opening prayer by Reverend Gaddis, a delegate from Ohio, various committee reports were received. The Committee on the Order of Business reported its recommendations: on roll calls the states would be called in the traditional order with Maine being first and then southward and westward; states would be entitled to twice the number of votes they held in the Electoral College, with four of those votes cast by at-large delegates from each state and two votes from each congressional district; debate would be limited in that no delegate could speak more than once in the same issue and, without unanimous consent, no one delegate could speak more than five minutes on an issue. These rules were adopted by the convention.[57] While the convention went about its business, behind the scenes of the public show in the Front Street Theater, the politicking and jockeying over the vice presidential nomination continued.

The Committee on Credentials then submitted its report. Never before in American history had a political convention needed to decide the fundamental issue of whether states, not merely competing delegations from a state, could vote or not. The position of Lincoln and many in the North had always been that secession from the Union by any state was impossible and a nullity. Under that theory, if some of the purportedly seceding states had sent delegates to Baltimore, should not their votes be counted? But what about the order that was issued by the party's hierarchy in calling the convention, which had invited delegations from only those states that then had voting representatives in Congress, which excluded the states belonging to the Confederate States of America? What about the territories, some of which had applications pending before Congress for statehood that might, or might not, be approved between the time of the convention and the November election? The Committee on Credentials sorted through all of these issues and made the following recommendations: (1) the delegation from South Carolina (the birthplace of the rebellion) should be totally unrecognized for any purposes, (2) the delegations from the purportedly seceding states of Tennessee, Louisiana, Arkansas, Virginia, Louisiana, and Florida should be admitted "with all the rights and privileges of delegates, except the right to vote," (3) the delegations from the District of Columbia and from the territories (Nebraska, Colorado, and Nevada), should also be admitted with all privileges, except voting rights, and (4) of the two competing Missouri delegations that had been sent to Baltimore, the one known as the "Radical Union Delegation" should be seated, with voting rights.[58]

The debate over the report of the Committee on Credentials went on for hours. Some wanted the delegations from the South and the territories admitted with full voting rights. A Connecticut delegate objected and questioned how the convention could possibly admit voting delegations "from states where the Federal Government ... can barely plant its foot upon the soil and territory of those states ... [and] from territories that have no votes ... [in the] House of Representatives, [and] will have none between now and the November election."[59] A New York delegate who favored full voting rights responded to an argument that the convention would be setting a bad precedent by the expansion of voting rights and stated, "I hope we shall never have a condition of affairs in this country (and I do not believe we ever shall) when things done now may properly be quoted as precedent for things done then."[60]

There was a long debate over the two competing Missouri delegations. Some proposed admitting both delegations but not counting their votes unless both agreed on an issue.[61] The delegation that was not favored by the Committee on Credentials, known as the Conservative delegation, was actually preferred by Lincoln and his convention floor leaders over the Radical delegation, as they were more philosophically in tune with Lincoln. The decision not to mount a floor fight over this, in an effort to appease the Radicals at the convention, apparently came from Lincoln himself. Years later, an Illinois delegate, Clark E. Carr, recounted how the Illinois delegation, while meeting in conference in a parlor room at Barnum's Hotel on the eve of the convention, had their collective minds on the Missouri issue changed by a visitor from Washington:

> With scarcely an exception, every Illinois delegate favored the Conservatives, and we went into that conference without any doubt that we would so declare....
>
> Just as we were about to vote upon the question, a young man ... arose in a corner of the room and modestly asked to be heard for a moment. He said that he only wished to say a word — that he wanted to voice his own opinion, and not that of any one else ... and then gave as his opinion that, after all, under the circumstances, he thought Illinois had better favor the admission of the delegates of the Radical convention of Missouri. That was all. There was perfect silence for a few moments after he closed.... By this time, every delegate knew who he was. It was John G. Nicolay, President Lincoln's private secretary. Earnest as he was in the declaration that he was speaking only for himself, we very soon realized that through his lips, Abraham Lincoln was speaking to us. We at once voted in favor of seating the Radicals....
>
> It did not take long for us to get into our dull heads the reason for, nor for us to see the wisdom of, admitting the Radicals to the convention.... We saw that when we admitted this Radical delegation upon an equality with all other delegates and gave them a right to be heard, gave them their day in court, they were, like us, committed to the action of the convention and its candidates....
>
> Mr. Lincoln was great enough and wise enough to see all this. A less sagacious man would no doubt ... have imperiled his own success and that of the party and of the country. In the only way possible without directly taking part in the management of the proceedings of the convention, he quietly indicated to the delegates from his own State, and through them to the whole great convention, his views, upon which we acted.[62]

At the conclusion of the credentials debate, several roll call votes were taken. The lead of Lincoln's own state of Illinois was followed and the Radical delegation from Missouri was admitted with full voting rights by an overwhelming vote of 440 yeas and only 4 nays. One of Lincoln's cabinet members, Gideon Welles, strongly disagreed with the vote that his boss had apparently engineered. After Welles heard the news in Washington by telegraph, he fumed to his diary that night: "The wrong Delegates [from Missouri] were admitted by an almost unanimous vote. A strange perversion. There was neither sense nor reason or justice in the decision. Rogues, fanatics, hypocrites, and untruthful men secured and triumphed over good and true men. Prejudice overcame truth and reason. The Convention exhibited great stupidity."[63]

On the other credentials issues before the convention, Tennessee was singled out for a vote by itself, obviously because of the issue of Andrew Johnson for vice president that would soon come before the convention. Overruling the committee's recommendation, the Volunteer State's fifteen delegates present in Baltimore were admitted with full voting rights, by a vote of 310 yeas to 151 nays, with the majority of the negative votes coming from Massachusetts, Pennsylvania, Maryland, and Kentucky.[64] Delegate Horace Maynard of Tennessee expressed his state's "profound sense of gratitude for the expression of confidence in the patriotism, the loyalty, and the devotion to country of our constituents at home."[65] A separate vote was then taken on admitting the delegations from Arkansas and Louisiana with full voting rights, which passed with 317 yeas to 167 nays.[66] The theory behind this was that these two states, along with Tennessee, had "free state organizations" in place and had taken initial steps toward Reconstruction under Lincoln's plan. Feeling generous with the granting of voting rights, the convention then approved, without a roll call, the granting of voting rights to the territories of Nebraska, Colorado, and Nevada, after being assured that each of those territories had elections fixed for statehood votes in September and, if those votes were for admission as states, as anticipated, then they would be entitled to vote in the November presidential election.[67] The final result after all of the votes on credentials was that most of the states and territories were fully in, except the delegations from the District of Columbia, Virginia, Florida, and the territory of New Mexico, which could stay but not vote. Only South Carolina was denied any recognition. Its delegates could pack their bags and head back south.

The convention then received the report of the Committee on Resolutions, which was read by the committee's chairman, Henry J. Raymond, a New York delegate and the editor of the *New York Times*. The eleven-plank platform called for a full prosecution of the war and "not to compromise with Rebels, or to offer them any terms of peace, except such as may be based upon unconditional surrender." It called for "bringing punishment due to the Rebels and Traitors," but did not specify the punishment sought or needed. It called for slavery's "utter and complete extirpation from the soil of the Republic" and for a constitutional amendment to "terminate and forever prohibit the existence of slavery." The platform expressed gratitude to the fallen and wounded soldiers and sailors during the war. It applauded Abraham Lincoln for "the practical wisdom, the unselfish patriotism, and the unswerving fidelity to the constitution and to the principles of American liberty" with which he had guided his administration. A vaguely worded plank called for "harmony to prevail in the national councils," which was later interpreted as a call for the firing or resignation of the conservative Montgomery Blair, a Marylander, from his position as postmaster general in the Lincoln cabinet.[68] Other planks called for full protection of soldiers under the "laws of war," encouraged "a liberal and just policy" on immigration, the "speedy construction of a railroad to the Pacific Coast," economy in public expenditures, and reaffirmation of the Monroe Doctrine. The full platform was passed unanimously and without debate.[69]

The convention then moved to its primary business — the nomination of the party's presidential ticket. The outcome of the vote for the top half of the ticket was not in doubt, but for the bottom half, it was anybody's guess. When a Pennsylvania delegate, Simon Cameron, jumped up and made a motion to nominate both Lincoln for president and Hamlin for vice president by acclamation, he was shouted down with cries of "No, No!" at the mention of Hamlin's name, and his motion was tabled.[70] Another motion to nominate just Lincoln for the presidency by acclamation was withdrawn when a New York delegate, Henry J. Raymond, who had chaired the Committee on the Platform, questioned the wisdom of this, in light of the fact that some in the press and in the country had tried to "convey the impression that the nomination of Abraham Lincoln is to be rushed though the convention by some demonstration that will not allow the exercise of individual opinion."[71] Thus, the roll call of the states began, starting with Maine in the northeastern corner of the country. All votes, as expected, went to Lincoln, until Missouri was reached. Missouri was the state whose Radical delegation had been admitted, without objection from the Lincoln forces, over the Conservative delegation from Missouri that they had actually preferred. The chairman of the Missouri delegation rose and explained to the convention, "It is a matter of much regret that we now differ from the Convention which has been so kind to the Radicals of Missouri, but we come here instructed ... and [we] intend to obey our instructions ... [and cast our votes for] the man who stands at the head of the fighting Radicals of the Nation, Ulysses S. Grant."[72] The convention was stunned. One Missouri delegate later recounted that "I hadn't any doubt for a few moments but that we would be picked up, every man of us, and thrown out into the street."[73] After this aberration, the roll call continued with a final tally of 484 votes for Lincoln and only Missouri's 22 votes for Grant. Missouri then switched its votes to Lincoln and the decision was unanimous. The delegates and galleries rose to their feet, with applause and cheering, and the band in the theater played "Hail Columbia" and "Yankee Doodle."[74] A reporter described the scene: "Men hurrahed, embraced one another, threw up their hats, danced in the aisles or on the platform, jumped up on the benches, waved flags, yelled ... the racket was so intolerable that I involuntarily looked up to see if the roof of the theater were not lifted by the volume of sound."[75] Abraham Lincoln had just become the first incumbent president of the United States in twenty-four years to be nominated by his party for a second term.

Following the Lincoln nomination, a contentious late afternoon battle was fought in Baltimore over the second office in the land. There were a total of ten candidates placed in nomination as Lincoln's running mate, with Hamlin, Johnson, and Dickinson being the top three contenders. At the conclusion of the roll call on the first ballot, the unofficial tally had Johnson in the lead with 200 votes, compared to 150 for Hamlin and 108 for Dickinson, with the remaining votes scattered among the lesser candidates.[76] While the roll call was still going on, the Pennsylvania and New York delegations, which had been called early in the list of states that started in the Northeast, continued to confer. Cameron of Pennsylvania, who had cast all of his state's fifty-two votes for Hamlin, offered to switch them to Dickinson if the New Yorkers would unite behind him. The Seward New York faction flatly rejected this proposal.[77] This would have given Dickinson an additional ninety votes and would have likely resulted in his nomination. Instead, the momentum swung to Johnson. Before the first ballot was declared official, Kentucky, Oregon, and Kansas switched their votes to Johnson. Cameron then switched Pennsylvania's votes to the Tennessean, over the objection of Thaddeus Stevens of the Keystone State, an arch–Radical who supported Hamlin, and who turned to another Pennsylvania delegate and muttered: "Can't you find a candidate for vice president in the United States without going down to one of those damned rebel provinces to pick one up?"[78] Other states then joined the Johnson bandwagon and, by the time the first ballot was officially completed, Johnson had an overwhelming total of 494 votes, with only 17 for Dickinson and 9 for Hamlin.[79] The Republicans would soon find out, as the Whigs had in 1840, that nominating someone as a vice presidential candidate, to be a heartbeat away from the presidency, who was not a tried and true member of their own party was not a wise move. Before adjourning, the convention passed a resolution of thanks to the Baltimore City Council for having prepared and provided the Front Street Theater for use by the convention. An announcement was also made that an invitation had been received from Patterson Park Hospital in Baltimore, where over one thousand Union soldiers were being treated, advising that the soldiers "will

ABRAHAM LINCOLN,
OF ILLINOIS.

ANDREW JOHNSON,
OF TENNESSEE.

Abraham Lincoln was nominated for a second term in the White House at the 1864 Republican convention held in Baltimore. Years later, a controversy arose in the national press over whether Lincoln actively engineered the nomination of Andrew Johnson of Tennessee, a Democrat, to be his running mate on the Republican ticket in 1864, replacing Hannibal Hamlin of Maine *(Library of Congress)*.

be gratified to meet their delegates" and the delegates were encouraged to visit the war wounded before leaving the city.[80]

During the evenings following both days of the convention, as with conventions in the past, Baltimore's Monument Square was the scene of political rallies. On the evening of June 7, after the first day's proceedings, a large crowd gathered in the square and heard speeches from various politicians, and "the meeting was kept up until a late hour."[81] The next night, after the nominations were made, a formal ratification convention was held in the square. Beginning shortly after eight o'clock, the rally elected officers for the evening and heard from Baltimore's mayor, John L. Chapman, a Union Party member. A resolution was adopted strongly endorsing the nominations of Abraham Lincoln and Andrew Johnson and a committee of two was appointed to go to Washington and advise the president of the ratification of his nomination by the gathering. The throng then heard a speech from "Parson" Brownlow of Tennessee, whose speech had closed the convention's proceedings on the prior day, who spoke "in his usual style" to a cheering crowd.[82]

The roll call of the states for the presidential nomination had concluded in the early afternoon on a Wednesday. A few hours, later, around 4:30 P.M., forty miles to the south of Baltimore, a tall, bearded gentleman was at the telegraph office in the War Department building, next to the White House, communicating with General Grant about the Battle of Cold Harbor, when the telegraph receiver started clicking incessantly. It brought news of Johnson's nomination for vice president, which surprised Lincoln, who had not yet heard of his own nomination a few hours earlier. Confused, he queried the telegraph operator, "What, do they nominate a vice president before they do a president?" and muttered something about putting "the cart before the horse." When told by the operator that news of his own nomination had come over the wire a few hours earlier, while Lincoln was at lunch, and had been sent to the White House, which he somehow missed, the president responded with a low-key "What, I am renominated?" He asked that the news be delivered immediately to his wife, for "she will be more interested in it than I am." That night, Lincoln engaged in one of his favorite pastimes, going to Grover's Theater in Washington, alone, and taking in a play. The next day, a committee from the Union League, the organization whose meeting on the night before the convention had severely criticized Lincoln before being swayed otherwise by Senator Lane of Kansas, visited the White House and there were smiles all around. Lincoln, the man who always had an anecdote or joke to tell, advised his amused guests who had gathered in the East Room: "I have not permitted myself, gentlemen, to conclude that I am the best man in the country, but I am reminded, in this connection, of a story of an old Dutch farmer, who remarked to a companion once that 'it was best not to swap horses when crossing streams.'"[83]

Democratic Convention

Almost three full months after Lincoln was renominated in Baltimore in early June, the Democratic Party met for its convention in Chicago on August 29, 1864. All of Chicago's grand hotels — the Richmond House, the Tremont House, the Sherman House, and others — were filled to capacity as Democrats from across the country congregated for the convention. Hotel space was so tight that some Democrats visiting the city, swallowing their pride, asked if they could sleep on the floor of the offices of the staunchly Republican *Chicago Tribune*, prompting the newspaper to speculate that this showed "either a change in sentiment is arrived at, or the extremity to force such a sacrifice must be awful."[84] As the convention neared, it was noted that the prices of "fashionable drinks at popular saloons are going up with fearful rapidity" and were expected to peak at fifty cents per drink by the time the gavel fell.[85]

Like the Republicans, who were divided between the Radicals and the more moderate Lincoln supporters, the Democrats were also divided into two factions — one seeking an immediate end to the war at any cost, and a more moderate faction which supported the war, but not the way the Republicans had administered and fought it. Throughout American history, before and since 1864, the political party not in power during a time of war has walked a fine line between being the loyal opposition and being considered treasonous. It was so with the Federalists in the War of 1812, with the Whigs in the Mexican War, and with the Democrats in the Civil War. There was no clear leader of the Democratic Party in 1864. Its 1860 nominee, Stephen A. Douglas, had died at the young age of forty-eight in 1861. Still, with the war having gone on for so long and having gone so badly for the North, the Democrats were optimistic for victory in 1864. The fact that they did not hold their convention until late August (almost three months later than the normal time for conventions of the era) was a sign of the times. The longer they delayed, the more likely that bad news from the war could help their cause, and the more likely that Republican opposition to Lincoln would strengthen. Wealthy Democratic bankers and railroad men from the east controlled the moderate faction of the party, and their candidate for the nomination was former General George B. McClellan. Known to his troops by the nickname of "Little Mac," McClellan had led the Union army in the east early in the war, but had been removed from command by Lincoln on two occasions over frustration with McClellan's lack of aggressiveness in planning and conducting his military campaigns. McClellan was a pro-war Democrat, but the majority of the delegates to the convention were believed to be from the party's more extreme peace faction. Several of this faction's leaders had been arrested at various points during the war by the Lincoln administration on charges of aiding and abetting the enemy with words or actions. The Peace Democrats had no clear candidate of their own for the nomination, but two governors, both of whom were named Seymour — Thomas H. Seymour, a former governor of Connecticut, and Horatio Seymour, the sitting governor of New York — and Congressman George H. Pendleton of Ohio were frequently mentioned. Both Democratic Party factions favored a cease-fire or armistice with the Confederacy, to be followed by a national convention to work out the terms of ending of hostilities. The difference between the two was that the moderate faction would condition any cease-fire upon the South's prior commitment to reenter the Union. The peace faction, however, would impose no pre-conditions, which could result in the Confederacy surviving after the war as an independent nation. McClellan was thought to be the frontrunner going into the convention, but the outcome was not certain. Noah Brooks, a reporter for the *Sacramento Daily Union* who was covering the convention, met with Lincoln in the White House shortly before departing for Chicago and later recalled that the president was acutely aware of the need for the opposition party to unify both factions and the dilemma it faced: "They must nominate a Peace Democrat on a war platform, or a War Democrat on a peace platform; and I personally can't say that I care much which they do."[86]

On the Saturday evening prior to the opening of the convention, the McClellan forces staged a mass rally at Bryan Hall, a large auditorium in Chicago. As one newspaper noted, "It was evident that they had determined on making a grand effort at effecting an imposing demonstration — one which should awe the opposition into submission." Everything did not go according to plan. The square outside of Bryan Hall was decorated with American flags and "an imposing galaxy of lights." The highlight of the elaborate decorations was "coil upon coil of gas pipe, with jets," spelling out "McClellan, Our Only Hope." Unfortunately for the organizers of the event, the gas jets would not burn. The Republican-leaning *Chicago Tribune* joked that "the failure of the jets was, however, compensated by an additional supply of gas of the windy kind, the speaking being resumed when it was found that their light was gone out."[87] The speakers blasted the Lincoln administration for its handling of the war, for the loss of civil liberties, and displayed sympathy and respect for the South. Typical were the remarks of one O. E. Perrine:

> We did not come here to speak to men by the acre, but one would suppose that this was our mission.... We have come here to consider whether we have a country, and rights; whether we can lift up our voices for constitutional rights. All parties are rallying for a common country. The question is to be determined whether we are to exercise our rights under martial law, or at the point of bayonets.... We will bring down all who would trample upon our rights.... We will support the Government, but we will not support Lincoln and his administration.... Our enemies have unmasked themselves and we are going to take the government from their hands. We are going to elect another man, and that man will be George B. McClellan.... When he is elected we will go to our erring brothers with the olive branch of peace in one hand and the implements of war in the other and will propose to take them back and to give them all their Constitutional rights.
>
> We have been told that the South had no resources, that their soldiers are naked and unfed. If they fight so well without anything to eat or wear, what in God's name will become of us if they ever get anything to wear or eat.[88]

The McClellan effort in Chicago was being spearheaded by Congressman Samuel S. Cox of Ohio, who was also known by the interesting nickname of "Sunset." Cox's job was to line up midwestern delegates for Little Mac. He visited multiple delegations prior to the opening of the convention and, by all accounts, was very successful in securing support for his candidate.[89]

If there was a politician who represented the heart and soul of the Peace Democrats, or Copperheads, as they were called, it was Clement Vallandigham, a former congressman from Ohio. Having openly stated that he believed the war was unconstitutional on the part of the Lincoln administration and that he wanted the South to win, Vallandigham was convicted by a military tribunal in 1863 for violation of military orders in Ohio that made it a crime to be in the "habit of declaring support for the enemy" and was sentenced to two years in a military prison. Lincoln commuted the sentence to banishment from the United States, and Vallandigham made his way to Richmond and eventually ended up in Windsor, Canada, just across the border from Detroit, where he continued to speak out against the war and the Lincoln administration. He returned to Ohio in June 1864. While the former congressman's presence on American soil was in violation of the terms of Lincoln's commutation of his sentence and could make him subject to arrest, federal authorities decided to leave him alone, lest they make him a martyr by throwing him back in prison.[90] Vallandigham came to Chicago for the convention and his suite of rooms at the Sherman House became the headquarters of the Peace Democrats, with numerous politicians and delegates coming and going at all hours of the day and night. In front of the Sherman House, a "triumphant mob surged at all hours about this hostelry, and its cries of 'Speech!' 'Speech!' would bring to the balcony first one and then another of the popular favorites — the measure of acclaim with which their appearance was greeted usually being in proportion to the lengths of time they had served in some 'Lincoln bastile.'"[91] In contrast to their remarks from the floor of the convention, speakers tended to be more extreme in their comments at these evening rallies, where they were eager to respond to the sentiments of the crowd, and where their remarks would not be transcribed as part of an official record.

The ninth presidential nominating convention of the Democratic Party was held in a building called the Amphitheater, a large circular structure located near Lake Michigan at Michigan Avenue and Eleventh Street. It was a huge wooden structure, similar to the Wigwam in the same city that had hosted the Republican convention in 1860. Two bands had been hired from Springfield to entertain the audience during the convention. A large gallery on the north side of the building, which had no seats and which could hold up to 8,000 people, was open to the public without any ticket required. The smaller gallery on the south side had benches for sitting, one-third of which were reserved for gentlemen accompanied by ladies, and two-thirds of which required tickets that had been given to the delegates for distribution by them. A larger than expected crowd gathered outside the Amphitheater in the hours before the convention's scheduled opening time of noon on Monday, August 29. When the doors for the large unticketed standing room only gallery opened at 11:00 A.M., a mass of humanity rushed in. The weight proved to be too much for one section of the gallery. According to the *Chicago Tribune*, "The fragile timbers commenced to creak most ominously, and ere the doors had been opened for half an hour, about thirty feet of the 'standing' platform fell with a loud crash ... burying about sixty people in the ruins. Happily, no one was more seriously injured than slightly bruised."[92]

The convention was called to order by August Belmont of New York, the chairman of the Democratic National Committee. Aware of the divisions among the delegates over the pending war, and of the need for compromise, Belmont's opening speech reminded delegates of the disastrous last convention that the party had held in 1860: "Gentlemen, let us now, at the very outset of our proceedings, determine that the dissentions [sic] at the last Democratic convention was one of the principal causes which gave the reins of government into the hands of our opponents; and let us beware that we do not fall into the same error."[93] William Bigler of Pennsylvania was named the temporary president of the gathering, and gave the first of what would be many speeches from the podium denouncing the war and calling for peace at the earliest opportunity: "At the end of three years of a war unparalleled in modern times, and for its barbarous desolations ... after the whole land has been literally drenched in fraternal blood, and wailings and lamentations are heard in every corner of our common country, the hopes of our Union, our cherished object, are in nowise improved."[94] The convention then established the standard committees, a Committee on Organization, a Committee on Credentials, and a Committee on Resolutions, with the traditional one member from each of the twenty-three states represented in Chicago. When the name of Ohio's representative on the Committee on Resolutions, Clement Vallandigham, was read from the podium, it was greeted with great applause from the delegates and the galleries.[95] His presence on the platform committee was seen as almost a guarantee that the committee would come back to the convention with a strongly worded peace plank. With the committees established, the convention adjourned its first day of proceedings.[96]

When the convention resumed for its second day on Tuesday, August 30, the first order of business was receipt of committee reports. The Committee on Credentials was first up, and reported that the only dispute as to delegates was in Kentucky, which had sent two delegations to Chicago. The committee recommended that both be seated, with the right to cast one-half of Kentucky's allotted votes, which was approved. The Committee on Permanent Organization nominated Horatio Seymour of New York for the position of permanent president, and a vice president from each of the states represented at the convention, which were approved. After an opening prayer and a long speech by Seymour, the Committee on Resolutions was called on for its report. Its chairman announced that they had not completed their work and, as a result, the convention recessed until 4:00 P.M. After its recess, the Committee on Resolutions gave its report. There were six planks in the platform, but all eyes and ears in the hall were focused on the secretary of the committee as the long-anticipated second resolution, the so-called peace plank, was read. It called the war "four years of failure" and provided that "the public welfare demand that immediate efforts be made for a cessation of hostilities with a view to an ultimate convention of the states, or other peaceable means, to that end that at the earliest practicable moment peace may be restored on the basis of the Federal Union of the States."[97] There were no preconditions — stop the war now, and the terms of the peace (hopefully, but not necessarily, with the Union intact) can be worked out later. According to reporter Brooks, the party's chairman, Belmont, "looked profoundly sad" as the peace plank of the platform was read.[98] But he was in the minority. This is what the Peace Democrats had come to Chicago to hear and they welcomed it with enthusiasm. According to the official proceedings of the convention:

> The deep, almost breathless attention of the vast audience was unbroken until the middle of the second resolution, when the popular approbation found vent in cheers which rendered the latter portion of the resolution unintelligible, the voice of the Secretary being totally drowned in the deep volume swelling up around from the lips of thousands. Order having been restored, the resolution was again read, and was listened to in silence until its close, when the audience again surrendered itself to the wildest enthusiasm, which died away and was renewed a half dozen times before the third resolution could be received.[99]

The platform was adopted by the delegates on a voice vote, with only a couple of dissenting voices being heard.[100]

The convention next moved to the nomination of candidates for the presidency. New Jersey nominated General George B. McClellan. Delaware nominated Lazarus W. Powell of Kentucky. Powell, a delegate to the convention, and immediately took the floor and declined to have his name placed in nomination, feeling that the candidate of the party should be from a non-slaveholding state. Ohio then nominated former governor Thomas H. Seymour of Connecticut. Kentucky then brought forward a surprising name, former president Franklin Pierce of New Hampshire, to which a Massachusetts delegate responded that Pierce absolutely did not want his name brought before the convention.[101]

Perhaps the most dramatic moment of the convention came when a Maryland delegate, Benjamin G. Harris, a member of Congress, took the floor, purportedly to make a seconding speech for Thomas Seymour. Instead, he launched into a virulent denouncement of McClellan. Harris lambasted Little Mac for his actions as one of Lincoln's generals early in the war, for having members of the Maryland legislature arrested, and for other military actions that Harris argued made McClellan unfit to even be considered a potential nominee by the Democratic Party. Rarely in American history has a party's prospective nominee been so personally attacked at his party's own convention. Harris's diatribe went on for quite some time:

> We have come here from the down-trodden State of Maryland and we do not desire to see placed in nomination the man most active in oppressing her.... All our rights have been trampled upon and the strong arm of the military has been over us, and ... it was instituted by your nominee....
>
> I claim it as a right to state that one of the men you have nominated is a tyrant.... Gen. McClellan was the very first man who inaugurated the system of usurping State rights. What you ask me to do is, in reality, to support the man who stabbed my own mother; and I for one — and I believe for the whole delegation from Maryland — will never do it....
>
> George B. McClellan, in September, 1861, broke up the Legislature of a sovereign State, deliberately and with full purpose, in order to exercise tyranny and oppression in advance of Abraham Lincoln. Now ... you ask men who are still smarting under the wrongs ... McClellan inflicted, to go to the polls and cast their free votes for such an one as he!
>
> What, then, have you to say in his favor? Why, as a military man, he has been defeated everywhere.... The siege of Richmond was not, I think, a success; the battle of Antietam was not a success, and in him as a military leader you have nothing whatever to brag of, while you have combined with military incapacity the fact that he has interfered with and destroyed the civil rights of the people.[102]

Harris went on and on, eventually going to the podium to complete his remarks, frequently being interrupted by cheers and applause but also at times by hisses. When Harris finally returned to his seat in the Maryland delegation, a New York delegate called him a traitor as he passed by. In response, Harris punched him, "leading to a scene of general uproar and riotous confusion."[103] The back-and-forth continued as other speakers took to the floor to defend McClellan, while others criticized him, each side interrupting the other. McClellan's detractors appeared to have more support in the huge convention hall than his defenders. One reporter at the convention observed of the general tone of the gathering: "It was noticeable that peace men and measures and sentiments were applauded to the echo, while patriotic utterances, what few there were, received no response from the crowd. The playing of 'Dixie' was cheered, while Union tunes were met with virtual silence."[104] In the midst of the speeches over the merits of McClellan as a nominee, an Ohio delegate placed the name of the convention's president, Horatio Seymour, into nomination. Seymour ruled him out of order.[105] By late afternoon, the debate raged on and it was clear that no nomination vote would be completed that day. The Amphitheater was not equipped with gas lights for an evening session and tempers were on edge. One Ohio delegate moved for adjournment, complaining that "I, for one, now state, that I do not propose to sit here in the dark." Convention president Seymour, noting that "it is utterly impossible to transact business in this confusion," agreed. A motion to adjourn was finally passed, and the second day of the convention ended.[106]

That night, the usual evening rallies took place around Chicago. The weather had been perfect for the convention, with late summer bright and sunny skies, and mild evenings with cool breezes blowing in from Lake Michigan. The Tuesday night rallies were less well attended than those on Saturday and Monday, perhaps because the McClellan supporters were concerned over the verbal drubbing that their man had received at the convention that afternoon and were worried what the next day would bring. The *Chicago Tribune* wondered if the McClellan crowd had "been betting their money on a losing horse" and commented that they "have evidently lost heart. They are very much like a rooster under a cart on a wet day. Their wings are ragged and drooping, and their tail feathers are bedraggled with mud and covered with mire." There were evening rallies at the Sherman House, at Court House Square, and at the Tremont House, but the level of enthusiasm of the prior nights was not repeated.[107]

When the convention resumed for its third day of proceedings on Wednesday, August 31, it quickly became evident that any "Stop McClellan" movement had fizzled overnight. The Peace Democrats knew that they could not put forward the name of the semi-fugitive Vallandigham as the party's nominee, and they had failed to unite behind another candidate. Having gotten the platform that they wanted, most of the Peace Democrats swallowed hard and reluctantly voted for McClellan. The roll call itself was not very suspenseful. With a total of 226 delegate votes, under the two-thirds rule that was again adopted by the Democrats at this convention, 151 votes were needed to win the nomination. On the initial results of the first ballot, McClellan had an overwhelming lead with 174 votes, with only 38 for Thomas Seymour of Connecticut, 12 for Horatio Seymour of New York, and two votes for other candidates. Various delegates who had supported the losers quickly jumped on the bandwagon, and the revised first ballot tally was 202 for McClellan and 28 for Thomas Seymour.[108] Delegates who had the previous day applauded statements that McClellan was a tyrant and a puppet of Abraham Lincoln then rose as one applauded him as the nominee of the Democratic Party for the presidency. According to the official proceedings, "Shout after shout from the assembled thousands, mingling with the thunders of cannon and the swelling strains of music, swept out of that building. For over fifteen minutes the tumultuous applause continued. Gentlemen upon chairs swung their hats. Ladies waved their handkerchiefs. Everyone joined in the grand shout of joy, caught up and echoed back again by the eager and enthusiastic thousands who were unable to gain admission." A group of McClellan supporters from New York then entered the hall carrying a large banner with the nominee's portrait on it and the words "McClellan, Our Country's Hope and Pride." The banner was taken to the area of the platform behind the desk of the convention president and was elevated toward the rafters, keeping the demonstration going strong for a few more minutes.[109] The love-fest not yet over, the leader of the Peace Democrats, Vallandigham, rose and moved that the nomination of McClellan be made unanimous.[110] The convention then took up its last task, the nomination of a candidate for vice president. A total of eight names were placed in nomination and, at the end of the first ballot, the two leaders were James Guthrie of Kentucky with 65 votes and Congressman George Pendleton of Ohio with 55 votes. On the second ballot, state after state switched their votes to Pendleton, who was known as a staunch Peace Democrat, and he was unanimously named to be McClellan's running mate. Pendleton, who was a delegate at the convention, then took the podium and made some brief remarks of thanks.[111] McClellan, age thirty-seven, and Pendleton, age thirty-nine, were at the time, and still remain, the youngest ticket nominated by any major American political party.

By tradition, once the ticket was nominated, presidential nominating conventions of the nineteenth century adjourned using the Latin phrase *sine die*, meaning that no future meetings were planned or anticipated. Curiously, the 1864 Democratic convention did not. Instead, the delegates approved a motion made by a delegate Wickliffe of Kentucky that the convention be placed in a state of suspension, subject to the call of the party's National Executive Committee "at any time and place" that might be designated.[112] This was clearly an anti–McClellan measure. The Peace Democrats, having been forced to accept a military man and a War Democrat as their party's nominee, wanted leverage over McClellan with the ability to reconvene, if necessary, and name a new nominee, if circumstances warranted such an action.[113] When McClellan's written acceptance of the nomination was received a few days later, many thought the suspension resolution needed to be invoked, for the candidate rejected the key plank of the platform of the convention that had nominated him. McClellan repudiated the language of the peace plank calling for "immediate efforts" for a cease-fire and stated that he favored, instead, a cessation of hostilities only after the South committed to rejoining the Union. The nominee wrote, "The re-establishment of the Union in all its integrity is, and must continue to be, the indispensible condition in any settlement. So soon as it is clear, or even probable, that our present adversaries are ready for peace, upon the basis of the Union, we should exhaust all the resources of statesmanship ... to secure such peace, re-establish the Union, and guarantee for the Union the constitutional rights of each State. The Union is the one condition of peace — we ask no more."[114] Vallandigham, back in Ohio, was furious and threatened to bolt the party and to take many of the Peace Democrats with him. After a lot of diplomacy and stroking of his ego, however, party leaders managed to keep him in the tent and he actually made some speeches during the fall campaign for the ticket of McClellan and his Ohio friend Pendleton.[115] A reconvening of the Democratic convention was never called for by the party's leadership. The divisions in the party so evident at the convention never healed and, as a result, many of the Peace Democrats never ardently support the McClellan candidacy.[116]

If the 1864 convention was not entirely successful for the Democratic Party, the opposite could be said of the City of Chicago. For the second presidential election in a row, Chicago had been the focus of the nation's attention and had proved itself worthy as a convention host city. East Coast cities would no longer be the exclusive territory for presidential nominating conventions. Shortly after the convention's closing gavel, a hometown newspaper, the *Chicago Tribune*, gave the Windy City a pat on the back: "It is fresh proof that Chicago has a way in such matters that is very satisfactory to our visitors and a source of just pride to our residents. We know how to attend to crowds. Our capacities are vast, with the utmost elasticity. We can always accommodate a few more. Chicago holds her lap, and her railways pour in their teeming thousands, and we can feed, lodge, and care for them."[117]

The Campaign and Election

The surprisingly smooth renomination of Lincoln in Baltimore in early June 1864 did not end the drama and intrigue as to whether Lincoln would have the support of the Radical

Republicans come November, and certainly did not settle the question as to whether he would be reelected. News from the battlefront got worse over the summer. Just before and during the Republican convention in early June, the Union army suffered defeat and massive losses at the Battle of Cold Harbor, adding to defeats and stalemates incurred earlier in the year.[118] In early July, Confederate general Jubal Early led a raid through Maryland and succeeded in reaching the outskirts of Washington, cutting the city's communications with the outside world for a few days and sending a shockwave of panic through the Federal City.[119] The same month, Lincoln pocket-vetoed the Wade-Davis Act, a Reconstruction bill passed by the Radical Republicans in Congress, which contained harsher terms and more stringent requirements than his own proposals for the South's readmission to the Union at the war's end.[120] On July 30, Grant's troops, who were laying siege to Petersburg, near Richmond, suffered a humiliating defeat at the Battle of the Crater.[121] By late summer, the prospects for a second Lincoln term were looking slim: "Grant seemed to be accomplishing nothing; Lee appeared invincible; three years of war and hundreds of thousands of casualties had gone for naught; Sherman was apparently getting nowhere; Early had almost seized Washington. Lincoln was at odds with his own party on war aims and reconstruction and had offended his Congress."[122] On August 23, 1864, Lincoln called his cabinet together and had each member sign the back of a folded and sealed piece of paper, the front of which he did not show them, and the contents of which he would not disclose until after the election. On the front, the pessimistic sixteenth president of the United States had written: "This morning, as for some days past, it seems exceedingly probable that this Administration will not be reelected. Then it will be my duty to so co-operate with the president elect, as to save the Union between the election and the inauguration; as he will have secured his election on such ground that he cannot possibly save it afterwards."[123] Calls were made for a new Republican convention, to be held in September in Cincinnati or Buffalo, to select a new nominee. By late August, the optimism of early June had turned into despair.

Lincoln's reelection to the presidency rested with the Union army and a much-needed victory to turn the tide of the war and of the election. General William Tecumseh Sherman delivered. On September 3, 1864, only three days after the end of the Democratic convention in Chicago, Sherman's telegraphic message to Washington was succinct: "Atlanta is ours, and fairly won." Combined with a naval victory the same week by Admiral David Farragut at Mobile Bay, Alabama, the fall of the Confederacy's largest city gave confidence to the northern public that the war could be won and imparted the determination to reelect Lincoln to see it to a conclusion. New York's Republican boss, Thurlow Weed, wrote to his close friend Secretary of State William Seward, that, with these military successes, the "conspiracy against Mr. Lincoln collapsed."[124] The much-touted new Republican convention set for September was never held.[125] The other Republican in the race, General John C. Frémont, who had been nominated at a Radical Republican convention in Cleveland in May, withdrew from the presidential contest on September 22. The next day, Lincoln asked for and received the resignation of Postmaster General Montgomery Blair of Maryland from his cabinet. Blair, who was viewed as the most conservative member of the cabinet, was hated by the Radicals, and his ouster was the purported object of the call for "harmony in national councils" in the platform of the Baltimore convention. The timing of Frémont's withdrawal from the campaign and the forced resignation of Blair the next day has been viewed by most historians as not being mere coincidence.[126]

The election on November 8, 1864, turned out to be anticlimactic, given the difficulties Lincoln faced for much of the spring and during the summer. He became the first president since Andrew Jackson in 1832 to be elected to a second term, with a vote total of 2,206,938 to McClellan's 1,803,787. With a victory margin of more than 400,000, Lincoln increased his percentage of the vote to fifty-five, fifteen percent more than he had won in 1860. Even more significant was the Electoral College tally, which was a Lincoln landslide of 212 to only 21 for McClellan. Little Mac won only three states, New Jersey (where he resided), Delaware, and Kentucky. Secretary of War Stanton, General Grant, and the Union army had arranged for hundreds of thousands of soldiers to vote, by absentee ballot where permitted, and by massive furloughs at election time in states where voting in person was required. Historians generally agree that Lincoln carried the soldier vote by a large margin over his former general and that their votes were decisive in several states, including New York, Pennsylvania, and Maryland.[127] And there was a new vice-president-elect, pro-war Democrat Andrew Johnson of Tennessee, whose nomination had been steered through the Baltimore convention in June with much political skill by those involved. Within five months, Lincoln would be dead by an assassin's bullet, Johnson would be president, and the Republican Party would soon regret its choice for the second spot on its 1864 ticket.

CHAPTER 12

1868: Let Us Have Peace

We are ready for the fight, we will struggle for the right.
And we know that Grant is true, his arm is strong.

He is once more at our head, as he was when late he led.
And the battle cry of freedom was our song

Grant, Grant, Grant! The country's calling
Goodbye Andy, you must go![1]

Republican campaign song, 1868

History repeats itself. In 1840, the Whigs, in an attempt to broaden their support in the election, nominated for vice president John Tyler, a former Democrat who was not a true Whig. In 1864, the Republicans, in an attempt to broaden their support in the election, nominated Andrew Johnson for vice president, who was a Democrat and not a true Republican. In both instances, only a month after the start of the new presidential term of office, the president was dead. The new vice president was elevated to the presidency, vetoed the signature legislation of the party that nominated him, and was then disowned by that party.

Shortly after taking the oath of office on April 15, 1865, Andrew Johnson proclaimed his determination to pursue lenient terms with the South for readmission to the Union, which was the policy that Lincoln had implied he would pursue in his second inaugural address. Since Congress would not be in session until December 1865, Johnson, upon taking office, instituted his own program of presidential reconstruction and began the process of having the southern states form new state governments and constitutions, having their citizens take loyalty oaths to the United States Constitution, and electing representatives to Congress. The Radical Republicans in Congress stopped Johnson's plan dead in its tracks. When the congressional session resumed in December, they refused to seat as members the southerners elected under Johnson's policies. Determined to have the Reconstruction process controlled by Congress, they passed the Freedman's Bureau Bill and the Civil Rights Act, both of which Johnson vetoed. Northern public opinion supported the Radicals' more stringent policies toward the South and, in the mid-term elections of 1866, the Radicals won veto-proof majorities in both the House and the Senate.

When the new congressional session began in 1867, the Radical Republicans in Congress proceeded to enact their agenda. Over Johnson's vetoes, the South was divided into five military districts, southern black males were enfranchised, many southern white males remained disenfranchised, and new state governments in the South were established under the rules set by the Radicals. The Radicals also passed the Tenure of Office Act, which required Senate approval of the president's dismissal of high civilian and military officials. When Johnson fired Secretary of War Edwin M. Stanton, an ally of the Radicals, during a congressional recess, the Senate, upon its return to Washington, refused to consent to the dismissal. Stanton evicted his successor from the War Department, lived day and night in his office, and had the building guarded by federal troops. The House of Representatives on February 24, 1868, passed eleven different articles of impeachment against President Johnson, nine of which related to his alleged violation of the Tenure of Office Act. At a trial in the Senate, the Radicals' case was presented by Senator Benjamin F. Butler of Massachusetts, a former Democrat who had jumped to the Republicans shortly after the war. It was Butler who had been offered the vice presidential spot on the Republican/Union Party ticket by Lincoln in the spring of 1864, only to decline it. Butler thus led the effort to remove Johnson from the presidential chair, a chair upon which he himself could have been sitting. The Republicans controlled the fifty-four-member Senate with forty-two seats, compared to only twelve held by the Democrats. Under the Constitution, a vote of two-thirds, or thirty-six senators, was required for conviction and removal of the president from office. After a six-week trial, on May 16, 1868, thirty-five guilty votes were cast in the Senate against Johnson, compared to nineteen not guilty votes, saving the Johnson presidency by a single vote. Forty-one-year-old Republican senator Edmund G. Ross of Kansas, who, unlike most of his colleagues, had not stated his opinion during the trial, is credited by historians as the man who cast the decisive vote.[2]

As the impeachment trial ended, the 1868 presidential campaign season began in earnest. For the first time since nominating conventions began in 1832, nine elections ago, Baltimore would be only an observer of the process. It would not host any political conventions in 1868. The Republicans returned to Chicago, the city where they had first nominated Lincoln in 1860, and, for the first time ever, the nation's largest city, New York, became a convention city and hosted the Democrats. The battle for the White House in 1868 would be played out over support for, or opposition to, the policies of the Radical Republicans in Congress since the death of Lincoln. One party was absolutely certain who its nominee and standard-bearer in the fall election would be; the other party did not have a clue.

Republican Convention

Only four days after Johnson's acquittal in the Senate, the fourth presidential nominating convention of the Republican Party opened on Wednesday, May 20, 1868, at Crosby's Opera House in Chicago. This building, located on the north side of Washington Street between State and Dearborn Streets, opened in late April 1865, its original opening date having been delayed by the news of Lincoln's assassination. Chicago in the 1860s did not have the public demand for a for a full slate of opera performances and, as a result, Crosby's became a venue for multiple types of entertainment for citizens of the Windy City, hosting "promenade concerts, charity balls (the first given in Chicago), regular opera and opera bouffe ... a medley of entertainments, including pantomime performances, exhibitions of trained animals, gymnastic feats and bellringers."[3] In May 1868, trained animals of the political kind took to the stage of Crosby's and followed a pre-convention script that had no suspense as to the outcome. General Ulysses S. Grant, the Union's most prominent military leader during the Civil War, was the consensus choice of Republicans to be their nominee for the presidency.

Crosby's Opera House was the site of the 1868 Republican convention, where Ulysses S. Grant was nominated for his first term as president. By 1868, Chicago was replacing Baltimore as the city of choice for conventions *(Library of Congress)*.

More than 20,000 visitors, including approximately 500 reporters, descended on Chicago for what was officially called the convention of the National Union Republican Party. On the eve of the convention, downtown streets were "blocked up with people to such an extent as to render walking, except at a very slow rate, exceedingly difficult."[4] Lodging was at a premium. Outraged delegates found that rooms in the best hotels — the Sherman House, the Richmond House, and the Tremont House — were going for more than twenty dollars a night. As a reporter for the *New York Times* noted of the innkeepers, "It is their harvest-time, and they are making the most of it."[5] A national soldiers' and sailors' convention and a Union League convention, also meeting in Chicago the same week, added to the overcrowding. The outside of the Opera House gave no indication that the convention was being held inside, although huge pictures of Grant were hung from some of the adjacent buildings. Anyone within a block of Crosby's who was seen wearing an official convention badge "immediately became the centre of a throng of ticket seekers." On the streets, there was a carnival atmosphere, and "vendors of Grant badges, and Grant breast pins and Grant photographs, the bootblacks and newsboys, and the sellers of Arabian dates and Turkey figs, drove a thriving business." Silk pictures of Abraham Lincoln, imported from Switzerland, sold for one dollar each and were suitable for wearing as badges.[6] The thousands outside were kept advised of the goings-on inside by a man "with great lung power" who appeared periodically at a balcony window and announced "to the multitude below what was the engrossing subject then occupying the attention of the convention."[7]

Inside, more than 3,000 people could be seated in Crosby's Opera House for the proceedings. Although there were an additional 2,000 standing-room spaces scattered around the building, this gathering would not have the massive crowds of more than 10,000 people that had packed the prior Chicago conventions at the Wigwam in 1860 and at the Amphitheater in 1864. This would be a more subdued gathering. The various state delegations consisted of "active, intelligent men; of middle-aged men, the bone and sinew of the land; of soldiers who have fought and now came to counsel; of prudent, thoughtful men, slow but sure in action."

Unlike most conventions of the era, there were only a few ladies in attendance on the opening day and, scanning the audience, one saw a "sea of black coats and hats. Here and there a green veil, a blue hat or a waving fan indicated a gap in the masculine ranks." Chicago police manned the entrances to the Opera House and greeted the crowd with two instructions — show your tickets and drop your cigars — as smoking was not permitted inside. Red, white, and blue decorations covered the stage, with a large American flag and curtain at the rear concealing a surprise that was to be revealed to the delegates once General Grant was formally nominated.[8] The presiding officers, distinguished guests, and some reporters were seated on the stage. More reporters were in the orchestra pit and the delegates were seated on the main floor of the theater and in the dress circle. Two upper balconies accommodated the ticketed guests of the convention.[9]

As the delegates began to stroll in during the late morning for the opening session scheduled to begin at noon, most entered casually and in small groups — except for the delegates from Empire State. Those New Yorkers knew how to make an entrance. The massive delegation of sixty-six men marched in as a group, with their heads held high, as if in formation. They were led by one of their own, General Daniel Sickles, on crutches because of a leg lost at Gettysburg, who clutched a flag that his troops had carried into battle. The stirring scene elicited overwhelming applause from the galleries. As one reporter commented, "There is no mistaking the New Yorkers. Irreproachable in raiment, solid in watch chains, *au fait* in the matter of whiskers ... they are the trained political athletes, skilled in parliamentary law, practiced in point of order, and motions and resolutions, good fluent speakers and solid votes. In a convention, they are in their element and their vote is like a bombshell."[10]

In the opening session, Carl Schurz, a leader of German Americans and a leading Republican from Missouri, was named the convention's temporary president. He later handed the gavel over to Joseph Hawley of Connecticut, the permanent president of the proceedings.[11] Just after the convention got underway, Henry Lane, a senator from Indiana, "who boils over with gushing enthusiasm at the mere mention of Grant," according to a contemporary, took to the floor and moved that Grant be nominated by acclamation.[12] Why wait? he pleaded. Calmer and more patient heads prevailed. The Committee on Credentials had not yet even determined who the proper voting delegates would be at the convention, nor had any rules been established. Lane was persuaded to withdraw his motion and the convention went about its business in an orderly fashion. The speeches at the convention were generally forgettable, with a recurring theme of expressing regret over the decision at the 1864 Republican convention to place the now despised Andrew Johnson on the ticket with Lincoln. Typical was the statement that "our policy was thwarted by the very person, whom, in an unfortunate moment, we had put on the road to power."[13] The convention's delegates included a dozen African American men from four southern states, the first time in American history that African Americans had been certified as delegates to a major party's presidential nominating convention.[14] There were some interesting decisions on rules and procedures. Although Colorado was not yet a state, the Colorado delegation was given full voting rights, under the reasoning that it would be a state had not President Johnson vetoed the bill for its admission. The Republicans felt that any decision made by Johnson could be ignored.[15] With Colorado added, thirty-eight states were represented at the convention. The delegations from the territories, as well as the District of Columbia, were given seats on the floor and were allotted two votes each. Two delegate votes were allotted for each state's Electoral College votes and a majority rule was established for nomination. In all, there were approximately 650 delegate votes. After all of the issues concerning credentials, rules, and procedures were adopted, the convention's opening day ended with the announcement that copies of a new campaign song were available on the stage for the delegates to pick up, the song to be sung at the appropriate time later in the proceedings.[16]

When the convention resumed for its second day on the morning of Thursday, May 21, there were more ladies in the galleries than on the opening day. Unfortunately, there was little for them to see. No official business could be conducted, since the Committee on Resolutions had not yet completed its work on the platform, and the rules required that the platform be adopted before the nominations could commence. Thus, there was time to kill. As a reporter noted, "there was an hour for evil or for good."[17] A New York delegate proposed reading the resolutions adopted by the Union League, which had also been meeting in Chicago the same week. The Union League had strongly denounced the Republican senators who had voted the previous week to acquit Andrew Johnson at his Senate trial, and the apparent purpose of having this presented to the convention was to put pressure on the Committee on Resolutions to adopt similarly strong language. After some discussion, it was agreed to read the Union League's resolutions, but with the understanding that the reading of them was not their adoption. The portion concerning the repudiation of fellow Republicans stated, "We especially feel called upon to condemn the traitorous conduct of the Senators who disappointed the hopes of every loyal heart in the land in voting for the acquittal of Andrew Johnson ... who deserted the country in the hour of its peril; and we class them ... traitors to their party and country ... with the assurance that a traitor's doom awaits them."[18] The convention still waited for the report on the platform, and in the meantime speeches were called for. Delegate Hassaurek of Ohio launched into an address, only to stop after a couple of minutes to complain to convention president Hawley of noise coming from the lobby and that no one could hear or was listening to him: "I do not believe that this convention is in a humor, now, to hear a discourse on the political questions of the day ... and would rather be excused until that is over." After Hawley directed the Committee on Arrangements and the police in the hall to "correct the evil," Hassaurek resumed his speech, going on for some time.[19] The next speaker, an Illinois delegate, General John Palmer, told the convention that the Baltimore convention "made a mistake in 1864," and even went so far as to imply that, had Johnson not been nominated for vice president, Abraham Lincoln would still be alive, through the twisted logic that Booth shot Lincoln in order to put the Democrat Johnson in the White House.[20] Of course, Palmer ignored the fact that Booth and his co-conspirators had also planned to assassinate Johnson on the same night as Lincoln. With still more time to fill, various speakers were called for, several of whom declined to address the convention, some for physical reasons, some apparently for lack of any prepared remarks, and some of whom were not present in the hall. The band in the hall filled the void by playing tunes such as "Columbia, Gem of the Ocean" and "Hail Columbia."[21]

Finally, in the late morning, the Committee on Resolutions appeared with its report on the party's platform. It praised the Radical Republicans in Congress for taking control of the reconstruction of the defeated southern states, and supported "equal suffrage to all loyal men of the South," which included African American males. The fact that African American males were still denied voting rights in several northern states in 1868 was finessed by stating that the issue, in those states, "belongs to the people of those states." The platform called for economy in government and reducing the national debt. A hot economic issue in 1868 was whether holders of government bonds should be repaid in gold or in less valuable paper money, referred to as greenbacks. The Republican platform came down squarely on repayment in gold: "National honor requires the payment of the public indebtedness in the utmost good faith to all creditors at home and abroad, not only according to the letter, but the spirit of the laws under which it was contracted." It further denounced the Johnson administration, went on the record to "profoundly deplore the untimely and tragic death of Abraham Lincoln, and regret the accession of Andrew Johnson to the presidency," and then listed a litany of Johnson's alleged transgressions, for which he "has been justly impeached for high crimes and misdemeanors, and properly pronounced guilty thereof by the vote of thirty-five senators."[22] Unlike the Union League's resolutions, the Republican platform, which was quickly approved by the convention, did not go so far as to name as traitors those Republican senators who voted for acquittal of Johnson.

The nomination process then began. After a "brief and eloquent" speech by Senator John Logan of Illinois nominating Ulysses S. Grant, the roll call of the states began. The chairman of the Ohio delegation, the state where Grant was born, perhaps exaggerated the effect of a Grant victory in the election: "Ohio is in line, and on that line Ohio proposes to follow this great Captain, that never knew defeat ... until victory shall be secured, and all the stars that glitter in the firmament of our glorious constellation shall again be restored to their proper order, and all the sons of freedom throughout the whole earth shall shout for joy."[23] The roll call was quickly completed and Grant received all of the 650 votes cast.[24] When the final tally was announced, "The Opera House rang from floor to ceiling, from balcony to curtain, and from the stage to the gallery, with the wildest cheers ... until it seemed as though the roof itself must give way under the volume and sound which surged upward to the ceiling."[25] As

As the Union's most popular general during the Civil War, Ulysses S. Grant was the consensus choice of Republicans to be their nominee in 1868. The Chicago convention nominated Schuyler Colfax of Indiana to be Grant's running mate *(Library of Congress)*.

the cheering continued, two surprises greeted the delegates. A dove (some thought it was a pigeon), painted red, white, and blue, was let loose from one of the proscenium boxes near the stage to symbolize the dramatic moment. Instead of soaring gracefully, as hoped for, the frightened bird flew about the hall "in great agitation, not liking the tremendous roaring about him."[26] When the scared creature finally landed on the stage, the band struck up "Hail to the Chief," at which time a curtain in the back of stage was dropped, revealing a painting which filled the entire rear of the stage. Done by the famous cartoonist Thomas Nast, it depicted the portico of the White House, with Grant, in uniform, on the right side, seated on a pedestal, underneath which was written "Chicago Nominee 1868." On the left side, there was an empty pedestal, underneath which was written "Democratic Nominee New York 1868." Above all of this was a depiction of the mythical figure Columbia, representing America, pointing to the two pedestals, one with Grant and one vacant, and stating the words "Match Him!" A new campaign song, entitled "Fight It Out Here, On the Old Union Line," the lyrics having been distributed to the delegates the day before, was sung with gusto by all and was "received with great favor."[27]

The issue of the vice presidency was not so quickly accomplished. There were four major candidates nominated, each of whom it was thought could walk away the winner: Schuyler Colfax of Indiana, who was the Speaker of the House of Representatives, Senator Benjamin Wade of Ohio, a longtime leader of the Radical Republicans (who many thought was the favorite going into the convention), Governor Reuben Fenton of New York, and Senator Henry Wilson of Massachusetts.[28] Wade was the president *pro tempore* of the Senate and, under the law of presidential succession in effect in 1868, he would have become president a few days before the convention if Andrew Johnson had been convicted in his Senate trial and removed from office. Some criticized him for participating in the trial and for voting to convict Johnson, given his own self-interest in the outcome. During the convention, tracts were circulated at the major hotels by unknown opponents of Wade, warning against nominating the sixty-seven-year-old Radical Republican for the vice presidency "on the ground that his age, infirmities, and declining powers, physically and mentally, rendered him unfit for the office."[29] Although Wade led on the first four ballots, Colfax pulled ahead on the fifth ballot and won the nomination.[30]

In his written acceptance letter a few days after the convention, Grant proclaimed "Let us have peace," which became the slogan for his campaign, a status desperately wished for by Americans after the tumult of the war and the political battles of the Johnson presidency.[31]

Democratic Convention

Six weeks later, on July 4, 1868, the Democratic Party opened its national convention at Tammany Hall in New York City. It was the first time that New York hosted a presidential nominating convention. The building was the headquarters of the New York political organization of the same name. Over the course of more than a century, a total of four separate buildings served as the home of New York's Tammany Hall and the 1868 Democratic convention was held in the third of these, located on the north side of Fourteenth Street, between Third Avenue and Irving Place. The hall was an elegant and spacious room topped by an ornate oval ceiling.[32] Recently completed, it could hold up to 4,000 people and was "garishly decorated" for the convention. Several former Confederate soldiers and politicians showed up in New York for the convention, including General Nathan Bedford Forrest, reaffirming the view of many in the North that the Democrats were the party of disloyalty and treason.[33]

The Democrats held their 1868 convention in Tammany Hall, the first major party convention to be held in New York City. This building was the third of four different structures over the years to bear the name Tammany Hall *(Library of Congress).*

Unlike the Republicans, there was no preordained nominee for the Democrats in their first post-war convention. To the contrary, in the weeks leading up to the convention, the names of more than forty potential candidates surfaced and it was anybody's guess as to who would emerge as the nominee. The frontrunners were perceived to be former congressman George H. Pendleton of Ohio (who had been the party's vice presidential nominee in 1864), Senator Thomas Hendricks of Indiana, Francis P. Blair, Jr., of Missouri, and General Winfield Scott Hancock. There was also a behind-the-scenes movement to nominate Salmon P. Chase of Ohio, a former Republican and Lincoln's secretary of the treasury, who in 1872 was the chief justice of the Supreme Court of the United States and who had presided over the recent Senate trial of President Johnson. Chase's daughter, Kate, who had been her father's popular hostess in Washington during his tenure there, was in New York during the convention and actively promoted her father as the Democratic nominee.[34]

In addition to their differences over a potential nominee, the delegates were also divided over an economic issue — greenbacks. Eastern investors, who had purchased federal bonds during the war, wanted repayment in gold, while westerners felt that repayment should be made in paper currency — greenbacks — which had less value. Pendleton of Ohio was a leader of the pro-greenback movement. His Ohio supporters walked around the streets of New York with fake five-dollar bills pinned to their lapels to show their support for the greenback cause.[35]

The tenth presidential nominating convention of the Democratic Party began at noon on Independence Day, a Saturday, with an opening address by August Belmont, the chairman of the Democratic National Committee. Belmont minced no words in stating that the Radical Republicans who controlled Congress were determined now to also control the presidency and the rest of the federal government, that the trampling of civil liberties that had occurred since the end of the Civil War would only increase under their continued rule, and that a military dictatorship was their ultimate goal:

> Instead of restoring the Southern states to their Constitutional rights, — instead of trying to wipe out the miseries of the past by a magnanimous policy, dictated alike by humanity and sound statesmanship, and so ardently prayed for by the heart of the generous American people, — the Radicals in Congress, elected in an evil hour, have placed the iron heel of the conqueror on the South.... These men, elected to be legislators, and legislators only, trampling the Constitution under their feet, have usurped the functions of the Executive and the Judiciary.... In order to carry out this nefarious programme, our army and navy are kept in a time of profound peace on a scale which involves a yearly expenditure of from one to two hundred millions.... And now this same party, which has bought all these evils on the country, comes again before the American people, asking again for their suffrages; and whom has it chosen for its candidate? The general commanding the armies of the United States. Can there be any doubt left as to the designs of the Radicals, if they should be able to keep their hold on the reins of government? They intend Congressional usurpation of all of the branches and functions of the government, to be enforced by the bayonets of a military despotism![36]

After Belmont's speech, the convention moved to the initial organizational matters required of all such gatherings. The seemingly routine action of adopting the procedural rules of the House of Representatives was controversial, since some delegates felt that the Radical Republicans in control of Congress might have changed the rules, since they have otherwise "done so much damage, so much mischief, so much outrage, and so much of wrong." As a result, to avoid this issue, the rules governing the last Democratic convention in 1864 were proposed and were adopted.[37] The standard committees to address permanent organization of the convention, credentials, and the platform were all appointed, with the usual one member from each state. A proposal to have an evening session was not favorably received, as the convention was meeting on a Saturday and it was the Fourth of July. A New York delegate opposed meeting any further until Monday morning: "This being the national anniversary, the City of New York has made great preparations for a proper celebration of the day, at its close." The convention decided to hear a reading of the Declaration of Independence and to call it a day, no doubt so that all could enjoy New York's Fourth of July fireworks.[38] The sheer size of New York drew criticism from some visiting delegates, who found that it took too long to get around the city. On the opening day, one Ohio delegate telegraphed a complaint to a Cincinnati newspaper:

The unfitness of New-York as a place for holding a national convention is pretty well demonstrated already. Delegates and others who have come here in the interest of the Convention are scattered at such great intervals, over such a vast extent of territory, that great difficulty is met in securing meetings or consultations. It seems almost impossible, owing to this fact, to secure perfect concert of action. The result is especially unfavorable to Western men, many of whom are unacquainted with the city and its magnificent distances.[39]

When the convention resumed on Monday, July 6, Horatio Seymour of New York was named the permanent president of the convention, repeating the position he had filled at the party's 1864 convention in Chicago.[40] Seymour, a wealthy lawyer and businessman from Utica, had been a leading figure in the conservative wing of the New York Democratic Party for years. After serving a two-year term as governor in the early 1850s, he was again elected to a two-year term as governor of the Empire State in 1862, making him one of the nation's more prominent Democratic officeholders during the Civil War. He had been mentioned as a possible nominee prior to the convention, but let it be known that he was not interested. Seymour favored Chief Justice Chase for the nomination and, with the nomination race wide open, his position as president of the convention was seen as a favorable development for Chase's chances.[41] After a speech from Seymour, the convention spent most of the day offering proposed resolutions to be included in the platform, arguing over whether to proceed to the nominations before the platform was adopted (it was decided to have the platform finalized first), and welcoming a committee from a soldiers' and sailors' convention that was also meeting in New York, who were "received with loud cheers, the delegates rising."[42] With little of substance accomplished, the convention adjourned for the day.

This drawing depicts the interior of Tammany Hall during the 1868 Democratic convention. The delegates deadlocked for days before deciding on a reluctant nominee, Horatio Seymour of New York *(Library of Congress)*.

On its third day, July 7, the convention heard the platform being recommended by its Committee on Resolutions. It was pro-western and pro-southern. On the primary economic issue before the country, it supported the use of greenbacks, instead of gold, to repay government bonds: "Where the obligations of the government do not expressly state upon their face ... that they shall be paid in coin, they ought, in right and in justice, be paid in the lawful money of the United States." On the issue of the Radical Republicans in Congress and their policies for reconstruction of the South, the platform called for "immediate restoration of the States to their rights," for amnesty for all former Confederates, for regulation of the franchise by the states, for reductions in the size of the army and navy, and for "the abolition of the Freedman's Bureau; and all political instrumentalities designed to secure negro [sic] supremacy." President Johnson was also praised for "resisting the aggressions of Congress upon the constitutional rights of the States and the people." Surprisingly, despite the fact that a substantial number of delegates from the East, particularly from New York, were known to oppose the greenback plank, the platform was approved unanimously and without debate.[43]

As the balloting started, there was no clear frontrunner. Initially, there were eight names placed in nomination by various state delegations: George Pendleton by Ohio, General Winfield Scott Hancock by Maine, President Andrew Johnson by Tennessee, James English by Connecticut, Joel Parker by New Jersey, Sanford Church by New York, Asa Packer by Pennsylvania, and James Doolittle by Wisconsin.[44] Several of these were "favorite son" candidates of the states who nominated them — someone to throw their support to until it could be determined which way the political winds were blowing. Church was seen as a stalking horse put forward by New York investors, who hoped to bring Chief Justice Chase forward as the balloting went on. The Democratic Party's two-thirds rule for nomination was again adopted, making it almost impossible for any one candidate to win with so many in the race. With a total of 317 delegates at the convention, 212 votes were needed for nomination. Pendleton led the voting on the first ballot, with 105 votes. His three closest pursuers were President Johnson with 65, Church with 34, and Hancock with 33. After a total of six ballots, with little movement among the frontrunners, the convention agreed to adjourn for the day at midafternoon.

When the convention met for its fourth day, July 8, Indiana introduced a new candidate and nominated its own Thomas Hendricks. Pendleton peaked at 156 on the eighth ballot and then began a slow decline. The roll call of the states was read a dozen more times. There was a surge for Hancock, and the new man in the race, Hendricks, ran well, picking up New York's large bloc of votes. By the eighteenth ballot and the end of the day, however, no candidate had a majority of the votes, much less the two-thirds required for nomination. At the day's adjournment, Hancock was up to 144 votes, Hendricks was in second with 87 votes, and Pendleton had faded to 56 votes.[45]

As the convention resumed for its fifth day of proceedings on July 9, its president, Horatio Seymour of New York, who had been overseeing the stalemate, was waiting for the convention to deadlock. At the appropriate moment, he planned to put forward the name of Chief Justice Chase. Much to Seymour's surprise, however, it was his own name that was put forward, by the Ohio delegation, as the compromise candidate. During the twenty-second ballot, the head of the Ohio delegation sent a shock wave of excitement through the convention by announcing, when the Buckeye State was reached during the roll call, Ohio's intention to "place in nomination against his inclination, but no longer against his honor, the name of Horatio Seymour of New York.... Let us vote Mr. Chairman and gentlemen of the convention, for a man whom the Presidency has sought, but who has not sought the Presidency."[46] Seymour's home state delegation quickly chimed in and voiced its support. A visibly upset Seymour immediately took the podium and protested against his name being introduced as a candidate:

> I do not stand here as a man proud of his opinions, or obstinate in his purposes; but upon a question of duty and of honor I must stand upon my own convictions against the world.... Gentlemen, when I said here at an early day, that honor forbade my accepting a nomination by this Convention, I meant it. When, in the course of my intercourse with those of my own delegation and my friends, I said to them that I could not be a candidate, I meant it.... Gentlemen, I thank you, and may God bless you for your kindness to me, but your candidate I cannot be.[47]

The Ohio and New York delegations had clearly colluded to bring Seymour's name forward, and they proceeded to totally ignore his objections. Neither state favored Hancock. Chase, as an Ohioan, was acceptable to the Buckeye State, but New York, having lost out to the West on the platform with the adoption of the pro-greenback plank, wanted a candidate from the East as the nominee. Of Seymour's comments, the chairman of the Ohio delegation was blunt: "Ohio will not accept his declination, and her twenty-one votes shall stand in his name." New York's chairman, likewise, would hear none of Seymour's reluctance. By declining, he had done all that an honorable man was required to do to avoid being accused of hypocrisy or opportunism over his pre-convention statements that he did not desire to be the nominee: "but, now, that his honor is safe, his duty to his country ... requires that he shall let the judg-

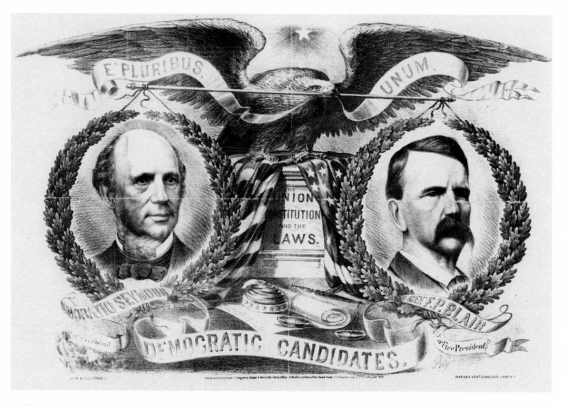

Horatio Seymour, a former governor of New York, was the president of the 1868 Democratic convention. Against his wishes, he was nominated on the twenty-second ballot to break a deadlocked convention and won the nomination. Francis Blair of Missouri was nominated as Seymour's running mate (*Library of Congress*).

ment of the delegates of this Convention prevail."[48] Seymour then left the hall, perhaps in disgust, perhaps not of his own choice. One story has it that Seymour was, in effect, kidnapped by several of his friends before he could get to the podium again, was taken from the convention hall to the nearby Manhattan Club, and was kept there while the balloting continued.[49] As the twenty-second roll call of the states continued, states began falling like dominoes for Seymour — Kentucky, Massachusetts, North Carolina, and others. Once it became clear that the Seymour bandwagon was rolling, "[a] scene of the wildest enthusiasm followed, the chairmen of a dozen delegations present springing from their seats to obtain a recognition of the chairman pro tem, to change their votes for Seymour."[50] No politician ever wants to be at the end of a parade. As state after state began the process to make Seymour's nomination unanimous, a cannon outside Tammany Hall began firing salutes, and "the discharges were answered by those inside the hall rising to their feet with vociferous cheers and the waving of handkerchiefs."[51]

Known to history as "The Great Decliner," the reluctant Seymour was persuaded to accept the nomination and did so publicly the next day.[52] After the stampede for Seymour, Francis Blair, Jr., of Missouri was named his running mate by a unanimous vote on the first ballot.[53] Blair had been a Union general during the Civil War. He was the nephew of Montgomery Blair of Maryland, who had been in Lincoln's cabinet as postmaster general. The elder Blair had been viewed as too conservative by the Radical Republicans during Lincoln's administration and, as a result, had been forced out of the cabinet during Lincoln's 1864 reelection campaign. Now, four years later, his nephew and Seymour would be taking on the candidate of the Radicals, Grant, and his running mate, Colfax.

The Campaign and Election

The campaign of 1868 followed the standard custom of the era, with the two candidates doing little, if any, active campaigning. Grant, who was still a general, did take a western trip to Colorado in the summer, purportedly to inspect the army's peacekeeping efforts with the Indians. He took along with him on the tour two other popular generals, William T. Sherman and Philip Sheridan, but declined to make any political speeches. Grant then went to his home in Galena, Illinois, for the remainder of the campaign. As he was the perceived frontrunner, there was little need for him to do anything else. The Democrats argued that the election of Grant would result in a military dictatorship. They accused him of being a drunkard and of fathering an illegitimate Indian daughter. The Republicans "waved the bloody shirt," charging the Democrats with being supported by traitors who had caused a war that resulted in the deaths of hundreds of thousands of Union soldiers. Seymour was accused of being a coward (he had not served in the military during the war) and it was alleged that hereditary insanity ran in his family.[54]

When the votes were counted, as expected, Grant was the victor, but not by as large a margin as had been predicted. He received 3,012,833 votes, compared to 2,703,249 for Seymour, a margin of just over 300,000. It is estimated that up to one-half million black men in the South voted, which likely provided the margin of victory. Blacks were still not permitted to vote in several northern states. Out of the thirty-four states that participated in the election, black votes were counted in only sixteen, eight of which had been part of the Confederacy. In the Electoral College, Grant won over Seymour by a tally of 214 to 80, winning twenty-six states to Seymour's eight. Votes from Virginia, Texas, and Mississippi were not counted, since those states had not yet been formally readmitted to the Union under the Reconstruction Acts established by the Radical Republicans in Congress. If approximately 30,000 Grant votes had gone to Seymour in several close states, Seymour would have prevailed in the Electoral College.[55]

For the fifth time, the nation had elected a military general to the office of president of the United States. The victor proclaimed "Let us have peace." It remained to be seen whether peace would come.

CHAPTER 13

1872: Strange Bedfellows

To swell our gallant army, come from hill and plain,
Grant shall win the victory, for President again.

He's a gallant hero, and noble statesman, too,
He's safely brought our Ship of State, the darkest dangers through;

The sons of freedom in their might, have come from hill and plain,
To make the brave Ulysses, our President again.[1]

Republican campaign song, 1872

"I never said all Democrats were saloonkeepers; what I said was all saloonkeepers are Democrats."[2] It was not a compliment, nor was most of what the speaker had to say or write about the Democratic Party. The words were spoken by Horace Greeley, the former Whig turned Republican, longtime editor of the *New York Tribune* and a critic of, and a thorn in the side of, the Democratic Party for his entire career. This is the same Horace Greeley who was the nominee of the Democratic Party for president of the United States in 1872. How did this happen?

Horace Greeley was an American original. As the founder and editor of the *New York Tribune*, including its nationally distributed weekly edition, Greeley was one of the country's best-known figures in the mid–nineteenth century. Born in New Hampshire in 1811 into a poor farming family, he had little formal schooling but was a child prodigy and was able to read books by the age of four. He was always perceived as having an eccentric personality. Some have speculated that Greeley may have had Asperger's syndrome (undiagnosed in the nineteenth century), which is a mild form of autism, usually in males, that is typically characterized by intellectual brilliance, obsession with facts, focusing on one object to the exclusion of others, and social isolation.[3] Greeley's career path was analogous to that of another famous American, Benjamin Franklin, a century earlier. Apprenticed to a Vermont printer at the age of fifteen, he, like Franklin, learned the printer's trade and then became a famous editor and writer. Greeley's first political activity was in the Anti-Mason movement in the late 1820s and early 1830s. After his Vermont apprenticeship ended, Greeley worked for a brief time as a printer in western Pennsylvania, where his family then lived, and then moved, almost penniless, to New York City in 1831.[4] By the mid–1830s, Greeley closely identified himself with the new Whig Party and Henry Clay became his idol. In preparation for the 1838 midterm elections, he was hired by New York Whig political boss, Thurlow Weed, to publish a weekly pro–Whig newspaper called the *Jeffersonian*, which brought him into contact with not only Weed, but also William H. Seward and other Whig leaders.

In 1841, Greeley began publishing the *New York Tribune*, the newspaper that, by the time of the Civil War, would be the most influential paper in the nation, and which would be his legacy. By this time his eccentric physical features were well known. Standing nearly six feet tall, he looked shorter due to hunched shoulders that resulted from constantly being stooped over his editor's desk. He had blond hair, blue eyes, a pink baby face, white throat whiskers, and wore thick wire-rimmed glasses. His attire was equally noticeable. He almost always wore an old white Irish linen coat, boots, and baggy black pantaloons, and he topped his wardrobe off with a beaver hat that he wore cocked back on his forehead.[5] Greeley probably was not the originator of the phrase for which he is credited and best known, "Go West, young man!," but he did constantly promote in the *Tribune* western settlement as a way to better the quality of life in New York City and elsewhere in the East of young men, who were trapped in lives of unemployment and poverty.[6] From the pages of the *Tribune*, Greeley, over a generation, expressed his opinions on almost every issue facing the American public. His political philosophy was difficult to define and pigeonhole. He was anti-slavery, but he was not an abolitionist. Although a strong capitalist, during his career he associated with socialists and even hired Karl Marx as a writer for the *Tribune*.[7] He was initially against Abraham Lincoln when the Illinoisan first arrived on the national scene, but he then supported Lincoln and later turned against and criticized him during the Civil War. He did not favor Lincoln's reelection in 1864.[8] Greeley was hated in the South for his anti-slavery views, but he supported full amnesty for southerners after the war's end and was also one of a handful of people who guaranteed the bail bond of former Confederate president Jefferson Davis in 1867, allowing Davis to be released from prison.[9] Known fondly as "Uncle Horace" throughout much of the nation, Greeley had a reputation for being blunt and passionate in his beliefs, and for his honesty and integrity. It was a reputation that many hoped would propel the *Tribune* editor into the White House in 1872.

The nation was in need of honesty and integrity in government after the first term of President Ulysses S. Grant. The man who was the nation's most successful general during the Civil War had become one of its least successful presidents. Although immensely popular, Grant presided over an administration of corruption. By the end of his first term, speculators who were friends of the president had cornered the gold market, based in part on bribes and inside information from a Grant brother-in-law.[10] In 1872, the Crédit Mobilier became public, wherein it was discovered that Union Pacific Railroad officials had bilked the government out of millions of dollars and had bribed Republican congressmen to cover their misdeeds.[11] Northern politicians flooded the South to control state governments elected through the enfranchisement of former slaves and the disenfranchisement of former Confederates. An uncontrolled spoils system resulted in political appointees whose main goal was to profit from holding public office, whether by outright acceptance of bribes or otherwise.

Liberal Republican Convention

In reaction to the corruption of the Grant administration, a group of Republicans formed their own third party to challenge Grant for a second term in 1872. Calling themselves Liberal Republicans, this movement began in Missouri and was led by Carl Schurz, one of that state's senators. Schurz had come to the United States after a failed revolution in his native Germany in 1848 and became a leader of the Republican Party. He was Lincoln's minister to Spain early in the Civil War, and then served as a Union general for the remainder of the conflict. He had supported Grant in 1868, but led the opposition to the president in 1872. The new party had succeeded in electing one of its own, Benjamin Gratz Brown, to the Missouri governorship in 1870, and then began to organize nationwide. In early 1872, the Liberal Republicans called for a national nominating convention, to be held in Cincinnati in May, to choose candidates for president and vice president. They favored civil service reform, free trade, amnesty for former Confederates, and local self-government.[12]

When the Liberal Republican convention opened at Exposition Hall in Cincinnati on May 1, Horace Greeley was in the running, but was not considered the leading candidate for the nomination. The pre-convention favorites were Charles Francis Adams (son of former president John Quincy Adams and Martin Van Buren's running mate on the Free-Soil ticket in 1848), Governor Benjamin Gratz Brown of Missouri, Judge David Davis of Illinois (a key figure in Lincoln's nomination in 1860), and Lyman Trumbull of Nebraska (a Democrat turned Republican who was one of the Republican votes in the Senate against Andrew Johnson's impeachment in 1868). The party's leader, Schurz, did not favor Greeley as the nominee of his new party. Schurz himself was ineligible for the presidency under the Constitution, due to his foreign birth. Whitelaw Reid, the managing editor of the *New York Tribune*, led the

The corruption of the first term of the Grant administration led a group of Republicans to break with the party and form a third-party movement of their own. These Liberal Republicans met in convention at Exposition Hall in Cincinnati in 1872 and nominated Horace Greeley as their candidate for the presidency *(Cornell University Library)*.

Greeley forces at the Cincinnati convention, which included support from almost all of the large New York delegation. One potential problem for Greeley was that he differed with the Liberal Republicans on a major economic issue — they favored free trade, while he was a protectionist. Reid, however, had a plan to minimize any objections to Greeley over this issue. He proposed to the party's leaders that the issue of free trade versus tariffs be left up to Congress, without interference by the president.[13] The rules adopted by the party in advance of the convention allowed two delegates for each state's Electoral College votes, which meant that there would be more than 700 delegates in Cincinnati.[14]

On the eve of the convention, the *New York Times*, a pro–Grant newspaper, mocked the gathering of "soreheads" and what its reporter perceived as the light turnout of delegates and onlookers: "Cincinnati is a provincial town in hotel accommodations, and there are to-night empty beds in Cincinnati hotels." Estimating that there were less than two thousand people in town for the convention, the *Times* joked that there was "great anxiety to learn the whereabouts of those armies of soreheads who are reported to have left various cities, and have disappeared on the journey."[15] As the convention opened, the hottest rumor favored an Adams/Trumbull ticket.[16] The chair upon which President John Adams had sat when he signed the Declaration of Independence was transported from Philadelphia to be used by the convention's president,[17] perhaps with the anticipation that Adams' grandson would be the nominee. Suffragists Susan B. Anthony and Laura de Force Gordon were permitted to have seats on the podium of the Liberal Republican convention in Cincinnati, which they took "amid cheers and hisses," but Gordon lost her attempt to be named by the credentials committee as a delegate from California.[18] It would be another twenty-eight years, in 1900, before the first female would be seated as a delegate at a presidential nominating convention.[19] As expected, Missouri senator and party founder Schurz was named the permanent president of the proceeding. In his address to the convention, he stressed the reform nature of the party: "There is something more wanted than to beat Grant.— We don't want a mere change of persons in the administration of the government. We want the overthrow of a pernicious system; we want a government which the best people of the country can be proud of."[20]

On the first ballot, Adams led with 203 votes. Greeley was in second place with 147, followed by Trumbull with 100, Brown with 95, and Davis with 92 . Brown then threw his support to Greeley and it became a two-man race between Adams and Greeley. Each led at times over the next few ballots, but neither gained a majority, which was required for nomination. Finally, on the sixth ballot, Greeley snatched the nomination in a close tally with 332 votes, compared to 324 for Adams.[21] Upon the nomination being made official, "Hoary-haired, hard-eyed politicians, who had not in twenty years felt a noble impulse, mounted their chairs and with faces suffused with a seraphic fervor, blistered their throats hurraying for the great and good Horace Greeley. The noise bred a panic. A furor, artificial at first, became real and ended in a stampede."[22] Brown was nominated for the vice presidency as Greeley's running mate on the Liberal Republican ticket. The platform adopted by the Liberal Republicans in Cincinnati called for the following: equality of all men before the law; no reopening of the issues settled by the thirteenth, fourteenth, and fifteenth amendments to the Constitution at the end of the Civil War; immediate removal of "all disabilities imposed on account of the rebellion"; local self-government rather than centralized government in Washington; reform of the civil service; one term of office for the president; a speedy return to specie payments; gratitude to soldiers and sailors; no further government land grants to railroads; and treatment of all foreign nations with fair and equal terms. On the potentially divisive free trade versus tariffs issue, the convention adopted the proposal of Greeley's floor manager at the convention,

Reid, and recognized "that there are in our midst honest but irreconcilable differences of opinion." It resolved to have the matter decided by the elected representatives of the people in Congress, without interference from the executive. Finally, the platform declared that the party "cordially welcomes the co-operation of all patriotic citizens without regard to previous political affiliation."[23]

Reaction to the nomination of Greeley was mixed. The nation's political leaders were dumbfounded — could the eccentric Greeley actually be the next president of the United States? Greeley's former mentor, a fellow New York editor, and political boss, Thurlow Weed, wrote to a friend, "Six weeks ago I did not suppose that any considerable number of men, outside of a Lunatic Asylum, would nominate Greeley for president."[24] President Grant reportedly told a visitor that he viewed the Greeley nomination "as a joke."[25] The newspapers that supported the Liberal Republican cause, such as the *Chicago Tribune*, the *Cincinnati Commercial*, the *Springfield Republican*, and of course Greeley's own *New York Tribune*, supported the nomination, although some felt that Adams would have made a stronger candidate. Pro-Grant newspapers theorized that, by the time of the election, most of the Liberal Republicans would return to the main party and would support the president for reelection. Most felt that Greeley would not run well in the South, due to his long-standing and well-known anti-slavery views before the war.

The real question was — what would the Democratic Party do in response to the Greeley nomination? The chairman of the party's National Executive Committee, August Belmont, called the Cincinnati nominations "a bombshell," but added, "I will do most anything to beat this administration."[26] The week after the Liberal Republican convention in Cincinnati, Belmont's committee met in New York and selected July 9 as the opening date for the party's 1872 convention. With twenty-one of the committee's votes, Baltimore was selected as the site for the convention, compared to four votes each for St. Louis and Louisville, and one vote for Cincinnati. It was reported that Baltimore was selected "principally on the ground urged that in that city less undue outside influence would be brought to bear on the proceedings of the convention than elsewhere."[27] It was likely felt that a Democratic convention held in the Midwest, where the Liberal Republican Party was born and was strongest, would be more influenced by that party's nominations in Cincinnati than if the convention was held in Baltimore. In any event, for the first time in twelve years, since the debacle in 1860 that split the party, the Democrats would return to the Monumental City to select their presidential nominee.

Republican Convention

Before the Democrats met in Baltimore, the regular Republican Party met in Philadelphia on June 5, 1872, for its fifth presidential nominating convention. The gathering was held at the Academy of Music (originally American Academy of Music), located at Broad and Locust Streets. Built in 1857, the brick structure was an opera house and had a massive crystal chandelier hanging from the center of its ornate ceiling, lit by 240 gas jets. There was no suspense as to the nominee — delegates from thirty-four of the thirty-seven state delegations were known to have instructions from their state parties to support President Ulysses S. Grant for a second term in the White House. The delegates met in the elaborately decorated concert hall and sat through two days of speeches while the convention completed its business.

The temporary president of the proceedings, Morton McMichael of Philadelphia,

Philadelphia's Academy of Music was the site of the 1872 Republican convention, which nominated Ulysses S. Grant for a second term. The building still stands and is listed as a National Historic Landmark *(Library of Congress)*.

welcomed the delegates to his hometown and disparaged the two other parties in the field in 1872, the Liberal Republicans and the Democrats, and the possibility that Horace Greeley may be the nominee of both: "The malcontents who recently met at Cincinnati were without a constituency; the Democrats who are soon to meet at Baltimore will be without a principle ... the former, having no motive in common but personal disappointment, attempted a fusion of repelling elements, which has resulted in explosion; the latter, degraded from the high estate they once occupied, propose an abandonment of their identity, which means death."[28] The standard committees were appointed: a Committee on Credentials, a Committee on Permanent Organization, a Committee on Resolutions, and a Committee on Rules and Order of Business. Although the committees consisted of the usual single member from each state, a representative from each territory and the District of Columbia were also included.[29] The delegates then heard from a succession of speakers urging the reelection of Grant. The chairman of the New York delegation, Gerritt Smith, who was a well-known abolitionist before the war and had been the presidential candidate of the Liberal Party in 1848, dismissed the charges of corruption under Grant as nothing more than is typical in any administration:

It is said, too, that Grant has made mistakes. Oh yes; he has. All presidents make mistakes. To err is human — human in the broadest sense.... It is said that some of his appointments have turned out badly. Yes; some of the appointments of all Presidents turn out badly. They are not all gifted with clairvoyance. They don't all read character in advance ... but we find ample consolation in this fact, that notwithstanding the industrious efforts — and as venomous as industrious — to bring home to him corruption in these appointments, to foist upon him money making or other corrupt motives, all this has signally failed.[30]

In other words, Grant might be a poor judge of character, or even stupid, but he is not a crook. A series of Republican officeholders then addressed the convention extolling the reasons why a second Grant term was necessary for the survival of the nation.

Then occurred a first in American political convention history. A delegate from Arkansas, William H. Grey, rose amidst cheers to address the convention. What was unique about Grey was his race — he was the first African American delegate to address a major party presidential nominating convention:

For the first time, perhaps, in the history of the American people, there stands before you in a National Convention assembled, a representative of that oppressed race that has lived amongst you for two hundred and fifty years, lifted by the magnanimity of this great nation, by the power of God and the laws of war, from the degradation of slavery to the proud position of American citizenship.... Words fail me, upon this occasion, to thank you for this evidence of the grandest progress in civilization, when a people of such magnitude, the grandest and greatest nation upon the face of the earth ... have, in convention assembled, been willing to listen not only to the greatest of her orators, but to the humblest citizens of this great Republic....

I scarcely know where to begin upon an occasion like the present. If I raise the curtain of the past, then I open the doors of the sarcophagus from which we have but just emerged....

But this is scarcely necessary. We are ready to say in the words of the Good Book, "let the dead bury its dead." While we remember these errors, while we remember all these degradations, there is no vengeance, thank God, found in our hearts. No revengeful feelings, no desire of retaliation...

Therefore we urge upon the American people to give us Ulysses S. Grant for our candidate, for his name is a tower of strength at the South, and the only name that unrepentant rebels respect.... He is the man who is to work out the great problem now being solved in this country by the great Republican party.... The full measure of our citizenship is not yet complete.....

All we ask is a fair chance in the race of life. Give us the same privilege and opportunities that are given to other men. I hope the action of this Convention will be such that we may be able to go home rejoicing. So far as the colored people of the South are concerned, they are a unit to-day for Ulysses S. Grant.... God grant that the Republican party may close up its ranks and solidly march together, and victory will perch on its banners in the coming contest.[31]

After more speeches, the convention adjourned for the day.

When it resumed for its second day on June 6, the delegates to the 1872 Republican convention heard still more speeches. A former Confederate officer from Texas, George W. Carter, now a Republican, proclaimed that the war had taught him a lesson: "I came out of the war with only two planks in my platform. One was ... if I could not get what I wanted to take what I could get. The other was a philosophical plank, to have no prejudices, and that a whipped man was not entitled to his prejudices.... We have come through the war, and we have learned lessons which we think will be valuable. I think our people down there are learning. One of the lessons we have learned is this, that the will of the American people is to be respected."[32]

The convention then moved to its purpose, the nomination of the Republican Party's candidate for president of the United States. Only one name was placed in nomination, that of Ulysses S. Grant, at which time the convention reached its most dramatic moment. At the conclusion of the nominating speech,

> A scene of the wildest excitement followed.... The spacious Academy was crowded with thousands of spectators in every part; and on the stage, in the parquet, and in tier upon tier of galleries, arose deafening, prolonged, tumultuous cheers, swelling from pit to dome. A perfect wilderness of hats, caps and handkerchiefs waved to and fro in a surging mass....
>
> The band appeared to catch the prevailing enthusiasm, and waved their instruments as though they had been flags. Amid cries of "Music!" "Music!" they struck up "Hail to the Chief."
>
> As the majestic strains of this music came floating down from the balcony, a life-size equestrian portrait of Grant came down as if by magic, filling the entire space of the back scene, and the enthusiasm knew no bounds.[33]

As the alphabetical roll call of the states proceeded, the chairmen of the delegations of several states could not resist making the most of their moment in the spotlight. Maine gave

Despite the corruption of his first term, President Grant remained popular with most Republicans and easily won renomination by the party in 1872 at its Philadelphia convention. The bottom half of the ticket was changed, however, with Henry Wilson of Massachusetts replacing Schuyler Colfax of Indiana as the party's vice presidential nominee *(Library of Congress).*

"her grateful heart, and her fourteen votes" to Grant. Michigan "cast twenty-two votes for Ulysses S. Grant, and only wish we had forty-four to cast." Referring to one of Grant's several prewar jobs as a tanner, Nebraska gave "her six votes for the tanner who will tan the hide of Horace in the vat of Democratic disunion, corruption, and damnation — Ulysses S. Grant." South Carolina, "whose first hostile gun made Grant a possibility ... to-day, standing redeemed, regenerated, disenthralled, a State of law and order, casts her fourteen votes for Ulysses S. Grant." Tennessee cast its votes "for the most gallant soldier that the world ever saw." The chairman of the District of Columbia's delegation noted that his city "has a desirable house to rent, desirable for habitation, and much sought after" and that the city "desires that it shall be relet to the same tenant for another four years." The vote was unanimous, with Grant receiving all 752 votes cast.[34] At the conclusion of the balloting, a lead singer and a choir appeared in the balcony with the band and sang as the band played the "Grant Campaign Song," specially written for the occasion, the lyrics of which are quoted at the beginning of this chapter.[35]

The only controversy at the convention was over the vice presidential spot, with the incumbent vice president, Schuyler Colfax of Indiana, being replaced on the ticket, in a close vote, by Massachusetts senator Henry Wilson.[36] Some thought Colfax was dumped because he was involved in the emerging Crédit Mobilier scandal, while others believed that Grant thought Colfax was too ambitious and simply wanted him out of the administration.[37]

There were now two nominees officially in the race — Greeley and Grant. The remaining question for the campaign of 1872 was — would there be a third?

Democratic Convention

In the early 1870s, Baltimore's entertainment venues reached a new level of elegance with the opening of Ford's Grand Opera House. Owned by John T. Ford, the same Ford who owned the infamous theater in Washington where John Wilkes Booth assassinated Abraham Lincoln in April 1865, Ford's Grand Opera House opened to the public in October 1871. Ford was a native of Baltimore and had been managing theaters in the city for years. He was active in civic affairs, serving on the Baltimore City Council and even briefly as acting mayor in the late 1850s. He then expanded his business interests to Washington and opened the theater there bearing his name on Tenth Street in 1861. Ford knew and was friends with Booth, a leading actor of the era, and he happened to be in Richmond, the just-fallen capital of the Confederacy, at the time of the assassination on April 14, 1865. All of this raised suspicions as to his involvement in the plot of Booth and his cronies.[38] Upon his return to Maryland a few days later, Ford was arrested at his Baltimore home and was imprisoned, along with two of his brothers, under orders of Secretary of War Edwin M. Stanton. No evidence linking the Ford brothers to Booth's conspiracy was ever produced and, after six weeks, the trio was released from prison. The United States government confiscated Ford's Theater in Washington, eventually paying Ford $100,000 for the building and property. His Washington business interests at an end, Ford continued to manage a theater owned by others in Baltimore and, six years after the end of the war, he was able to open his own theater bearing his name in his hometown. He chose the title Ford's Grand Opera House for his new venture.[39]

Located on the north side of Fayette Street, just east of Eutaw Street, Ford's Grand Opera House lived up to the "grand" adjective in its name. Three stories tall with a mansard roof, the brick structure faced Fayette Street and was referred to as a "temple of the drama." It had

Ford's Grand Opera House in Baltimore was the site of the 1872 Democratic convention. It was owned by John T. Ford, the same man who owned the theater in Washington, D.C., where Abraham Lincoln was assassinated in 1865 *(Enoch Pratt Free Library)*.

a large stage, an elegant interior with walnut woodwork, twenty gas-lit chandeliers, and "particularly beautiful was 'an exquisite balustrade of iron-fretted work which extends around the balcony, surrounded by a rail covered with green plush, complementing the gilding below and the green carpet.' Buff walls and a ceiling frescoed to represent a cloud-filled sky completed the picture."[40] Ford's opened in fall 1871 and quickly became Baltimore's leading theater. Like one of its Baltimore competitors, the Front Street Theater, it would, in the summer of 1872, play host to a uniquely American political drama, a presidential nominating convention, for the Democrats selected Ford's as the location of their Baltimore convention.

In 1872, the Democratic Party was still reeling from a dozen years of defeat. It had no national leader who was viewed as capable of beating the incumbent President Grant. The choice of Baltimore for the party's convention was not seen by many as a good omen, since it was there that the final steps in the party's self-destruction in 1860 had taken place. With respect to Baltimore, a New York newspaper, the *Brooklyn Eagle*, cautioned that "[t]here is a warning in the very name of that city," but expressed a hope that "the troubles of the republic can be brought to a close on the very spot on which they had their origin. At Baltimore the political revolution began. It can be terminated there." Noting the late date of July 9 for the opening of the Democratic convention, the *Eagle* felt that this favored a Greeley nomination in Baltimore also, since the time frame from the close of the convention to the election in November would be too short to put a totally new candidate before the country and to organize an effective campaign.[41] In the weeks leading up to the convention, Democrats around the nation gradually warmed up to the idea of their old nemesis, Horace Greeley, who had harangued against their party for years in the *New York Tribune*, being their own nominee for the presidency. The Democratic governor of North Carolina stated the facts bluntly: "If the Baltimore Convention puts Greeley in our hymn book, we will sing him through if it kills us."[42] Potential Greeley opponents, on the eve of the convention, backed away from any challenge. One potential candidate, Chief Justice James Thompson of Pennsylvania, telegraphed friends in Baltimore that placing his name in nomination "would meet with his most decided disapproval." Another, General Winfield Scott Hancock, who had been a leading contender for the Democratic nomination in 1868, let it be known that, if his name was presented to the convention, "such an act would not be regarded as one of friendship."[43]

As usual, Baltimore was alive with pre-convention activity in the days before the opening of the 1872 convention of the Democratic Party on Tuesday, July 9, 1872. There was "great bustle and animation" at the city's major hotels. Hundreds of extra mattresses had been ordered by the hotels, to be spread on floors, if necessary. Some delegates did not travel lightly. One observer noted, "The amount of baggage was in some instances very remarkable, and plain looking delegates of sober demeanor had trunks trailing in size and weight of those of a fashionable belle en route for the springs." In the heat of a Baltimore summer, restaurants and saloons that supplied a "concoction of cooling drinks" thrived. Some interesting characters showed up in the Monumental City for the convention. One, "a robust old fellow, who styles himself the modern Franklin ... and whose occupation is the peddling of quack nostrums, came over from the capital city, and wandered disconsolately around, attracting but little attention." Another well-known figure from Washington, Bean Hickman, made the trek to Baltimore. Hickman was an amiable bum, resembling a character out of a Dickens novel. Tall and lean, with a face like a wizened apple, he generally wore a top hat, a dingy coat, faded pantaloons, and used a foppish cane. Bean would often be seen in the lobbies of Washington hotels and other public places, always willing to tell a story or a joke for a few tokens or a meal. He was supposedly born a Virginia gentleman, and it was "the pride of his heart that he never did anything useful in his life."[44] In Baltimore, Hickman managed to con a room at the Gibbons Hotel and gave a speech in the lobby of one of the larger hotels, telling jokes and stories and no doubt picking up a few coins in the process.[45]

Several visitors from the West "expressed great surprise at the large number of well kept and admirably appointed hotels to be found in Baltimore." A Missouri man noted that St. Louis, "which makes so much pretension," paled in comparison to the accommodations available in Baltimore.[46] A major new hotel, the Carrollton Hotel, had opened in the city since Baltimore had last hosted a convention in 1864. Located on the east side of Light Street, it occupied the entire space between Baltimore Street and what is now Redwood Street. Completed just a few months before the start of the 1872 Democratic convention, the Carrollton was named for that venerable Maryland patriot, Charles Carroll of Carrollton, who had received, in his nearby home, delegates from the first Baltimore conventions held forty years earlier. The massive hotel was six stories tall, had a mansard roof, and contained 350 elegant guest rooms.[47] It was the new fashionable place for visitors to stay while in Baltimore, rivaling the aging Barnum's City Hotel. The Carrollton was the "favorable place of resort," with Democratic politicians and power brokers from around the nation crowding its lobbies on the eve of the convention.[48]

All of Baltimore's hotels "were like bee hives" on the Monday before the convention's Tuesday opening. Storefronts sold handheld Greeley fans, with the face and ears of the *Tribune* editor on the front, complete with a fringed snowy beard. Pre-convention headquarters for the Democratic National Executive Committee was at Raine's Hall, located at the corner of Baltimore Street and Post Office (now Customs House) Avenue. It was there that visitors would be formally welcomed to the Monumental City. Baltimore Democrats had arranged for a reception committee of 200 people, with ten from each of the city's twenty political wards. Monday, July 8, would be a busy day for them. At 11:30 A.M., the committee went to the Camden Station of the B & O Railroad and met approximately one hundred and fifty members of the Washington Democratic Club and escorted them back to Raine's Hall, where welcoming speeches and a lunch were held, following which the Washingtonians were escorted off to their hotel, the Eutaw House. Next up, at 3:30 P.M., was the Americus Club from Philadelphia, one of that city's leading Democratic organizations, whose approximately one hundred members were clad in light pants, dark coats, and white hats, and carried small white flags with the club's logo, an owl encircled with an English garter. They were met by the reception committee at Calvert Station and brought with them their own band, McClung's Cornet Liberty Band, whose members wore white uniforms on a hot July day. After welcoming speeches and a reception, they were escorted to the St. Clair Hotel (formerly the Gilmor House) on Monument Square, their temporary home while in Baltimore. Then, at 7:30 P.M., the process was repeated with another Philadelphia group, the Keystone Club, who were met at the same railroad station, escorted to Raine's Hall for welcoming speeches and a reception, and then were seen off to their hotel, the St. Nicholas Hotel on Holliday Street. Amid all this activity at Raine's Hall, the Democratic Party's National Executive Committee had tried to have an afternoon meeting, but gave up and adjourned "as the din and confusion of the reception proved antagonistic to a calm deliberation."[49] Hotel registrations in Baltimore since Saturday showed more than 950 new guests at Barnum's, 700 at the Carrollton, 400 at the Maltby House, 325 at the Eutaw House, 250 at St. Clair's Hotel, and hundreds of others at the city's smaller hotels and in private boarding houses.[50]

Ford's Grand Opera House was decorated for the convention as no other convention hall had ever been. Prior conventions had bunting, banners, flags, and portraits of political leaders, but the elaborate preparations at Ford's in 1872 set a new standard. A portico was added to the main entrance of the theater, facing south onto Fayette Street, and was covered in evergreens and red, white, and blue bunting. Above the portico was an 1840 quotation from Baltimore lawyer and politician John V. L. McMahon: "Every mountain has sent forth its rill, every valley its stream, every river its flood, and lo!, the avalanche of the people is here." It was an interesting quotation to be adorning the entrance to a Democratic convention, for McMahon was a Whig and had made the statement at the great Whig rally and ratification convention held in Baltimore in May 1840, of which he was the president.[51] Perhaps, however, it was appropriate, since this Democratic convention was about to name Horace Greeley, a Republican, as its presidential nominee. Above the main entrance were other quotations. On the west front near Eutaw Street were words of Andrew Jackson: "The constitution is still the object of our reverence, the bond of our Union; our defense in danger, the source of our prosperity in peace." On the east front near Howard Street was a quotation from Thomas Jefferson: "The whole art of government consists in the art of being honest," a not-so-subtle reference to corruption of the Grant administration. In between the Jackson and Jefferson words of wisdom were four quotations from George Washington's farewell address, all "covered with bunting, the stars and stripes being gracefully draped and interwoven with evergreens, forming frames for the patriotic mottoes." On top of the theater, there were thirty-seven white triangular flags with blue borders, each with the name of one of the states written in red.

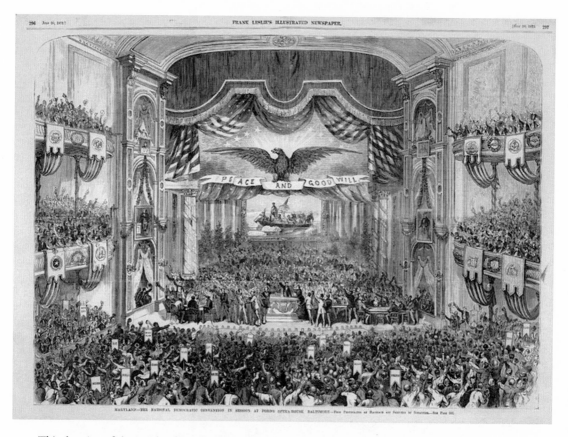

This drawing of the inside of Ford's Grand Opera House during the 1872 Democratic convention shows some of the elaborate decorations used for the convention *(Cornell University Library).*

The decorations inside the theater were no less elaborate. Above the stage was a proscenium border, consisting of a folded American flag with an eagle at its center, holding in its claws a scroll reading "Peace and Good Will." The chandeliers were trimmed in blue cloth with gilt stars. Suspended above the balcony and hanging from the walls were large banners, each with the coat of arms of one of the states. A life-size portrait of George Washington hung to the right of the stage, while an equally large portrait of the great Whig Henry Clay was stage left.[52] Above the balcony boxes were more portraits, of Washington (again), Jefferson, Van Buren, and Maryland's own Charles Carroll of Carrollton. Steps were built from the main aisle to the stage, bisecting the orchestra pit. On the stage, a raised platform for the president was at the center and, slightly lower, there was seating on the platform for the vice presidents and secretaries of the convention. Accommodations for reporters were at the rear of the stage and in the orchestra pit. Three "refreshment saloons" in the building were equipped with "soda and mineral water, as well as beer and something stronger — 'Bourbon' included." The seating for the delegates was divided into forty-six sections, for the thirty-seven states then in the Union, eight territories, and the District of Columbia, each one marked with a flag of blue silk with gold lettering. The home state of Maryland received no seating preference, with the Old Line State's delegates placed in the extreme rear of the theater, "behind even the eight territories."[53]

On the Monday afternoon before the convention's opening day, Ford's was open to the public for two hours and a stream of Baltimore citizens walked in one side, were permitted to observe the decorations, and were then led out of the other side. A total of 2,500 tickets were distributed to the public for each day of the convention, which was far more than the seating capacity of the gallery, the organizers presuming that all would not show up at one time. Each of the more than 700 delegates was given two tickets, with ten tickets distributed to each of the members of the Democratic Executive Committee, and approximately 150 given to Baltimore Democratic officeholders and party activists.[54]

On Tuesday, July 9, the eleventh presidential nominating convention of the Democratic Party of the United States opened at Ford's Grand Opera House. A crowd had begun to gather that morning several blocks away in Monument Square, near many of the major hotels, as early as 4:00 A.M. When the barbershops opened, "a rush took place for the chairs, and faces were lathered and chins scraped at a rate that could not have been altogether pleasant for a nervous man." Closer to Ford's, by midmorning the streets surrounding the theater were packed with people, with police doing their best to keep the sidewalks clear. Several bands played patriotic music on neighboring street corners and at the front of the nearby Eutaw House hotel. It was a hot July day, typical of Baltimore in the early summer. Mechanics Hall, located directly across Fayette Street from Ford's, was "thronged all day with thirsty people, drinking cool lager, and keg after keg was opened, and the cool foaming beverage dispensed to the hundreds before the long counter waiting for it." Outside, those without tickets had "some satisfaction in the spectacle presented by the gaudy decorations, the numerous flags, streamers, mottoes, and other adornments, with which the exterior meeting place was bedecked." For those fortunate enough to get inside, the heat was stifling and almost everyone had either a palm leaf fan or a new Greeley fan. Packed with people and full of decorations, the theater seemed smaller than it was in reality.[55]

The convention was called to order by party chairman August Belmont, using an oak gavel made from wood of the old frigate *Constitution*, ten minutes after the scheduled noon starting time.[56] He reminded the audience that he had predicted at their last gathering in 1868 that the election of General Grant would lead to military despotism, a prediction he alleged had come true. He then focused on the tasks before the delegates — to nominate a man previously considered their enemy and the need for the party to unite behind the Liberal Republicans and Greeley, for the sake of the country:

> The wisest and best men of the Republican party have severed themselves from the Radical wing, which is trying to fasten upon the country another four years' reign of corruption, usurpation, and despotism; and, whatever individual opinion we may entertain as to the choice of the candidate whom they have selected in opposition to Gen. Grant, there cannot be any doubt of the patriotic impulses which dictated their action, nor can any fault be found with the platform of principles upon which they have placed their candidate....
>
> The resolutions of the Cincinnati Convention are what the country requires.... In the struggle which is before us we must look to principles and not men, and I trust that no personal predilections or prejudices will deter us from doing our duty to the American people.... Gen. Grant was a good and faithful soldier during our civil war ... but he has most singely and sadly failed in the discharge of the high trust imposed upon him by the confidence of a grateful people. He is at this moment the very personification of the misrule which is oppressing us...
>
> On the other hand, Mr. Greeley has been heretofore a bitter opponent of the Democratic party, and the violent attacks against myself individually, which have from time to time appeared in his journal, certainly do not entitle him to any sympathy or preference at my hand. Mr. Greeley represents the National and Constitutional principle of the Cincinnati platform ... and by his admirable and manly letter of acceptance, he has shown that he is fully alive to their spirit.... Should you, therefore, in your wisdom, decide to pronounce in favor of the Cincinnati candidates, I shall for one bury all past differences, and vote and labor for their election with the same zeal and energy with which I have supported heretofore, and mean to ever to support, the candidates of the Democratic party.... However much you might desire to fight the coming battle for our rights and liberties under one of the trusted leaders of the Democratic party, it will become your duty to discard all considerations of party tradition if the selection of a good and wise man outside of our own ranks offers better chances of success.[57]

Belmont's speech was received with great applause and enthusiasm by the delegates. Prior to the convention, there had been some discussion of just endorsing the Cincinnati nominees and platform, rather than a formal nomination, but the reaction to Belmont's remarks indicated that there would be a formal and enthusiastic nomination of Greeley. As reported by the *Baltimore Sun*, whenever Belmont "mentioned the name of Mr. Greeley, the wildest enthusiasm prevailed, cheer after cheer rent the air, the whole vast crowd, delegates and all rose, and continued in the wildest demonstrations for some time."[58] It was clear that the party was going to swallow its pride, do what it perceived was necessary for victory in the election, and make Horace Greeley the Democratic nominee for the presidency.

Belmont then introduced the temporary president of the convention to the delegates, whose mere presence was a public relations coup for the party. The name of Thomas Randolph was better recognized when his middle name, Jefferson, was included. As the eighty-year-old grandson of the man who authored the Declaration of Independence, was the third president of the United States, and was the founder of the Democratic Party, took the podium, the band inside the hall started playing "Dixie," amid a loud ovation from the audience. As a young man and a member of the Virginia legislature in 1832, "Jeff" Randolph had introduced a bill for the gradual emancipation of slaves in that state, a bill which, had it passed, could possibly have averted the Civil War a generation later. It was a stance that caused him to be defeated for reelection in 1833. When the war came, Randolph, like most Virginians, supported the Confederacy. He had nearly gone bankrupt as a result, but had sworn an oath of loyalty to the United States at the war's end.[59] Now, in Baltimore, he would be performing the last political act of a long life. Distinguished looking, standing six feet and four inches tall, with white locks of hair, Randolph was characteristically modest in his address to the delegates, acknowledging it was not he who had earned their respect: "I am aware that the very great honor conferred on me by this body is due to no personal merit on my own, but is a token of respect to the State from which I come; and a recognition of other circumstances." Noting that he vividly recalled every presidential election since the first election of his grandfather in 1800, Randolph stated "I can say with truth that I remember none which involved higher questions of personal liberty, local self government, honest administration, and constitutional freedom, than the present.... It strikes me as the duty of this hour and of the body to wrest the Government from the hands of its present despotic and corrupt holders, and to place it in honest hands."[60] The old gentlemen's remarks were brief, but poignant, and provided another link between a Baltimore convention and the nation's founding fathers, just as the 1832 conventions had done by inviting Charles Carroll of Carrollton to their proceedings and as the 1860 Constitutional Union Party's convention had done in hearing a moving speech from the grandson of Patrick Henry.

After an opening prayer, the convention then got down to the initial organization required of all such gatherings. A Committee on Credentials and a Committee on Permanent Organization were named, with one delegate from each state. When the roll call of the states for the appointment of committee members began, one delegate objected to the states being called in the traditional geographic order, starting with Maine in the northeast, and suggested an amendment requiring that an alphabetical roll call be used.

The amendment was adopted and the Democrats had finally jettisoned one of their long-standing convention traditions.[61] Others, such as the two-thirds rule for nomination and the unit rule, they would keep until the twentieth century. The convention then, at 1:15 P.M., adjourned its morning session.

When the afternoon session's scheduled starting time of 4:00 P.M. arrived, no officials were on the stage and a band entertained the crowd until the proceedings finally got underway about a half hour later. The delay was apparently caused by the absence of the man proposed to be the convention's permanent president, who was not yet in the theater. When the proceedings got underway, the Committee on Permanent Organization announced that it was nominating James R. Doolittle of Wisconsin as the permanent president of the convention, which was received with great cheers and applause. The usual appointments of the multiple vice presidents, one from each state, and several secretaries for the convention were also made.[62] Doolittle had originally been a Democrat, but became a Republican and served as a senator from Wisconsin during the war, and then switched back to the Democrats in the late 1860s. He was the embodiment of the unity that the Democrats were seeking with disaffected Republicans in 1872. After being escorted to the podium, Doolittle gave a rousing speech to the convention, tracing the history of the Liberal Republican movement since its origin in Missouri, its commonality with the concerns of Democrats, and the need for unity to remove the Grant administration from office:

> Two years ago, nearly five years after the bloody period of the civil war had closed, the Liberal Republicans of Missouri ... determined to organize a movement to restore equal rights to all our citizens, white as well as black, to restore self-government, and to arrest the further centralization of Federal power, they then said, This thing has gone far enough, if not too far; the time has come when all honest and patriotic Republicans must say "halt!"...

They resolved to invite the Liberal Republicans in all the States to meet them in national convention in Cincinnati on the 1st day of May. That invitation was accepted. There was indeed a great response. They came by thousands....

That convention presented a platform and presented candidates to the country — for President, Horace Greeley, and for Vice President, B. Gratz Brown, and that convention, for the promotion and success of the principles declared in that platform there enunciated, and the support of the candidates nominated by that convention, have invited and cordially welcomed the cooperation of all patriotic citizens, without regard to pervious political affiliations.... As between the Liberal Republicans and the followers of the Grant Administration, the issue is now clearly made up. It is Grant or Greeley.... Shall we accept this invitation to cooperate with the Liberal Republicans? Shall we nominate the same candidates, and shall we elect them, or shall we refuse to cooperate, nominate other candidates, and strive to elect them over both tickets in the field? Gentlemen, these are the questions which you are to decide here....

What means all this?... It means to-day for all the other States of the South what it has already done in Missouri. Instead of proscriptive test oaths, suspension of habeas corpus, and military despotism, it means personal freedom for the individual, and republican government for all. It means equal rights to all men, white as well as black. Instead of thieving governments organized to plunder subjugated States, it means the domination once more of intelligence and integrity, instead of strife, hate, and robbery. It means justice, liberty, peace, loyalty, and good will; and, gentlemen, for our whole country, East, West, North, and South, it means, instead of a war President, trained only in a military school, and whose whole character has been formed in the ideas, arts, habits, and despotism of military life — instead of this, it means a peace President, trained in the ideas, arts, blessings, and republican simplicity of peace and universal freedom, of peace not enchained, of liberty not under arrest awaiting trial, sentence, and execution by drum-head court-martial, but that liberty and that peace which the Constitution secures by placing the civil law above the sword, by preserving in full vigor the sacred writ of *habeas corpus*, and by the right of trial by jury.

It means another thing, and perhaps the most important of them all; it means to arrest the centralization of power in the Federal Government. It means to assert the vital principal of our republican system, in which it lives and moves and has its very being, that constitutions are made by the people in their sovereign capacity for the express purpose of defining and limiting the powers of government, State or national.... It means also a genuine civil service reform, beginning with the presidential office. It means to put an end forever to certain practices which have grown up with this Administration ... practices which never existed under any other Administration, which are but too well known to all the world, and which our nation's good reputation will be best consulted by not even naming.... It means to place in the highest offices of our Government men of whom all the world will say, "They are honest and they are capable." Gentlemen, I have thus briefly stated the situation, the duties, and the purpose which bring us here. A great responsibility rests upon this convention. If its action shall be such (and I doubt not it will be) as to put an end to the misrule which for the last few years had afflicted our beloved country, this generation and generations to come after us will remember with pride and gratitude the convention at Baltimore of the 9th of July, 1872.[63]

At the conclusion of Doolittle's crowd-pleasing speech, a Committee on Resolutions was appointed to decide on the party's platform, again with one member from each state. All resolutions of a policy nature were referred to the committee including, for the first time at a Democratic convention, a proposal (which the committee would vote to reject) that "accepting the Constitution as it is, with the fourteenth amendment, declaring all persons born or naturalized in the United States ... citizens ... we are logically compelled to admit that women, being citizens are possessed of the right to vote."[64] The Committee on Credentials then presented its report, which was non-controversial. It concluded that there were no contests as to any delegate seats, that 732 delegates were certified, and recommended that delegates from the territories be seated on the floor of the convention, but without voting rights. A roll call of the states was then held for each state to name its member of the party's National Executive Committee, with the most recognized name read being that of inventor of the reaper, Cyrus H. McCormick, as the Illinois member, which elicited a round of cheers from the crowd. The convention then adjourned for the day, with the Committee on Resolutions scheduled to meet that evening at the Carrollton Hotel and the new National Executive Committee to meet at the same time at Ford's.[65]

As Doolittle left the stage, he was approached by two suffragists, Susan B. Anthony and Isabella Beecher Hooker. The women had been making the rounds of all of the 1872 conventions, trying to get at least one party to insert a plank in its platform favoring voting rights for women. They had struck out with the Liberal Republicans in Cincinnati and with the Republicans in Philadelphia and this was their last chance. Hooker did most of the talking in the encounter, asking Doolittle that they be permitted "to appear before the convention and state their views." The *Baltimore Sun* noted that "they seem to be fully convinced that if this privilege is accorded to them that their eloquence will be so convincing that a woman suffrage plank will at once be inserted in the platform." Doolittle, who seemed taken aback by their persistence, told them he had little influence with the platform, that he did not agree with their views, and excused himself to go to dinner.[66]

The end of the convention's official session did not mean the end of politicking in Baltimore for the day. As with past Baltimore conventions, Monument Square was the hub of evening activity and a mass meeting was held there. Speakers addressed the crowd of thousands from the balcony of Guy's Hotel, located on the northeast corner of Fayette Street and Monument Square. They praised Greeley as the man who could unite the country. An Iowan proclaimed, "Horace Greeley says to the people of the South, 'You have made your gallant fight; now let us shake hands over the bloody chasm that has divided us.'" Another speaker, an Alabaman who had attended the Liberal Republican convention in Cincinnati a couple of months earlier, told the crowd that "the politicians did not want Greeley nominated but that he was the choice of the people." The Americus Club of Philadelphia, a Democratic club that had accompanied that city's delegation to Baltimore, and which had brought along its own brass band, then marched, "followed by a large concourse of persons, amounting to several thousand," several blocks to Franklin Street and the home of Thomas Swann, who had been the governor of Maryland immediately following the war and who was a Democratic congressman from Maryland at the time of the 1872 convention. After the band played "Maryland, My Maryland," Swann appeared at a window and gave a brief speech, denouncing "in strong terms the usurpation, tyranny and rascality of those in power," following which he invited the club members and the band into the house. While the Philadelphia band played inside, two other political clubs, the Keystone Club and the Washington Club, also showed up in front of Swann's home, also with their own bands, also playing "Maryland, My Maryland." and also asking for a speech. Swann, however, "was unable to respond on account of his being at the time engaged with the Americus Club." The Americus Club members then, at about 10:30 P.M., moved on to the front of the Eutaw House for more speeches and more music. The *Baltimore Sun* reported another interesting evening sighting: "Our neighbors at the

Gazette, last evening made a very brilliant and neat gas-jet display in front of their office. The words 'Greeley and Brown' appeared in large, flaming letters along the lower line of a bright bordering of gas jets. The space between the tops of the letters in the upper lines of the border was so great, however, as to suggest the idea that it had possibly been originally intended for some other lettering as a prefix to Greeley and Brown, which, under a better view of things, had been deemed proper to omit."[67]

It is not known whether the unlit words on the *Gazette*'s sign were "Anyone But," or some similar anti–Greeley prefix, but it was clear that the Democratic opposition to Greeley's nomination burned out and fizzled in Baltimore. As in 1860, there was a competing Democratic convention scheduled in Baltimore for the same date and time as the event at Ford's Grand Opera House, originally organized by Joseph R. Flanders of New York. A circular had been sent to Democrats across the country to meet in Baltimore on the same day as the party's convention, July 9, to oppose any nomination of Greeley.[68] The leaders of this movement were several Democrats who had been jailed by the Lincoln administration during the Civil War and who opposed Greeley because he had supported Lincoln's actions. Baltimore proponents of this movement had secured the Hall of the Maryland Institute for their meeting, the same building where the rump convention of southern Democrats had met in 1860 and nominated John Breckinridge for the presidency. This 1872 effort, however, met with much less success. At a preliminary meeting on the Monday before the convention, only about two hundred people showed up, many of them members of the press.[69] The convention did meet, but its participants did little other than vent anger at their Democratic brethren. John C. Bayard of New Jersey was named president of the proceeding and proclaimed to the few assembled that: "A conspiracy for the destruction of the party had been formed for several months.... We consider that we represent vast masses who are not represented in the convention at the Opera House, which is carrying out the objects of said conspiracy.... There are millions of people opposed to the conspiracy whose voices are only heard at the polls. Political coalitions never succeed." How could the great Democratic Party, Bayard asked, support "the nomination of a man who for years has been the most bitter and implacable enemy of the democratic party which the country has known." The actions of the convention at Ford's is "far from being binding as the action of the democratic party, should be spurned by all true democrats, and resisted with unyielding tenacity, and to the uttermost extremity." No nominations were made at this Maryland Institute gathering, but those assembled did pass a resolution calling for another meeting in Louisville on September 3, "to take such steps as may be deemed prudent and essential."[70]

After an opening prayer, the regular Democratic convention at Ford's began its second and last day of proceedings at 10:00 A.M. on Wednesday, July 10. The initial item of business was the report from the Committee on Resolutions, whose chairman reported that the committee recommended adoption of the Cincinnati platform of the Liberal Republicans, without any changes or additions. One hour of debate was permitted on the proposed platform, and the opposition to it was led by Senator James A. Bayard, Jr., of Delaware. While there was much in the Cincinnati platform that Bayard supported, he argued that it was unwise to not write an independent document:

> But I think it becoming the dignity of this grand National organization ... that we should at least be permitted to have an unrestrained moderate, straightforward expression of our own opinions, without having the words of other men, unchosen by us, forced down our throats. Now, gentlemen, I ask you, will not the Democratic masses of the country demand of this Convention that the expression which you shall give shall not be merely the

cut-and-dried language of another, but that it shall be the expression of the unterrified, clear, outspoken wishes of the Democratic party itself? Are we not entitled to it? ... [W]e stand here to-day and shall probably, according to the expression of this assembly, go before the country, for the first time in the history of our party, without an independent expression of its cherished sentiments. Is the Convention ready for it? I am not.[71]

Notwithstanding the Delaware delegate's protestations, as well as those of a few others, the Democratic convention approved the Liberal Republican platform, word for word, by a vote of 670 yeas to 62 nays.[72]

The Cincinnati platform having been adopted, the next item of business was whether the Cincinnati nominees would be as well. Only one name, that of Horace Greeley, was officially placed in nomination. The alphabetical roll call of the states then began. When the first state, Alabama, cast all of its twenty votes for Greeley, the announcement "called forth a burst of applause, the entire audience rising and waving hats, handkerchiefs and fans, the ladies in the galleries and boxes joining in the demonstration." The unanimity for the editor of the *Tribune* continued until Delaware was reached. The chairman of that delegation announced that all six of his state's votes were being cast for their own Senator Bayard, who had just led the opposition to the platform, including Bayard's own vote, which was being cast for him under the unit rule and over his own objection. The chairman of the Illinois delegation announced that his delegation was "here to contribute her aid to save the country, rather than to sustain a party" and cast all forty-two votes for "the philosopher, statesman, and patriot, HORACE GREELEY." Referring to the motto clutched in the claws of the decorative eagle above the stage, the chairman of the Mississippi delegation proclaimed, that "It is inscribed on the platform above your head 'Peace and Good Will'; Mississippi accepts these as the watchwords of the campaign, and casts her sixteen votes for the illustrious apostle of peace and good will — HORACE GREELEY." Missouri cast its thirty votes for Greeley, its chairman announcing that his state would give the nominee the largest majority of any state in the Union. When Greeley's home state of New York was called, the entire seventy-member delegation rose as one, with the Empire State's governor, John T. Hoffman, as their spokesman. For a moment, the entire theater was silent, and then the whole mass of delegates rose and erupted with three cheers for New York, and then three cheers for Governor Hoffman. The governor was unable to be heard, as "cheer followed cheer, and the galleries rose, the audience waving hats and handkerchiefs, while the enthusiasm became irrepressible." When it finally quieted down, Hoffman announced that, while he had great respect for Missouri, "I tell them, and I tell you, and I ask you to take it kindly, that New York will give a larger majority for Horace Greeley than all the votes which Missouri shall cast."[73] Hoffman then addressed those Democrats in the hall who did not support Greeley. The Liberal Republicans were heading in the correct direction, he argued, and "the good of the country requires that all who seek that end should act together. By so doing we make success certain.... The acceptance of the Liberal Republican ticket here is the work of the Democratic masses.... Mr. Greeley will go into the presidential chair not by force of any combination of political leaders. The crisis is too grave to admit of schemes for personal advancement, for bargains or coalitions and temporary advantages. He will not be embarrassed by any feeling of obligation to party leaders. He will owe his election purely and solely to an uprising of the people." Hoffman then cast all of the Empire State's seventy votes for its own Horace Greeley, which was followed by continuous applause and cheers.[74] When the last state, Wisconsin, had cast its votes, the clerk announced that Greeley had won 686 votes, compared to only 15 for Bayard of Delaware, 21 for Jeremiah S. Black of Pennsylvania, 2 for William S. Groesbeck of Ohio, and 8 blank bal-

lots.[75] For the first time in American history, a major political party had adopted the nominee of a third party. Greeley would go into the election as the official nominee of two parties. A Pennsylvania delegate then moved to make the nomination unanimous. This was approved and, at the same moment, at the rear of the stage, a painted curtain was dropped depicting the White House, the hoped-for home of the new nominee.[76]

The convention then moved to its remaining business. The issue of the vice presidency was resolved quickly, also on the first ballot, with Governor Benjamin Gratz Brown of Missouri, the nominee for the second spot by the Liberal Republicans, also being named the nominee of the Democrats, with 713 votes, compared to 6 for John W. Stevenson of Kentucky and 13 blank ballots.[77] After that, only a few housekeeping matters remained. It was barely past noon. Resolutions were passed thanking two Baltimoreans for their hospitality to the convention: to attorney Frederick Raine for use of the "commodious building known as Raine's Hall" by the party's National Executive Committee before and during the proceedings, and to John T. Ford "for the gratuitous use by the Convention of his Opera House." The man who had endured a presidential assassination in one of his theaters had now seen a presidential candidate nominated in another. Thanks were also extended to "the citizens of Baltimore for their generous payment of all the expenses of the National Committee incurred in holding the Convention, and to John W. Davis and others, of the Baltimore Committee, for their valuable services in the arrangement for the Convention." Ford, who had been acting unofficially as the sergeant-at-arms of the convention, was formally given that title and was also named as "chief marshal" to escort the New York and Missouri delegations from the Opera House back to their hotels, with bands playing and banners flying. After a committee of one delegate from each state was named to formally notify Greeley and Brown of their nominations, there was one more speech. A New York delegate, Thayer, took the floor and reminded the delegates that, in the closing moments of the Republican convention in Philadelphia a few weeks earlier, a large canvas painting of Grant was lowered at the back of the stage of the convention hall depicting Grant on horseback, "shining in military boots, and in all the array of a warrior chieftain." In contrast, the new nominee of the Democratic Party was decidedly non-military, a civilian who was "a plain American citizen, in humble attire, but with a broad and radiant brow, countenance full of benevolence, speaking peace and harmony, and as pure and genuine a type of American character as was ever born on this soil. The country will hail him as the man whose reconciling genius shall span the dividing stream that rolls between the sections; and before a twelve months of his administration has passed, the dark and bloody chasm will be filled."[78]

Outside of Ford's, a large crowd had been waiting all morning in stifling heat, with the temperature in the nineties. Boys selling ice water and fans did a thriving business. Bands entertained the crowd with patriotic music, including "Hail Columbia," "The Bonnie Blue Flag," "Dixie," "The Star Spangled Banner," and "Yankee Doodle." Just before 1:00 P.M., when the nominations were completed inside, a large banner was unfurled from the front of Ford's, with the portraits and names of Greeley and Gratz Brown on either side and above them the words "The People's Choice." Canes, with their tops bearing a likeness of Greeley's head, showed up for sale on the streets of Baltimore. In the midafternoon, as many of the delegates

Opposite: Horace Greeley, the well-known Republican editor of the *New York Tribune,* was a constant critic of the Democratic Party. In a strange turn of events, Greeley became the nominee of the Democratic Party for president in 1872, as well as of the Liberal Republican third-party movement. His running mate was Governor Benjamin Gratz Brown of Missouri *(Library of Congress).*

were leaving their hotels and headed for the train stations, "Uncle Horace" himself made an appearance on Baltimore Street. A mask with the exaggerated facial features of Greeley "was placed on the shoulders of some adventuresome youth" who also wore an old white coat and beaver hat, and who, with several followers, strode up the middle of the street waving to onlookers and making a "a very laughable counterfeit presentation" of the original.[79]

According to the *New York Times*, there was more than one mask being worn in Baltimore that hot July day. The newspaper that was the chief rival of Greeley's *Tribune*, and a strong supporter of Grant and the Republicans, repeatedly ridiculed in its columns the Democratic convention in Baltimore and called the whole proceeding a ruse to bring New York's Tammany Hall–style corruption to Washington. Under a headline of "Midsummer Madness," the *Times* characterized the last day of the convention as follows: "At last the agony is over. With many expressions of extreme disgust, with some weak and vain attempts to like the dose, the Democracy swallowed Greeley, Brown, and the Cincinnati platform. From first to last the affair has been the ghastliest of political shows." In contrast to the descriptions in the *Baltimore Sun* of wildly enthusiastic delegates and galleries giving three cheers at every mention of Greeley's name, the *Times* portrayed a much more subdued scene, with on "one or two occasions perhaps a third of the Convention had risen and yelled with some degree of vigor ... from the start there was an evident straining for enthusiasm that never appeared."[80] One detects sour grapes in the convention stories published by the *New York Times*, its owners perhaps envious that the editor of their main competitor, after securing the Democratic nomination in Baltimore, might well be on his way to holding the highest office in the land. The irony of the Democrats having nominated their old foe, Horace Greeley, as their candidate for the presidency was not lost on the country. One joke that made the rounds in several newspapers had two Democrats discussing the outcome of the convention:

> FIRST DEMOCRAT: Er you goin' to vote fer Greeley?
> SECOND DEMOCRAT: Yes, but I don't like it. What er you goin' to do?
> FIRST DEMOCRAT: Well, I kin eat crow, but I don't hanker after it.[81]

Of the Democratic convention, one Republican officeholder wrote to another, "Had the Philadelphia Republican convention given Jefferson Davis the nomination for the presidency, it would not have been more preposterous ... than this strange nomination of their bitterest reviler, and hitherto most unrelenting foe."[82]

The Campaign and Election

The modern view is that it was a foregone conclusion that Ulysses S. Grant would be reelected. That was not the impression in the country in summer of 1872. At that time, since Andrew Jackson, the only president to have been reelected was Abraham Lincoln, but that was in the midst of war. Moreover, the Republican Party was split, with a significant minority of its members joining the third-party Liberal Republican movement, and the Democrats had united with them behind the same candidate, Horace Greeley, one of the best-known personalities in the country. Republican and future president Rutherford B. Hayes wrote in his diary that he thought Greeley would be the next president. Former President Andrew Johnson endorsed the New Yorker, as did Johnson's nemesis and the man who had led the effort to remove him from office, Radical Republican senator Charles Sumner of Massachusetts. Greeley himself felt confident enough to write his daughter in late July that "I guess we shall all go to

Washington next winter."[83] Even Grant's running mate, Henry Wilson, reported to a friend that he thought he and Grant were likely going to lose the election.[84]

Another party did enter the contest late in the game. The call by the disaffected Democrats at their Maryland Institute meeting in July in Baltimore for another meeting in Louisville in early September was heeded. This convention of what were called "Straight-Out Democrats" did meet in Louisville and nominated New York attorney Charles O'Conor as their standard-bearer. Interestingly, O'Conor, although he supported the movement, declined the nomination. Despite their own candidate's protests, this rump element of Democrats, who could not stomach Greeley as their party's official nominee, was successful in getting O'Conor's name on the ballot in twenty-three of the thirty-seven states.[85]

Just as the nominating process in 1872 was different from past elections, so was the campaign. Greeley actually campaigned, and vigorously so. The only prior candidate to have earnestly done so was Democrat Stephen A. Douglas in 1860, who had traveled the country, particularly late in the campaign, more in an attempt to save the Union than to promote his own candidacy. Greeley conducted the first whistle-stop campaign in American politics. He went from Maine to Texas, often speaking from the rear of his train, and making up to fifteen or twenty speeches per day. As a Greeley biographer has noted, his "personality and fame as a fearless editor and reformer, more than his political philosophy, made him a serious candidate. He symbolized virtue over corruption, reform over reaction, reconciliation over revenge, generosity over greed."[86] One commentator called it a campaign between a man with no ideas (Grant) and a man with too many ideas (Greeley).[87] Mud, in the form of insults and unfounded allegations, was slung freely. The Grant forces were merciless in their attacks on Greeley who, as a newspaper editor for his entire career, had a record of public comment on virtually every issue of the last generation. He was attacked as being "a secessionist, a pacifist, a traitor, disloyal, cowardly, unqualified, erratic, favoring miscegenation, a friend of Tammany Hall, a supporter of the Ku Klux Klan, a Democrat, and a supporter of Free Love."[88] Thomas Nast of *Harper's Weekly* bitterly attacked Greeley in his popular cartoons. Greeley had said many times since the end of the Civil War that he hoped for a reunion between the North and the South by "clasping hands over the bloody chasm." This phrase became a favorite target of Nast. One Nast cartoon depicted Greeley shaking hands with John Wilkes Booth over Lincoln's grave.[89] Greeley's co-signing of ex-Confederate Jefferson Davis' bail bond was emphasized by the Grant forces in the North. Near the end of the campaign, Greeley would write in despair, "I hardly knew whether I was running for the Presidency or the penitentiary."[90] Grant did not actively campaign, and he stayed in the White House, also spending some time at the New Jersey seashore. He was also attacked, alleged to be a military despot, a drunkard, a crook, and basically stupid.[91] Near the end of the campaign, personal tragedy struck Greeley. His wife, Molly, who had been an invalid for years, took a turn for the worse and Greeley left the campaign trail in mid–October to be with her. She died on October 30, a week before the election.[92]

When the votes were counted, it was a Grant landslide. The fondness of northern voters for the general who had won the Civil War had not faded. Grant racked up 3,597,132 votes, compared to 2,834,079 for Greeley, for a winning percentage of 55.6, compared to 43.8 percent for the loser. The Straight-Out Democratic candidate, O'Conor, received only 29,489 votes and was not a factor in the contest. The Electoral College count was just as lopsided, with Grant winning thirty-one of the thirty-seven states and 286 of the 349 electoral votes at stake. Greeley ran best in the border states, winning four of them — Missouri, Kentucky, Tennessee, and Maryland — but won only two southern states, Texas and Georgia, and won nothing in the North or West.[93]

Greeley was devastated. The loss of his wife and a humiliating defeat in the election sent him into a tailspin. Around the same time, after an absence from work for months while campaigning, he also became aware that others at the *New York Tribune* were taking control of his beloved newspaper. Greeley was a man who was not in robust health before the campaign. Shortly after the election, within a matter of days, he faded both physically and emotionally. The available evidence strongly suggests that he had a nervous breakdown. By November 20, restless and delirious, he was placed in a private asylum near his New York home. The end came quickly and Horace Greeley died on November 29, 1872, only three weeks after the election. He is the only presidential candidate in American history to have won electoral votes and to die before the meeting of the Electoral College.[94] Most of Greeley's electors decided to cast their votes for Democrat Thomas A. Hendricks of Indiana, who had not been a candidate in the election. Georgia's three electors stood by Greeley and cast their votes for him, only to have their votes thrown out by Congress, which decided that electors could not cast votes for a dead man.[95]

With the Democratic convention of 1872, Baltimore's reign of forty years as the primary city for hosting presidential nominating conventions ended.[96] There were various reasons. As the population center of the nation shifted westward after the Civil War, so did the conventions. Railroads made travel to and from most parts of the country relatively easy. The national committees of the major parties, which by then were selecting the location of the conventions, tended to favor other cities. With the telegraph and improved communications, Baltimore's proximity to Washington became less of a factor in the selection of convention sites. Chicago, which had already hosted three presidential nominating conventions in the 1860s, became the next city of choice for conventions. It would host nine such gatherings between 1860 and the end of the nineteenth century. After 1872, a new generation of presidential nominating conventions would begin, with the politics of the antebellum era and of the Civil War receding into memory and with new issues and challenges facing the nation.

CHAPTER 14

Conclusion

From their humble beginning in the 1830s, presidential nominating conventions have grown in size and scope and remain today a uniquely American experience, by which members of a political party from throughout the country meet and select their choice of a candidate to be the nation's next leader. The creation and development of the convention system was a democratic reform and was an improvement over the prior congressional caucus system for selecting nominees for the presidency.

Decisions made at the early presidential nominating conventions changed the course of American history. In analyzing the conventions, it is hard to resist not speculating on what might have been. The seemingly insignificant decision by the Democratic Party at its first convention in 1832 to require a two-thirds vote for nomination, which came to be honored as precedent and tradition by later conventions, had far-reaching consequences. Without the two-thirds rule, Martin Van Buren would have won the Democratic nomination over James K. Polk in 1844. If Van Buren, or the Whig nominee, Henry Clay, had won the 1844 election, there likely would not have been an annexation of Texas by the United States, nor a Mexican War. Without annexation of Texas and the territory gained in the Mexican War, the map of the United States would likely look much different today. If Henry Clay had defeated Van Buren in the 1844 election, could Clay, as president, have implemented his policy of gradual emancipation of slaves and, if so, could this have averted the Civil War? Without the two-thirds rule, Stephen Douglas would have won the Democratic nomination in 1860, likely on the first ballot in Charleston. Could he then have united his party and gone on to defeat Abraham Lincoln in the election? Or, if Lincoln's team in Chicago at the 1860 Republican convention had not so adroitly outmaneuvered the other favored candidates for the nomination, would the monument standing today at the end of the reflecting pool in Washington, D.C., be named for William Seward? If Daniel Webster had decided a few hours earlier to drop out of the contest for the Whig Party's nomination in 1852, would Millard Fillmore have been nominated by the Whigs and won the election, or at least have avoided the massive defeat of Winfield Scott and enabled the Whig Party to survive? One could go on. We will never know the answers to these questions, but merely asking them underscores the relevance and importance to modern Americans of the decisions made at the early conventions.

For all of their faults, presidential nominating conventions have served the interests of the nation well. As one commentator has noted, "If one considers the nominating devices of other nations, if one takes a realistic view of politics and politicians ... if one is willing to admit the impossibility ... of often achieving truly representative government, it is hard not to conclude that the convention is one of history's most ingenious and practical political inventions.... Beyond that, it is a ... rain dance by which political parties and populace are reminded of tradition and assured of identity."[1] While some consider them now to be unnecessary, the modern presidential nominating convention "still possesses an automatic, visceral fascination — the proverbial cast of thousands, the rhetoric and symbols of a rich national history, the high drama and low comedy of democratic politics in action."[2]

Many of the convention traditions that began with the first conventions held in the 1830s and 1840s still exist — the opening prayer, the selection of temporary and then permanent presiding officers, and the formation of the standard committees for credentials, rules, and organization. The dramatic roll call of the states survives, as does the adoption by the delegates of a platform of principles and policies upon which the party will stand before the country. The tradition, started with the first conventions, of using a state's number of Electoral College votes to determine its number of convention delegates is still part of the calculation of a state's delegate allocation, but both parties now have complicated formulas for delegate allotment that also include the party's showing in recent elections in that state, the number of the party's federal and state officeholders in that state, as well as other factors.[3] The Democrats finally got rid of the two-thirds rule for nominating a candidate in 1936, but the unit rule, requiring that the entire vote of a state be cast according to the majority vote of that state's delegates, lasted until 1968.[4]

While much remains of the procedures established at the first conventions, these gatherings have evolved over time and much has changed. From less than 200 delegates at the first conventions, the number of delegates has grown with the growth of the country. The recent conventions of the Democratic Party had more than 4,000 delegates, while recent Republican Party conventions had more than 2,000 delegates.[5] Perhaps the greatest change from the early conventions to their modern counterparts is the diversity of the delegates. The delegates to all of the nation's presidential nominating conventions from 1832 to 1864 were white males. The Republican convention in 1868 was the first to admit male African American delegates, and the Republican and Democratic conventions in 1900 were the first to have female delegates. Today, a majority of delegates to the conventions of both parties are either female or minorities.[6] The dissemination of news from political conventions has grown exponentially. From a small crowd huddled outside of the Capitol building in Washington in 1844 to hear the first telegraphic news from a convention in Baltimore, conventions have become media extravaganzas with thousands of reporters instantly conveying every tidbit of convention information to a waiting nation and, indeed, the world. Convention news was first transmitted by radio in 1924 and by television in 1940. Unlike their nineteenth-century counterparts, modern convention delegates now hear in person from their presidential nominee. It was not until 1932 that the taboo of the nominee appearing before the convention was broken, when Franklin D. Roosevelt went to Chicago to personally accept the Democratic nomination and to deliver a speech to the convention.[7] With Roosevelt's acceptance speech, a new convention tradition was born.

In the last half century, the role and power of conventions as deliberative bodies that select the party's nominee for the presidency has diminished. Some have argued this function and power have been totally eliminated and, with this, that conventions are anachronistic and should themselves be eliminated. This change has largely been brought about by a more democratic delegate selection process, due to the creation of, and the now predominant role of, state primary elections. While delegates to the mid–nineteenth-century conventions were generally selected at their party's local convention held in their congressional district, delegates today are chosen in the majority of states based upon the vote of the people in statewide presidential primaries, and by statewide caucuses in the remaining states. In modern times, candidates appeal to the people directly for their votes and support, as opposed to party leaders, and one usually picks up enough momentum in the primaries and caucuses to secure a majority of the party's delegates for the nomination. As a result, the convention has become more of a ratification of the will of the voters in the primaries and caucuses, rather than a body that chooses the nominee. The last major party conventions to go past the first ballot in selecting a presidential nominee were in 1952. This does not mean, however, that all conventions in the future will have preordained nominees, and scenarios could easily develop where a convention is divided and brokered deals at the convention lead to the choice of a nominee. In recent years, two nomination races (the Republican contest in 1976 between Gerald Ford and Ronald Reagan and the Democratic contest in 1980 between Jimmy Carter and Edward Kennedy) went down to the wire and, in such a race, only a few uncommitted delegates, or delegates committed to a candidate other than the two frontrunners, could prevent a majority vote and a first ballot nomination.

Beyond the nomination of a presidential candidate, conventions still serve the important role that Henry Clay predicted they would in a letter written in 1830, before the first nominating convention was ever held. Conventions, wrote Clay, would be a place where the party's leaders and rank-and-file members would meet and "form acquaintances, exchange opinions and sentiments, catch and infuse animation and enthusiasm, and return with a spirit of union and concert."[8] At conventions, party activists get the opportunity to meet each other, to renew old acquaintances, and to make new connections. Aspiring politicians meet the people who can advance their careers. Many of those attending a convention are more focused on the presidential contest four or eight years in the future than on the one at hand. The tradition of the presidential nomination convention provides continuity of the American political experience. As one commentator has stated:

> Conventions play an important role in the political socialization process. Delegates bring their children and other family members along to experience the circus atmosphere and to learn about the political process. Important values — such as resolving political differences through the use of persuasion tactics and not violence — of our political society are passed on to the next generation. Thus, the republic is reenergized once every four years as the parties convene.
>
> Of all the rituals of American politics, only the presidential inauguration ceremony provides some of the same important — and intangible — benefits by emphasizing the republic's basic values of civil partisanship and conflict resolution. The conventions, however, represent unique opportunities for participatory politics. Concerns expressed over the modern conventions' lack of suspense ... fail to acknowledge the important contributions that they make to the republic.[9]

Moreover, conventions provide a way for the parties to unify and prepare for the upcoming campaign, to formally introduce their nominee to the country, to select a vice presidential nominee, and to receive an abundance of free media coverage. Even with their changed role, it is a safe bet that presidential nominating conventions will continue to exist as long as the nation.

While political conventions remain with us in the twenty-first century, tangible evidence of the mid–nineteenth-century conventions in the cities where they were held is scarce. In Philadelphia, the Chinese Museum, where the 1848 Whig Convention was held, was destroyed by fire in 1854. The current building on the site, at 834 Chestnut Street, is The Franklin

Residences, the former Benjamin Franklin Hotel, now converted into apartments.[10] Charleston's Institute Hall, the site of the first portion of the 1860 Democratic convention, was the victim of a massive fire in that city a few months after the start of the Civil War, in December 1861, which burned more than five hundred buildings.[11] All of the convention halls of Chicago discussed in this book are no more. The Wigwam, the site of Lincoln's first nomination for president by the Republican Party in 1860, was not built to be a lasting structure. For a while, it was converted into ten large retail stores, but it burned to the ground in about 1869.[12] Today, the site of the Wigwam, at 191 North Wacker Drive, is occupied by a thirty-seven-story office building. The Amphitheater, where McClellan was nominated by the Democratic Party in 1864, and Crosby's Opera House, where Grant was nominated by the Republicans in 1868, were victims of the Great Chicago Fire of 1871.[13] The Tammany Hall building in New York where the Democrats nominated Horatio Seymour in 1868 was demolished in 1928 for the expansion of the adjacent Consolidated Gas Company (now Consolidated Edison) office building.[14]

Unfortunately, as in Chicago and New York, in Baltimore, where most of the conventions discussed in this book were held, none of the buildings that served as convention halls between 1832 to 1872 survive, all victims of either fire or the wrecking ball.

The Athenaeum, the location of the first three nominating conventions held in Baltimore during the 1832 presidential campaign (Anti-Mason, National Republican, and Democratic), was destroyed by fire in February 1835. Although the cause of the fire was never determined, it was thought to be arson due to mob violence that occurred in Baltimore at that time related to the failure of one of the city's leading banks. The current building on the site, at the southwest corner of St. Paul and Lexington Streets, and directly across from the St. Paul Street entrance of the Clarence M. Mitchell, Jr., Courthouse of the Circuit Court for Baltimore City, is a seven-story hotel.

The First Presbyterian Church, known as the Two Steeple Church, which was the location of the 1835 Democratic convention and the 1860 Constitutional Union Party convention, was sold in 1859 by the congregation to the United States government and a new sanctuary for the church was built elsewhere in Baltimore. The old building was then razed to make way for a new federal courthouse, which opened in the mid–1860s and which lasted until the 1930s. The site, at the northwest corner of Fayette Street and Guilford Avenue, is currently occupied by a portion of Courthouse East of the Circuit Court for Baltimore City.

The location of the Assembly Rooms, the site of the 1840 Democratic convention, at the northeast corner of Fayette and Holliday Streets, is now an open plaza near the front of Baltimore's City Hall. The Assembly Rooms building later became the home of Baltimore City College, a public high school. In 1873, the structure was totally destroyed by a fire that spread from the adjacent Holliday Street Theater.[15]

Diagonally across the same plaza, on Gay Street near Fayette Street, the site of Odd Fellows Hall, where the 1844 Democratic convention was held, is also now open space. The hall remained the Baltimore home of the Grand Lodge of Odd Fellows until 1892, when a new Odd Fellows Temple was opened a few blocks away. At that time, the old structure was abandoned and was eventually torn down.

The Universalist Church at the northeast corner of North Calvert and East Pleasant Streets, where the 1844 Whig and the 1848 Democratic conventions were held, later became St. Francis Xavier Catholic Church, Baltimore's first African American Catholic parish. The structure was eventually demolished in 1942 and is currently the location of a three-story office building.

The Hall of the Maryland Institute, perhaps the most impressive Baltimore structure to host political conventions in the city, was a victim of the Great Baltimore Fire, which started on February 7, 1904, burned out of control for thirty hours, and destroyed more than seventy blocks and more than 1,500 buildings in the heart of the city. The building that was the home to both the Whig and Democratic conventions in 1852, the Whig convention in 1856, the rump Democratic convention of southerners in 1860, and the meeting of the Straight-Out Democrats in 1872, and which was once considered the grandest meeting hall in the United States, was reduced to a pile of charred rubble.[16] The site is now where Baltimore's Port Discovery Children's Museum and Power Plant Live entertainment complex are located.

The Front Street Theater did not have a noble ending. The site of the 1860 Democratic convention and the 1864 Republican/Union Party convention was never Baltimore's premier performing arts venue and, by the 1890s, was frequently hosting boxing matches. Tragedy struck the theater on the night of December 22, 1895, when a full house of 2,500 people were attending an opera. Shortly after the orchestra began playing, the smell of gas was noticed. An employee lit a match to search for the source of the odor, which caused a jet of fire from a punctured gas pipe. Amid cries of "Fire! Fire!" the main gas line to the theater was shut off, plunging the public areas into total darkness. As the crowd panicked and struggled to get out of the building, twenty-three people, including fifteen children, were trampled to death.[17] Shortly after this tragedy, the Front Street Theater was condemned. It escaped destruction in the fire of 1904, but was torn down a year later. Now, an abandoned factory stands on its ground at the northeast corner of Front and Low Streets.

The building that hosted the last convention analyzed in this book, the Democratic convention of 1872, survived the longest of the Baltimore convention sites.[18] Ford's Grand Opera House, on Fayette Street, near Eutaw Street, lasted for ninety-three years. From its opening in 1871, the building, later renamed simply Ford's Theater, remained as Baltimore's premier theatrical venue for half a century. Its ownership remained with the Ford family until the 1920s. The first act of Cole Porter's famous musical *Kiss Me, Kate*, which debuted in 1948, is set in Baltimore's Ford Theater. On February 1, 1964, a capacity crowd of almost 2,000 people saw the last show at Ford's. Two days later, the wrecking balls began their work and the site became a parking lot.[19] Currently, it is a parking garage.

All of Baltimore's grand, and not so grand, hotels that accommodated delegates attending the nineteenth-century political conventions are gone. Barnum's City Hotel began a gradual decline in quality after the Civil War. Located on the southwest corner of Calvert and Fayette Streets, the hotel developed a reputation during the Civil War as a meeting place for Confederate sympathizers. The alleged ringleader of a Baltimore plot to assassinate Abraham Lincoln in the city while the president-elect was en route to his inauguration in February 1861 was a barber who worked in the basement of the hotel.[20] In the early 1890s, Barnum's was torn down and a new ten-story office tower, the Equitable Building, was constructed on the site. It remains there at present.[21]

The city's other luxury hotel of Baltimore's convention era, the Eutaw House, lasted until the early twentieth-century. In 1912, an explosion in the basement caused a fire in the massive five-story structure. The Eutaw House never fully recovered from the fire and was partially torn down in 1914 for the construction of the Hippodrome Theater, which now stands on part of its location, with the remaining portion having been torn down in 1916.[22] The Carrollton Hotel, newly opened just months before the 1872 Democratic convention and the height of elegance at the time, was also a victim of the Great Baltimore Fire of 1904.[23] Similarly, Chicago's great convention hotels of the 1860s, the Sherman House, the Richmond House, and the Tremont House, were all destroyed in the Great Chicago Fire of 1871.

What remains of the buildings that hosted and were associated with America's first generation of presidential nominating conventions? Most of Pennsylvania's convention sites survive. The Zion Lutheran Church, located at 15 South Fourth Street in Harrisburg, Pennsylvania, the site of the Whig convention in 1839, still exists and is still home to a Lutheran congregation.[24] The Musical Fund Hall, site of the 1856 Republican convention, in Philadelphia and located at 808 Locust Street, still exists, but has been substantially renovated and turned into condominiums.[25] Also in Philadelphia, the Academy of Music, located at the corner of Broad and Locust Streets, the site of the 1872 Republican convention, still stands. It is the oldest opera house in continuous use in the United States, and is listed as a National Historic Landmark.[26] In Cincinnati, where the 1856 Democratic convention was held, the building that was once Smith & Nixon's Hall still stands, located at 8 East Fourth Street. Its façade and interior have been substantially modified over the years, and it now houses a retail business and offices.[27]

In Baltimore, although no convention halls still exist, other structures identified with the nineteenth-century conventions provide a tangible link to the past for the modern observer. The Baltimore & Ohio Railroad's Camden Station, where so many delegates attending the conventions arrived and departed from the city, has been refurbished and is currently a sports museum, adjacent to Oriole Park at Camden Yards. A portion of one of the city's other historic train stations, the President Street Station, remains, and has most recently been used as a Civil War museum. The Battle Monument, which was the center of evening rallies and speeches during most of the Baltimore conventions, still stands, but its once grand square has now been reduced to a traffic island in the middle of Calvert Street. The city's most famous monument, the Washington Monument, which was visited by many of the delegates and whose majesty and beauty was commented upon during speeches at many of the conventions, still proudly rises toward the sky in Mount Vernon Square. Also surviving is the Carroll Mansion, at Lombard and Front Streets, the home of Charles Carroll of Carrollton, where the aged patriot graciously received delegates from the National Republican and Democratic conventions during the 1832 campaign.

Beyond these few physical remains, however, Americans of the twenty-first century are left only with the historical record of a generation in the mid–nineteenth-century when a new and more democratic system for selecting the nation's leader was created, refined, and became a tradition. We are left with only our imaginations to picture where buildings once stood in which decisions were made that would shape the course of history. We are left to reflect upon a time when, then as now, every four years, the nation's attention focused on its convention cities for the drama and excitement of a uniquely American institution, the presidential nominating convention.

Notes

Preface

1. Paul O'Neil, "Conventions: Nomination by Rain Dance," in *Life Special Issue: The Presidency*, July 5, 1968, p. 28.

2. H. L. Mencken, *On Politics: A Carnival of Buncombe,* edited by Malcolm Moos (Baltimore: Johns Hopkins University Press, 1956), p. 33.

Chapter 1

1. There are two modern exceptions, Maine and Nebraska, which allot two electoral votes to the winner of the state popular vote, with the rest apportioned to the winner of each congressional district.

2. David M. Potter, *The Impending Crisis 1848–1861*. Completed and edited by Don E. Fehrenbacher (New York: Harper & Row, 1976), p. 405.

3. United States Constitution, Article 2, Section 1.

4. United States Constitution, Article 2, Section 1.

5. Edward Stanwood, *A History of Presidential Elections* (Boston: James R. Osgood, 1884) p. 1.

6. This famous description of Washington was delivered in a funeral eulogy before Congress by his fellow Virginian, Henry "Light-Horse Harry" Lee, the father of General Robert E. Lee.

7. Gary C. Byrne and Paul Marx, *The Great American Convention: A Political History of Presidential Elections* (Palo Alto: Pacific Books, 1976), p. 18.

8. It was not until the election of 1824 that popular vote totals were available. South Carolina, until the time that it seceded from the Union in 1860, still had its electors chosen by its state legislature, rather than by the majority vote of the people.

9. Stefan Lorant, *The Glorious Burden* (Lenox, MA: R. R. Donnelley & Sons, 1976), p. 1058.

10. Charles S. Thompson, *An Essay on the Rise and Fall of the Congressional Caucus as a Machine for Nomination Candidates for the Presidency* (New Haven, CT, 1902), pp. 22–23.

11. Lorant, p. 1058.

12. U.S. Constitution, 12th Amendment.

13. Byrne and Marx, p. 32.

14. Thompson, p 29.

15. Benjamin Austin, *Constitutional Republicanism, in Opposition to Fallacious Federalism* (Boston: Adams and Rhoades, 1803), p. 87.

16. *Niles Weekly Register*, Vol. 21, p. 338; Boller, p. 34.

17. Thompson, p. 30.

18. Paul F. Boller, Jr. *Presidential Campaigns from George Washington to George W. Bush* (Oxford: Oxford University Press, 2004), pp. 33–34.

19. The Constitution provides that only the top three Electoral College finishers are candidates in the House of Representatives. Thus Clay, who was the fourth-place finisher, was excluded.

20. *Niles Weekly Register*, Vol. 21, p. 404.

21. Joseph B. Bishop, *Presidential Nominations and Elections* (New York: Scribner's, 1916), p. 6.

Chapter 2

1. Joseph W. Cox, "The Origins of the Maryland Historical Society: A Case Study in Cultural Philanthropy," *Maryland Historical Magazine* 74:2, 1979, p. 108.

2. Cox, p. 108.

3. Nagal, p. 315.

4. *Niles Weekly Register*, Vol. 33, p. 113.

5. Aquila Randall Monument, The Historical Marker Database, http://www.hmdb.org (retrieved October 17, 2010).

6. *Niles Weekly Register*, Vol. 33, p. 113.

7. *Niles Weekly Register*, Vol. 33, p. 114.

8. Clayton C. Hall, editor, *Baltimore, Its History & Its People, Vol. I* (New York: Lewis Historical Publishing, 1912), p. 129.

9. John F. Weishampel, *The Stranger in Baltimore* (Baltimore: J. F. Weishampel, Jr., Booksellers and Stationers, 1866), pp. 85–86.

10. Sinclair Hamilton Collection of American Illustrated Books, Library of American History (Cincinnati: U. P. James, 1896), pp. 202–03.

11. Ralph D. Gray and Gerald E. Hartdagen, "A Glimpse of Baltimore Society in 1827: Letters by Henry D. Gilpin," *Maryland Historical Magazine*, Vol. 69:3 (1974), p. 258.

12. *Baltimore Sun*, October 17, 1839, and November 11, 1849.

13. Writers Program of the Work Projects Administration, *Maryland: A Guide to the Old Line State* (New York: Oxford University Press, 1940), p. 226.

14. John Thomas Scharf, *History of Baltimore City and County* (Philadelphia: Louis H. Everts, 1881), p. 516.

15. Varle, p. 80.

16. Letitia Stockett, *Baltimore: A Not Too Serious His-*

tory (Baltimore: Johns Hopkins University Press, 1997), p. 51.

17. Stockett, p. 208.

18. Weishampel, p. 145.

19. James S. Buckingham, *America: Historical, Statistic, Descriptive* (London: Fisher, Son, 1841).

20. Scharf, pp. 514–16.

21. John F. Stover, *History of the Baltimore & Ohio Railroad* (West Lafayette, IN: Purdue University Press, 1984), p. 25.

22. Stover, p. 15.

23. Stover, p. 33.

24. Stover, pp. 41–43.

25. Michael J. Kline, *The Baltimore Plot: The First Conspiracy to Assassinate Abraham Lincoln* (Yardley, PA: Westholme Publishing, 2008), p. 15.

26. For a history of the Philadelphia, Wilmington, & Baltimore Railroad and of the Northern Central Railroad, see Scharf, pp. 342–351.

27. Robert C. Keith, *Baltimore Harbor: A Picture History* (Baltimore: Johns Hopkins University Press, 2005), pp. 134–35.

28. Varle, pp. 75–76.

29. Stover, pp. 12–13.

30. Charles H. Bohner, *John Pendleton Kennedy: Gentleman from Baltimore* (Baltimore: Johns Hopkins University Press, 1961), p. 31.

31. Hamilton, Vol. II, pp. 10–11.

32. Hamilton, Vol. II, p. 14.

33. Cox, p. 110.

34. Cox, p. 109.

35. In 1830, Baltimore had a free black population of approximately 15,000 and a slave population of about 4,000. By 1860, the number of free blacks had almost doubled, to 26,000, while the number of slaves had dropped by half, to almost 2,000. Charles M. Christian, *Black Saga: The African American Experience* (Boston: Houghton Mifflin, 1995), p. 171.

36. Eugene H. Roseboom, "Baltimore as a National Nominating Convention City," *Maryland Historical Magazine* 67:3 (1972), p. 217.

Chapter 3

1. "No You Don't, Old Harry," New Patriotic Songs, in "Printed Ephemera" R1 1822–1879, Maryland Historical Society.

2. On the Anti-Masonic movement, see, generally, Howe, pp. 266–70; Holt, pp. 12–15.

3. Robert Morris, *William Morgan; or Political Anti-Masonry, Its Rise, Growth and Decadence* (New York: Robert Macoy, Masonic Publisher, 1883), pp. 21–23.

4. Morris, pp. 110–12.

5. Leslie H. Southwick, *Presidential Also-Rans and Running Mates, 1788 Through 1996*, Second Edition (Jefferson, NC: McFarland, 1998), pp. 159–61.

6. *Diary of John Quincy Adams*, March 14, 1833.

7. Harriet A. Weed, editor, *Autobiography of Thurlow Weed* (New York: Houghton Mifflin, 1884) , p. 389. McLean was wrong about Calhoun, who was the incumbent vice president. Instead of running for president in 1832, the South Carolinian decided to resign from the vice presidency, which he did near the end of Jackson's term and, instead, sought and obtained a South Carolina seat in the Senate.

8. Mary Ellen Hayward and Frank R. Shivers, Jr., editors, *The Architecture of Baltimore: An Illustrated History* (Baltimore: Johns Hopkins University Press, 2004), pp. 114–16.

9. Laws of Maryland, Chapter 7, Vol. 629, p. 9 (1824).

10. Charles Varle, *A Complete View of Baltimore* (Baltimore: Samuel Young, 1833), p. 35.

11. *Baltimore Sun*, September 10, 1891.

12. *Proceedings of the Second United States Anti-Masonic Convention Held at Baltimore, September, 1831* (Boston: Boston Type and Stereotype Foundry, 1832), p. 3; Stanwood, p. 104.

13. *Proceedings of 1831*, p. 2.

14. *Proceedings of 1831*, p. 5.

15. *Proceedings of 1831*, p. 14; *Maryland Republican*, October 1, 1831.

16. With twelve years in the office, Wirt still holds the record as the nation's longest-serving attorney general.

17. Southwick, p. 133.

18. Howe, p. 354–56.

19. See http://charlescarrollhouse.com (retrieved July 20, 2010).

20. To make matters even more confusing, there were still more Charles Carrolls in Maryland history. Charles Carroll of Homewood was the ne'er-do-well son of Charles Carroll of Carrollton, who lived in the Homewood House, a wedding gift from his father, and which is now owned by the Johns Hopkins University in Baltimore. Charles Carroll the Barrister (1723–1783) was a distant cousin of Charles Carroll of Carrollton and, as his name indicates, was a prominent attorney. He was a Protestant, and resided at Mount Clare Mansion on the western edge of Baltimore, another Carroll family home that remains open to the public today.

21. *Proceedings of 1831*, p. 13.

22. Weed, p. 390.

23. One Maryland newspaper mockingly commented: "We see no committee upon the self-created secret association of *Odd Fellows*. The convention pay no respect to our suggestions. We shall have to denounce their whole proceedings, or get up an Anti–Odd-Fellow Convention of our own." *Maryland Republican*, October 1, 1831.

24. *Proceedings of 1831*, pp. 17–18.

25. *Proceedings of 1831*, pp. 18, 19, 35.

26. Weed, pp. 390–91.

27. *Proceedings of 1831*, p. 59.

28. Southwick, p. 136.

29. *Proceedings of 1831*, p. 59.

30. *Proceedings of 1831*, p. 60.

31. *Proceedings of 1831*, p. 61.

32. *Proceedings of 1831*, p. 65.

33. *Proceedings of 1831*, p. 65–66.

34. *Proceedings of 1831*, p. 67.

35. John Pendleton Kennedy, *Memoirs of the Life of William Wirt* (Philadelphia: Lea and Blanchard, 1849), pp. 345–46.

36. Kennedy, p. 356.

37. Kennedy, p. 356–57.

38. Kennedy, p. 360.

39. Kennedy, p. 369.

40. Kennedy, p. 381.

41. Knupfer, p. 61.

42. Kennedy, p. 347.

43. Holt, p. 17, Kennedy, p. 381.

44. The focus by the Jacksonians upon the 1824 popular vote totals, implying that their candidate was cheated out of the election, was misleading. In 1824, Jackson led Adams by slightly fewer than 40,000 popular votes (152,901 to 114,023), but six states, including New York and Vermont, had no popular votes cast in the election. They still had their Electoral College votes cast through their state legislatures. Adams won in the Electoral College in both New York and Vermont and, if popular votes had been conducted in those states, Adams might well have overtaken Jackson in the nationwide popular

vote, or at least significantly closed the gap. For the 1824 vote totals, see Lorant, p. 1060.

45. *Niles Weekly Register*, Vol. 40, March 12, 1831, reprinting article from the *Annapolis Republican*, February 19, 1831.
46. Remini, p. 367.
47. *Journal of the National Republican Convention in Baltimore, December 1831* (Washington: Office of the National Journal, 1831), p. 4.
48. *Journal of 1831*, p. 7.
49. *Journal of 1831*, pp. 7–8.
50. *Journal of 1831*, p. 8.
51. Miller Center of Public Affairs, University of Virginia, American President: An Online Reference Resource. http://millercenter.org/academic/americanpresident/jqadams/essays/cabinet/166.
52. Southwick, pp. 78–84. An excellent biography of Clay's long career is Robert Remini, *Henry Clay: Statesman for the Union* (New York: W. W. Norton, 1991).
53. *Journal of 1831*, p. 8.
54. *Journal of 1831*, p. 8.
55. *Journal of 1831*, p. 9.
56. *Journal of 1831*, p. 9.
57. *Journal of 1831*, p. 10.
58. *Journal of 1831*, p. 10.
59. *Journal of 1831*, p. 10.
60. Roseboom, p. 224.
61. *Journal of 1831*, p. 12.
62. *Journal of 1831*, p. 12.
63. Southwick, pp. 126–32.
64. *Journal of 1831*, pp. 14–15.
65. *Journal of 1831*, p. 15.
66. *Journal of 1831*, pp. 15–26.
67. *Niles Weekly Register*, Vol. 42, May 26, 1832, p. 235.
68. A thorough biography of Van Buren is John Niven, *Martin Van Buren: The Romantic Age of American Politics* (Newtown, CT: American Political Biography Press, 2000).
69. A good biography of Calhoun is Irving H. Bartlett, *John C. Calhoun: A Biography* (New York: W. W. Norton, 1994).
70. Robert V. Remini, *The Life of Andrew Jackson* (New York: Penguin Books, 1988), p. 174, Louis McLane to James A. Bayard, February 19, 1829, Bayard Papers, LC.
71. Remini, p. 199.
72. Remini, p. 197.
73. James Parton, *Life of Andrew Jackson, Vol. III* (New York: Mason Brothers, 1860), p. 287. On the Eaton affair, see Howe, pp. 335–42; Remini, pp. 173–74; 190–94.
74. Howe, p. 341; Remini, p. 246.
75. Remini, pp. 198–99; Howe, pp. 340–41.
76. Remini, pp. 195–97.
77. Remini, p. 225; Thomas Hart Benton, *Thirty Years View, Vol. I* (New York: D. Appleton, 1854), p. 219.
78. Remini, p. 225, Andrew Jackson to Van Buren, February 12, 1832, Van Buren Papers, Library of Congress.
79. Sumner, p. 140.
80. Austin Ranney, *Curing the Mischief of Faction: Party Reform in America* (Berkeley: University of California Press, 1975), p. 69.
81. Sumner, p. 273.
82. Scharf, p. 120; Remini, p. 225–26; *Niles Weekly Register*, Vol. 42, May 26, 1832, p. 234.
83. *Niles Weekly Register*, Vol. 42, p. 234.
84. *Niles Weekly Register*, Vol. 42, p. 234.
85. *Niles Weekly Register*, Vol. 42, p. 234.
86. *Niles Weekly Register*, Vol. 42, p. 234.
87. *Niles Weekly Register*, Vol. 42, pp. 234–35.
88. Bishop, p. 10.
89. *Niles Weekly Register*, Vol. 42, p. 235.
90. *Niles Weekly Register*, Vol. 42, p. 235.
91. Niven, p. 301.
92. *Niles Weekly Register*, Vol. 42, p. 235.
93. Sumner, p. 273.
94. Sumner, p. 273.
95. *Niles Weekly Register*, Vol. 42, p. 235.
96. *Niles Weekly Register*, Vol. 42, p. 236.
97. Roseboom, pp. 217–18.
98. *Niles Weekly Register*, Vol. 42, p. 236.
99. *Niles Weekly Register*, Vol. 42, p. 238.
100. Daniel Walker Howe, *What Hath God Wrought: The Transformation of America, 1815–1848* (New York: Oxford University Press, 2007), pp. 489–91.
101. Howe, pp. 496–97.
102. Roger Matuz, *The Presidents Fact Book* (New York: Black Dog & Leventhal Publishers, 2004), p. 129; Lorant, pp. 138–39; 1061.

Chapter 4

1. Reprinted in *Niles Weekly Register*, Vol. 48, pp. 80–81.
2. Niven, p. 395.
3. Roseboom, p. 219.
4. Niven, p. 395.
5. *Niles Weekly Register*, Vol. 48, p. 226.
6. Scharf, p. 548; Backus, p. 71.
7. *Niles Weekly Register*, Vol. 48, p. 206.
8. *Niles Weekly Register*, Vol. 48, p. 227.
9. William Reynolds , *A Brief History of First Presbyterian Church of Baltimore* (Baltimore: Williams and Wilkins, 1913), p. 13; Varle, p. 49.
10. John H. Gardner, Jr., "Presbyterians of Old Baltimore," *Maryland Historical Magazine* 35:3 (1940), p. 253.
11. Williams, p. 51; Gardner, p. 253.
12. Williams, p. 68.
13. *Niles Weekly Register*, Vol. 48, p. 244.
14. *Niles Weekly Register*, Vol. 48, p. 227.
15. *Niles Weekly Register*, Vol. 48, p. 227.
16. *Baltimore Chronicle*, May 21, 1835.
17. *Niles Weekly Register*, Vol. 48, p. 227.
18. *Niles Weekly Register*, Vol. 48, p. 229.
19. Niven, pp. 395–96.
20. Niven, p. 395.
21. Miller Center of Public Affairs, University of Virginia, American President: An Online Reference Resource. http://millercenter.org/academic/americanpresident/vanburen/essays/vicepresident/1862 (retrieved April 20, 2010).
22. Ibid.
23. Niven, p. 396.
24. Niven, p. 396.
25. Niven, p. 396.
26. *Niles Weekly Register*, Vol. 48, p. 273. *See also* Austin Ranney, *Curing the Mischief of Faction: Party Reform in America* (Berkeley: University of California Press, 1975), p. 107.
27. *Niles Weekly Register*, Vol. 48, p. 229.
28. *Niles Weekly Register*, Vol. 48, p. 229.
29. *Niles Weekly Register*, Vol. 48, p. 229.
30. *Maryland Republican*, May 26, 1835.
31. *Niles Weekly Register*, Vol. 48, p. 229.
32. *Niles Weekly Register*, Vol. 48, p. 248.
33. Stanwood, p. 116.
34. *Niles Weekly Register*, Vol. 48, p. 248.
35. *Maryland Republican*, May 26, 1835.
36. *Niles Weekly Register*, Vol. 48, p. 273.
37. Sumner, p. 376; Boller, p. 60.
38. Holt, p. 29
39. Niven, p. 401.

40. Holt, p. 39.

41. Holt, p. 39.

42. Holt, p. 4.

43. Samuel G. Heiskell, *Andrew Jackson and Early Tennessee History, Vol. I* (Nashville: Ambrose Printing, 1920), pp. 644–649.

44. Southwick, pp. 148–56. For a good biography of Webster, see Robert V. Remini, *Daniel Webster: The Man and His Time* (New York: W. W. Norton, 1997). Remini also wrote leading biographies of Andrew Jackson and Henry Cary, which are cited elsewhere in this book.

45. Holt, p. 43–44; Howe, pp. 486–87.

46. Lorant, p. 165.

47. Howe, p. 491.

48. Holt, pp. 44–49; Howe, 487–88; Lorant, pp. 148–49, 1062.

49. United States Constitution, Article 2, Section 1.

50. Niven, p. 403.

Chapter 5

1. "Tippecanoe and Tyler, Too," Oscar Brand, singer, *Presidential Campaign Songs: 1789–1996* (Washington: Smithsonian Folkways Recordings, 1999).

2. Boller, p. 65; *United States Magazine and Democratic Review, VIII*, p. 198 (September 1840).

3. John J. Reed, "Battleground: Pennsylvania — Anti-Masons and the Emergence of the National Nominating Convention," *Pennsylvania Magazine of History and Business* 122:1–2 (1998), pp. 96–98.

4. *Proceedings of the Democratic Whig National Convention Which Assembled at Harrisburg, Pennsylvania on the Fourth of December, 1839* (Harrisburg: R. S. Elliott, 1839), p. 3.

5. *Niles National Register*, Vol. 57, p. 250.

6. Bishop, pp. 11–12.

7. *Niles National Register*, Vol. 57, p. 248.

8. Howe, pp. 586–88.

9. Bishop, pp. 12–13.

10. *Proceedings at Harrisburg in 1839*, pp. 3–6; *Niles National Register*, Vol. 57, p. 225.

11. *Proceedings at Harrisburg in 1839*, pp. 15–16; Freeman Cleaves, *Old Tippecanoe: William Henry Harrison and His Time* (Newtown, CT: American Political Biography Press, 1939), p. 317; Bishop, p. 13.

12. *Niles National Register*, Vol. 57, p. 249.

13. Holt, p. 103.

14. *Proceedings at Harrisburg in 1839*, p. 20; *Niles Weekly Register*, Vol. 57, p. 250.

15. Reed, p. 112.

16. Holt, p. 102; Bishop, p. 15; Reed, pp. 112–13.

17. Reed, p. 113.

18. Remini, p. 554.

19. Holt, p. 104.

20. Holt, p. 104.

21. Boller, p. 66.

22. Boller, pp. 68–69.

23. *Proceedings at Harrisburg in 1839*, p. 25.

24. Robert G. Gunderson, *The Log-Cabin Campaign* (Lexington: University of Kentucky Press, 1957), p. 13.

25. Norton, p. 95.

26. Norton, p. 95.

27. Bohner, p. 140.

28. Gunderson, p. 13.

29. Baltimore Whig Convention Quick Step, The Lester S. Levy Collection of Sheet Music. http://www.library.jhu.edu/collections/specialcollections/sheetmusic/musictours/baltimore/whig.html (retrieved September 12, 2010).

30. Norton, pp. 101–02.

31. *Baltimore Clipper*, May 5, 1840.

32. Norton, pp. 106–07.

33. McMaster, p. 571.

34. Boller, p. 67.

35. *Baltimore Clipper*, May 5, 1840.

36. Norton, p. 109.

37. Norton, p. 112.

38. Gunderson, pp. 12–13.

39. Boller, p. 68; Edward Stanwood, *A History of Presidential Elections* (Boston: James R. Osgood, 1884), pp. 129–30.

40. Gil Troy, See *How They Ran: The Changing Role of the Presidential Candidate* (New York: Free Press, 1991), p. 21

41. *Baltimore Clipper*, May 5, 1840, *U.S. Gazette*, May 6, 1840, p. 2, *Baltimore American*, May 6, 1840.

42. Scharf, p. 849.

43. Norton, p. 112–13.

44. Norton, p. 119.

45. Norton, pp. 120–22.

46. Gunderson, p. 16.

47. James F. Schneider, "Reverdy Johnson's House," *The Baltimore Barrister, Newsletter of the Bar Association of Baltimore City*, Vol. I, No. 3, 1979, pp. 35–37.

48. Howe, pp. 502–04.

49. Scharf, p. 679.

50. Varle, pp. 34–35.

51. Hayward and Shivers, p. 64.

52. *Proceedings of the National Democratic Convention, Held in the City of Baltimore, on the 5th of May, 1840* (Baltimore: Office of the Republican, 1840), hereinafter cited as *Proceedings of 1840*, p. 3.

53. *Proceedings of 1840*, p. 3.

54. *Niles National Register*, Vol. 58, p. 148.

55. *Niles National Register*, Vol. 58, p. 148.

56. As the only state since the 1830s to still have its electors to the Electoral College appointed by the state legislature (which it would continue until after the Civil War), there was no real reason for South Carolina to send delegates to political conventions. The political bosses in the legislature would decide who would get their state's electoral votes for president — not delegates to a convention, nor the majority of the popular vote of the people of their state.

57. *Niles National Register*, Vol. 58, p. 149.

58. *Niles National Register*, Vol. 58, p. 149.

59. Niven, pp. 462–63.

60. *Niles National Register*, Vol. 58, pp. 149–50.

61. *Niles National Register*, Vol. 58, p. 150.

62. *Proceedings of 1840*, pp. 10–19.

63. *Proceedings of 1840*, p. 19.

64. *Proceedings of 1840*, p. 20.

65. *Niles National Register*, Vol. 58, p. 152.

66. *Niles National Register*, Vol. 58, p. 152.

67. *Baltimore Clipper*, May 5, 1840.

68. Holt, p. 110.

69. Holt, p. 110.

70. Troy, p. 25.

71. Troy, pp. 5–29.

72. Holt, pp. 111–12.

73. Howe, p. 574.

74. Howe, p. 576.

75. As usual, South Carolina's electoral votes were cast by its legislators, rather than by the popular votes of the people of that state. The Palmetto State did not cast its vice presidential electoral votes for the Democratic vice presidential candidate, Richard Johnson; it voted instead for L. W. Tazewell of Virginia. Lorant, p. 1063.

76. For analysis of the 1840 election results, see Cleaves, pp. 327–28, Holt, pp. 111–21, Howe, pp. 575–76; Lorant, pp. 168, 1063.

Chapter 6

1. "Jimmy Polk of Tennessee," Oscar Brand, singer, *Presidential Campaign Songs: 1789–1996*, (Washington: Smithsonian Folkways Recordings, 1999).

2. Howe, p. 594; Lorant, p. 171, Matuz, p. 176.

3. Lorant, p. 171.

4. Since Tyler, as Harrison's vice president, had assumed the presidency upon the death of Harrison, there was no vice president and, had Tyler been killed on the *Princeton*, the line of succession in effect at that time would have elevated the president *pro tempore* of the Senate, Senator Willie P. Mangum of North Carolina, a Whig, to the presidency. It would not be until 1967, with the enactment of the 25th Amendment to the Constitution that a procedure for filling vacancies in the vice presidency would be established.

5. Niven, pp. 516–73; *New York Times*, October 17, 1915; Steven E. Woodworth, *Manifest Destinies: America's Westward Expansion and the Road to the Civil War* (New York: Alfred A. Knopf, 2010), pp. 116–19.

6. Howe, pp. 679–80.

7. Seigenthalaer, p. 75.

8. Howe, p. 680.

9. Niven, p. 526.

10. Niven, p. 527.

11. *Maryland Republican*, May 4, 1844.

12. John Seigenthaler, *James K. Polk* (New York: Henry Holt, 2003), pp. 76–77.

13. Seigenthaler, p. 76.

14. Howe, p. 680.

15. Seigenthaler, pp.56–69; see also Matuz, pp. 185–88.

16. Seigenthaler, p. 80.

17. Seigenthaler, p. 80.

18. *Maryland Republican*, May 11, 1844.

19. Robert V. Remini, *Henry Clay: Statesman for the Union* (New York, W. W. Norton, 1991), p. 644.

20. Scharf, p. 543.

21. *Baltimore Sun*, May 2, 1844.

22. *Baltimore Sun*, May 2, 1844.

23. *Baltimore Sun*, May 2, 1844.

24. *Baltimore Sun*, May 2, 1844.

25. *Baltimore Sun*, May 2, 1844.

26. Southwick, pp. 184–86.

27. Lurton D. Ingersoll, *The Life of Horace Greeley* (Chicago: Union Publishing, 1873), p. 161.

28. *Maryland Republican*, May 11, 1844.

29. *Baltimore Sun*, May 3, 1844.

30. The Calvert Hall School moved to Cathedral and Mulberry Streets in Baltimore in 1891 and, much later, in 1960, relocated to the Baltimore suburb of Towson.

31. Oliver P. Chitwood, *John Tyler: Champion of the Old South* (Newtown, CT: American Political Biography Press, 1939), pp. 375–76.

32. Chitwood, p. 376.

33. *Baltimore Sun*, May 29, 1844.

34. *Baltimore Sun*, May 28, 1844.

35. *Baltimore Sun*, May 28, 1844.

36. *Baltimore Sun*, May 28, 1844.

37. *Baltimore Sun*, May 29, 1844.

38. *Baltimore Sun*, May 28, 1844.

39. Chitwood, pp. 381–84.

40. *Atlantic Monthly*, Vol. 46 (Boston: Houghton Mifflin, 1880), p. 673.

41. Eugene I. McCormac, *James K. Polk: A Political Biography* (Berkeley: University of California Press, 1922), p. 230.

42. McCormac, p. 233.

43. McCormac, p. 234.

44. Varle, pp.41–42.

45. Weishampel, pp. 131–32.

46. *Baltimore Sun*, May 28, 1844.

47. Niven, pp. 534–35.

48. Niven, p. 575.

49. This Benjamin Franklin Butler, of New York, was a former law partner of Van Buren and had served as attorney general of the United States under President Andrew Jackson. He should not be confused with another Benjamin Franklin Butler, of Massachusetts, who would take a leading role at the Democratic convention a quarter of a century later, in 1860, and who will be discussed in later chapters.

50. Niven, p. 536.

51. *Baltimore Sun*, May 28, 1844.

52. *Baltimore Sun*, May 28, 1844.

53. Niven, p. 537.

54. *Baltimore Sun*, May 29, 1844.

55. *Baltimore Sun*, May 29, 1844.

56. *Baltimore Sun*, May 29, 1844.

57. Niven, pp. 532–33.

58. Niven, p. 533.

59. Niven, pp. 538–38.

60. McCormac, p. 240.

61. Niven, pp. 539–540, Seigenthaler, p. 84.

62. Scharf, p. 503.

63. *Maryland Republican*, June 1, 1844.

64. *Baltimore Sun*, May 30, 1844.

65. *Baltimore Sun*, May 30, 1844. It was well known that the great Whig Henry Clay had been in to two duels, one in 1809 when he was in the Kentucky legislature and against a fellow member of that body, Humphrey Marshall. The second occurred in 1826, when Clay was secretary of state under John Quincy Adams, and was against Senator John Randolph of Virginia. Clay and Marshall inflicted minor flesh wounds on each other, while Clay and Randolph each missed with their shots. *New York Times*, August 4, 1856; Remini, pp. 55, 294–95.

66. Ransom H. Gillet, *The Life and Times of Silas Wright*, Vol. 2 (Albany: Argus, 1874), p. 1526.

67. *Harper's New Monthly Magazine*, Vol. 24, p. 226.

68. Scharf, p. 504.

69. *Baltimore Sun*, May 31, 1844.

70. *Baltimore Sun*, June 3, 1844.

71. Troy, p. 30.

72. Howe, p. 173

73. Lorant, p. 177.

74. Troy, p. 30.

75. Troy, p. 32.

76. Howe, p. 180.

77. Troy, p. 36.

78. Howe, p. 188.

79. Lorant, p. 1063.

80. Howe, p. 198.

81. Howe, p. 194; Lorant, pp. 183, 1063.

82. Florida had been admitted as the twenty-seventh state during the time that the Texas issue was brewing.

Chapter 7

1. "Old Zack Upon the Track," Northern Illinois University Libraries Digitization Projects. http://lincoln.lib.niu.edu/cgi-bin/philologic/getobject.pl?c.1303:1.lincoln (viewed July 12, 2011)

2. Locofocos was a name for the Democratic Party, generally used derisively by the Whigs, which referred to a meeting of New York Democrats at Tammany Hall when the majority tried to end a meeting by turning out the gaslights and the minority lit matches, which were called locofocos, to illuminate the room and keep the meeting going. Bucktails was the name given to the anti–DeWitt Clinton faction of

the New York Democratic Party shortly after the War of 1812, who were known to wear deer tails in their hats. Wide Awakes were young Republicans in the campaign of 1860 who wore oilcloth caps, black capes, and marched in torchlit evening rallies. Hunkers were a New York Democratic faction that favored the Wilmot Proviso and its prohibition against slavery in land gained in the Mexican War. Barnburners, the opposing New York Democratic faction, were against the Wilmot Proviso. See *Harper's New Monthly Magazine*, Vol. LI (1875), pp. 139–40, and *Gaskell's Political Dictionary*, http://people/virginia.edu/~rmf8a/gaskell/poldict.htm (retrieved December 3, 2010), for discussion of several other nineteenth-century political faction nicknames.

3. Potter, pp. 70–72, Howe, pp. 830–31, Matuz, p. 205.

4. Potter, pp. 236–37; Potter, p. 297.

5. The city of Fort Worth, Texas, is named for this general.

6. *Baltimore Sun*, May 17, 1848.

7. *Baltimore Sun*, May 2, 1848.

8. Niven, p. 579.

9. *Baltimore Sun*, May 17, 1848.

10. *Baltimore Sun*, May 19, 1848, and May 21, 1848.

11. *Baltimore Sun*, May 22, 1848.

12. *Baltimore Sun*, May 23, 1848.

13. *Baltimore Sun*, May 28, 1844.

14. *Baltimore Sun*, May 23, 1848.

15. South Carolina remained the only state to continue to have its electors to the Electoral College chosen by its state legislature, rather than by the popular vote of its people. Since the people had no direct voice in choosing electors, it made little sense to send delegates to a political convention to nominate candidates for whom the people could vote.

16. Unlike Rucker, the South Carolinian, a man named Major Commander (a fitting last name for a military man), had been duly appointed a delegate to the Baltimore convention by a Democratic Party convention in South Carolina.

17. *Baltimore Sun*, May 23, 1848.

18. *Niles National Register*, Volume 74, p. 75.

19. *Niles National Register*, Volume 74, p. 75.

20. In years to come, Hamlin would join the Republican Party and serve as vice president under Abraham Lincoln during his first term.

21. *Baltimore Sun*, May 24, 1848.

22. *Baltimore Sun*, May 24, 1848.

23. *Baltimore Sun*, May 24, 1848.

24. *Baltimore Sun*, May 24, 1848.

25. *Niles National Register*, Vol. 74, pp. 75–77; *Baltimore Sun*, May 24, 1848.

26. Roseboom, p. 224.

27. *Niles National Register*, Vol. 74, p. 326.

28. The Northwest Territory ultimately became the states of Ohio, Illinois, Indiana, Michigan, and Wisconsin.

29. *Niles National Register*, Vol. 74, p. 325.

30. *Baltimore Sun*, May 24, 1848.

31. *Niles National Register*, Vol. 74, p. 325.

32. *Niles National Register*, Vol. 74, p. 325.

33. *Niles National Register*, Vol. 74, p. 328.

34. Southwick, pp. 206–11.

35. Roseboom, p. 224.

36. *Niles National Register*, Vol. 74, p. 329.

37. Potter, pp. 80–81.

38. Minor, p. 224.

39. John S. D. Eisenhower, *Zachary Taylor* (New York: Henry Holt, 2008), pp. 80–81.

40. Henry A. Minor, *The Story of the Democratic Party* (New York: Macmillan, 1928), p. 223.

41. Howe, p. 828; Bauer, p. 228.

42. Bauer, p. 231.

43. Troy, p. 48.

44. Bauer, p. 230.

45. John Thomas Scharf and Thompson Westcott, *History of Philadelphia: 1609–1884, Vol. II* (Philadelphia: L. H. Everts, 1884), pp. 948–49.

46. Bradley R. Hoch, "The Lincoln Landscape: Looking for Lincoln's Philadelphia: A Personal Journey from Washington Square to Independence Hall," *Journal of the Abraham Lincoln Association* 25:2 (2004). http://www.historycooperative.org/journals/jala/25.2/hoch.html (Viewed July 24, 2011).

47. Bauer, p. 235.

48. Bauer, pp. 235–36.

49. Rayback, pp. 185–86; Matuz, pp. 213–14; Bauer, pp. 236–37.

50. Hoch.

51. Bishop, pp. 27, 32; Troy, p. 49; Bauer, p. 244.

52. Malcolm C. McMillan, "Joseph Glover Baldwin Reports on the Whig National Convention of 1848," *The Journal of Southern History* 25:3 (August 1959), pp. 375–76.

53. Niven, pp. 581–89.

54. Troy, p. 48; Bauer, p. 249.

55. Holt, pp. 351–61; Bauer, pp. 243–44.

56. Bauer, pp. 245–57; Lorant, p. 1064.

Chapter 8

1. "Pierce and King," Oscar Brand, singer, *Presidential Campaign Songs: 1789–1996* (Washington: Smithsonian Folkways Recordings, 1999).

2. Taylor developed severe indigestion after attending a Fourth of July celebration in Washington and sitting for hours in the hot sun while eating cherries in iced milk. He died five days later. K. Jack Bauer, *Zachary Taylor: Soldier, Planter, Statesman of the Old Southwest* (Baton Rouge: Louisiana State University Press, 1985), pp. 314–316. Conspiracy theorists speculated for years that he was poisoned, and his body was actually exhumed in 1991, but no excessive levels of arsenic or other toxins were found.

3. *See* Potter, pp. 90–144, for a detailed discussion of the Compromise of 1850, its path through the Congress, and its provisions.

4. John E. Semmes, *John H. B. Latrobe and His Times 1803–1891* (Baltimore: Norman, Remington, 1917), pp. 412–17.

5. Bernard C. Steiner, "History of Education in Maryland," in *United States Bureau of Education Circular of Information No. 2* (Washington, DC: Government Printing Office, 1894), p. 318.

6. Semmes, p. 415.

7. Hayward and Shivers, p. 137.

8. *New York Times*, September 23, 1854.

9. Southwick, p. 209.

10. Potter, p. 141.

11. *New York Times*, June 1, 1852.

12. *Baltimore Sun*, May 31, 1852.

13. Charles Duff and Tracey Clark, *Baltimore Architecture (Then & Now)* (Charleston: Arcadia Publishing, 2006), p. 29.

14. *New York Times*, May 30, 1852.

15. *Baltimore Sun*, June 2, 1852.

16. *Baltimore Sun*, June 2, 1852.

17. William Hincks and F. H. Smith, *Proceedings of the Democratic National Convention Held in Baltimore, June, 1852* (Washington, DC: Buell & Blanchard Printers, 1852), hereinafter cited as *Proceedings of 1852*, pp. 8–9.

18. *Baltimore Sun*, June 2, 1852.

19. *Baltimore Sun*, June 3, 1852.

20. *Proceedings of 1852*, pp. 20–21.

21. Potter, p. 142.

22. *Baltimore Sun,* June 4, 1852.

23. *Baltimore Sun,* June 4, 1852.

24. *Proceedings of 1852,* p. 24.

25. *Proceedings of 1852,* p. 24. It would not be until the passage of the Twenty-third Amendment to the Constitution in 1961 that the District of Columbia would be granted votes in the Electoral College.

26. *Proceedings of 1852,* pp. 28–29.

27. *Baltimore Sun,* June 4, 1852.

28. *Baltimore Sun,* June 5, 1852.

29. Roy F. Nichols, *Franklin Pierce: Young Hickory of the Granite Hills* (Newtown, CT: American Political Biography Press, 1931), p. 193.

30. John S. D. Eisenhower, *Agent of Destiny: The Life and Times of General Winfield Scott* (New York: Free Press, 1997), pp. 311–18.

31. Nichols, p. 198

32. Nichols, p. 200.

33. Nichols, p. 202.

34. Nichols, p. 203.

35. A post-convention letter written by one of the Virginia delegates indicates that a small group of them had wanted to support Pierce on Saturday morning, but were overruled when most of the delegation decided to go with Dickinson. After Dickinson declined their support from the floor of the convention, however, the pro–Pierce delegates then circulated Pierce's letter to Major Lally, wherein Pierce firmly supported all elements of the Compromise of 1850, including enforcement of the Fugitive Slave Act. It was only after reading this letter that the rest of the Virginians were persuaded to support Pierce. *Baltimore Sun,* June 11, 1852.

36. *New York Times,* June 7, 1852; *Baltimore Sun,* June 7, 1852.

37. King was the Washington roommate of another loser in the contest for the nomination, Senator James Buchanan of Pennsylvania. There was some gossip at the time, and some modern speculation, that the relationship between Buchanan and King was more than that of congressional colleagues and friends.

38. *New York Times,* June 7, 1952; *Baltimore Sun,* June 7, 1852.

39. Boller, p. 89.

40. *Baltimore Sun,* April 22, 1852.

41. *Baltimore Sun,* April 27, 1852.

42. *Baltimore Sun,* May 11, 1852.

43. *Baltimore Sun,* May 27, 1852.

44. *Baltimore Sun,* June 14, 1852.

45. Holt, p. 682.

46. *Baltimore Sun,* June 16, 1852.

47. *Baltimore Sun,* June 17, 1852.

48. *Baltimore Sun,* June 16, 1852.

49. *Baltimore Sun,* June 14, 1852.

50. *Baltimore Sun,* June 16, 1852; *New York Times,* June 16, 1852.

51. *New York Times,* May 18, 1884.

52. *Baltimore Sun,* June 17, 1852.

53. *Baltimore Sun,* June 17, 1852.

54. *Baltimore Sun,* June 16, 1852.

55. *Baltimore Sun,* June 17, 1852.

56. *Baltimore Sun,* June 17, 1852.

57. *Baltimore Sun,* June 18, 1852.

58. *Baltimore Sun,* June 19, 1852.

59. Holt, p. 719.

60. Remini, p. 736.

61. *Baltimore Sun,* June 19, 1852.

62. Remini, p. 734.

63. *Baltimore Sun,* June 21, 1852.

64. *Baltimore Sun,* June 21, 1852.

65. *Baltimore Sun,* June 21, 1852.

66. Raymond had been one of the pro–Scott New York delegates who was denied a seat by the Committee on Credentials, but he was later admitted as a substitute delegate when one of the regular New York delegates became ill during the convention and had to leave Baltimore. *Baltimore Sun,* June 22, 1852.

67. Holt, p. 719.

68. *Baltimore Sun,* June 21, 1852.

69. Rayback, p. 358.

70. Holt, p. 721.

71. Robert V. Remini, *Daniel Webster: The Man and His Time* (New York: W. W. Norton, 1997), p. 738.

72. Holt, p. 721.

73. *New York Times,* June 28, 1884.

74. Holt, p. 722.

75. Remini, p. 738.

76. *Baltimore Sun,* June 22, 1852.

77. *New York Times,* June 28, 1884.

78. *Baltimore Sun,* June 22, 1852.

79. *Baltimore Sun,* June 22, 1852; Troy, p. 41.

80. *Baltimore Sun,* June 22, 1852.

81. Southwick, pp. 229–31.

82. Bishop, pp. 33–34.

83. *Baltimore Sun,* June 22, 1872.

84. *Baltimore Sun,* June 22, 1872.

85. Lorant, pp. 210–12; Holt, p. 263.

86. Troy, p. 50.

87. Troy, p. 53.

88. Holt, pp. 745–46.

89. Lorant, p. 212; Holt, p. 746.

90. Troy, p. 56.

91. Holt, p. 742.

92. Nichols, pp. 209–10; Lorant, pp. 208–10.

93. Potter, p. 143.

94. Lorant, p. 1064.

Chapter 9

1. "Buchanan and John Breckinridge," Oscar Brand, singer, *Presidential Campaign Songs: 1789–1996,* (Washington: Smithsonian Folkways Recordings, 1999).

2. Rayback, p. 383.

3. Roy F. Nichols and Philip S. Klein, "Election of 1860," in Arthur M. Schlesinger, Jr., editor, *The Coming to Power: Critical Presidential Elections in American History* (New York: Chelsea House, 1971), pp. 94–95.

4. Potter, pp. 145–69.

5. Potter, p. 167.

6. Rayback, p. 383.

7. Rayback, p. 377

8. Rayback, p. 379–80, Nichols and Klein, pp. 97–98.

9. Morris L. Radoff, editor, *The Old Line State: A History of Maryland* (Baltimore: Twentieth Century Printing, 1971), p. 201.

10. Potter, p. 252–53.

11. Potter, pp. 254–55.

12. Nichols and Klein, p. 104, Lorant, p. 224.

13. Potter, p. 257.

14. William E. Gienapp, *The Origins of the Republican Party 1852–1856* (New York: Oxford University Press, 1987), p. 330; Lorant, p. 224.

15. Potter, p. 257.

16. Nichols and Klein, pp. 106–07.

17. *Official Proceedings of the National Democratic Convention Held in Cincinnati, June 2–6, 1856* (Cincinnati: Enquirer Company Steam Printing Establishment, 1856), hereinafter cited as *Official Proceedings of 1856,* p. 3.

18. *Cincinnati Magazine*, August 1972, p. 12.
19. Nichols and Klein, p. 105.
20. *Cincinnati Magazine*, August 1972, p. 12.
21. *New York Times*, June 3, 1856.
22. *Official Proceedings of 1856*, pp. 13–14; *New York Times*, June 3, 1856.
23. *Official Proceedings of 1856*, pp. 13–15.
24. *Official Proceedings of 1856*, p. 16.
25. *Official Proceedings of 1856*, p. 17.
26. *Official Proceedings of 1856*, p. 18.
27. *New York Times*, June 3, 1956; *Cincinnati Magazine*, August 1972, p. 12.
28. *New York Times*, June 4, 1856.
29. *Official Proceedings of 1856*, p. 21.
30. *Official Proceedings of 1856*, p. 26.
31. *Official Proceedings of 1856*, p. 29.
32. *Official Proceedings of 1856*, pp. 34–37.
33. *Official Proceedings of 1856*, p. 39.
34. *Official Proceedings of 1856*, p. 43.
35. *Official Proceedings of 1856*, p. 45.
36. *Official Proceedings of 1856*, p. 46.
37. *Official Proceedings of 1856*, p. 58.
38. *Official Proceedings of 1856*, pp. 63–67; Nichols and Klein, pp. 105–06; Lorant, pp. 222–23.
39. Nichols and Klein, p. 106.
40. Musical Fund Society Hall, Philadelphia, Pennsylvania. National Historic Landmarks Program. www.nps.gov/nhl/DOE_dedesignations/Musical.htm (viewed July 3, 2011).
41. Gienapp, p. 334.
42. *New York Times*, June 18, 1856.
43. Gienapp, p. 334.
44. *Proceedings of the First Three Republican National Conventions of 1856, 1866 and 1864* (Minneapolis: Harrison & Smith, Printers, 1893), pp. 18–20.
45. *Proceedings of the First Three Republican National Conventions of 1856, 1866 and 1864,* pp 43–44.
46. Gienapp, pp. 308–318.
47. Matuz, p. 192.
48. Nichols and Klein, pp. 110–11.
49. *Proceedings of the First Three Republican National Conventions of 1856, 1866 and 1864,* pp. 50–54.
50. *New York Times*, June 20, 1856.
51. *Proceedings of the First Three Republican National Conventions of 1856, 1866 and 1864*, p. 66.
52. Rayback, pp. 381–82.
53. Rayback, pp. 387–88.
54. Rayback, p. 395.
55. Rayback, pp. 396–97.
56. Rayback, pp. 398–400.
57. *Baltimore Sun*, September 19, 1856.
58. *Baltimore Sun*, September 17, 1856.
59. *Baltimore Sun*, September 18, 1856.
60. *Baltimore Sun*, September 18, 1856.
61. *Baltimore Sun,* September 18, 1856.
62. *Baltimore Sun*, September 19, 1856.
63. *Baltimore Sun*, September 19, 1856.
64. *Baltimore Sun*, September 19, 1856.
65. *Baltimore Sun*, September 19, 1856.
66. Nichols and Klein, pp. 111–15.
67. Radoff, p. 201.
68. Nichols and Klien, pp. 113–117; Lorant, p. 1065.

Chapter 10

1. "Lincoln and Liberty," Oscar Brand, singer, *Presidential Campaign Songs: 1789–1996* (Washington: Smithsonian Folkways Recordings, 1999).
2. *New York Times*, February 22, 1860.
3. Reynolds, p. 68.
4. *Baltimore Sun*, May 9, 1860.
5. *New York Times*, May 10, 1860.
6. Southwick, p. 299.
7. Murat Halstead, *A History of the National Political Conventions of the Current Presidential Campaign* (Columbus: Follett, Foster, 1860), p. 110.
8. Donald W. Curl, "The Baltimore Convention of the Constitutional Union Party," *Maryland Historical Magazine* 67:3 (1972), pp. 257–58.
9. Curl, p. 260.
10. *New York Times*, May 10, 1860.
11. Halstead, p. 107.
12. *New York Times*, May 10, 1860; Curl, pp. 261–62.
13. *New York Times*, May 10, 1860; Curl, p. 262.
14. *New York Times*, May 11, 1860; Curl, p. 263.
15. *Baltimore Sun*, May 11, 1860, Curl, p. 265.
16. Curl, p. 265.
17. Halstead, pp. 114–15.
18. *Baltimore Sun*, May 11, 1860, Curl, pp. 267–68.
19. Halstead, p. 117.
20. Halstead, p. 118.
21. Curl, p. 269.
22. *Baltimore Sun*, May 11, 1860.
23. Halstead, pp. 118–19, Curl, pp. 269–70; *Baltimore Sun*, May 11, 1860.
24. Halstead, p. 120, *Baltimore Sun,* May 11, 1860.
25. Knupfer, pp. 59–60.
26. Knupfer, p. 57; *New York Daily Tribune*, May 22, 1860.
27. Knupfer, p. 59.
28. Scharf, p. 690.
29. Scharf, p. 534.
30. *Baltimore Sun*, December 10, 1850.
31. Horace Greeley and John F. Cleveland, editors, *A Political Text-Book for 1860* (New York: Tribune Association, 1860), p. 25.
32. Betty D. Greeman, "The Democratic Convention of 1860: Prelude to Secession," *Maryland Historical Magazine* 67:3 (1972), pp. 225–26; Charles W. Mitchell, "The Madness of Disunion: The Baltimore Conventions of 1860," *Maryland Historical Magazine* 100:3 (2005), p. 329
33. Mitchell, p. 328.
34. Greeman, p. 327–30.
35. Mitchell, p. 327.
36. Institute Hall/"The Union Is Dissolved!" The Historical Marker Database. www.hmdb.org/marker.asp?marker=39371 (viewed July 2, 2011).
37. Greeman, p. 231; Mitchell, p. 329.
38. Greeman, p. 232; Mitchell, pp. 330–31.
39. Greeman, p. 233–234; Mitchell, p. 332.
40. Mitchell, p. 332; Greeman, p. 234.
41. Mitchell, p. 334; Greeman, p. 235.
42. *Baltimore Sun*, June 18, 1860.
43. *Baltimore Sun*, June 18, 1860; Greeman, p. 245.
44. Mitchell, pp. 339–40.
45. *Democratic National Convention, 1860, at Charleston and Baltimore, Proceedings at Baltimore, June 18–23 (1860)*, hereinafter cited as *Proceedings at Baltimore 1860*, p. 94.
46. *Proceedings at Baltimore 1860*, pp. 95–96.
47. *Proceedings at Baltimore 1860*, p. 98.
48. Interestingly, the resolution had initially been proposed by delegate Church, who was from New York. The majority of the New Yorkers likely remembered with anger the attempt at the 1848 convention to impose a loyalty oath on the Barnburner and Hunker factions from the Empire State and wanted no part of it in 1860, despite the fact that they were likely opposed to the bolted southerners.

49. *Baltimore Sun*, June 19, 1860; Halstead, pp. 160–66.
50. *Proceedings at Baltimore 1860*, p. 102.
51. *Proceedings at Baltimore 1860*, pp. 102–03.
52. Halstead, pp. 170–71; *Baltimore Sun,* June 19, 1860.
53. Halstead, p. 171.
54. *Proceedings at Baltimore 1860*, p. 108.
55. Halstead, pp. 175–76; *Baltimore Sun*, Jun 19, 1860.
56. *Proceedings in Baltimore 1860*, p. 105.
57. *Proceedings in Baltimore 1860*, p. 107.
58. *Baltimore Sun*, June 20, 1860.
59. *Proceedings at Baltimore 1860*, pp. 108–09.
60. *Baltimore Sun*, June 20, 1860.
61. Halstead, p. 178.
62. *Proceedings at Baltimore 1860*, pp. 110–11.
63. *Latter Day Saints' Millennial Star*, Vol. XXII, No. 30, July 28, 1860; Dianne Neal and Thomas Kremm, *Lion of the South: General Thomas C. Hindman* (Macon, GA: Mercer University Press, 1993), p. 75.
64. *New York Times*, June 21, 1860.
65. Halstead, p. 186; *Latter Day Saints' Millennial Star*, Vol. XXII, No. 30, July 28, 1860.
66. *Baltimore Sun*, June 22, 1860.
67. Halstead, p. 179.
68. *Proceedings in Baltimore 1860*, p. 111.
69. *Baltimore Sun*, June 22, 1860.
70. *Proceedings at Baltimore 1860*, p. 114.
71. *Proceedings at Baltimore 1860*, p. 116.
72. *Proceedings at Baltimore 1860*, p. 120.
73. *Proceedings at Baltimore 1860*, p. 117.
74. *Proceedings at Baltimore 1860*, p. 118–19.
75. *Proceedings at Baltimore 1860*, p. 121.
76. *Proceedings at Baltimore 1860*, pp. 123–24.
77. Halstead, p. 185.
78. *Proceedings at Baltimore 1860*, p. 125.
79. Greeman, p. 249.
80. Halstead, pp. 186–87.
81. *Proceedings at Baltimore 1860*, p. 133.
82. *Proceedings at Baltimore 1860*, p. 137.
83. *Proceedings at Baltimore 1860*, p. 140.
84. *Proceedings at Baltimore 1860*, p. 141.
85. *Proceedings at Baltimore 1860*, p. 142.
86. *Baltimore Sun*, June 23, 1860.
87. Halstead, p. 194.
88. Halstead, p. 195.
89. *Proceedings at Baltimore 1860*, p. 146.
90. Halstead, p. 196.
91. *Proceedings at Baltimore 1860*, pp. 144–45.
92. *Proceedings at Baltimore 1860*, pp. 145–46.
93. *Proceedings at Baltimore 1860*, p. 146
94. *Proceedings at Baltimore 1860*, p. 148.
95. *Proceedings at Baltimore 1860*, p. 148.
96. Halstead, pp. 198–99.
97. Halstead, p. 199.
98. Halstead, pp. 200–01.
99. *Proceedings at Baltimore 1860*, p. 150.
100. *Proceedings at Baltimore 1860*, pp. 152–53.
101. *Proceedings at Baltimore 1860*, pp. 155–56.
102. Halstead, p. 205.
103. *Proceedings at Baltimore 1860*, pp. 156–67.
104. *Baltimore Sun*, June 25, 1860.
105. Halstead, p. 206.
106. *Proceedings at Baltimore 1860*, p. 158.
107. *Proceedings at Baltimore 1860*, pp. 159–60.
108. *Proceedings at Baltimore 1860*, p. 163.
109. *Proceedings at Baltimore 1860*, p. 164.
110. *Proceedings at Baltimore 1860*, p. 166.
111. *Proceedings at Baltimore 1860*, p. 166.
112. *Proceedings at Baltimore 1860*, p. 168.
113. *Proceedings at Baltimore 1860*, p. 169.

114. *Proceedings at Baltimore 1860*, pp. 169–70.
115. *Proceedings at Baltimore 1860*, pp. 170–71.
116. *Proceedings at Baltimore 1860*, pp. 172–73.
117. *Proceedings at Baltimore 1860*, pp. 184–85.
118. *Proceedings at Baltimore 1860*, p. 185.
119. *Proceedings at Baltimore 1860*, pp. 176–77.
120. *Baltimore Sun*, June 25, 1860.
121. Halstead, p. 219.
122. *Baltimore Sun*, June 25, 1860.
123. *Baltimore Sun*, June 25, 1860.
124. *Baltimore Sun*, June 25, 1860.
125. *Baltimore Sun*, June 25, 1860.
126. *Baltimore Sun*, June 25, 1860.
127. Halstead, pp. 226–27.
128. *Chicago Press and Tribune*, May 16, 1860.
129. Frederick F. Cook, *Bygone Days in Chicago* (Chicago: A. C. McClurg, 1910), p. 194.
130. Goodwin, p. 239; Potter, p. 418.
131. Josiah S. Currey, *Chicago: Its History and its Builders, Volume 2* (Chicago: S. J. Clarke Publishing, 1912), p. 92.
132. Currey, p. 92.
133. Goodwin, pp. 215–16, 241–43.
134. Leslie M. Scott, "Oregon's Nomination of Lincoln," *Oregon Historical Quarterly* 17:1 (1916), pp. 204–07.
135. John Tweedy, *A History of the Republican National Conventions from 1856 to 1908* (Poughkeepsie, NY: A. V. Haight, 1910), p. 38.
136. Halstead, p. 122.
137. Tweedy, p. 39.
138. *Chicago Press and Tribune*, May 22, 1860.
139. *Chicago Press and Tribune*, May 17, 1860.
140. *Chicago Press and Tribune*, May 17, 1860.
141. *Chicago Press and Tribune*, May 18, 1860.
142. William E. Baringer, *Lincoln's Rise to Power* (Boston: Little, Brown, 1937), p. 184.
143. *Chicago Press and Tribune*, May 18, 1860.
144. *Chicago Press and Tribune*, May 18, 1860.
145. *Chicago Press and Tribune*, May 18, 1860.
146. Larry Tagg, *The Unpopular Mr. Lincoln: The Story of America's Most Reviled President* (New York: Savas Beatie, 2009), p. 65.
147. *Chicago Press and Tribune*, May 22, 1860.
148. Bruce Chadwick, *Lincoln for President: An Unlikely Candidate, an Audacious Strategy, and the Victory No One Saw Coming* (Naperville, IL: Sourcebooks, 2009), pp. xxvii–xviii.
149. Goodwin, p. 246.
150. Perhaps the rumors of cabinet seats being promised for support of Lincoln were true. Simon Cameron would ultimately be offered by Lincoln, and would accept, the post of secretary of war. Due to the Union army's defeats early in the Civil War and poor oversight of the department, he would last only nine months, resigning in January 1862 and being replaced by the more able Edwin M. Stanton. Randall and Donald, pp. 320–24.
151. Tagg, p. 67.
152. Goodwin, p. 249.
153. *Chicago Press and Tribune*, May 22, 1860.
154. Scott, p. 210.
155. Halstead, p. 232.
156. Potter, pp. 440–41. Douglas, who had a rough lifestyle that included heavy alcohol use, developed a severe case of rheumatism in spring 1861, which was complicated by liver problems and an ulcerated throat. He never recovered, and died at the young age of forty-eight on June 3, 1861, only three months after Lincoln's inauguration. Southwick, p. 264.
157. Randall and Donald, p. 133; Lorant, p. 1066.

158. Lorant, pp. 249–50, 1066.
159. Randall and Donald, pp. 136–41.

Chapter 11

1. "Old Abe and Little Mac" in Tremaine Brothers, *Lincoln and Johnson Campaign Song-Book* (New York: American News, 1864), p. 12.
2. Schlesinger/Human, p. 144.
3. Lorant, p. 262.
4. Lorant, p. 260–61.
5. Lorant, p. 262.
6. *New York Times*, June 4, 1864.
7. *New York Times*, April 27, 1864, April 30, 1864.
8. Alexander K. McClure, *Old Time Notes of Pennsylvania, Vol. II* (Philadelphia: John C. Winston, 1905), p. 137.
9. Lorant, p. 1066.
10. Kline, pp. 214–16.
11. Kline, pp. 257–65.
12. Kline, pp. 348–50.
13. J. G. Randall and David H. Donald, *The Civil War and Reconstruction*, Second Edition (Lexington, MA: DC Heath, 1969), pp. 232–33.
14. Kline, pp. 374–375.
15. Edward McPherson, *The Political History of the United States of America During the Great Rebellion* (Washington, DC: Philp and Solomons, 1864), p. 153.
16. *New York Times*, September 18, 1860; Kline, pp. 374–75.
17. Flood, p. 133.
18. Gideon Welles, *Diary of Gideon Welles, Volume II (April 1, 1864–December 31, 1866)* (Boston: Houghton Mifflin, 1911), p. 30, May 13, 1864; Waugh, p. 187.
19. *Baltimore Sun*, May 18, 1864.
20. D. F. Murphy, *Proceedings of the National Union Convention Held in Baltimore June 7th and 8th, 1864* (New York: Baker & Godwin, 1864), hereinafter cited as *Proceedings of 1864*, p. 3.
21. *New York Times*, June 6, 1864.
22. *Baltimore Sun*, June 8, 1864.
23. *New York Times*, June 7, 1864; *Baltimore Sun*, June 7, 1864.
24. *Baltimore Sun*, June 6, 1864.
25. *Baltimore Sun*, June 8, 1864.
26. Charles B. Flood, *1864: Lincoln at the Gates of History* (New York: Simon & Schuster, 2009), pp. 123–24.
27. *Proceedings of 1864*, p. 4.
28. *Proceedings of 1864*, p. 5
29. *Proceedings of 1864*, p. 9.
30. *Baltimore Sun*, June 6, 1864.
31. *Proceedings of 1864*, pp. 22–24.
32. *Proceedings of 1864*, p. 27.
33. Flood, p. 136.
34. *Proceedings of 1864*, p. 29.
35. Flood, p. 137.
36. John C. Waugh, *Reelecting Lincoln: The Battle for the 1864 Presidency* (New York: Crown, 1997), pp. 183–84.
37. Welles, p. 44.
38. Welles, p. 45.
39. Waugh, p. 184.
40. Waugh, p. 184.
41. *Baltimore Sun*, June 6, 1864.
42. Waugh, pp. 185–87; Flood, pp. 130–33.
43. Hans L. Trefousse, *Andrew Johnson: A Biography* (New York: W. W. Norton, 1989), pp. 177–80; Flood, pp. 122–23.
44. Trefousse, pp. 188–90, 315–28.
45. *New York Times*, August 10, 1891.
46. *New York Times*, August 10, 1891.

47. Benjamin F. Butler, *Autobiography and Personal Reminiscences of Major-General Benjamin F. Butler* (Boston: A. M. Thayer, 1892), p. 634.
48. *Baltimore Sun*, July 8, 1891.
49. *Baltimore Sun*, July 9, 1891.
50. *Baltimore Sun*, July 13, 1891.
51. *Baltimore Sun*, July 10, 1891.
52. *Baltimore Sun*, July 13, 1891.
53. James F. Glonek, "Lincoln, Johnson, and the Baltimore Ticket," in *The Abraham Lincoln Quarterly*, Vol. VI, No. 5 (March 1951), pp. 260–61.
54. Glonek, p. 265.
55. Glonek, p. 266.
56. Glonek, p. 267.
57. *Proceedings of 1864*, p. 32–33.
58. *Proceedings of 1864*, p. 33.
59. *Proceedings of 1864*, p. 39.
60. *Proceedings of 1864*, p. 38.
61. *Proceedings of 1864*, p. 38.
62. Clark E. Carr, *My Day and Generation* (Chicago: A. C. McClurg, 1908), pp. 141–44.
63. Welles, p. 46.
64. *Proceedings of 1864*, p. 51.
65. *Proceedings of 1864*, p. 52.
66. *Proceedings of 1864*, p. 54.
67. *Proceedings of 1864*, pp. 54–55.
68. Flood, pp. 139–40.
69. *Proceedings of 1864*, pp. 57–58.
70. Curiously, Cameron was the man whom Lincoln had sent to the war zone in Virginia in spring 1864 to sound out General Butler for a spot on the ticket and was one of the delegates, along with McClure, later alleged to have been recruited by Lincoln to promote Andrew Johnson for vice president in Baltimore. Why would he then nominate Hamlin? Historians speculate that this was all part of a plan to bring the issue of the vice presidency to the forefront before Lincoln was nominated. Perhaps it was all staged, along with the shouts of "No!" to Hamlin's name, for Cameron did not pursue his motion with any vigor. *See* Flood, pp. 140–41.
71. *Proceedings of 1864*, p. 58.
72. *Proceedings of 1864*, p. 63.
73. Waugh, p. 195.
74. *Proceedings of 1864*, p. 65–66.
75. Flood, p. 141.
76. *Proceedings of 1864*, p. 73.
77. Glonek, p. 270.
78. Flood, p. 142.
79. *Proceedings of 1864*, p. 73.
80. Tweedy, p. 77.
81. *Baltimore Sun*, June 8, 1864.
82. *Baltimore Sun*, June 9, 1864.
83. Flood, pp. 143–43; Goodwin, p. 626.
84. *Chicago Tribune*, August 28, 1864.
85. *Chicago Tribune*, August 28, 1864.
86. Noah Brooks, "Two War-Time Conventions," *The Century Illustrated Monthly Magazine*, November 1894–April 1895 (New York: Century), p. 732.
87. *Chicago Tribune*, August 28, 1864.
88. *Chicago Tribune*, August 28, 1864.
89. Frank L. Klement, *The Limits of Dissent: Clement L. Vallandigham & the Civil War* (New York: Fordham University Press, 1998), pp. 279–82.
90. William D. Pederson and Frank J. Williams, editors, *The Great Presidential Triumvirate: Washington, Jefferson, and Lincoln* (New York: Nova Science Publishing, 2006), pp. 143–47.
91. Cook, p. 80.
92. *Chicago Tribune*, August 30, 1864.
93. *Official Proceedings of the Democratic National Con-*

vention Held in 1864 at Chicago (Chicago: Times Steam Book and Job Printing House, 1864), p. 3.

94. *Proceedings of 1864 at Chicago*, p. 4.
95. *Chicago Tribune*, August 30, 1864.
96. *Proceedings of 1864 at Chicago*, p. 6.
97. *Proceedings of 1864 at Chicago*, p. 27.
98. Brooks, p. 733.
99. *Proceedings of 1864 at Chicago*, pp. 27–28.
100. *Proceedings of 1864 at Chicago*, p. 29.
101. *Proceedings of 1864 at Chicago*, pp. 29–30, 36.
102. *Proceedings of 1864 at Chicago*, pp. 30–32.
103. Brooks, p. 733.
104. Goodwin, p. 654.
105. *Proceedings of 1864 at Chicago*, p. 38.
106. *Proceedings of 1864 at Chicago*, pp. 41–42.
107. *Chicago Tribune*, August 31, 1864.
108. *Proceedings of 1864 at Chicago*, pp. 43–46.
109. *Proceedings of 1864 at Chicago*, p. 46.
110. *Proceedings of 1864 at Chicago*, p. 47.
111. *Proceedings of 1864 at Chicago*, pp. 54–56.
112. *Proceedings of 1864 at Chicago*, p. 43.
113. Waugh, p. 292.
114. *Proceedings of 1864 at Chicago*, p. 60.
115. Klement, pp. 288–90.
116. On the 1864 Democratic convention in Chicago, *see* Goodwin, pp. 653–65; Randall and Donald, p. 474; Hyman, pp. 159–61.
117. *Chicago Tribune*, September 1, 1864.
118. Randall and Donald, pp. 419–20; William F. Zornow, "The Unwanted Mr. Lincoln," *Journal of Illinois State Historical Society* 45 (1952), p. 147.
119. Doris Kearns Goodwin, *Team of Rivals: The Political Genius of Abraham Lincoln* (New York: Simon & Schuster, 2005), pp. 640–44; Randall and Donald, p. 436.
120. Lincoln's reconstruction plan, announced in December 1863, granted pardons to Confederates who took an oath of loyalty to the United States Constitution. When one-tenth of the number of people in a state who had voted in the 1860 election had taken such an oath, a state government could be established. If that state government agreed to abolish slavery, the state could be readmitted to the Union. Under the Wade-Davis Act, however, a provisional governor would be appointed in each of the seceded states and would conduct a census of the adult white male population in that state. When a majority of that population in a state took a loyalty oath, a constitutional convention could be called for the establishment of a new state government, which would have to abolish slavery. No officeholders under the Confederacy were permitted to vote or hold office under the new state constitution. *See* Randall and Donald, pp. 552–54. The "Davis" of the Wade-Davis Act was Congressman Henry Winter Davis of Maryland, the same man who had arranged for the Maryland Institute in Baltimore to be rented for the week of the National Union Party convention in early June, resulting in the convention that renominated Lincoln being held in Baltimore's Front Street Theater.
121. Goodwin, pp. 645–46.
122. Randall and Donald, p. 473.
123. Hyman, p. 159.
124. Goodwin, pp. 654–66.
125. Zornow, p. 160.
126. Goodwin, pp. 658–59; Zornow, p. 161.
127. Hyman, pp. 164–65; Goodwin, pp. 660–66.

Chapter 12

1. "Grant, Grant, Grant!," Oscar Brand, singer, *Presidential Campaign Songs: 1789–1996* (Washington: Smithsonian Folkways Recordings, 1999).

2. For details of the battle between the Radical Republicans and Johnson, and of the Johnson impeachment trial in the Senate, *see* Trefousse, pp. 272–334; Lorant, pp. 272–93.
3. Josiah S. Currey, *Chicago: Its History and its Builders, Volume 3* (Chicago: S. J. Clarke Publishing, 1912), p. 253.
4. *Chicago Tribune*, May 20, 1868.
5. *New York Times*, May 20, 1868.
6. *Chicago Tribune*, May 20 and 21, 1868.
7. *Chicago Tribune*, May 22, 1868.
8. *New York Times*, May 21, 1868.
9. *Chicago Tribune*, May 21 and 22, 1868.
10. *Chicago Tribune*, May 21, 1868.
11. *Proceedings of the National Union Republican Convention Held at Chicago May 20 and 21, 1868* (Chicago: Evening Journal Press, 1868), p. 8
12. *New York Times*, May 21, 1868; *Proceedings of 1868 at Chicago*, pp. 30–31.
13. *New York Times*, May 21, 1868.
14. Donald Richard Deskins, Hanes Walton, and Sherman C. Puckett, *Presidential Elections 1789–2008: County, State and National Mapping of Election Data* (Ann Arbor: University of Michigan Press, 2010), p. 189.
15. *Proceedings of 1868 at Chicago*, pp. 14–17. Historians generally agree that Johnson had legitimate reasons to veto the bill for Colorado statehood, given lack of sufficient population and conflicting votes in Colorado as to whether its citizens wanted to remain a territory or pursue statehood. Colorado did not become a state until 1876.
16. *Proceedings of 1868 at Chicago*, p. 63; *New York Times*, May 21, 1868.
17. *New York Times*, May 22, 1868.
18. *Proceedings of 1868 at Chicago*, p. 67; *New York Times*, May 22, 1868.
19. *Proceedings of 1868 at Chicago*, p. 70.
20. *Proceedings of 1868 at Chicago*, p. 81.
21. *Proceedings of 1868 at Chicago*, pp. 82–84; *New York Times*, May 22, 1868.
22. *Proceedings of 1868 at Chicago*, pp. 84–85; Lorant, pp. 295–96.
23. *Proceedings of 1868 at Chicago*, p. 94.
24. *Proceedings of 1868 at Chicago*, p. 95.
25. *New York Times*, May 22, 1868.
26. McFeely, p. 277.
27. *Proceedings of 1868 at Chicago*, p. 97; *New York Times*, May 22, 1868.
28. *Proceedings of 1868 at Chicago*, p. 132; *Baltimore Sun*, May 22, 1868.
29. *Chicago Tribune*, May 20, 1868.
30. *Chicago Tribune*, May 22, 1868.
31. McFeely, p. 277.
32. Nathan Silver, *Lost New York, Second Edition* (New York: Houghton Mifflin, 2000), pp. 54–55.
33. Ellis P. Oberholtzer, *A History of the United States Since the Civil War, 1868–1872, Vol. II* (New York: Macmillan, 1922), p. 171.
34. Oberholtzer, pp. 173–74.
35. Oberholtzer, p. 172.
36. *Official Proceedings of the National Democratic Convention Held at New York, July 4 to 9, 1868* (Boston: Rockwell & Rollins, Printers, 1868), pp. 4–5.
37. *Proceedings of 1868 at New York*, pp. 6–8.
38. *Proceedings of 1868 at New York*, pp. 18–20; *New York Times*, July 5, 1868.
39. *New York Times*, July 5, 1868.
40. *Proceedings of 1868 at New York*, pp. 21–22.
41. Lorant, pp. 299–302; Albert B. Hart, *Salmon Portland Chase* (Boston: Houghton Mifflin, 1899), pp. 367–68.
42. *Proceedings of 1868 at New York*, pp. 42–47.

43. *Proceedings of 1868 at New York*, pp. 58–61.
44. *Proceedings of 1868 at New York*, pp. 68–72.
45. *Proceedings of 1868 at New York*, p. 137.
46. *Proceedings of 1868 at New York*, p. 152.
47. *Proceedings of 1868 at New York*, p. 153.
48. *Proceedings of 1868 at New York*, p. 154.
49. Oberholtzer, p. 180; Lorant, pp. 302–04.
50. *Proceedings of 1868 at New York*, p. 155.
51. *Proceedings of 1868 at New York*, p. 156.
52. Oberholtzer, p. 180.
53. *Proceedings of 1868 at New York*, p. 170.
54. Josiah Bunting III, *Ulysses S. Grant* (New York: Times Books, 2004), pp. 83–85; McNeely, pp. 279–83; Lorant, pp. 304–06.
55. Bunting, p. 85; McNeely, pp. 278–79, 283–84; Lorant, pp. 306–07.

Chapter 13

1. "Grant Campaign Song," *Proceedings of 1872*, p. 43.
2. Robert A.. Rutland, *The Democrats: From Jefferson to Clinton* (Baton Rouge: Louisiana State University Press, 1979), p. 123.
3. Robert C. Williams, *Horace Greeley: Champion of American Freedom* (New York: New York University Press, 2006), p. 10.
4. Williams, pp. 24–25.
5. Williams, pp. xi, xii, 33, and 53.
6. Williams, pp. 42 and 308.
7. Williams, pp. 131–36.
8. Williams, pp. 195–99, 217–20, 256–58.
9. Williams, pp. 272–73.
10. William S. McFeely, *Grant: A Biography* (New York: W. W. Norton, 1981), pp. 319–29.
11. McFeely, pp. 381–83.
12. Williams, pp. 290–92, 296–97; McNeely, pp. 380–82; Lorant, pp. 309–11.
13. *Baltimore Sun*, April 30, 1872.
14. *Baltimore Sun*, April 30, 1872.
15. *New York Times*, May 1, 1872.
16. *Baltimore Sun*, May 2, 1872.
17. *Baltimore Sun*, May 2, 1872.
18. *Baltimore Sun*, May 3, 1872.
19. The first female delegate to a major party national convention was Frances Warren of Wyoming, who was elected a delegate to the Republican convention in 1900. The same year, Elizabeth Cohen of Utah was elected as an alternate delegate to the Democratic convention and took a seat at the convention as a result of the illness of another delegate. Lynne E. Ford, *Encyclopedia of Women and American Politics* (New York: Infobase Publishing, 2008), p. 515.
20. *Baltimore Sun*, May 3, 1872.
21. Lorant, p. 312; Williams, pp. 297–99.
22. Williams, p. 298.
23. *Baltimore Sun*, May 4, 1872.
24. Lorant, p. 312.
25. *Baltimore Sun*, May 18, 1872.
26. *Baltimore Sun*, May 6, 1872.
27. *Baltimore Sun*, May 9, 1872.
28. Francis H. Smith, *Proceedings of the National Union Republican Convention Held at Philadelphia, June 5 and 6, 1872* (Washington: Gibson Brothers, 1872), p. 6.
29. *Proceedings of 1872 at Philadelphia*, pp. 7–10.
30. *Proceedings of 1872 at Philadelphia*, p. 12.
31. *Proceedings of 1872 at Philadelphia*, pp. 19–20.
32. *Proceedings of 1872 at Philadelphia*, p. 29.
33. *Proceedings of 1872 at Philadelphia*, p. 36; *Philadelphia Public Ledger*, June 7, 1872.

34. *Proceedings of 1872 at Philadelphia*, pp. 38–42.
35. *Proceedings of 1872 at Philadelphia*, p. 43.
36. *Proceedings of 1872 at Philadelphia*, p. 55.
37. McFeely, pp. 380–82; Lorant, pp. 316–17.
38. Booth and two conspirators planned three assassinations for the night of April 14, 1864, not only of President Lincoln, but also of Vice President Andrew Johnson and Secretary of State William Seward. Booth was the only one to accomplish his goal. Booth crony George Atzerode got drunk, lost his nerve, and did not attempt to shoot Johnson in his Washington hotel. Another conspirator, Lewis Powell, did attack the bedridden Seward in his Washington home, stabbing him about the face and neck several times. A neck brace that Seward was wearing as a result of a recent carriage accident likely absorbed some of the blows and saved the secretary of state's life.
39. Scharf, p. 696; *Baltimore Sun*, January 26, 1964.
40. *Baltimore Sun*, January 26, 1964.
41. *Brooklyn Eagle*, reprinted in *Baltimore Sun*, May 17, 1872.
42. Lorant, p. 319.
43. *Baltimore Sun*, July 9, 1872. Hancock eventually became a candidate and won the Democratic nomination in 1880, but narrowly lost the election that year to Ohio's James Garfield. Lorant, pp. 354, 362.
44. Mary Clemmer Ames, *Ten Years in Washington: Life and Scenes in the National Capital* (Hartford, CT: A. D. Worthington, 1874), pp. 158–59.
45. *Baltimore Sun*, July 8 1872, July 11, 1872.
46. *Baltimore Sun*, July 8, 1872.
47. Scharf, p. 514–15.
48. *Baltimore Sun*, July 8, 1872.
49. *Baltimore Sun*, July 9, 1872.
50. *Baltimore Sun*, July 9, 1872.
51. Scharf, p. 122.
52. The presence of a portrait of Henry Clay adorning a Democratic convention likely had Andrew Jackson spinning in his grave.
53. *Baltimore Sun*, July 8, 1872.
54. *Baltimore Sun*, July 8, 1872.
55. *Baltimore Sun*, July 10, 1872.
56. *New York Times*, July 10, 1872.
57. *Official Proceedings of the National Democratic Convention Held at Baltimore, July 9, 1872* (Boston: Rockwell & Churchill, 1872).
58. *Baltimore Sun*, July 10, 1872.
59. Alan Pell Crawford, *Twilight at Monticello* (New York: Random House, 2008), pp. 258–59, 261–64.
60. *Proceedings of 1872*, pp. 5–6; *Baltimore Sun*, July 10, 1872.
61. *Proceedings of 1872*, pp. 7–13; *Baltimore Sun*, July 10, 1872.
62. *Proceedings of 1872*, pp. 12–15.
63. *Proceedings of 1872*, pp. 15–20 (annotations to applause, etc. omitted).
64. *Proceedings of 1872*, pp. 20–23.
65. *Baltimore Sun*, July 10, 1872, *Proceedings of 1872*, pp. 24–38.
66. *Baltimore Sun*, July 10, 1872.
67. *Baltimore Sun*, July 10, 1872.
68. *New York Times*, June 26, 1872.
69. *Baltimore Sun*, July 9, 1872.
70. *Baltimore Sun*, July 11, 1872.
71. *Proceedings of 1872*, pp. 45–47.
72. *Proceedings of 1872*, p. 56; *Baltimore Sun*, July 11, 1872.
73. *Proceedings of 1872*, p. 61.
74. *Proceedings of 1872*, pp. 62–63.
75. *Proceedings of 1872*, pp. 65–66; *Baltimore Sun*, July 11, 1872.

76. *Proceedings of 1872*, p. 67; *Baltimore Sun*, July 11, 1872.

77. *Proceedings of 1872*, pp. 71–72.

78. *Proceedings of 1872*, p. 73, *Baltimore Sun*, July 11, 1872.

79. *Baltimore Sun*, July 11, 1872.

80. *New York Times*, July 11, 1872.

81. Martin W. Littleton, *The Democratic Party of the State of New York* (New York: J. F. Tapley, 1905), pp. 414–15.

82. John Bigelow, *Retrospections of an Active Life, Vol. V 1872–1879* (New York: Doubleday, Page, 1913), p. 38.

83. Williams, p. 303.

84. McFeely, p. 384.

85. Darcy G. Richardson, *Third-Party Politics from the Nation's Founding Fathers to the Rise and Fall of the Greenback-Labor Party* (Lincoln, NE: iUniverse, 2000), pp. 381–91.

86. Williams, p. 303.

87. Boller, p. 129.

88. Williams, pp. 303–04.

89. Boller, p. 129.

90. Boller, p. 129.

91. Lorant, pp. 323–34; Boller, p. 130.

92. Williams, p. 305.

93. Lorant, p. 1068; Williams, p. 305; Boller, p. 130.

94. Williams, pp. xii, 305–07; McFeely, pp. 384–85; Lorant, pp. 324, 1068.

95. Lorant, p. 1068.

96. The only other time that a political party returned to Baltimore for a convention was in June 1912, when the Democratic Party came back to the city for its convention, which was held at the Fifth Regiment Armory. It was a contentious affair, with Governor Woodrow Wilson of New Jersey emerging the victor after nearly a week and forty-six ballots. The preconvention front-runner had been Congressman Champ Clark of Missouri, who was the Speaker of the House of Representatives. Others in the race included Governor Judson Harmon of Ohio and Congressman Oscar W. Underwood of Alabama. Although Clark had a majority of votes on some ballots, the Democrats in 1912 still had their two-thirds rule for nomination. Clark faded on later ballots and Wilson eventually crossed the two-thirds threshold. *See* John A. Thompson, *Woodrow Wilson* (London: Pearson Education, 2002) pp. 58–60. With the Republican Party split in 1912 between the incumbent president, William Howard Taft, and former president Theodore Roosevelt's Bull Moose Party, Wilson waltzed into the White House with an easy win.

Chapter 14

1. O'Neil, p. 22.

2. Byron E. Shafer, *Bifurcated Politics: Evolution and Reform in the National Party Conventions* (Cambridge, MA: Harvard University Press, 1988), p. 290.

3. John Haskell, *Fundamentally Flawed: Understanding and Reforming Presidential Primaries* (Lanham, MD: Rowman & Littlefield Publishers, 1996), pp. 35–36.

4. Emmett H. Buell, Jr. and William G. Mayer, editors, *Enduring Controversies in Presidential Nominating Politics* (Pittsburgh: University of Pittsburgh Press, 2004), p. 100.

5. Buell and Mayer, p. 100.

6. A study of delegates to the 2004 conventions revealed that 50 percent of the Democratic Party's delegates and 46 percent of the Republican Party's delegates were female, while 32 percent of the Democratic delegates and 15 percent of the Republican delegates were minorities. *See* Costas Panagopoulos, *Rewiring Politics: Presidential Nominating Conventions in the Media Age* (Baton Rouge: Louisiana State University Press, 2007), p. 55.

7. Conventional Facts. *Smithsonian Magazine*. http://www.smithsonianmag.com/history-archaeology/conventional-facts.html (viewed January 22, 2011).

8. Remini, p. 367.

9. J. Mark Wrighton, "The Utility of Party Conventions in an Era of Low Visibility and Campaign Finance Reform," in Costas Panagopoulos, editor, *Rewiring Politics: Presidential Nominating Conventions in the Media Age* (Baton Rouge: Louisiana State University Press, 2007), p. 89.

10. Scharf and Westcott, p. 950; The Franklin Residences. http://www.kormancommunities.com/franklinresidences/contact.html (viewed July 5, 2011).

11. *New York Times*, December 18, 1861.

12. Dominic A. Pacyga, *Chicago: A Biography* (Chicago: University of Chicago Press, 2009), p. 50.

13. Currey, *Chicago: Its History and Its Builders, Volume 3*, p. 254.

14. Silver, p. 55.

15. Scharf, p. 680; *New York Times*, September 10, 1873.

16. Peter B. Peterson, *The Great Baltimore Fire* (Baltimore: Maryland Historical Society, 2004), pp. 15, 24, 39, and 179.

17. *New York Times*, December 23, 1895, *Baltimore Sun*, February 24, 1896.

18. The one Baltimore political convention not discussed in this book, the Democratic convention of 1912, was held at the Fifth Regiment Armory, which still stands.

19. *Baltimore Sun*, January 26, 1864, and February 2, 1864.

20. Kline, pp. 60, 120, 474.

21. *Baltimore Sun*, July 16, 1890, May 20, 1891.

22. Alexander D. Mitchell IV, *Baltimore Then and Now* (San Diego: Thunder Bay Press, 2001), pp. 94–95.

23. Peterson, p. 39.

24. Zion Lutheran Church. The Historical Marker Database. http://www.hmdb.org/marker.asp?marker=6662 (viewed July 5, 2011).

25. Musical Fund Society Hall, Philadelphia, Pennsylvania. National Historical Landmarks Program. http://www.nps.gov/nhl/DOE_dedesignations/Musical.htm (viewed July 3, 2011).

26. The Academy of Music. http://www.academyofmusic.org/home.php (viewed July 3, 2011).

27. E-mail with Linda Bailey, Curator of Prints and Photographs, Cincinnati Museum Center (July 15, 2011).

Bibliography

BOOKS

Ames, Mary Clemmer. *Ten Years in Washington: Life and Scenes in the National Capital.* Hartford: A. D. Worthington, 1874.

Atlantic Monthly, Vol. 46. Boston: Houghton Mifflin, 1880.

Austin, Benjamin. *Constitutional Republicanism, in Opposition to Fallacious Federalism.* Boston: Adams and Rhoades, 1803.

Baringer, William E. *Lincoln's Rise to Power.* Boston: Little, Brown, 1937.

Bartlett, Irving H. *John C. Calhoun: A Biography.* New York: W. W. Norton, 1994.

Bauer, K. Jack. *Zachary Taylor: Soldier, Planter, Statesman of the Old Southwest.* Baton Rouge: Louisiana State University Press, 1985.

Benton, Thomas Hart. *Thirty Years View, Vol. I.* New York: D. Appleton, 1865.

Bigelow, John. *Retrospections of an Active Life, Vol. V, 1872–1879.* New York: Doubleday, Page, 1913.

Bishop, Joseph B. *Presidential Nominations and Elections.* New York: Scribner's, 1916.

Bohner, Charles H. *John Pendleton Kennedy: Gentleman from Baltimore.* Baltimore: Johns Hopkins Press, 1961.

Boller, Paul F., Jr. *Presidential Campaigns from George Washington to George W. Bush.* Oxford: Oxford University Press, 2004.

Buckingham, James S. *America: Historical, Statistic, Descriptive.* London: Fisher, Son, 1841.

Buell, Emmett H., Jr., and William G. Mayer, eds. *Enduring Controversies in Presidential Nominating Politics.* Pittsburgh: University of Pittsburgh Press, 2004.

Bunting, Josiah, III. *Ulysses S. Grant.* New York: Times Books, 2004.

Butler, Benjamin F. *Autobiography and Personal Reminiscences of Major-General Benjamin F. Butler.* Boston: A. M. Thayer, 1892.

Byrne, Gary C., and Paul Marx. *The Great American Convention: A Political History of Presidential Elections.* Palo Alto: Pacific Books, 1976.

Carr, Clark E. *My Day and Generation.* Chicago: A. C. McClung, 1908.

Chadwick, Bruce. *Lincoln for President: An Unlikely Candidate, an Audacious Strategy, and the Victory No One Saw Coming.* Naperville, IL: Sourcebooks, 2009.

Chitwood, Oliver P. *John Tyler: Champion of the Old South.* Newtown, CT: American Political Biography Press, 1939.

Christian, Charles M. *Black Saga: The African American Experience.* Boston: Houghton Mifflin, 1995.

Cleaves, Freeman. *Old Tippecanoe: William Henry Harrison and His Time.* Newtown, CT: American Political Biography Press, 1939.

Cook, Frederick C. *Bygone Days in Chicago.* Chicago: A. C. McClurg, 1910.

Crawford, Alan Pell. *Twilight at Monticello.* New York: Random House, 2008.

Currey, Josiah S. *Chicago: Its History and its Builders, Volume 2.* Chicago: S. J. Clarke Publishing, 1912.

_____. *Chicago: Its History and its Builders, Volume 3.* Chicago: S. J. Clarke Publishing, 1912.

Deskins, Donald Richard, Hanes Walton, and Sherman C. Puckett. *Presidential Elections 1789–2008: County, State and National Mapping of Election Data.* Ann Arbor: University of Michigan Press, 2010.

Duff, Charles, and Tracey Clark. *Baltimore Architecture (Then & Now)*. Charleston, SC: Arcadia Publishing, 2006.

Eisenhower, John S. D. *Agent of Destiny: The Life and Times of General Winfield Scott*. New York: Free Press, 1997.

_____. *Zachary Taylor*. New York: Henry Holt, 2008.

Flood, Charles B. *1864: Lincoln at the Gates of History*. New York: Simon & Schuster, 2009.

Ford, Lynne E. *Encyclopedia of Women and American Politics*. New York: Infobase Publishing, 2008.

Gienapp, William E. *The Origins of the Republican Party, 1852–1856*. New York: Oxford University Press, 1987.

Gillet, Ransom H. *The Life and Times of Silas Wright, Vol. 2*. Albany: Argus, 1874.

Goodwin, Doris Kearns. *Team of Rivals: The Political Genius of Abraham Lincoln*. New York: Simon & Schuster, 2005.

Greeley, Horace, and John F. Cleveland, eds. *A Political Text-Book for 1860*. New York: Tribune Association, 1860.

Gunderson, Robert G. *The Log-Cabin Campaign*. Lexington: University of Kentucky Press, 1957.

Hall, Clayton C., ed. *Baltimore, Its History & Its People*, Vol. I. New York: Lewis Historical Publishing, 1912.

Halstead, Murat. *A History of the National Political Conventions of the Current Presidential Campaign*. Columbus: Follett, Foster, 1860.

Hart, Albert B. *Salmon Portland Chase*. Boston: Houghton Mifflin, 1899.

Hasell, John. *Fundamentally Flawed: Understanding and Reforming Presidential Primaries*. Lanham, MD: Rowman & Littlefield Publishers, 1996.

Hayward, Mary Ellen, and Frank R. Shivers, Jr., eds. *The Architecture of Baltimore: An Illustrated History*. Baltimore: Johns Hopkins University Press, 2004.

Heiskell, Samuel G. *Andrew Jackson and Early Tennessee History, Vol. I*. Nashville: Ambrose Printing, 1920.

Howe, Daniel Walker. *What Hath God Wrought: The Transformation of America, 1815–1848*. New York: Oxford University Press, 2007.

Hyman, Harold M. "Election of 1864." In Arthur M. Schlesinger, Jr., editor, *The Coming to Power: Critical Presidential Elections in American History*. New York: Chelsea House, 1972.

Intersoll, Lurton D. *The Life of Horace Greeley*. Chicago: Union Publishing, 1873.

Keith, Robert C. *Baltimore Harbor: A Picture History*. Baltimore: Johns Hopkins University Press, 2005.

Kennedy, John Pendleton. *Memoirs of the Life of William Wirt*. Philadelphia: Lea and Blanchard, 1849.

Klement, Frank L. *The Limits of Dissent: Clement L. Vallandigham & the Civil War*. New York: Fordham University Press, 1998.

Kline, Michael J. *The Baltimore Plot: The First Conspiracy to Assassinate Abraham Lincoln*. Yardley, PA: Westholme Publishing, 2008.

Knupfer, Peter. "Aging Statesmen and the Statesmanship of an Earlier Age: The Generational Roots of the Constitutional Union Party." In David W. Bright, and Brooks D. Simpson, editors, *Union and Emancipation: Essays on Politics and Race in the Civil War Era*. Kent, Ohio: Kent State University Press, 1997.

Littleton, Martin W. *The Democratic Party of the State of New York*. New York: J. F. Tapley, 1905.

Lorant, Stefan. *The Glorious Burden*. Lenox, MA: R. R. Donnelley & Sons, 1976.

Matuz, Roger. *The Presidents Fact Book*. New York: Black Dog & Leventhal, 2004.

McClure, Alexander K. *Old Time Notes of Pennsylvania, Vol. II*. Philadelphia: John C. Winston, 1905.

McCormac, Eugene I. *James K. Polk: A Political Biography*. Berkeley: University of California Press, 1922.

McFeely, William S. *Grant: A Biography*. New York: W. W. Norton, 1981.

McPherson, Edward. *The Political History of the United States of America During the Great Rebellion*. Washington, DC: Philp and Solomons, 1864.

Mencken, H. L. *On Politics: A Carnival of Buncombe*. Edited by Malcolm Moos. Baltimore: Johns Hopkins University Press, 1956.

Minore, Henry A. *The Story of the Democratic Party*. New York: Macmillan, 1928.

Mitchell, Alexander D., IV. *Baltimore Then and Now*. San Diego: Thunder Bay Press, 2001.

Morris, Robert. *William Morgan; or Political Anti-Masonry, Its Rise, Growth and Decadence*. New York: Robert Macoy, Masonic Publisher, 1883.

Neal, Dianne, and Thomas Kremm. *Lion of the South: General Thomas C. Hindman*. Macon, GA: Mercer University Press, 1993.

Nichols, Roy F. *Franklin Pierce: Young Hickory of the Granite Hills*. Newtown, CT: American Political Biography Press, 1931.

_____, and Philip S. Klein. "Election of 1860." In Arthur M. Schlesinger, Jr., editor, *The Coming to Power: Critical Presidential Elections in American History*. New York: Chelsea House, 1972.

Niven, John. *Martin Van Buren: The Romantic Age of American Politics*. Newtown, CT: American Political Biography Press, 2000.

Oberholtzer, Ellis P. *A History of the United States Since the Civil War, 1868–1872, Vol. II.* New York: Macmillan, 1922.

Pacyga, Dominic A. *Chicago: A Biography.* Chicago: University of Chicago Press, 2009.

Panagopoulos, Costas, ed. *Rewiring Politics: Presidential Nominating Conventions in the Media Age.* Baton Rouge: Louisiana State University Press, 2007.

Parton, James, *Life of Andrew Jackson*, Vol. III. New York: Mason Brothers, 1860.

Pederson, William D., and Frank J. Williams, eds. *The Great Presidential Triumvirate: Washington, Jefferson, and Lincoln.* New York: Nova Science Publishing, 2006.

Peterson, Peter B. *The Great Baltimore Fire.* Baltimore: Maryland Historical Society, 2004.

Potter, David M. *The Impending Crisis 1848–1861.* Completed and edited by Don E. Fehrenbacher. New York: Harper & Row, 1976.

Radoff, Morris L., ed. *The Old Line State: A History of Maryland.* Baltimore: Twentieth Century Printing, 1971.

Randall, J. G., and David H. Donald. *The Civil War and Reconstruction, Second Edition.* Lexington, MA: DC Heath, 1969.

Ranney, Austin. *Curing the Mischief of Faction: Party Reform in America.* Berkeley: University of California Press, 1975.

Remini, Robert V. *Daniel Webster: The Man and His Time.* New York: W. W. Norton, 1997.

_____. *Henry Clay: Statesman for the Union.* New York: W. W. Norton, 1991.

_____. *The Life of Andrew Jackson.* New York: Penguin Books, 1988.

Reynolds, William. *A Brief History of First Presbyterian Church of Baltimore.* Baltimore: Williams and Wilkins, 1913.

Richardson, Darcy G. *Third-Party Politics from the Nation's Founding Fathers to the Rise and Fall of the Greenback-Labor Party.* Lincoln, NE: iUniverse, 2000.

Rutland, Robert A. *The Democrats: From Jefferson to Clinton.* Baton Rouge: Louisiana State University Press, 1979.

Scharf, John Thomas. *History of Baltimore City and County.* Philadelphia: Louis H. Everts, 1881.

_____, and Thompson Westcott. *History of Philadelphia: 1609–1884, Vol. II.* Philadelphia: L.H. Everts, 1884.

Seigenthaler, John. *James K. Polk.* New York: Henry Holt, 2003.

Semmes, John E. *John H. B. Latrobe and his Times 1803–1891.* Baltimore: Norman, Remington, 1917.

Shafer, Byron E. *Bifurcated Politics: Evolution and Reform in the National Party Conventions.* Cambridge, MA: Harvard University Press, 1988.

Silver, Nathan. *Lost New York, Second Edition.* New York: Houghton Mifflin, 2000.

Sinclair Hamilton Collection of American Illustrated Books, Library of American History. Cincinnati: U. P. James, 1896.

Southwick, Leslie H. *Presidential Also-Rans and Running Mates, 1788 Through 1996, Second Edition.* Jefferson, NC: McFarland, 1998.

Stanwood, Edward. *A History of Presidential Elections.* Boston: James R. Osgood, 1884.

Steiner, Bernard C. "History of Education in Maryland." In *United States Bureau of Education Circular of Information No. 2.* Washington, DC: Government Printing Office, 1894.

Stockett, Letitia. *Baltimore: A Not Too Serious History.* Baltimore: Johns Hopkins University Press, 1997.

Stover, John F. *History of the Baltimore & Ohio Railroad.* West Lafayette, IN: Purdue University Press, 1984.

Sumner, William G. *Andrew Jackson as a Public Man.* Boston: Houghton Mifflin, 1889.

Tagg, Larry. *The Unpopular Mr. Lincoln: The Story of America's Most Reviled President.* New York: Savas Beatie, 2009.

Thompson, Charles S., *An Essay on the Rise and Fall of the Congressional Caucus as a Machine for Nomination Candidates for the Presidency.* New Haven, CT, 1902.

Thompson, John A. *Woodrow Wilson.* London: Pearson Education, 2002.

Trefousse, Hans L. *Andrew Johnson: A Biography.* New York: W. W. Norton, 1989.

Tremaine Brothers. *Lincoln and Johnson Campaign Song-Book.* New York: American News, 1864.

Troy, Gil. *See How They Ran: The Changing Role of the Presidential Candidate.* New York: Free Press, 1991.

Tweedy, John. *A History of the Republican National Conventions from 1856 to 1908.* Poughkeepsie, NY: A. V. Haight, 1910.

Varle, Charles. *A Complete View of Baltimore.* Baltimore: Samuel Young, 1833.

Waugh, John C. *Reelecting Lincoln: The Battle for the 1864 Presidency.* New York: Crown, 1997.

Weed, Harriet A., ed. *Autobiography of Thurlow Weed.* New York: Houghton Mifflin, 1884.

Weishampel, John F. *The Stranger in Baltimore.* Baltimore: J. F. Weishampel, Jr. Booksellers and Stationers, 1866.

Welles, Gideon. *Diary of Gideon Welles, Volume II (April 1, 1864–December 31, 1866).* Boston: Houghton Mifflin, 1911.

Williams, Robert C. *Horace Greeley: Champion of American Freedom.* New York: New York University Press, 2006.

Woodworth, Steven E. *Manifest Destinies: America's Westward Expansion and the Road to the Civil War.* New York: Alfred A. Knopf, 2010.

Writers Program of the Work Projects Administration. *Maryland: A Guide to the Old Line State.* New York: Oxford University Press, 1940.

Newspapers and Periodicals

Atlantic Monthly
Baltimore American
Baltimore Chronicle
Baltimore Clipper
Baltimore Sun
Brooklyn Eagle
Century Illustrated Monthly Magazine
Chicago Press and Tribune
Chicago Tribune
Cincinnati Magazine
Harper's New Monthly Magazine
Journal of Southern History

Latter Day Saints' Millennial Star
Life
Maryland Republican
New York Times
New York Tribune
Niles National Register
Niles Weekly Register
Oregon Historical Quarterly
Pennsylvania Magazine of History and Biography
Philadelphia Public Ledger
Smithsonian Magazine

Articles

Cox, Joseph W. "The Origins of the Maryland Historical Society: A Case Study in Cultural Philanthropy," in *Maryland Historical Magazine* 74:2, 1979.

Curl, Donald W. "The Baltimore Convention of the Constitutional Union Party," *Maryland Historical Magazine* 67:3, 1972.

Gardner, John H., Jr. "Presbyterians of Old Baltimore," *Maryland Historical Magazine* 35:3, 1940.

Glonek, F. "Lincoln, Johnson, and the Baltimore Ticket," *The Abraham Lincoln Quarterly* VI, No. 5, 1951.

Gray, Ralph D., and Gerald E. Hartdagen. "A Glimpse of Baltimore Society in 1827: Letters by Henry D. Gilpin," *Maryland Historical Magazine* 69:3, 1974.

Greeman, Betty D. "The Democratic Convention of 1860: Prelude to Secession," *Maryland Historical Magazine* 67:3, 1972.

Mitchell, Charles W. "The Madness of Disunion: The Baltimore Conventions of 1860," *Maryland Historical Magazine* 100:3, 2005.

O'Neil, Paul. "Conventions: Nomination by Rain Dance," *Life Special Issue: The Presidency*, July 5, 1968.

Reed, John J. "Battleground: Pennsylvania — Anti-Masons and the Emergence of the National Nominating Convention," *Pennsylvania Magazine of History and Business* 122:1–2, 1998.

Roseboom, Eugene H. "Baltimore as a National Nominating Convention City," *Maryland Historical Magazine* 67:3, 1972.

Schneider, James F. "Reverdy Johnson's House," *The Baltimore Barrister, Newsletter of the Bar Association of Baltimore City*, Vol. I, No. 3, 1979.

United States Magazine and Democratic Review, VIII, September 1840.

Zornow, William F. "The Unwanted Mr. Lincoln," *Journal of Illinois State Historical Society*, Vol. 45, 1952.

Convention Proceedings

Democratic National Convention, 1860, at Charleston and Baltimore, Proceedings at Baltimore, June 18–23, 1860.

Hincks, William, and F. H. Smith. *Proceedings of the Democratic National Convention Held in Baltimore, June, 1852.* Washington, DC: Buell & Blanchard Printers, 1852.

Journal of the National Republican Convention in Baltimore, December 1831. Washington: Office of the National Journal, 1831.

Murphy, D. F. *Proceedings of the National Union Convention Held in Baltimore June 7th and 8th, 1864.* New York: Baker & Godwin, 1864.

Official Proceedings of the Democratic National Convention Held in 1864 at Chicago. Chicago: Times Steam Book and Job Printing House, 1864.

Official Proceedings of the National Democratic Convention Held at Baltimore, July 9, 1872. Boston: Rockwell & Churchill, 1872.

Official Proceedings of the National Democratic Convention Held in Cincinnati, June 2–6, 1856. Cincinnati: Enquirer Company Steam Printing Establishment, 1856.

Proceedings of the Democratic Whig National Convention Which Assembled at Harrisburg, Pennsylvania on the Fourth of December, 1839. Harrisburg: R. S. Elliott, 1839.

Proceedings of the First Three Republican National Conventions of 1856, 1866 and 1864. Minneapolis: Harrison & Smith, Printers, 1893.

Proceedings of the National Democratic Convention, Held in the City of Baltimore, on the 5th of May, 1840. Baltimore: Office of the Republican, 1840.

Proceedings of the National Union Republican Convention Held at Chicago May 20 and 21, 1868. Chicago: Evening Journal Press, 1868.

Proceedings of the Second United States Anti-Masonic Convention Held at Baltimore, September, 1831. Boston: Boston Type and Stereotype Foundry, 1832.

Smith, Francis H., *Proceedings of the National Union Republican Convention Held at Philadelphia, June 5 and 6, 1872.* Washington: Gibson Brothers, 1872.

Index